# Content

W9-BJU-642

**Published by Lonely Planet Publications Pty Ltd**
ABN 36 005 607 983

**Australia** Head Office, Locked Bag 1, Footscray,
Victoria 3011, ☎ 03 8379 8000, fax 03 8379 8111,
talk2us@lonelyplanet.com.au

**USA** 150 Linden St, Oakland, CA 94607,
☎ 510 893 8555, toll free 800 275 8555,
fax 510 893 8572, info@lonelyplanet.com

**UK** 72–82 Rosebery Ave, Clerkenwell, London,
EC1R 4RW, ☎ 020 7841 9000, fax 020 7841 9001,
go@lonelyplanet.co.uk

**France** 1 rue du Dahomey, 75011 Paris,
☎ 01 55 25 33 00, fax 01 55 25 33 01,
bip@lonelyplanet.fr, www.lonelyplanet.fr

# The Authors

## BECKY OHLSEN

Becky Ohlsen has spent the better part of 30 years trying to wriggle out from under the dual burdens of *lagom* (just right) and *ordning och reda* (orderliness), which she inherited, presumably, from the Swedish side of her family. She studied Swedish in order to discuss food with her grandmother, and modern art, trolls and ghosts with her grandfather. She has an unhealthy fondness for August Strindberg's *Occult Diary* and Torgny Lindgren's short stories. Her favourite thing about Sweden, other than Max von Sydow, is the existence of reindeer meat in a tube. She doesn't really like cloudberries, but she can appreciate their unique qualities. And she has spent enough time in Stockholm to know the secret locations of free public toilets in several neighbourhoods.

## JONATHAN SMITH

Raised in the Scottish Highlands, Jonathan Smith graduated from St Andrews University in 1994 with an MA in German. Unsure of what to do with his life, he took a flight to Vilnius in Lithuania and spent the next four years travelling around the former USSR. Having tried everything from language teaching to translating Lithuanian cookery books, Jon resolved to seek his fortune as a freelance travel photographer. Jon's byline has since appeared in over 50 Lonely Planet titles. Jon had a cool time in Stockholm, tiptoeing across frozen lakes, trudging through snowdrifts and sipping vodkas in the Icebar.

Lonely Planet Publications
Melbourne | Oakland | London | Paris

Becky Ohlsen

# Stockholm

## The Top Five

*1 Take a boat tour*
Explore Stockholm's waterways by boat (p50)

*2 Skansen*
Step into another time at this traditional open-air museum (p72)

*3 Kungliga Slottet*
Wear out your shoes touring the 608-room Royal Palace (p52)

*4 Gamla Stan*
Lose yourself in the winding streets of the Old Town (p51)

*5 Vasamuseet*
Admire the salvaged 17th-century flagship Vasa (p73)

# Introducing Stockholm

The city of Stockholm might have been arranged by some divine hand to serve as a canvas for the rarefied northern European light. Whether it is the coldest wash of blue-white in winter or the amber hues of an autumn afternoon, light is the defining element of the city and has fascinated its best artists, from Strindberg to Bergman to Zorn. In summer, the sun barely sets on Stockholm; in winter, the city huddles in semi-darkness. You can't be in Stockholm very long without noticing the light; it casts diamonds across the water on sunny days and brings warmth into people's homes in the dark of winter. It hits the earthy red, yellow and saffron buildings and makes them glow.

Scattered across a series of islands where the freshwater Lake Mälaren meets the Baltic Sea – Stockholm is undeniably beautiful. It's a compact city – defined by water on all sides – and has remained a manageable size even while its status as a cultural centre has grown. Despite its small extent and its remote location relative to most of Europe, Stockholm is seen as a world leader in design, architecture, theatre, film, science and literature, as well as less arty things like civic planning, progressive politics, gender equality and environmentalism.

Stockholmers like to keep ahead of trends, which gives the city a distinctly plugged-in

### Essential Stockholm

- Moderna Museet (p73)
- Thielska Galleriet (p73)
- Millesgården (p85)
- Kvarnen (p126)
- Mondo (p134)

buzz – and ensures that all the big names in fashion, footwear, accessories and interior design are represented in the city's posh boutiques. It's a shopper's paradise, even for the thrift-shop crowd; the bohemian neighbourhood of Södermalm boasts as many offbeat vintage shops, record shops and artists' co-ops as the city centre has designer-label boutiques. The forward-looking, hipster youth of Stockholm keep their eyes glued to New York City – so much so that they've nicknamed a Stockholm neighbourhood SoFo (South of Folkungagatan), only half-ironically.

If the city is bent on embracing the future, it's equally adept at preserving the past. Stockholm does museums like no place else – it's that lighting thing again, an innate understanding of how to build atmosphere and drama that makes what could be, say, a mundane exhibit of military history seem more like a 3D version of the latest Spielberg blockbuster. Of course, the city also has its own real-life, walk-through museum in Gamla Stan, the original 13th-century settlement that grew from a walled fortress on one island into the modern, cosmopolitan city that Stockholm is today.

Preserving the past and clinging to it are two different things, however, and Stockholm is finding itself in the midst of a series of changes that, while they aren't always free of tension, amp up the city's energy level in exciting ways. Waves of immigrants since WWII have brought diverse cultural influences affecting nearly every aspect of life in the city, from food to employment to politics. And speaking of politics, there's the EU and the question of the euro – perhaps playing to its stereotype, Sweden has remained aloof to the European Union and recently voted against adoption of the euro. Sweden's struggle to carve out a place for itself in the global milieu, as well as its own path for the future, promises to be an interesting one.

## Lowdown

**Population** 755,000

**Time zone** GMT/UTC + 1hr

**3-star double room** Skr1500–2000

**Coffee and cake** Skr35

**24hr T-bana pass** Skr80

**Husmanskost lunch at KB** Skr95–120

**Pint of lager** Skr35–52

**Movie ticket** Skr75

**Percentage of Stockholmers who'd voluntarily jump a queue** 0

# BECKY'S TOP STOCKHOLM DAY

My dream day in Stockholm would start with a *lussekatt* (saffron bun) and coffee at Thelins, then a leisurely trip to Moderna Museet and a stop at Svensk Form Designcenter on Skeppsholmen. After a stroll along Strömkajen and through Kungsträdgården in the sunshine (of course there would be sunshine!), I'd have lunch at Kulturhuset's Cafe Panorama. Afterwards, I'd either hop on the *tunnelbana* or stroll down busy Drottninggatan to Gamla Stan in time to catch the changing of the guard at Kungliga Slott, especially if the drummer on the warhorse is anywhere to be seen. Then I'd aimlessly wander the old town until it's time to *fika* (have coffee and cake). After that, it's off to Södermalm and the Hornspuckeln galleries, dinner at Östgötakällaren, drinks at the Vampire Lounge, further drinks at Kvarnen, and live music at Mondo. If it's early enough afterwards, I'll stop for a *grillad korv* and maybe pop into the Loft on my way home.

# City Life

# City Life

## STOCKHOLM TODAY

Style is everything in Stockholm – whether you're talking about this season's three acceptable colours for women's clothing or the prevailing model of light fixture being featured in chic new bars. The rigour and precision that are part of the Swedish character mean that things are generally kept in order, nobody ever gets very far out of style and no public places have an unpleasant ambience.

But this veneer of perfection hides some fairly serious issues that Stockholm, unlike its neighbours, has had little practice in dealing with. There are telltale signs that the façade may be cracking: muggings are occurring on subway trains in broad daylight; homeless people are much more visible than 10 years ago; and graffiti decorates tube stations and alleyways. Swedes are also worrying more than they used to – about the European Union (EU) and the euro, immigration and their economy.

But this isn't suggesting that Stockholmers don't know how to have a good time. There might be tension in the air, but it doesn't stop people from enjoying a good meal out or a drink with friends – and it vanishes completely around the 25th of the month, Stockholm's payday. Change may cause anxiety, but the flip side of that is excitement, and Stockholmers are excited about a lot of things these days: a fresh crop of visual artists and designers is beginning to achieve recognition; several new live music venues are opening up; restaurants are growing even more sophisticated and embracing cuisines once deemed exotic; and immigrant culture is brewing in the suburbs. Stockholm, in other words, may not be as rich, pristine or idyllic as it once seemed, but it certainly isn't boring.

### Hot Conversation Topics

- **The euro** Will they or won't they? A 2003 referendum on whether Sweden should adopt the EU's single currency resulted in a resounding 'no', but the question is certain to come up again.
- **Hammarby** No one even seems to care *how* the club is doing – they just love being its fans.
- **Rent** It's too high.
- **Taxes** Again – much too high.
- **Politics** Which three parties will team up to lead parliament this time?

Café life in Gamla Stan (p104)

## CITY CALENDAR

Annual events throughout Stockholm are listed here. For an extensive, updated list of current events, festivals, concerts, exhibitions and more, check the free monthly magazine *What's On – Stockholm*, produced by the tourist office.

Most of the city's public celebrations take place in the park Kungsträdgården, rain or shine. In winter there are also indoor events like the Lucia choirs in Centralstationen, holiday music in churches and, of course, the Christmas markets in squares across the city. Sporting events are timed according to season.

# JANUARY & FEBRUARY
## SWEDEN HOCKEY GAMES
☎ 725 10 00; www.globen.se

In the second week of February, this is an ice-hockey tournament with eight leading teams from around the world; tickets cost around Skr300.

## STOCKHOLM NEW MUSIC FESTIVAL
☎ 407 16 00; www.rikskonserter.se

This two-week festival for new music takes place at various venues around Stockholm in mid-February; it's organised by the Swedish Concert Institute, Sveriges Radio, and the concert halls Konserthuset and Berwaldhallen.

## VIKINGARÄNNET
☎ 55 63 12 45; www.vikingarannet.com

This immensely popular 80km ice-skating race on the third or fourth Sunday in February from Uppsala to Stockholm is open to everyone; fees are around Skr550.

# MARCH
## WINTER SPORTS WEEK
☎ 55 51 00 90

During week nine (early March), this winter sports and events fest is held in Kungsträdgården, featuring ice-skating, cross-country skiing, dog sledding, winter camping, reindeer, Sami huts, and music.

## STOCKHOLM ART FAIR
☎ 50 66 50 00; www.artfair.se

This fair on the second weekend of March brings artists, students, gallery owners and dealers, plus the public, together for seminars and exhibits on painting, sculpture, graphic design and photography, as well as video installations.

# APRIL
## STOCKHOLM FILMFESTIVAL JUNIOR
☎ 677 50 00; www.filmfestivalen.se

This film festival for children takes place in the first week in April (for five or six days) at various cinemas around the city.

## CIRKUS PRINCESSAN
☎ 660 02 00; www.bronett.se

From late April to late May, you can watch daily performances (twice on Saturday and Sunday) of an all-female circus gala.

# MAY
## BELLMANSFESTIVALE
☎ 789 24 90; www.stockholmto

This one-day festival is celeb with a free picnic in Hagapar a singing troubadour dressed Bellman and lots of other p century costume.

## SKÄRGÅRDSMARKNAD
☎ 789 24 90; www.stockholmtown.com

For one or two days on the last weekend in May, traders from the archipelago come to sell herring, lamb and other foods. Ask at the tourist office for this year's time and location (usually Gälarvarvet, near Nordiska Museet).

## ELITLOPPET
☎ 635 90 00; www.kjelletrot.com

On the last weekend in May, this trotting competition involves the finest Swedish horses and takes place at Solvalla *travbana* (racetrack) in Sundbyberg.

## TJEJTRAMPET
☎ 450 26 10; www.tjejtrampet.com in Swedish

This 51km-long event on the last Sunday in May starts in the Gärdet area and claims to be the world's biggest women's bicycle race.

## RESTAURANGERNAS DAG
☎ 789 24 90; www.stockholmtown.com

This five-day food festival (late May to early June) is held in tents on Kungsträdgården; besides sampling from the kitchens of some local restaurants, you can hear music, drink beer, dance, buy crafts and watch circus events.

# JUNE
## NATIONALDAG
☎ 442 80 00; www.skansen.se

Gustav Vasa was elected king of Sweden on 6 June 1523. The main celebration, which includes a parade and the presentation of Swedish flags to various organisations in the presence of the royal family, takes place on the Solliden stage at the open-air museum Skansen and is broadcast live on TV. Admission is free after 3pm, but you'll still have to pay the regular Skansen admission fee (see p72).

## STOCKHOLM MARATHON
☎ 667 19 30; www.marathon.se

On the second Saturday in June, around 13,000 people enjoy one of the finest marathon circuits

...rticipants must be over 17 years ... deadline for entries is 20 April.

## AYONNAISE OPEN
☎ 714 04 20; www.mayo.se

Held in the third week of June, this is the largest *boules* competition in northern Europe; it takes place on the park-like island Långholmen. There are tournaments for everybody, from beginners to the best players.

## SLOTTSGALA
☎ 50 62 24 00; www.slottsgala.nu in Swedish

On this day in the third week of June, various concerts are held in the grounds at the palace Ulriksdal Slott, including classical and contemporary music.

## EKEN CUP
☎ 726 18 79; www.ekencup.org

These handball competitions for teams in every category are played on 35 grass fields in the central city area on the third weekend in June. Registration forms and fees are posted on the website.

## MIDSUMMER'S EVE
☎ 442 80 00; www.skansen.se

The first Friday after 21 June is Midsummer's Eve. Raising the Midsummer pole and danc-

ing around it are traditional activities, still observed mainly in towns and villages in the countryside. Skansen is the best place to see the activities in the city, with around 30,000 visitors on Midsummer's Eve. However, folk costumes, music, dancing, pickled herring washed down with *snaps* (a form of vodka), strawberries and cream, and beer drinking, are common in rural areas around the city. Activities continue for two more days at Skansen.

# JULY

## STOCKHOLM SUMMER GAMES
☎ 22 21 60; www.summergames.se

This sports competition for young people at Stadion (Stockholm's Olympic stadium) in the first week in July features all the main track and field events.

## STOCKHOLM JAZZ FESTIVAL
☎ 55 69 24 40; www.stockholmjazz.com

This highly regarded festival held during the third week in July features Swedish and international jazz artists and draws some 30,000 spectators to the island Skeppsholmen. Tickets are also available from the tourist office.

## SKOKLOSTERSPELEN
☎ 018 38 61 00; www.skoklosterspelen.com

This fun medieval event takes place the third week in July at the palace Skokloster Slott (see p180) with 350 performances, including tournaments, theatre, music and weightlifting.

# AUGUST

## STOCKHOLM PRIDE WEEK
☎ 33 59 55; www.stockholmpride.org

Stockholm's Gay Pride festival is the biggest in Scandinavia, with a full five days of entertainment. It takes place in the first week of August, with a big parade on Saturday.

## STRINDBERGSFESTIVALEN
☎ 411 53 54; home.swipnet.se/~w-49963/

Held in Tegnérlunden Park, this festival includes poetry readings and discussions, as well as seminars and guided excursions to Strindberg sites around Stockholm, with some tours in English.

## KSSS CITY MATCH
☎ 717 03 65; www.ksss.se

This regatta, held during the fourth week in August, is organised by the Royal Swedish

---

## Quirky Holidays

- **Skärgårdsbåtens Dag** On Archipelago Boat Day, the first Wednesday in June, a parade of Stockholm's old-fashioned steamboats sails off to Vaxholm from Strömkajen; boats are met with music and an outdoor market at Vaxholm.
- **Annandag Jul** The day after Christmas, Annandag Jul, is also a holiday, and much of the city remains closed.
- **Luciadagen** Youngsters wear flames on their heads to mark the darkest time of the year, and everyone eats saffron bread and drinks *glögg*.
- **Stockholm Furniture Fair** Designers and their groupies from all over the world gather to reveal the newest trends at this fair, held on the second weekend in February and open to the public on the last day. The fair is a big draw, so plan ahead: many of Stockholm's hotels will be booked solid.
- **Valborgsmässoafton** (Walpurgis Night) On 30 April, in a holdover from pagan times, Stockholm celebrates the arrival of spring with bonfires, fireworks and choral singing.

Yacht Club and is great fun to watch. It takes place in the bay Riddarfjärden.

## TJEJMILEN
☎ 667 19 30; www.tjejmilen.se
Held on the last Sunday in August, this is the largest women's running race in northern Europe. Attracting around 26,000 participants, it follows a 10km route in the Gärdet area.

# SEPTEMBER & OCTOBER
## STOCKHOLM BEER & WHISKY FESTIVAL
☎ 662 94 94; www.stockholmbeer.se
This festival, held on the last two weekends of September, includes tastings, exhibitions, beer and whisky schools, and a vote on which is the best beer out of around 500 varieties. It takes place at Nacka Strand, a beach on the eastern edge of Stockholm, toward Saltsjöbaden.

## HEM & VILLA
☎ 749 41 00; www.stofair.se
This annual homes and interior design exhibition takes place on the first weekend in October and attracts around 50,000 visitors.

## LIDINGÖLOPPET
☎ 765 26 15; www.lidingoloppet.se
Held during the first weekend in October, this is the world's largest cross-country race, with around 25,000 participants, from juniors (from seven years) to veterans. Its length ranges from 5.6km to 30km, and there are two women-only races.

## STOCKHOLM OPEN
☎ 450 26 25; www.stockholmopen.se
You'll see some of Sweden's best tennis players at this competition held on the last weekend in October. It's arranged by tennis star Sven Davidson and draws around 40,000 spectators.

## POETRY FESTIVAL
☎ 612 10 49; www.00tal.com
Held at Dramatiska teatern (Royal Dramatic theatre) in Nybroplan on the last weekend

## Great Crowns of Fire
Luciadagen (Lucia Festival) on 13 December has little to do with the Italian St Lucia of Syracuse, but is connected with restrictions after the Reformation and appears to be related to traditions from western Sweden. Popular throughout the country since the 1930s, the festival is a major part of holiday celebrations.

The main feature of the tradition of St Lucia is a procession of carol-singing children in white gowns led by Miss Lucia, who wears a crown of candles. Most Lucias these days are 'electric Lucias', due to the obvious fire risk. Lucia traditionally visits schools, workplaces and private homes, usually in the afternoon, and serves coffee, buns called *lussekatten* and gingerbread. Adult Swedes also enjoy their favourite Christmas drink, *glögg*, which is a spicy mulled wine. Lucia parades and choir singing take place at most major churches around Stockholm, and there's usually a large choral performance at midnight.

in October, this festival offers poetry, theatre, music and dance.

# NOVEMBER & DECEMBER
## STOCKHOLM INTERNATIONAL FILMFESTIVAL
☎ 677 50 00; www.filmfestivalen.se
At this prestigious 10-day festival held during the third week in November, more than 150 films from around 40 countries are screened at various city cinemas.

## JULAFTON
The main Christmas holiday in Sweden is Julafton (Christmas Eve) on 24 December. Everyone has the day off, gifts are exchanged and festive meals are served.

## NYÅRSAFTON
☎ 442 80 00; www.skansen.se
On 31 December, Swedish New Year's Eve celebrations include traditional singing broadcast live on TV from the Solliden stage at Skansen, followed by magnificent firework displays at Skansen and the city centre.

# CULTURE
## IDENTITY
Nearly everyone has an opinion on Stockholmers – and it's quite frequently less than flattering. Visitors often accuse the Swedes of being chilly and even rude to strangers, uptight about alcohol, and spoiled by a consistently high standard of living. As with

most stereotypes, these accusations have some basis in fact, but are generally more about misunderstanding.

It's true that Stockholmers are naturally reserved and often shy; their lack of effusiveness in greeting strangers can indeed seem rude to visitors, though it is seldom intentional. To a Swede, grinning cheerily at someone as if you know him when you don't is presumptuous and impolite. But Swedes are, in fact, exceptionally polite people – the old joke about Scandinavians using the word 'thanks' 15 times while buying a newspaper holds true in Stockholm. And when it comes to the Swedes' legendary defensiveness about alcohol and the country's high standard of living, these two factors have been slowly changing with Sweden's involvement in the EU.

Stockholmers are extremely proud of their city, although many of the city's young cultural movers and shakers seem to wish it were more like New York. Locals view the international media's fascination with their stylish capital – *Wallpaper\** magazine in particular – with anything from eye-rolling disgust to grudging pride.

An interesting development in recent years has been the shift of the cultural trend-watching spotlight out towards the suburbs. Long the domain of Stockholm's immigrant population, suburban areas, such as Rinkeby and Tensta, have suddenly garnered the interest of the *über*-stylish city-centre residents. The music, cuisine and artwork being produced in newly established cultural centres in these areas are gaining rapid respect and recognition in the rest of the city; examples include the music of the Latin Kings (see p22) and the photography of Ann Eriksson, whose documentation of diverse cultures in Stockholm's suburbs has appeared at the Nordiska Museum.

Stockholm, overall, is growing – more people are moving into the city each year than leaving. The city has a population of 754,948 (as of December 2001), but the population of greater Stockholm (which includes 22 municipalities within 'commuting' distance, such as the satellite cities of Solna, Sollentuna, Täby and Södertälje) is 1,838,882.

Most of Stockholm's population is considered to be of Nordic stock. These people are thought to have descended from central and northern European tribes who migrated northward after the end of the last Ice Age around 10,000 years ago and are the indigenous peoples of southern and central Scandinavia.

There are also about 80,000 foreigners of more than 80 nationalities living in Stockholm, but there are even more people of foreign extraction who have Swedish citizenship. The largest single group is the Finns, who number around 14,000 and form 18% of the total population. The next four largest groups are Iraqis, Somalis, Turks and Iranians – including many Kurds who fled Kurdistan and settled in Sweden before tightening of the previously liberal immigration laws in the late 1990s. British and American populations each number about 2500 in the city.

Sweden has been a fairly secular land ever since the church-smashing reign of Gustav Vasa (see p42), and the trend has continued. In 1994 a law was passed declaring that citizens don't legally acquire a religion at birth but may become members of a faith voluntarily. Although the vast majority of the population are officially members of the Church of Sweden, a denomination of Protestant Evangelical Lutheranism headed by the Archbishop of

## Reading Up on Stockholm Life

There's an interesting collection of articles about life in modern Stockholm in *Stockholm* by Ingmarie Froman (1997). *I Love Stockholm* by Teddy Brunius et al (1998) is a collection of essays by local artists, writers and other cultural figures. *The Soul of Stockholm* by Erland Josephson et al (1999) is a fine photographic book with essays by local experts in a range of fields. The large format coffee-table book *Stockholm Horizons* by Jeppe Wikström (1996) has more than 800 photos, from panoramas to close-ups.

If you're interested in Swedish festivals, try *Maypoles, Crayfish and Lucia – Swedish Holidays and Traditions*, by Jan-Öjvind Swahn (1997). For an interesting and accurate guide to cultural behaviour, read *Culture Shock! – Sweden: A Guide to Customs and Etiquette* by Charlotte Rosen Svensson (1998). *Smörgåsbord* by Kerstin Törngren (1996) features 20 recipes for the classic Swedish buffet, including herring, *gravad lax* (marinated salmon) and meatballs. Most of these books can be found or ordered from the Sweden Bookshop (see p144), run by the Swedish Institute.

Uppsala, less than 10% of the population regularly attends church. Complete separation of church and state took place on 1 January 2000, and Evangelical Lutheranism is no longer the official state religion.

The populace is uniformly well educated. From the age of six or seven, every child in Stockholm faces nine years of compulsory *grundskolan* (comprehensive school) education. The performance of 14-year-olds (compared with other industrialised nations) is good in reading, below average in mathematics and average in science. Depending on interest and ability, almost all pupils then move on to the three-year *gymnasieskolan* (upper secondary school), where they can study academic courses specifically designed for university entrance, or take a variety of vocational courses. Within Europe, Sweden has one of the lowest rates of students who leave school without a certificate.

The universities and a variety of other higher-education institutions attract around one third of young Swedes within five years of their completion of *gymnasieskolan*, but most students study short courses rather than complete a three-year degree. Stockholm University, founded in 1878, is north of the city centre at Frescati. Another important educational establishment is Kungliga Tekniska Högskolan (Royal Technical College).

Education, books and lunches in the municipality-run schools are provided free of charge. Teaching at the mainly state-run higher-education institutions is free and students can obtain loans on very good terms. A basic student grant, dependent on parental income for students under 20, is available to all and is usually worth around Skr1500 per month.

# LIFESTYLE

One of the first things a visitor may notice when wandering around Stockholm is the prevalence of men with baby strollers. Gender equality has advanced further in Sweden than in many other countries, and families in which the mother works while the father handles the bulk of the childcare duties are quite common.

Going out is an expensive proposition in Stockholm. Locals tend to save up for the weekend; a Monday or Tuesday night in the city centre during the off season can be very quiet. Conversely, every bar is packed full and sports a mile-long queue out the door on the days following the 25th of each month, when Stockholmers get paid.

Although Stockholm is a large city, rural connections are still strong and the summer cottage is almost *de rigueur* – there are thousands of little red cabins in the archipelago, and anyone who doesn't have one at least has plans for one. And many people exercise their right of common access to the countryside – called *allemansrätten* (see p173)– especially during the berry- and mushroom-picking seasons in summer.

Nationaldag (Swedish National Day) is on 6 June. This is one of several days in the year when the distinctive Swedish flag (blue, with a yellow cross) is unfurled and hauled aloft on countless flagpoles around the country. Midsummer poles, although an imported concept from elsewhere in Europe, are central to the extensive Swedish Midsummer and Midsummer's Eve festivities. For more details on all festivals, see City Calendar (p8).

Styles of traditional folk dress, known as *folkdräkt*, vary around the country and may be different in adjacent communities. The national version, which can be used everywhere, was designed in the 20th century. Women wear a white hat, yellow skirt and a blue vest with white flowers over a white blouse. Men wear a simpler costume of knee-length trousers (breeches), white shirt, vest and wide-brimmed hat. Folkdräkt comes out of the cupboard on Nationaldag and Midsummer, and for weddings, feasts, birthdays and church visits.

Queuing by number is a favourite Swedish pastime, and you'll have to do this in shops, bakeries, some Systembolaget shops (state-owned alcohol shops), banks, government offices, police stations, post offices etc. Don't miss your turn or you'll have to go back to the end – and don't even think of jumping the queue unless you want to be frowned at relentlessly.

The traditional handshake is used liberally in both business and social circles when greeting friends or meeting strangers. In the latter case, customary introductions will include your full names.

If you're an informal guest in a Swedish home, particularly in the countryside, it's polite to remove your shoes before entering the living area; many people habitually carry a pair of house slippers with them when they visit. It's customary to present your host with a small gift of sweets or flowers on arrival. At meals, avoid sipping your drink before the host or hostess makes the toast, *skål*, which you should answer in return. This traditional ritual is most frequently accompanied by direct eye contact with whoever offered the toast, symbolising respect and absence of guile.

# FOOD

Two things leap to mind when you think of Swedish cuisine: meatballs (*köttbullar*) and the Muppets. Of course, there's a lot more to the food scene in Stockholm than *köttbullar* and a cracked Swedish chef. It's true that classic Swedish *husmanskost* (literally 'plain folks food') is based on simply prepared combinations of meat, potatoes and fish. But the restaurant scene, like nearly every other aspect of Stockholm life, embraces the avant garde. The Swedish national cooking team, with its deft adaptations of global cooking trends, consistently does better than its competitive sports teams. People here take a keen interest in food, especially (but not exclusively) the food from other cultures. Dining out is seen as a cultural experience on par with visiting a museum or attending a concert.

Stockholmers don't typically go out for a full, cooked breakfast (*frukost*); most people start their day with coffee and a pastry (*wienerbröd* or *kanelbulle*), or cereal with yogurt or *fil*, a type of buttermilk.

Most cafés and restaurants serve a daily lunch special (or a choice of several) called *dagens rätt* at a fixed price. It's a practice originally supported and subsidised by the government with the goal of keeping workers happy and efficient all day, and it's still one of the most economical ways to sample upscale Swedish cooking.

You won't be in Sweden very long before hearing or seeing the word *fika*, which roughly means to meet friends for coffee and cake in the afternoon (around 3pm, although it can happen at any time of day and isn't technically restricted to coffee). Nearly every museum or tourist attraction in the city has a respectable café so as to prevent the crankiness of *fika*-deprived visitors.

Dinner in Stockholm presents a vast range of possibilities. Thanks to the influx of immigrants in the past decade, the range of available cuisines is increasingly broad; you can easily find authentic Turkish, Spanish, Lebanese, Indian, Cuban, Greek, Japanese, Chinese and Thai restaurants within the city centre. One of the most talked-about restaurants to open recently is Eyubi (p108), where Kurdish-Persian specialities are served in a converted car park.

# FASHION

Stockholmers are a rigorously fashionable bunch, especially the women. Shops enforce the latest styles as handed down by runway magazines – they simply don't carry anything uncool. It's not unusual to walk past the windows of three different clothing shops, say H&M, VeroModa and Åhléns, and see the exact same three colours (plus black) and the same basic outfits. Like all the other fashion capitals, Stockholm is currently undergoing an '80s renaissance in women's fashion, with slinky off-the-shoulder tops, miniskirts with leggings, black-and-white striped tights and *Flashdance*-style legwarmers. Men's fashion is fairly classic in the mainstream,

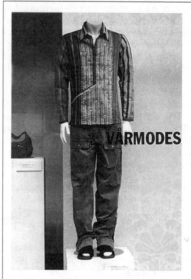

*Fashions at NK department store (p145)*

but hipsters and indie-rock youth lean towards a '60s-nerd look, which seems to be fairly universal.

## SPORT

Ice hockey, bandy and football are all big team sports in Stockholm. The main clubs are AIK, Djurgården and Hammarby, with Hammarby being the coolest. *Bandy*, a game similar to ice hockey (for more information, see the Entertainment chapter, p137), is among the most popular sports in Sweden, with nearly 120,000 licensed players in 1300 registered clubs.

The winter sports season runs from September to April. For a more DIY version, check out the iced-over pools at Kungsträdgården or Medborgarplatsen (the citizens' square) on any winter day, where pick-up bandy and ice-hockey games are played constantly.

As this is Sweden, fans don't get too riled up or cheer too loudly, but that doesn't mean they're any less enthusiastic at heart. Mostly they congregate in local pubs – Kvarnen is a Hammarby hang-out, and the bars around Zinkensdamms Idrottsplats are always brimming with bandy and ice-hockey enthusiasts.

Other big sports in Stockholm include tennis and golf, and a visit to Stockholm affords numerous options to watch or play both (see the Entertainment chapter for details, p137). Horse racing is also popular.

Past and present stars on the Swedish athletic scene include diver Anna Lindberg, tennis god Björn Borg, ice-hockey stud Peter Forsberg and Olympic gold medal–winning skiers Ingemar Stenmark and Pernilla Wiberg.

## MEDIA

Stockholm's media faces the same challenges as in most other major metropolitan areas: increasing control of a few large corporations; the resultant dumbing-down of the news; and the growing influence of commercial interests. While the main daily newspapers in Stockholm are still highly regarded, journalists have expressed concern about declining news standards and diminishing readership.

Swedish TV was once dominated by public-service broadcasting. Like the publicly owned Swedish radio, it was renowned for its creativity and well-produced programs. The more recent influx of commercial stations, both in radio and TV, seems to have put the fear of boredom into the public stations; they're now glutted with flashy programs that mimic the commercial stations. In fact, when watching Swedish TV it can be hard to tell you're not in the American Midwest. SVT, the first public TV station, still carries mostly public-service shows about Swedish culture and history, but they're far overshadowed by the 'edgier' stuff on the privately run TV4 and Kanal 5.

International magazines and all major European papers are sold at Press Stop newsstands, Pressbyrå shops and tobacconists. The reading room at Internationella Bibliotek (see p198) has fairly recent copies of many European newspapers, including London's *Times* and the *Observer*.

## LANGUAGE

Swedish is a Germanic language, belonging to the Nordic branch, and is the first language of the majority of people in Stockholm. Swedes, Danes and Norwegians can make themselves mutually understood, although Danes understand Swedish better than Swedes understand Danish. There are volumes' worth of intra-Scandinavian linguistic jokes, prejudices and tensions that most outsiders find difficult to fully appreciate. In films and on TV, it's not uncommon to see characters from Sweden marooned in Norway, for example, and unable to make themselves understood; see Lars von Trier's *The Kingdom* for one example, and Erik Skjoldbjærg's *Insomnia* starring Swedish film star Stellan Skarsgård for another.

Most Swedes speak English as a second language – and love any opportunity to show it off. Trying your hand at a bit of Swedish, however, will be met with appreciation if not some amusement. Since English and Swedish share common root words and the Old Norse language left sprinklings of words in Anglo-Saxon, you'll find many similarities between the two languages. The pronunciations differ, though, and there are sounds in Swedish that aren't found in English: try repeating the correct pronunciation of 'Yxsmedsgränd'. Also, there are three extra letters at the end of the Swedish alphabet – å, ä and ö.

For more extensive coverage of Swedish, see the Language chapter (p207), or Lonely Planet's *Scandinavian phrasebook*.

# ECONOMY & COSTS

Stockholm was founded to control trade in the Baltic region and, despite the economic crisis of the early 1990s, the city remains the strongest trading centre in the area. In fact, Stockholm is a leading European economic area and only 13 out of 200 EU regions have a higher per capita GDP.

Unemployment in the county of Stockholm was approximately 3.6% in early 2004. Since the end of the economic crisis (in 1994), Stockholm has accounted for around 90% of the increase in Sweden's employment figures.

The following figures refer to the percentage of the total workforce in each industry in Stockholm: banking, insurance and other financial services (25.3%); trade and communications (20%); medical care and social welfare (15.1%); personal and cultural services (12.7%); energy production and manufacturing (8.6%); education and research (8.5%); public administration (6.1%); construction (3.2%); and agriculture and fishing (0.2%).

The average Swede earns Skr26,000 per month. In Stockholm, 80% of the workforce is in the service sector. The largest employers, in descending order, are the city council, the postal service, Ericsson Radio Systems, Telia telecommunications company, Skandinaviska Enskilde Banken, Stockholm University, Ericsson Telecom and the Konsum group of cooperative supermarkets. Tourism employs around 62,000 people.

> ## How Much?
>
> - Litre of petrol Skr9.50
> - Litre of milk Skr6.60
> - Weekend admission to a Stureplan club Skr150
> - Arne Jacobsen's Myran chair Skr2900
> - 0.7 litre of renat brännvin (classic, purified Swedish vodka) Skr204
> - 20 cigarettes Skr36.40
> - Men's haircut Skr210
> - Women's haircut Skr300 to Skr400
> - Newspaper Skr10.90
> - Cinema ticket Skr75

The private sector is larger in Stockholm than elsewhere in Sweden. Several Swedish companies have their head offices and research and development units located in the capital but production units may be elsewhere in the country or abroad. One fifth of companies are at least half foreign-owned. Of the total industrial production, 35% is exported, but the share of exports from the high-technology industries is 70%.

More than 150,000 companies operate in Stockholm, but 98% are companies with fewer than 20 employees or single-person companies, with no employees. In private sector employment, small companies account for 35%, medium-sized 22% and large (over 200 employees) 43%.

Accommodation will be your primary expense in Stockholm, followed by food. The average rate at a mid-range hotel is Skr600 to Skr800 a night, while a top-end place will be closer to Skr1500 to Skr2500. Meals at mid-range and top-end restaurants cost anywhere from Skr85 to Skr250, depending on the time of day and the restaurant's style quotient.

# GOVERNMENT & POLITICS

The city council consists of a mayor (who heads the finance department and chairs the Council of Mayors and Stockholm City Executive Board meetings) along with seven vice mayors and 92 ordinary council members. All 101 members of the city council are elected by the people of Stockholm, who are aged 18 or over, once every four years. The council members then elect a mayor and the vice mayors.

The city council has responsibility for standards of municipal services, bylaws, and appropriate expenditure of tax revenue. It determines the rate of local income tax and the level of any fees to be charged, and also approves the budget and accounts from each of its committees and corporations.

The 13-member City Executive Board drafts items of business for the twice-monthly city council meetings. At these meetings, the council deals with resolutions referred to it by the district councils or the committees, who actually run most of the city's affairs. Public attendance at council meetings is extremely low, averaging only 1.5 people per meeting.

Currently, the city has 18 district councils (slimmed down from 24 in 1999), most with 13 members and 13 deputies, all of whom are appointed by the city council. Each district has a full-time director who is responsible for implementation of decisions – interestingly, most city council decisions are made at this level.

The entire city administration employs around 51,500 people. More information about the city council can be found on the Internet at www.stockholm.se.

The county of Stockholm consists of the city and 25 other *kommun* (municipalities). The low-key *landsting* (county council), elected by popular vote at the same time as the city council, has responsibility for regional public transport and health care. It raises income tax to pay for its expenses, and owns Storstockholms Lokaltrafik (SL; the regional transport network) and appoints its board members. For more details, visit www.sll.se/international /default.asp.

Voter turnout is consistently high, around 78% and up. Currently, the Swedish parliament is controlled by a three-party team consisting of the left-wing Social Democratic Party, the Left Party and the Green Party. The most pressing issues up for debate in parliament in the near future are likely to focus on the EU, adoption of the euro and domestic economy issues.

# ENVIRONMENT

Ecological consciousness among Swedes is high and is reflected in their concern for native animals, clean water and renewable resources. Although concern for the environment has only become widespread since the 1970s, Sweden and Stockholm now have good records when it comes to environmental policies. Industrial and agricultural waste is highly regulated, sewage disposal is advanced and efficient, recycling is popular, there's little rubbish in waterways and on streets, and general tidiness is highly prioritised in both urban and rural environments.

Stockholm takes pride in the fact that you can swim and fish for trout and salmon in the waters by the city centre. The city also has the world's first national city park, Ekoparken, which stretches 14km from the Fjäderholmarna islands to the northern suburbs.

For general environmental details on Sweden, check the Swedenvironment website at www.swedenvironment.environ.se. You can also contact the following organisations:

**Naturvårdsverket** (Swedish Environmental Protection Agency; ☎ 698 1000; www.internat.environ.se/index.php3; Blekholmsterrassen 36, SE-10648 Stockholm) This agency has a highly informative website that includes details on national parks.

**Svenska Naturskyddsföreningen** (Swedish Society for Nature Conservation; ☎ 702 6500; www.snf.se/english.cfm; Box 4625, SE-11691 Stockholm) It has around 175,000 members and has successfully protected endangered species, including peregrine falcons.

## THE LAND

Stockholm is built on a collection of islands, which has had a tremendous impact on the city's development. Gamla Stan (the Old Town), for example, is well preserved partly because it's contained on its own little island.

Water makes its presence known everywhere in Stockholm in the canals and channels separating the various islands; one of the city's marketing slogans is 'Beauty on Water'. Perhaps the most interesting geological formation in the area, however, is the Stockholm archipelago. Its scenic appeal and accessible location mean it lures locals and visitors alike out of the city by the thousands; for more on the archipelago, see the Excursions chapter (p171).

# GREEN STOCKHOLM

Recycling is extremely popular and Swedes strongly support the sorting of household waste – paper, organic matter, glass, plastics, tyres and car batteries – for collection. The country is the world leader in recycling aluminium cans; the recycling of glass and paper, though not quite as successful, stands at 59% and 50% respectively.

# URBAN PLANNING & DEVELOPMENT

A characteristic Stockholm planning venture in recent years was the Million Program, a scheme designed by the Swedish government based on the 1964 campaign slogan of the Social Democrats, 'A million homes in 10 years'. Sweden's strict rent controls and lack of investment in new housing had created a massive housing shortage, with hundreds of thousands of people waiting for apartments. The Million Program involved government loans to private builders to build huge housing complexes in suburbs across Sweden. This resulted in some pretty grim human-filing-cabinet-style buildings, many of which lurk in Stockholm suburbs like Tensta, Rinkeby and Brandbergen. The program basically ended in the 1970s after the government enacted tax breaks to make it easier for people to own their own homes rather than rent. Despite the aesthetic weaknesses of some of the buildings, the Million Program is considered a success for solving a pressing problem rather quickly while continuing to provide high-quality housing for many of the country's lower-income residents.

# Arts

# Arts

Aside from design, for which Sweden is acknowledged as a defining force and trend-setter, film and literature have historically been the country's twin champions in the world of the arts. They remain strong today, with Swedish film in particular undergoing a renaissance and talented young Swedish filmmakers like Lukas Moodysson and his peers gaining recognition worldwide. On the literary side, high-profile Swedish novels, such as Per Olov Enquist's *The Royal Physician's Visit* (2002), routinely become bestsellers in several languages. In popular literature, Stockholm-born mystery writer Henning Mankell is a publishing phenomenon on par with American writer John Grisham.

The visual arts scene in Stockholm is also thriving, chiefly on the fringes of town and among innovative, unorthodox groups like Magasin 3 and the Nursery. Similarly, the highest energy levels in Stockholm theatre are to be found in the city's scrappy little experimental theatres (although Bergman himself is still directing occasional plays at the Royal Dramatic Theatre).

Sweden has always had a keen interest in jazz and classical music; the pop and rock scenes have occasionally struggled, but hope for renewal always follows in the wake of internationally successful bands like the Hives, who swept the charts in 2002–03.

In short, Stockholm's arts scene is alive and kicking.

## MUSIC

Despite what their exported pop records might lead you to believe, Swedes have a profound appreciation for music, as highlighted by the fact that they buy more recorded music per capita than any other nationality. Stockholmers' musical literacy covers everything from trad jazz, fusion, blues and funk to reggae, techno, rock and death metal. The live music scene tends to die down in one area only to revivify in another; at the time of research, young pop bands playing '60s-influenced indie-rock were all the rage among hipsters, and you could find enthusiastic blues jams any night of the week. Salsa concerts and Cuban dance clubs are also popular.

### Top Five Stockholm CDs

- **ABBA** *Arrival* (1976) 'Dancing Queen' will never get old.
- **The Hives** *Veni Vidi Vicious* (2002) The Swedish punk-rock Rolling Stones.
- **The Cardigans** *Life* (1992) A band made for MTV.
- **Roxette** *Look Sharp!* (1988) Admit it, you loved this album!
- **The Latin Kings** *The Latin Kings* (2004) Head rapper Dogge Doggelito and his homies rap in suburban Swedish slang plus Turkish and Spanish – they're HUGE in Stockholm.

## CLASSICAL

Although Sweden has never produced a classical composer to match Norway's Edvard Grieg, there has been no shortage of contenders.

One of the earliest was the serious Franz Berwald (1796–1868), who wrote chamber music, operas and four symphonies, but wasn't fully appreciated as one of Sweden's finest composers until the 20th century. Berwaldhallen, the concert hall just east of the city centre, is named after him. Wilhelm Stenhamrar (1871–1927) was a fine composer of symphonic, vocal and chamber music, but his work has appealed more to musical experts than to the people at large.

The Wagnerian Wilhelm Peterson-Berger (1867–1942) composed musical dramas with a strong flavour of Swedish folk culture. Peterson-Berger's opera *Arnljot* became the Swedish national opera, but he's better known for his lyrical piano miniatures.

Hugo Alfvén (1872–1960), one of Sweden's greatest symphonists, also conducted several tours abroad as leader of a men's choir. One of his finest works, *Svensk rapsodi nr 1, Midsommarvaka*, completed in 1903, was influenced by a wedding he attended in the Stockholm archipelago.

Opera flourished after the opening of the Royal Opera House in Stockholm (1782), and since 1922 several other venues have appeared, including the Drottningholm Court Theatre and the proletarian-friendly Folkoperan, which brings the audience into close contact with the singers.

# FOLK

Interest in Swedish folk music really took off in the 1970s and 1980s, assisted by the annual Falun Folk Music Festival (in Dalarna). Some say it's the fastest-growing area in Swedish music, with folk rock and other avant-garde variants becoming increasingly popular. Traditional Swedish folk music revolves around the triple-beat *polska*, originally a Polish dance. Instruments commonly played include the fiddle, accordion, harp, violin and (more rarely) the bagpipes. Although most folk events take place in rural areas, folk music and dancing can also be experienced in Stockholm – the outdoor stage at Skansen, for example, frequently hosts folk singers and dancers.

The immensely popular troubadour Cornelis Vreeswijk (1937–87) wrote both amusing and serious lyrics and sang in perfect Swedish, although he was born in the Netherlands.

Ethnic minority folk music includes a wide range of styles brought in by immigrants from around the world. Stallet is the principal folk-music concert venue in Stockholm (see p135).

# JAZZ

Between the 1930s and 1960s, jazz was all the rage. Sweden produced a series of artists who excelled in the guitar, saxophone and clarinet, although early musicians were heavily influenced by American jazz. In the late 1930s the Sonora Swing Swingers – a jazz group with an ever-changing line-up led by bass player Thore Jederby – released a series of excellent records, including 'Lady Be Good' and other classics. During WWII, when Sweden was virtually cut off from the outside world, home-grown jazz expanded rapidly. Many excellent soloists appeared on the scene, including the trumpeter Rolf Ericson (1922–97), the saxophonist Carl-Henrik Norin (1920–67) and the clarinettist Putte Wickman (1924–).

In the 1950s the leading Swedish jazz musician was Lars Gullin (1928–76), who excelled as a baritone sax, travelled abroad and cooperated closely with visiting American musicians. His career was tragically curtailed due to drug abuse. Bernt Rosengren (1937–), a tenor saxophonist, was the main star of the 1960s, along with the pianist Jan Johansson (1931–68), who succeeded in blending jazz and folk in a peculiar Swedish fashion.

The rise of jazz-rock during the 1970s and 1980s, and a good selection of young vocalists in the 1990s, has ensured that jazz is an important music genre in Stockholm. There are three excellent jazz clubs in the city – the Glenn Miller Cafe (p136), Stampen (p136) and Jazzclub Fasching (p136) – each of which has live performances on most evenings.

*Record stall at Hötorget flea market*

## Mamma Mia, Here we go Again…

The Swedish group ABBA, consisting of two couples, was founded in the 1970s and soon became one of the most successful popular music acts of the decade. The individual members were all show business veterans in their native Sweden before the band was launched.

The name ABBA, an acronym of the names Agnetha, Björn, Benny and Anni-Frid, was a nickname invented by band manager Stig Anderson for convenience, but when a newspaper competition came up with the same name, the decision was made and ABBA was born. There was already a Swedish canned-fish company with the same name, but when Anderson asked if it would mind lending its name to a popular music group, fortunately, the herring purveyors didn't object.

ABBA won the Eurovision Song Contest in 1974 with 'Waterloo', topping the charts in several countries and reaching the top five in several others, including the USA. It went from success to success – ABBA toured the world, made a film and recorded many hit records. The band's last year together was 1982, but in 1992 the compilation album *ABBA Gold* became the group's biggest seller ever, topping charts the world over. Despite this revival success, no reunion is on the cards.

On 6 April 1999, 25 years to the day after ABBA won the Eurovision Song Contest, Benny Andersson and Björn Ulvaeus' new musical, *Mamma Mia*, featuring 27 of ABBA's legendary songs, received its world premiere at London's Prince Edward Theatre.

At the group's 30th anniversary, in April 2004, there was talk of another whole-group reunion; the Benny & Björn theatrical projects were an unabashed success, selling out in the thousands worldwide. Rumours of an Agnetha and Anni-Frid reunion tantalised fans, but nothing concrete had been established at the time of publication.

# POP & ROCK

After the Beatles visited Sweden in 1963, the pop scene exploded and more than 100 new bands were formed in a few weeks, many of them in Stockholm. Initially, groups were just imitations of British or American bands and styles, for example the bizarrely named Ola & the Janglers and the space-age Spotniks, who became internationally renowned.

By the 1970s a more distinctive Swedish pop tradition was growing. ABBA is the best-known group from this time (see the boxed text, p22), although its blatant commercialism caused controversy in Sweden. In the late 1970s anarchic punk groups, such as Ebba Grön, arose in Stockholm, as in most big cities, to 'fight the system'. The still-active band Refused is among the internationally best-known Swedish political hardcore/punk bands.

In 1986 the pop-rock group Europe, originally from the Stockholm suburb Upplands Väsby, achieved a number one hit around the world with 'The Final Countdown'. Since then, the tenacious pop duo Roxette and MTV-friendly groups such as the Cardigans and Ace of Base have held international attention. In the late 1980s and early '90s, the extreme 'death metal' scene in Stockholm developed an immense audience with a vast number of bands. Its roots lie in the northern part of the country; founding bands include Nihilist, Unleashed, At the Gates and the still-touring Entombed, one of the first bands on the genre-defining Earache record label.

One of Sweden's latest rock exports is the Hives, a garage band whose 2000 album *Veni Vidi Vicious* seized the MTV audience by their artfully tousled hair and shook the wrinkles out of their retro suits. An equally big sensation in Stockholm are the Latin Kings, a hip-hop group doing its best to support the theory that cultural epicentres have shifted to the suburbs. Its members have their roots in Latin America, live in the multicultural Stockholm suburbs of Tensta, Rinkeby and Alby, and rap in a particularly suburban-Stockholm pastiche of Swedish slang, Spanish, Turkish and English.

Perhaps the most influential Swede on the international music scene is not a rock star at all. Stockholm producer/songwriter Max Martin, who worked at the successful music studio Cheiron before shutting it down and starting his own, is the man behind the teen-pop revival of the 1990s. Martin has written about 300 hit songs and produced albums for the likes of Britney Spears, The Backstreet Boys and *N Sync.

# LITERATURE

The best-known members of Sweden's artistic community historically have been writers, chiefly the influential dramatist and author August Strindberg (1849–1912) and – at the opposite end of the emotional spectrum – the widely translated children's writer Astrid Lindgren (1907–2002).

Strindberg's *Röda Rummet* (Red Room), a satire based at Berns Salonger and completed in 1879, was a breakthrough for him and is widely considered the first modern Swedish novel. Ignored by the Nobel Prize committee but beloved by the Swedish people, Strindberg represents the conflicted, moody, mercurial side of the Swedish soul. His *Occult Diary*, a journal of the artistic and spiritual quagmire he titled *Inferno* that seized him in midlife (see the boxed text, p28), makes for fascinating if heartbreaking reading; only excerpts are available in translation. Strindberg is, of course, best known for his plays, particularly *Miss Julie* (see Theatre, p27).

Lindgren's well-known fantasy characters, especially Pippi Longstocking and her pet monkey, Herr Nilsson, hold an enduring fascination for children – understandably, as Pippi lived alone in her own house, was invincible, had animals for friends and could do whatever she wanted. Lindgren's book *Pippi Longstocking* was first published in English in 1950.

Selma Lagerlöf (1858–1940) was also an early literary giant. Two of her best-known works are *Gösta Berling's Saga* (1891) and *Nils Holgerssons underbara resa genom Sverige* (The Wonderful Adventures of Nils; 1906–07); the latter book was read as a history and geography text by Swedish schoolchildren for decades. Lagerlöf hailed from Mårbacka in Värmland (west-central Sweden), but she studied at the Royal Women's Superior Training Academy in Stockholm, graduating as a teacher in 1882. Despite her vocal opposition to the Swedish establishment, Lagerlöf became literature's Nobel laureate in 1909 'in appreciation of the lofty idealism, vivid imagination and spiritual perception that characterises her writings'.

During WWII some Swedish writers bravely opposed the Nazis, including Eyvind Johnson (1900–76) with his Krilon trilogy, completed in 1943. Johnson was the joint Nobel laureate in literature in 1974 (with fellow Swedish writer Harry Martinson) and spent his later years in Stockholm. Also outspokenly opposed to the Nazi regime was the troubled poet, novelist and painter Karin Boye (1900–41), whose novel *Kallocain* was published to great acclaim in 1940 and is still discussed in reverent tones. Despite her talents, Boye was an unhappy woman and committed suicide in 1941.

Stig Dagerman (1923–54) embodied yet another aspect of Swedish grim humour. A compatriot of Eyvind Johnson, Dagerman wrote darkly existential novels, short stories and poetry, and was considered among the most promising writers of his generation (he was often called the 'Swedish Camus'). He committed suicide in 1954 just outside of Stockholm. His works today are difficult to find in English.

The social critic Karl Ivar Lo-Johansson (1901–90) wrote for more than 50 years, mainly about ordinary people and landless peasants; he received the Nordic Council literary prize in 1979.

Torgny Lindgren (1938–), though born in Norsjö in the far north of Sweden, is a member of Stockholm's Swedish Academy and a frequent media presence in the capital. He is a peculiar talent whose hypnotic novels and short stories delve into the human psyche, particularly that of rural Swedes.

Equally individualistic is the experimental work of novelist Kerstin Ekman (1933–), a onetime member of the Swedish Academy known internationally for her dark mysteries frequently set in Stockholm. Her novel *Blackwater* (1993), the first of her works to be translated into English, is a moody crime novel that goes from rural Swedish commune to Stockholm apartment and plumbs the depths of a mother-daughter relationship.

Born in Västerbotten but now living in Stockholm, writer Per Olov Enquist (1934–) is noted for the reportorial style of his novels, often compared to the 'literary journalism' of Truman Capote or Tom Wolfe. Before writing *The Legionnaires* (1968), a novel about Sweden's deportation of Baltic soldiers at the end of WWII, Enquist gathered masses of documentation and travelled extensively to interview former legionnaires. Enquist has also published journalism and literary criticism in Stockholm newspapers, including *Expressen* and *Svenska Dagbladet*.

The name of Henning Mankell (1948–) is impossible to miss in any bookshop in Sweden. Born in Stockholm, he is one of Sweden's best-known writers and has gained international acclaim for his nine-book series about morose Swedish detective Kurt Wallander.

Mankell's breakthrough as a crime writer came with the novel *Faceless Killers* (1989). Trivial tidbit: Mankell's wife, Eva, is Ingmar Bergman's daughter.

Twentieth-century Swedish poetry tended to dwell on political and social issues such as the Vietnam War, apartheid in South Africa and social conditioning at home. Some of the better-known poets from the Stockholm area include Karin Boye (see above) and Katarina Frostenson (1953–), whose haunting poems strike some of the most basic chords within human nature. Frostenson has also written several fine avant-garde dramas, and her works have been performed by the Royal Dramatic Theatre in Stockholm.

To the Swedish soul, however, the Gustavian balladry of Carl Michael Bellman is perhaps dearest. Bellman was born in Stockholm in 1740 and completed one of his best-known writings, *Fredmans Epistlar* (Fredman's Epistles), when he was only 30. Greek themes, with references to drunken revelry and Bacchus, the Greek and Roman god of wine, are strong features in this work.

Evert Taube (1890–1976), sailor, author, composer and painter, is known as Bellman's modern successor. Part of Riddarholmen is now named Evert Taubes Terrass in his honour, and you'll find a statue of him there.

## Swedish Fiction

The following are some Stockholm-related literary works we recommend for anyone interested in the city's cultural fabric. Many were written by important Stockholm authors, while others are set there or nearby.

- *Anna, Hanna och Johanna* (Hannah's Daughters), Marianne Fredriksson (1994) – In this sprawling, multi-generational novel, a woman tries to piece together the lives of her dying mother and her mysterious grand-mother.
- *Blackwater,* Kerstin Ekman (1996) – In this unconventional mystery, a woman misinterprets an act of violence she witnesses in the forest, which has repercussions for her and her family for decades.
- *Doctor Glas: A Novel,* Hjalmar Soderberg (1905) – A doctor contemplates murder in this tale of moral compromise when the woman he loves, who happens to be the minister's wife, complains about her husband's oppressive sexual demands.
- *The Emigrants* series, Vilhelm Moberg (1949–59) – This is the definitive series on Swedish immigrants to the United States.
- *Faceless Killers,* Henning Mankell (1989) – Introducing Kurt Wallander, a chronically discontented Swedish detective.
- *Firewater,* Henning Mankell (2003) – The latest volume of Stockholm-native Mankell's popular Kurt Wallander series, featuring a gloomy police inspector.
- *The Island of Doom,* Stig Dagerman (1946) – This allegorical tale pits five men and two women against the elements on a deserted Pacific island; each character represents one aspect of human frailty.
- *Kallocain,* Karin Boye (1940) – This classic Swedish novel, a precursor to dystopian fiction like Orwell's *1984*, depicts a totalitarian state in which drugs ensure the subservience of every citizen.
- *Kungsgatan,* Karl Ivar Lo-Johansson (1935) – This novel by Sweden's champion of the proles deals with a farm boy's experiences in a big city; it created a sensation for its frank description of prostitution.
- *Merab's Beauty,* Torgny Lindgren (1982) – Lindgren's impeccable short-story collection presents an impossibly bleak view of peasant life in rural Sweden.
- *Nils Holgerssons underbara resa genom Sverige* (The Wonderful Adventures of Nils), Selma Lagerlöf (1906–07) – Nils, a callow preteen, rides a goose across all of Sweden, meeting people, having adventures and learning geography.
- *Ondskan* (Evil), Jan Guillou (1981) – A tough adolescent boy from Stockholm, beaten regularly by his stepfather, carves out a path for himself in an abusive boarding school.
- *Pippi Longstocking,* Astrid Lindgren (1945) – The original tale of everyone's favourite pigtailed tomboy.
- *The Royal Physician's Visit,* Per Olov Enquist (2002) – An atmospheric novel based on the life of Johann Friedrich Struensee, a German who became the royal physician in the late 1760s and essentially ran Denmark in King Christian VII's name.
- *Röda Rummet,* August Strindberg (1879) – Strindberg's breakthrough novel is a satire on Stockholm society based at Berns Salonger.
- *The Snake,* Stig Dagerman (1945) – A snake slithers into an army barracks in this episodic novel about fear, sensuality and the reptilian nature of human evil.
- *The Way of a Serpent,* Torgny Lindgren (1982) – In this dark novella with biblical overtones, a wicked shopkeeper in a backwater village holds a man's wife in bondage until her husband's debt is paid off.

# VISUAL ARTS

Although some of Sweden's most significant painters lived outside Stockholm, their works are displayed in galleries and public buildings throughout the city.

Carl Larsson (1853–1919), Nils Kreuger (1858–1930) and their peers were leaders of an artistic revolution in the 1880s. Some of the best 19th-century oil paintings were painted by Larsson in a warm Art Nouveau style. Anders Zorn (1860–1920) is noted for his nudes and portraits of famous Swedes. August Strindberg's surprisingly modern landscapes have also come to the attention of the art world lately. The nature paintings of Bruno Liljefors (1860–1939) are well regarded and consequently sell for high prices at auction. The vivid Stockholm landscapes by Eugène Jansson (1862–1915) show the influence of Norwegian artist Edvard Munch. Sweden's Prince Eugene (1865–1947) lived and worked in an isolated mansion on Djurgården and produced many fine paintings.

Although there was an initially cautious approach to cubism, some artists embraced the concepts of surrealist and abstract art, albeit with their own Swedish style, such as the rather bizarre 'dreamland' paintings of Stellan Mörner (1896–1979). Otto Carlsund (1897–1948) was the driving force behind early abstract art in Sweden, which strongly impinged on the public conscience during the Stockholm exhibition of 1930 but didn't really become established until after WWII. Olle Baertling's postwar geometric-style paintings still sell well at auction.

In Sweden as elsewhere, more radical art movements in the 1960s and 1970s were influenced by diverse sources, including far left-wing politics, popular culture, minimalism and pop art. The intriguing paintings by Jan Håfström (1937–) remind observers how close many Swedes are to nature, and the vaguely disturbing *Will you be profitable, my little one?* by Peter Tillberg is clearly an attack on 1970s society and schooling. Peter Dahl, Norwegian-born but living in Stockholm, is noted for his paintings illustrating Bellman ballads.

Until fairly recently women artists have been on the fringes of the Stockholm art scene. Two artists are Swedish photographer Annica Karlsson Rixon (1962–), who is known for her provocative images, and Maria Lindberg (1958–), who is known for her outrageously humorous paintings and drawings.

Stockholm is noted for its excellent street sculpture, often in bronze. The leading sculptors active in the 20th century were Carl Milles (1875–1955), who lived on the island Lidingö (see p85), and Carl Eldh (1873–1954), whose studio was based in a superb location near Brunnsviken. There are various other works by sculptors around the city, including *Systrarna* at Mosebacke torg (Mosebacke square), *Little Elephant Dreaming* at Greta Garbos torg (Greta Garbo's square) in Södermalm and the superb *Non Violence* (a revolver with a knotted barrel) in the middle of the shopping street Sergelgatan.

## Top Five Museums & Galleries

Some of the coolest galleries and art exhibition spaces in Stockholm are out towards the city fringes, often in non-traditional buildings. Other than the larger museum galleries reviewed in the Neighbourhoods chapter (Moderna Museet, National Museum, Thielska Galleriet and Waldemarsudde, for example), the following places are worth checking out.

- **Magasin 3** ( ☎ 54 56 80 40; www.magasin3.com; Frihamnen; bus 1, 76) Housed in an old warehouse by the ports beyond Gärdet, this innovative space curates three to four ambitious shows a year; check its website for opening hours.
- **Projekt Djurgårdsbrunnsviken** ( ☎ 54 56 80 40; Djurgårdsbrunnsviken 68; bus 69) The folks at Magasin 3 put on occasional shows at this sprawling, waterside complex.
- **Färgfabriken** ( ☎ 645 07 07; Lövholmsbrinken 1, Liljeholmen; T-Liljeholmen) An experimental centre showcasing art, architecture and design.
- **Tensta Konsthall** ( ☎ 36 07 63; www.tenstakonsthall.com; Taxingegränd 10; T-Tensta) This exhibition hall is in one of Stockholm's most interesting multicultural suburbs.
- **Konstakuten** ( ☎ 641 77 90; www.konstakuten.com; Nackagatan 11; bus 46) An artist-run space in Hammarby harbour, the 'art emergency room' is a major player in the avant-garde Nordic art scene.

Another kind of street art – underground or 'guerrilla' art – is also big in Stockholm. Whether the medium is graphics or graffiti, radical artists are putting their marks all over the city in a most entertaining fashion. A line drawing of a deer looking alarmed appears a lot – it's the handiwork of the mysterious 'Sticker Peter'. Keep your eyes peeled for posters, flyers, logos and creative reworkings of billboards. For more details, check out the websites www.akayism.org, www.bigd.nu or http://lunattack.cjb.net.

# CINEMA & TV

Three of the most important names in classic Swedish cinema are Victor Sjöstrom, Ingmar Bergman and Sven Nykvist. Sjöstrom, often called the father of Swedish cinema, started directing in 1912. Though a well-known stage actor, his work as a director was vital in eradicating old-fashioned theatrical conventions from the Swedish scene. Famous for using his landscape almost as a character, Sjöstrom also helped make Lillian Gish a star (*The Wind*, 1928). His films include *Terje Vigen* (1917) and *The Outlaw and His Wife* (1918). Along with Mauritz Stiller, who directed such masterpieces as *Körkarlen* (The Phantom Carriage, adapted from a novel by Selma Lagerlöf), Sjöstrom created a golden age of silent film in the 1920s. The glory days were put on hold, however, when most of the stars, including Sjöstrom and Greta Garbo moved to Hollywood.

Acclaim for Swedish film returned with the work of Ingmar Bergman, whose films from the late 1940s to 1982 made his name virtually synonymous with Swedish cinema (see the boxed text, opposite). Bergman's partner-in-crime, cinematographer Sven Nykvist, is less well known; his skill working with light and shadow was absolutely vital to achieving the director's vision.

As in many other countries, the growing power of TV in the 1960s caused cinema audiences to dwindle. Government intervention to save the industry resulted in increasing

## Sweden on the Silver Screen

Though Ingmar Bergman has inarguably had a tremendous impact on the film industry in this country, Swedish films are more varied than you might expect. The following are some of our favourite examples.

- *The Seventh Seal*, Ingmar Bergman (1956) – A corpse-like young Max von Sydow plays chess with 'Death' in this chilling allegory set in the medieval plague years.
- *Persona*, Ingmar Bergman (1966) – An extremely creepy psychodrama that builds strange tension between an actress who refuses to speak and her nurse who can't stop confessing.
- *I am Curious: Yellow*, Vilgot Sjöman (1967) – Provocative political commentary was overshadowed by frank sexuality for many viewers of this morality tale.
- *The Emigrants*, Jan Troell (1970) – Together with *The New Land*, this touching drama follows Swedish families relocating to the USA.
- *My Life as a Dog*, Lasse Hallström (1985) – The story of a farm boy in the '50s, this sweet film has touches of magic realism.
- *The Best Intentions*, Bille August (1992) – This screenplay was written by Ingmar Bergman about his parents.
- *Fucking Åmål* (Show Me Love), Lukas Moodysson (1998) – This award-winning film by the promising young Moodysson is an all-girl high school romance à la *Foxfire*.
- *Together*, Lukas Moodysson (2000) – A charming look at Swedish hippies in the '70s trying to find love and harmony in a commune.
- *Light Keeps Me Company*, Carl-Gustaf Nykvist (2000) – A documentary about Bergman's cinematographer and partner in crime, this touching and illuminating film was directed by Sven Nykvist's son after his father was diagnosed with career-ending aphasia.
- *Songs from the Second Floor*, Roy Andersson (2000) – Hailed by critics internationally, this surreal film takes a grim but comic look at the idiocy of modern life.
- *Ondskan* (Evil), Mikael Håfström (2003) – A gripping adaptation of Jan Guillou's semi-autobiographical novel, in which a teenage boy who has grown up surrounded by violence struggles to overcome his aggressors without beating them senseless.
- *Kops*, Josef Fares (2003) – An off-kilter parody about four cops in a small town who start committing crimes in order to keep their jobs.

politicisation but failed to halt the decline. Only in the 1990s, with the rise of Scandinavian filmmaking in general, did the trend reverse itself. Young filmmakers such as the Danish Lars von Trier and his Dogme 95 school and Sweden's Lukas Moodysson, have rejuvenated cinema with new blood and new styles. This renaissance centres on an unlikely small town near Göteborg, called Trollhättan (and nicknamed Trollywood). Trollhättan is home to the cinema resource centre Film i Väst, which has co-produced nearly 100 feature films since it opened in 1992. The past three von Trier films and all of Moodysson's films have been filmed in Trollhättan, as have major releases by Colin Nutley, Bille August and others. This development has placed the centre of Scandinavian film squarely within Sweden's borders. Other new Swedish filmmakers to look out for are Josef Fares, Reza Parsa, Roy Andersson and Reza Bagher, whose distinct voices reflect a new diversity in a film industry once completely dominated by Bergman.

Statue in Millesgården (p85)

Arts – Theatre

Meanwhile, TV in Stockholm seems content with alternating between prosaic talk shows and imported sitcoms and reality shows. *Survivor* and *Queer Eye for the Straight Guy* are as inescapable on Stockholm's airwaves as anywhere else.

Despite its reputation for licentious filmmaking, little pornography is actually produced in Sweden. In fact, the world's oldest film censorship board (formed in 1911) is based in Sweden, and it can ban, cut and set minimum ages for any film screened in the country.

# THEATRE

After King Gustav III founded the Royal Theatre in Stockholm in 1773, interest in theatre and opera blossomed. Later, with the arrival of social democracy, theatres were built in functional style in Stockholm and other towns around the country, particularly from the 1920s to the 1950s, to encourage an appreciation among ordinary people. Stockholm today reportedly has more theatres per capita than any other city in Europe. About 30% of government funding for the arts goes to the theatre, but the art form still struggles in the face of intense competition from other pursuits.

It's impossible to discuss Swedish theatre without mentioning, first and foremost, August Strindberg. The larger-than-life figure is best known outside Sweden for *Miss Julie*, his most frequently performed play, in which a servant is seduced by his master's daughter. The two main characters serve as avatars in a battle over class and gender, unable to free themselves from societal constraints. Strindberg was rather obsessed with male-female relations (he's

## Ingmar Bergman

The great film director and screenwriter Ingmar Bergman, one of the major international successes in Swedish cinema, was born in Uppsala in 1918. He's also known at home for his theatre direction.

Bergman's first professional job was the film *Hets* (1944), but his arty psychological style wasn't initially popular with conservative producers or critics. However, after *Smiles of a Summer Night* received international acclaim in 1955, appreciation of Bergman's films became more widespread. The disturbing *Through a Glass, Darkly* and *Winter Light* (both 1962), and *The Silence* (1963), which investigates loneliness and loss of faith, are typical examples of his outlook. His last job as a film director, *Fanny and Alexander*, was released as long ago as 1982, but Bergman has since continued to direct for the stage and write screenplays, including *Sunday's Children* (1993), which was directed by his son, Daniel Bergman.

## August Strindberg

August Strindberg was born in Stockholm in 1849, but his mother died when he was 13 and the stage was set for the chaotic life of this tortured genius who eventually would be hailed as the 'writer of the people'.

Strindberg periodically studied theology and medicine at Uppsala University from 1867 to 1872, but left without a degree. He then worked as a librarian and journalist prior to becoming a productive author and writing novels, plays, poetry and over 7000 letters. He was also a talented painter of moody scenes.

His breakthrough as a writer came in 1879 with publication of the novel *Röda Rummet* (Red Room). In 1884 Strindberg became notorious after publication of *Marriage*, a collection of short stories which led to his trial (and acquittal) for blasphemy in the City Court of Stockholm. Much of his work deals with radical approaches to social issues, and it didn't go down well with the conservative Swedish establishment. In *Miss Julie* (1888), Strindberg's most frequently performed play, a count's daughter seduces her valet on Midsummer's Eve, but she's wracked with guilt and commits suicide the next day.

Strindberg married three times, but each marriage ended in divorce. His first wife was Siri von Essen (married 1877, divorced 1891) and they had four children. During his stay in Central Europe (1892–99), he hung around with other artists, such as Edvard Munch and Paul Gaugin, and had a short-lived marriage to the Austrian Frida Uhl (married 1893, separated 1894, dissolved 1897), which led to the birth of a daughter.

As his emotional instability deepened, Strindberg took an interest in the occult; this led to a mental and emotional crisis that peaked with the publication of *Inferno* (1897), an accurate description of his own emotional shambles. He documented his catastrophic mood swings, paranoias and unshakeable depressions in what is known as his *Occult Diary*, excerpts of which are available (with letters between Strindberg and Harriet Bosse) in English in the fascinating book *From an Occult Diary* (1963).

After returning to Stockholm in 1899, he married Norwegian actress Harriet Bosse in 1901 (divorced 1904) and had yet another daughter.

His work *Dance of Death* (1900) features an old couple who live on an isolated island. They celebrate their silver jubilee, but have always hated each other. In *A Dreamplay* (1901), the daughter of the god Indira visits Earth to find out how people are getting along and finds out how hard human life is.

In 1912 Strindberg was awarded an 'Anti-Nobel Prize' (funded by people around the country) as compensation for not receiving the Nobel Prize for literature. Although the conservative Swedish Academy snubbed him, Strindberg's work was appreciated by many Swedes. His death, in 1912, was seen as the loss of the country's greatest writer.

often unfairly viewed as a misogynist), and many of his early plays hammer at these themes; *Miss Julie* is particularly notable for developing the naturalistic style for which Strindberg became known.

Since Strindberg's day, mainstream theatre in Stockholm has coasted a bit; it can seem a little safe and stodgy, relying on classics. Nevertheless, some interesting new experimental theatres are beginning to crop up in small spaces. For specific venues, see p131.

# ARCHITECTURE

While greater Stockholm contains faceless office blocks and flats dating from the 1960s and 1970s, there's a wide variety of architectural gems around the city, in the surrounding towns and in the countryside. The finest examples include churches, palaces and many large public buildings from the 18th century onwards. Recently, as in many European cities, restoration of older buildings has become popular. Stockholm is notoriously conservative when it comes to new buildings, but the younger generation of architects is beginning to foment a shift in attitudes – although it will be many years before this manifests in the form of visible architectural innovations.

## ROMANESQUE & GOTHIC

Examples of Romanesque church architecture in east-central Sweden, primarily constructed in sandstone and limestone and characterised by archways and barrel-vaulted ceilings, include the substantial ruins of St Olaf (p180) and St Per (p180) in the historical town Sigtuna.

Also in Sigtuna, the fantastic church Mariakyrkan (completed in 1237; p180 features Gothic styles from the 13th and 14th centuries, mainly in brick rather than stone, as does Uppsala cathedral, which was consecrated in 1435. Part of the church Riddarholmskyrkan (p56) in Stockholm can also be described as Baltic-brick Gothic.

# RENAISSANCE, BAROQUE & ROCOCO

During and after the Reformation, monasteries and churches were plundered by the crown and wonderful royal palaces and castles were constructed (or rebuilt) instead. One such example is Gustav Vasa's Gripsholm Slott, 50km west of Stockholm, which has one of the best Renaissance interiors in Sweden. Part of the exterior of St Jakobs kyrka (p68), in central Stockholm, also features Renaissance styles.

Magnificently ornate baroque architecture arrived in Sweden (mainly from Italy) during the 1640s when Queen Kristina held the throne. The church Hedvig Eleonora kyrka, on Storgatan, has an octagonal baroque interior, and Storkyrkan cathedral (p55) has a baroque exterior and tower. Riddarhuset (House of Nobility; p54) is a large Dutch-style baroque building constructed from brick and sandstone. The palace Drottningholms Slott (p177), just west of Stockholm, designed by the court architect Nicodemus Tessin the Elder and completed in the 1690s, is now on Unesco's World Heritage list. Though it wasn't completed until 1754, Nicodemus Tessin the Younger designed the vast 'new' Kungliga Slottet (Royal Palace; p52) in Stockholm after the previous palace was gutted by fire in 1697. The exterior is baroque but most of the interior is 18th-century rococo.

Highly ornamented, asymmetrical rococo designs of mainly French origin are prevalent in many other grandiose 18th-century buildings, including the exterior of Arvfurstens palats (also called Princess Sofia Albertinas palace).

# NEOCLASSICAL, NEOGOTHIC & NEORENAISSANCE

Towards the end of the 18th century, neoclassical designs became popular, especially with Gustav III. A particularly good example of the king's interests can be seen at Gustav IIIs Paviljong (p84), in the park Hagaparken. Generaltullstyrelsen, the former customs building on Skeppsbron at Tullgränd, has a typical neoclassical façade with cornices and hollow cast-iron columns, but it's not open to the public.

Architecture of the 19th century known as the Carl Johan style clearly reflects that particular king's French neoclassical interests, including Skeppsholmskyrkan (no longer used as a church and closed to the public).

Later in the century, neogothic and neo-Renaissance architectural designs also began to appear, including Johannes kyrka (brick-built neogothic) on Johannesgatan and also Kungliga biblioteket (neo-Renaissance). The Norra Latin City Conference Centre (1876), on Norra Bantorget, is an extraordinary Florentine neo-Renaissance building; the four-storey central tower has an oval staircase and the stunning interior includes murals by many leading Swedish artists.

Grand neoclassical architecture continued to appear in Stockholm until the 1920s. Some of the finest later examples include Konserthuset (the Concert Hall; 1923–26; partly Art Deco; p58) and the art gallery Liljevalchs konsthall (1916; p71).

# NEOBAROQUE

The Italian-style neobaroque church Gustaf Vasa kyrka (1906; p57) dwarfs Odenplan

## Top Five Notable Buildings

- **Riddarhuset** (p54) Tall and elegant, this is simply one of the loveliest buildings in the country.
- **Skogskyrkogården** (p86) This impeccably designed cemetery is a Unesco World Heritage site.
- **Stadsbiblioteket** (Map pp236–8) Gunnar Asplund's cylinder-crowned building is internationally renowned as a prime example of 1920s Nordic classicism.
- **Kulturhuset** (p58) Both loved and loathed, the glass house stands at the core of contemporary Stockholm.
- **Stadshuset** (p75) The red brick city hall has been praised since it opened in 1923; highlights are the Blue Hall and mosaic-encrusted Golden Hall.

with its 60m-high cupola. Some of the finest baroque sculpture in Sweden (much older than the church) can also be seen inside.

Other examples of neo-baroque architecture in Stockholm include most of the Opera House and the original (eastern) part of the parliament building Riksdagshuset (p55).

# NATIONAL ROMANTICISM, RHENISH-ROMANESQUE & ART NOUVEAU

The late 19th century and early 20th century saw a rise in national romanticism, a particularly Swedish style mainly using wood and brick. The style produced such wonders as Stockholm's Rådhus (law courts; 1916), which resembles the castle Vadstena Slott, and the Stadshuset (p75), completed in 1923. Also built in national romantic style are Nordiska museet (1907; partly neo-Renaissance; p71), Stadion (National Stadium, completed for the 1912 summer Olympic games and reminiscent of the medieval wall around Visby; p138) and Kungliga Tekniska Högskolan (Royal Technical College; 1914–50).

There are comparatively few examples of Rhenish-Romanesque architecture in the Stockholm area, but Sofia kyrka (1906) on Södermalm is the most prominent, with heavy façades in granite and sandstone.

Many of the Art Nouveau buildings lying east of Nybroplan were built in the early 20th century. The finest of these is Dramatiska teatern (1908; p81), with its magnificent marble façade. The odd-looking Kungsholms församlingshus (Parish social centre), on Kungsholmen, has a granite basement and limestone upper parts. The Rörstrandsgatan apartment buildings, 600m west of St Eriksplan, also feature Art Nouveau styles.

# FUNCTIONALISM

From the 1930s to the 1980s, functionalism and the so-called international style took over, with their emphasis on steel, concrete and glass. Flat roofs and huge windows, hopelessly inappropriate to Swedish weather, were eventually abandoned by architects. Although some buildings from this period are quite attractive, ghastly ranks of apartment blocks are an unpleasant reminder of the dark side of Swedish socialism – conformity.

The most successful examples of functionalism include the student centre Kårhus KTH (1928–30), Stockholm's first building in that style. Another interesting building from this period is the Bromma airport control tower (1936). The Unesco World Heritage-listed Skogskyrkogården (p86), a graveyard and crematorium co-designed by the great Gunnar Asplund, features high-quality functionalist and vernacular neoclassical styles. You'll also see other examples of functionalist styles in the Gärdet area of the city.

# NEOMODERNISM

The latest styles in glass and chrome can be seen at the Channel 5 TV headquarters at Rådmansgatan 42. Other ultramodern buildings include the Nordic Light Hotel (2001; p158) near Centralstationen and, in central Södermalm, the extraordinary semicircular Bofills Båge (1992), which also has classical influences.

# Design

# Design

Austerity is the magic word when it comes to Swedish design. Clean lines, simple patterns, earth tones and lots of space are the basic elements, and the golden rule is 'the best possible for as many as possible'. After all, this is the land of Ikea, a business that exists because its founder, Ingvar Kamprad, had an epiphany at a 1950s trade show in Italy. The beautiful furniture on display struck him as a jarring contrast with the dreary stuff in most people's houses, and he thought, 'Why do poor people have to put up with ugly things?' And democratic design was born.

Kamprad, of course, was not the first to have such ideas. Back in 1899, Swedish social reformer Ellen Key – who believed that a pleasant home environment could uplift its inhabitants – wrote *Skönhet för alla* (Beauty for all), a book criticising the awful housing conditions of the poor juxtaposed with the garish tastes of the bourgeois. In it she wrote, 'Not until nothing ugly can be bought – when the beautiful is as cheap as the ugly – only then can beauty for all become a reality.'

Truth be told, though, Stockholmers in general have always made it a point to furnish their homes with beautiful things. Swedish interior design is no abstract concept; people live with Bruno Mathsson chairs and Josef Frank textiles, or at least with convincing knock offs.

## A HISTORY OF SWEDISH DESIGN

Since its inception, Swedish design has maintained a relatively consistent affinity for clean lines and simple elegance, though these themes have only gradually developed.

### THE 19TH CENTURY

The roots of current Swedish design can be traced back to the sparse elegance of German home design in the late 1800s, but it was codified in 1899 by Carl Larsson. The beloved and internationally popular Swedish painter and his wife, Karin, published a book that year called *Ett hem* (A home), filled with illustrations of the Larssons' country home in Dalarna province. The house, which has been preserved and is now a museum, combined a range of references and influences, including walls and ceilings painted by Larsson himself, but above all else it was simple and comfortable. The book became a huge bestseller and the style was adopted quickly and almost universally in homes across the country. Those images formed the template that has been used for Swedish home design ever since.

### ASPLUND & BEYOND

From there it was an easy step to the next phase of Swedish design, functionalism. Inspired by Le Corbusier's 1925 modernist pavilion and brought to the forefront of Swedish consciousness by architect Gunnar Asplund in 1930, functionalism *(funkisen)* implies a liberal use of natural light and open space, access to plant life and a general bringing in of the outdoors. This aesthetic carried over from home design to architecture and civic planning. Asplund's amazing renovation of the cinema Biografen Skandia (see p57) represents the ultimate achievement in this style, with its impeccably proportioned space seeming to open up to the sky and invite the stars themselves to come on down and watch the movie.

In the 1930s Viennese architect and designer Josef Frank came to Stockholm to join Estrid Ericson's company Svenskt Tenn. The shop was decidedly upmarket, and still is today, but its approach to home design as envisioned by Frank – a blend of modernism with urban Viennese and English-country influences – raised the bar for home décor.

It was after the 1937 Paris Expo that the American press first coined the term 'Swedish Modern' to describe the movement that would span some 30 years of design in Sweden. Explained as 'a movement toward sanity in design' (Denise Hagströmer, *Swedish Design*), it provided a counterpoint to the brutalist aesthetic that dominated much of Europe at the time. Some of the more important artists who were key to formulating Swedish Modern include Sigurd Persson, who worked mostly in silver and designed jewellery, utensils and practical items for the home; Bruno Mathsson, best known for his subtly curved tables and chairs; and Yngve Ekström, who made experimental furniture.

In the 1950s Swedish Modern gave way to 'Scandinavian design', a sleeker, more streamlined, industrial aesthetic that placed a strong emphasis on functionality and elegance. This style closely mirrored the political and social climate of the Nordic states at the time. As interpreted by Mathsson and others, it incorporated elements of Japanese design, particularly the integration of nature with a home environment.

The biggest development to occur in design in the 1960s was the use of plastic – especially plastic in bright primary colours – to make furniture. And to bring such designs to the masses, the first Stockholm Ikea shop opened in 1968.

The next wave of influence over Swedish design came in the form of artistic control. A group of 10 young designers, among them Tom Hedqvist and Birgitta Hahn, got together in 1970 and formed a cooperative in order to ensure that they'd have full control over their work in every aspect of its creation, from sketch to store. Originally something of an anti-establishment force, the 10-Gruppen (Group of 10) and its designs have since become part of the classic Swedish design canon, right along with Svenkst Tenn, Bruno Mathsson and Carl Malmsten.

Other influential Swedish designers over the years include glass designer Erik Höglund (1932–98); Sixten Sason (1912–67), an industrial designer who worked with Husqvarna and Electrolux; porcelain designer Stig Lindberg (1916–82); textile artist Astrid Sampe (1909–2002); and architecturally trained furniture designer John Kandell (1925–91). You'll find their creations, along with other designers inspired by them, on the shelves of Stockholm's many design boutiques. For the best of these, see Top Five Swedish Design Shops (p152) in the Shopping chapter.

# THE NEW SCHOOL

More recently, Stockholm designers who are gaining renown include Jonas Bohlin (1953–), whose signature Concrete chair might not be the world's most comfortable piece of furniture, but certainly makes an impression. Bohlin was also tapped to do the redesign of prominent Östermalm restaurant Sturehof (p119); a peek inside offers a quick lesson in contemporary Swedish interior design. You'll see many of the details Bohlin used at Sturehof echoed in other restaurants and design stores all over town.

Since the late 1990s, the prevailing style of Swedish design has been a sort of Nordic minimalism epitomised in chic bars like Storstad (p111) and hotels like the new Clarion Hotel in Södermalm (p161). It's this spartan, white-walled, clutter-free aesthetic that has so infatuated design magazine *Wallpaper\** – and, through it, half the civilised world.

# THE FUTURE OF SWEDISH DESIGN

Only time will tell where Swedish design is headed next. The current minimalism has obvious limitations; if it gets much more

*Bathroom at the Clarion Hotel (p161)*

## Icons of Swedish Style

There are certain things that just scream 'Swedish design!' the minute you look at them. Below are a few favourites; for more, check out www.scandinaviandesign.com.

- **Absolut Vodka bottle** This emblematic and unmistakable glass bottle was designed in 1980 by Hans Brindfors, Lars Börje Carlsson and Gunnar Broman for Absolut manufacturer Vin & Sprit; its antique shape is meant to recall bottles of medicine at an apothecary, transmitting a sense of purity and medicinal value.
- **Mellanmjölk cartons** A signature item in all Swedish supermarkets, these brightly coloured pinstripe suits for milk cartons were designed in 1990 by Tom Hedquist.
- **Solstickan matchbox cover** The ubiquitous white silhouette of a pudgy kid tromping across a blue background was designed in 1936 by Einar Nerman; the matchboxes are still seen everywhere.
- **Bruno Mathsson chairs** Mathsson's trademark chair, made without hinges or springs and seeming to float gracefully above the floor, was designed in the '30s. His collection is now manufactured by Dux.
- **Josef Frank floral patterns** Designed in the decades Frank worked for Svenskt Tenn (1930s–1960s), these patterns have become part of the fabric of Stockholm life; they're seen on everything from curtains to serviettes to breakfast trays.
- **Ikea couch** And the Ikea coffee table and the Ikea lounge chair and the Ikea mug and the Ikea packaging system...

extreme it will run the risk of actually turning buildings completely invisible. Will there be a backlash of heavy-handed, busy design? Unlikely. At the time of research, interior design in Stockholm seemed to be edging toward a retro, faux-'60s iteration of its characteristically spartan elegance. For examples of this style, check out the Rival Hotel (p162) or the bar/restaurant Metró (p117).

In the early 1990s Italian architect Andrea Branzi predicted that European globalisation would bring about a 'Second Swedish Modernism', and indeed several of the country's younger designers seem to have used increasing opportunities for cultural exchange as a way to revive Swedish design. Another important element being reflected in the latest designs is a reverence and concern for the environment; shapes and materials are being chosen not just for style but for sustainability.

# GLASS DESIGN

The latest young talent to emerge in glass design is the wild child of Orrefors, Per B Sundberg, whose glass sculptures push the boundaries of the medium (and, some protest, of good taste). His inspired creations include updates of the classic Swedish crystal snowball candleholder – but with sexy messages and nudie pictures hidden inside the wavy glass. Rather dull, restrained glass candleholders take on new energy when Sundberg remakes them with pulpy black-and-white cartoon frames inside. His plates shaped like bent Lego blocks are another big hit. The creepy, mysterious faces created by Bertil Vallien for Kosta Boda are also an interesting and continually evolving experiment in glass design. Both of these artists' work can be found at Swedish glassware shops all over Stockholm (for details, see the Shopping chapter).

# LIGHTING DESIGN

Lighting design is another area in which the Swedes reign supreme. From the simple elegance of a classic coffee-shop chandelier, lighting systems have evolved into wildly inventive functional sculptures. They are, of course, utilitarian, but unlike much Swedish design they also tend to be frivolous and fun. Camilla Diedrich's floor light, for example, can take at least five different forms, starting as a round white onion-shaped globe on a stick and ending up a scalloped ribbon of white light dancing around an axis. Judging from what's on offer in Stockholm's design stores, lighting seems to be the one area where designers feel free to cut loose – whether that means making lampshades that look like hanging ballerinas (as Bohlin uses in his design of Sturehof; see The New School, p33) or cutting up love letters in 10 different languages to piece together a romantic chandelier.

# FURNITURE DESIGN

Furniture is perhaps the easiest format in which to study the evolution of Swedish design. From the 1930s, when Bruno Mathsson's lounge chairs defined the industry – free of joints, hinges or corners of any kind and appearing to float on the air above the ground – to the 1980s, when Jonas Bohlin's chair 'Concrete' caused a miniature but long-lasting scandal in Stockholm's design scene, the innovations are memorable and easy to see. Unsurprisingly, the Mathsson lounge chairs are still wildly popular, proving that a skilful blend of beauty and function never goes out of style.

Carl Malmsten is another key figure in Swedish furniture design. Chafing against the establishment from his high-school days, Malmsten constantly sought to break the staid old models of furniture design teaching. His dream finally came to fruition in 1957, when he acquired Capellagården (Chapel Garden) at Vickleby and founded a residential crafts school there. The school became his pride and joy, and his teachings continue to influence unorthodox young furniture designers to this day.

# INDUSTRIAL DESIGN

In 1959 Sixten Sason designed the Saab 93F and launched the company's car into the international marketplace. Sason became a massively successful industrial designer, whose other works included Hasselblad's 1600 F camera, and products for Husqvarna and Electrolux.

Since then, industrial design in Sweden has come to focus on a combination of ergonomics and environmental ethics. More recently, the consumer-driven marketplace has led to a focus on products 'with attitude', or industrial design that represents something about the philosophy of its creators and its intended users. It has become a given that things will work and will be at least somewhat environmentally responsible; industrial designers also now seek to make products that are a symbol or an extension of their company.

The Swedish Industrial Design Foundation was formed in the 1980s to emphasise the value of designing products for smaller manufacturers and to educate businesspeople on the importance of functional design.

# GRAPHIC DESIGN

Swedish graphic design has gone from being rather bland in the 1980s to being lauded by the jury of the Excellence in Swedish Design Awards in 1998 as having 'a vibrancy that other fields can't measure up to'. Notable examples of this vibrancy include the universally recognised Absolut vodka bottle, co-designed by Hans Brindfors, and the striped milk cartons, designed by Tom Hedquist in 1990. Other important examples of Swedish graphic design include the total-package logo redesign that Björn Kusoffsky and his Stockholm Design Lab have done for SAS airlines.

The importance of information technology to Sweden's overall economy has also had a somewhat predictable impact on its graphic design, primarily making international cross-pollination almost effortless. This means that

*Designer furniture at Nordiska Galleriet (p151)*

## Top Five Books on Swedish Design

- *Swedish Design*, Denise Hagströmer (2002) – This authoritative paperback text published by the Swedish Institute is well written and richly illustrated.
- *Creating the Look: Swedish Style*, Katrin Cargill (1996) – An easy to find and easy to follow guide to reproducing the Swedish sense of design in your own home.
- *A Treasury of Viking Design*, Courtney Davis (2000) – Yes, even back in the Viking era, Swedes had strict aesthetic guidelines.
- *Swedish Design*, Susanne Helgeson (2002) – Taking samples of a few dozen Swedish designers from various disciplines, Helgeson probes the technique and philosophy behind their work.
- *The Swedish Room*, Ursula and Lars Sjöberg (1994) – The authors illustrate and analyse Swedish rooms from various periods in the country's history.

a distinctly Swedish influence in graphic design isn't as readily identifiable as it is in most other areas, but it also puts top Swedish graphic artists at the forefront of the international design scene.

# FURTHER SOURCES

For an understanding of Swedish design and how it developed, one of the best sources is Svensk Form (p74), the Swedish Society of Crafts & Design, formerly Svenska Slöjd-föreningen (Swedish Handicraft Association). The organisation changed its name in 1976 to promote Swedish design and improve the public's knowledge of the basic principles of good design.

Svensk Form publishes an excellent magazine, *Form*, available from design shops and newsstands all over Stockholm. It features new products, innovative ideas, trends in design and profiles of prominent Swedish designers, and it always includes a number of articles in English. Svensk Form also has a gallery and design centre on Skeppsholmen.

A good online resource is the Form Design Centre at www.scandinaviandesign.com, with listings of events, biographies of prominent designers and a product catalogue.

The related magazines *Forum* and *Arkitektur* (both at www.arkitektur-forlag.se) are also loaded with information and resources about architecture and design, in both English and Swedish. They're available at most design shops in Stockholm as well as newsstands. *Stockholm New* (www.stockholmnew.com) is a glossy magazine published roughly once a year; it frequently contains articles on style and cutting-edge design.

# History

# History

## THE RECENT PAST

Sweden's generally placid public image belies the internal friction it has felt in recent years, as its ambitions have clashed with its rapidly changing reality. Under a basically left-leaning government coalition made up of the Social Democrats, the Greens (Miljöpartiet) and the Left Party (Vänsterpartiet), the country has sought to maintain its goals of economic equality and a progressive society, while at the same time struggling with the twin pressures of large-scale immigration and less-than-enthusiastic membership in the European Union.

Since WWII more than a million immigrants have come to Sweden, with the influx peaking at 75,000 in 1970. Today some 20% of the population of Stockholm county are foreign-born or have immigrant backgrounds. Sweden stayed neutral during WWII – although, inevitably, its neutrality was ambiguous – and the country consequently became a safe haven for refugees from Finland, Norway, Denmark and the Baltic states. Finns make up the largest group of immigrants in Stockholm. Thousands of Jews settled in Stockholm during the war, fleeing persecution. In more recent years, refugees have come primarily from the Middle East.

Stockholm's postwar growth meant that many older buildings were sacrificed to make way for new bridges and apartment blocks. In 1941 the city council decided to construct the subway, and the first line (Slussen to Hökarängen) was opened in 1950. Throughout the 1950s new suburbs cropped up along these subway lines, creating a radial pattern still in evidence today. The suburban centres, many of them architect-driven urban planning experiments, had services, office buildings, churches, schools and sporting facilities, but often the homes themselves were grim Stalinist-style blocks of flats.

Meanwhile, large sections of the city centre (in Norrmalm) started to resemble the worst of bombed-out Europe as older buildings were demolished in a frenzy. Today the most

### Top Five History Books

The best and most comprehensive book on Stockholm's history has yet to be translated into English. It is Lars Ericson's *Stockholms historia under 750 år* (2002), written in conjunction with the celebration of the city's anniversary. If you can navigate a little Swedish, it's packed with valuable information and lots of illustrations, and it's now available in a cheaper paperback version.

*Stockholm's Annual Rings*, by Magnus Andersson (1998), is an ambitious and detailed look at the development of the city over the centuries, with a strong architectural slant. Unfortunately, the translation into English is rather poor and the book is inordinately expensive.

Most of the history books available in English cover all of Sweden, rather than just Stockholm, but many of them focus on the goings-on of the capital. *Swedish Politics During the 20th Century*, by Stig Hadenius (1999), sets out the causes and effects of the dramatic changes in Swedish politics since 1900.

*Neutrality and State-Building in Sweden*, by Mikael af Malmborg (2001), is a scholarly look at the difficulties of maintaining neutrality as well as the driving forces behind such a stance and how it meshes with Sweden's global ambitions.

*The History of Sweden* (2002) is an easily digested, general history of the country by Byron J Nordstrom. It's well illustrated and available in most gift shops at Stockholm museums in both Swedish and English editions as well as a few other languages.

| TIMELINE | c 800–1050 | 1252 | 1275 |
|---|---|---|---|
| | The Viking era | Birger Jarl founds Stockholm and starts building the Tre Kronor castle fortress | Magnus Ladulås becomes king |

obvious examples of this modernisation effort are the five towers of the Hötorgscity business complex between Sergels Torg and Hötorget, completed in 1965, as well as Sergels Torg itself and its anchor, Kulturhuset. The slash-and-burn construction of these modern buildings on the site of dilapidated but historic neighbourhoods was regretted almost immediately, and the new constructions universally reviled, but these days Stockholm's younger generation – particularly the architects – see the Hötorget towers and Kulturhuset as among the very rare examples of interesting, forward-looking buildings in the cityscape.

Further expansions of the city on to virgin land included Bredäng (1962), Skärholmen (1964) and Rinkeby. In the 10 years from 1965, the national government ordered a massive construction program to ease the housing shortage.

By 1971, with Stockholm's population at 744, 911, the city's headlong building boom had taken its toll. People were fed up with government indifference toward history and aesthetics. In a defining moment, when authorities planned to cut down several healthy elm trees in Kungsträdgården to make room for a new *tunnelbana* station, mass public protests forced them to reconsider; the elms to this day symbolise for many Stockholmers the triumph of popular will over misguided government. After continued protests and the 1973 oil crisis, which dampened the economy and slowed construction, tensions started to dissipate.

*Tower of Sankt Jakobs kyrka (p68)*

*Tower of Sankt Jakobs kyrka (p68)*

In 1977 the business and shopping complex at Kista Centrum was opened; this area has since developed into the Swedish equivalent of Silicon Valley, dominated by Ericsson Radio Systems and IBM since the 1980s. Housing complexes were built in Kista, Skarpnäck and other suburbs throughout the 1980s to accommodate IT workers. These took on a sombre air following the worldwide collapse of the IT economy during the 1990s, which hit tech-dependent Stockholm particularly hard. Recovery has been slow; industry leader Ericsson, which once employed some 9000 people in Stockholm, laid off thousands worldwide during 2002 and early 2003. At the time of writing, however, its stocks showed stronger-than-expected performances, and the company's fate – and IT in general – seemed to be taking a turn for the better.

In 1986 Sweden's confidence was shaken by the murder of Prime Minister Olof Palme, who was shot while walking home from the movies on Sveavägen in the city centre. The bungled police inquiry into the assassination caused many ordinary Swedes to doubt their country's institutions and its leaders; the Social Democratic party, to which Palme belonged, was hit hard and only slowly recovered. Conspiracy theories abound regarding Palme's still-unsolved killing. A brass plaque on the street marks the site of the murder, at the corner of Sveavägen and Tunnelgatan.

During the late 1980s and '90s, redevelopment of Hötorgscity, Kungsgatan, Stureplan and central parts of Södermalm began and economic revival took off as credit laws were relaxed. Building and property investment caused rents to soar, making Stockholm an

| 1350 | 1397 | 1520 | 1523 |
|------|------|------|------|
| The Black Death (plague) devastates Sweden, killing off about a third of its people | Kalmar Union unites Sweden-Finland and Denmark-Norway under Queen Margareta | Stockholm Bloodbath | Gustav Vasa becomes king |

even more expensive place to live. But once the 1990s world recession burst that bubble, the devaluation of the krona actually helped Stockholm – tourism within Sweden grew, and foreign tourists arrived in ever-increasing numbers. The easing of licensing restrictions on bars and restaurants – such as restrictions on the hours during which alcohol could be sold, the type of alcohol sold and the age of clientele – caused a huge increase in the number of licensed premises, which certainly didn't hurt the tourism industry or the country's mood in general.

In 1995 Sweden voted by a narrow margin to join the European Union (EU) and the economy recovered somewhat, due in part to an austerity program and massive cuts in welfare. Stockholm was the Cultural Capital of Europe in 1998, and that year saw a record number of visitors to the city. A 2003 referendum to decide whether or not Sweden would give up the krona for the euro failed; the vote was surrounded by controversy and tainted by the murder of Swedish foreign minister Anna Lindh, who had campaigned fiercely for the euro. At the time of writing it was unclear whether the euro question would again be put to the vote.

# FROM THE BEGINNING

## EARLY SETTLEMENT

Around 8000 BC, at the end of the last Ice Age, most of what is now east–central Sweden lay under water. Freed of its burden of ice, the land rose, islands appeared, and by 6000 BC, humans had arrived. Remains of early Stone Age settlements have been found at Tullinge, about 15km southwest of the centre of modern Stockholm.

The area remained lightly populated until medieval times. In the 11th century, a jetty was built in Strömmen, and a hundred years later the first defensive towers had been built on Stadsholmen (now called Gamla Stan), a strategically located island at the nexus of freshwater Lake Mälaren and the sea. The churches at Bromma and Spånga are the oldest buildings in Greater Stockholm and were consecrated in the late 12th century, not long after Sweden's official conversion to Christianity.

## MEDIEVAL STOCKHOLM

Although Swedish Viking political power had been centred around northern Mälaren and Sigtuna for centuries, it was forced to move to the lake's outlet when rising land made navigation between the sea and lake impractical for large boats. Around 1250 a town charter was granted and a trade treaty was signed with the Hanseatic port of Lübeck. In 1252 Sweden's most important chieftain, Birger Jarl, ordered the strengthening of the defences on Stadsholmen and work began on the fortress-like Tre Kronor castle. Around the same time, locks were built on either side of Stadsholmen to control trade, using timber stocks arranged as a fence or boom. It's thought that Stockholm, meaning 'tree-trunk islet', is named after this boom.

By the 1270s, Franciscan monks had established a monastery on the islet Riddarholmen. The first mention of St Nicolai kyrka (consecrated as the cathedral Storkyrkan in 1306) dates from 1279, and in the 1280s the Klara nunnery was set up in Norrmalm. When King Magnus Ladulås was buried in St Nicolai kyrka in 1290, the town had around 2000 residents.

The oldest surviving Stockholm seal (1296) shows a defensive wall, which ran around Gamla Stan's plateau; the next seal (from 1326) shows a much stronger wall with towers and gatehouses. In 1301 Helgeandshuset, a combined hospital, chapel and cemetery, opened on Helgeandsholmen (which at this point was connected to Norrmalm and Stadsholmen by

| 1524–25 | 1544 | 1628–40 | 1630–48 |
|---------|------|---------|---------|
| Lutheran Reformation | Sweden's monarchy made hereditary | Expansion demands the removal of Stockholm's medieval city walls | Sweden takes the side of the Protestants in the Thirty Years' War |

## Vikings

The Viking age, normally taken to have lasted from AD 800 to 1100, was the period when Scandinavians from Sweden, Norway and Denmark made their mark on the rest of Europe. Vikings travelled greater distances than the earlier Roman explorers, and they established trading posts and an impressive communications network. They settled in North America and Greenland, traded with eastern and southern Asia, fought for the Byzantine Empire and sacked and looted towns in southern Spain, among many other places.

Not all of the Vikings were warlike, but they were initially all pagans. Scandinavian Vikings spoke the same language and worshipped the same gods (see the boxed text 'Norse Mythology', p42). Burial of the dead usually included some possessions that would be required in the afterlife. In Sweden it was popular to cremate the dead, and then bury the remains in a clay pot under a mound. There are also a number of impressive stone-ship graves, consisting of upright stones arranged in the plan of a Viking longship, with larger stones at the prow and stern. Viking graves have yielded a large amount of information about the Viking culture.

Rune stones were often erected as memorials, or as markers for highways, graveyards or other important sites. Runic inscriptions were also carved on things such as metal and bone. Sweden has around 3000 such inscriptions, containing a wealth of information about the Viking world. The small town of Sigtuna, for example (see p180), is dotted with historic rune stones of varying importance.

Applied art was important to the Vikings for decorative purposes, but some of the most spectacular art appears along with runic inscriptions and usually features dragons, horses or scenes from ancient sagas that bear little or no relevance to the attached runes. For more about the Vikings, visit Stockholm's Historiska Museet (p81).

wooden bridges). Tre Kronor castle now had a 25m-high round tower and six rectangular castellated towers linked by a curtain wall. The oldest street in Stockholm, Köpmannagatan, was first mentioned in 1323.

In 1350 the arrival of the Black Death killed around a third of the Swedish population. The diminished workforce meant that Sweden's position on the top trade routes in the Baltic was vulnerable; merchants from the rest of the Hanseatic League took the opportunity to squeeze the Swedes out.

Stockholm was besieged by the Danish Queen Margareta Valdemarsdotter from 1391 to 1395, and in 1397 the crowns of Sweden, Norway and Denmark amalgamated under the Union of Kalmar. A governor directed Swedish affairs from the castle, but the Kalmar Union was not popular and there were frequent efforts to rebel over the years.

Several serious fires swept through Stockholm during medieval times. The worst occurred in 1407, where many people died and everything except stone buildings (including Tre Kronor castle) was razed to the ground.

By the late 15th century Stockholm had become a significant commercial centre with a population of around 6000. Much of its commercial success was based on the shipping of copper and iron to continental Europe, but this lucrative trade was dominated by German merchants, meaning most of the wealth was destined to leave Sweden along with the goods. Built up rapidly and then left unsupported, Stockholm's infrastructure entered a long period of decline.

In 1471, with many Swedes still chafing under Danish rule, the Danish king Christian I besieged Stockholm in an attempt to quell Swedish rebel Sten Sture the Elder, whom nationalists had dubbed 'Guardian of the Realm'. The Swedes routed Christian's 5000-strong army just outside the city walls at the Battle of Brunkenberg (the fighting took place between what is now Vasagatan, Kungsgatan and Sergels Torg). The Danes retreated to Copenhagen, but trouble between unionists and separatists within Sweden continued. Things escalated in 1520 when city burghers, bishops and nobles agreed to meet the Danish king Christian II in Stockholm, presumably to discuss their grievances. When the city leaders arrived at the banquet, the king had them all arrested. There followed a quick and farcical trial, in which

| 1686 | 1697 | 1700–21 | 1719 |
|---|---|---|---|
| The Tessin-designed Drottning-holm Slott completed | Tre Kronor castle destroyed by fire | Great Northern War; Sweden loses territory to Denmark and Russia | Sweden's new constitution gives power to parliament instead of the monarchy |

## Norse Mythology

Some of the greatest gods of the Nordic world, Tyr, Odin, Thor and Frigg, live on in the English language as the days of the week – Tuesday, Wednesday, Thursday and Friday, respectively. Norse mythology is very complex, so we're restricted to a limited description here. A vast number of gods, wolves, serpents and other creatures are involved in the heroic Nordic tales of chaos and death.

The one-handed Tyr was the god of justice, including war treaties, contracts and oaths. The principal myth regarding Tyr involves the giant wolf, Fenrir. The gods decided Fenrir had to be chained up, but nothing could hold him. Dwarfs made an unbreakable chain and the gods challenged Fenrir to break it. He was suspicious, but agreed on condition that one of the gods place his hand in his mouth. Tyr was the only one to agree. The gods succeeded in fettering Fenrir, but he retaliated by biting off Tyr's right hand.

The most eminent of the Nordic gods was the one-eyed Odin (the father of most of the other gods), whose eight-legged flying horse, Sleipnir, had runes etched on its teeth. As a god of war, Odin sent his 12 Valkyries (battle maidens) to select 'heroic dead' killed in battle to join him in everlasting feasting at the palace of Valhalla. Odin carried a spear called Gungnir, which never missed when thrown, and his bow could fire 10 arrows at once. Odin was also the god of poets, a magician and master of runes. Odin's great wisdom had been granted in exchange for his missing eye, but he also gained wisdom from his two ravens, Hugin and Munin, who flew every day in search of knowledge.

Thor is usually depicted as an immensely strong god who protected humans from the malevolent giants with his magic hammer Mjolnir, which would return to the thrower like a boomerang. Thor represented thunder, and the hammer was the thunderbolt. Thor's greatest enemy was the evil snake Jörmungand, and they were destined to kill each other at Ragnarök, the end of the world, when the wolf Fenrir would devour Odin. At Ragnarök, the other gods and humans would also die in cataclysmic battle, the sky would collapse in raging fire and the earth would subside into the sea.

Frigg was Odin's wife and is also known as a fertility goddess and the goddess of marriage.

the Swedes were found guilty of burning down the archbishop's castle near Sigtuna. The next day, 82 men were beheaded at Stortorget, the main square outside the royal palace. This ghastly event became known as the Stockholm Bloodbath; heavy rain caused rivers of blood from the bodies to pour down the steep alleys descending from the square. Once the news of the slaughter spread to Sweden's outlying areas, it served to solidify resistance to Danish rule.

## THE RENAISSANCE

One of the 82 men killed in the Bloodbath happened to be the father of a certain Gustav Eriksson Vasa, who had been outspokenly opposed to the Kalmar Union and taken prisoner by the Danes. Gustav Vasa escaped to Lübeck and eventually sneaked back into Sweden. After the Bloodbath, he fled on skis to Dalarna and tried to drum up support for a massive rebellion against Danish rule. (There is an annual ski race, Vasaloppet, that celebrates Gustav Vasa's journey and has been held on the first Sunday of March since 1922. More about the 56 mile/90km race, one of Sweden's biggest sporting events, can be found at www.vasaloppet.se.) Once word of the Bloodbath had spread (again by ski-messenger) to the provinces, Gustav Vasa was able to gather a growing army of peasants and other Swedish nationalists. After a two-year siege, he finally took Stockholm in 1523. He was crowned king of Sweden on 6 June 1523, now Sweden's national day.

The new king ruled the city with a heavy hand – the role of commerce dwindled and the Reformation snuffed out the Catholic Church entirely in 1527. Meanwhile royal power grew, and the city revolved around the court. The king ordered the reconstruction of Tre Kronor castle, and defensive towers were built on Riddarholmen – Birger Jarls Torn and

| 1740 | 1754 | 1792 | 1849 |
|---|---|---|---|
| Carl Michael Bellman born | Kungliga Slottet, designed by Nicodemus Tessin the Younger, is completed | King Gustav III shot after attempting to restore the monarchy's power | August Strindberg born in Stockholm |

the southern tower of Wrangelska palats are now the only parts of the medieval fortifications left above ground. An unfortunate result of Gustav Vasa's rather zealous secularism was the destruction of many of Sweden's monasteries and churches; in fact he nearly tore down Storkyrkan, but the public outcry persuaded him against it. Gustav Vasa's son Johan later had many of the looted and demolished churches rebuilt.

The famous *Vädersolstavlan* painting (also called the *Parhelion Painting*) shows a city built mostly of brick and wood, with steeples, windmills, a curtain wall, and castellated towers and gatehouses. Both Norrmalm and Södermalm (north and south of Gamla Stan, respectively) were dotted with buildings and houses by this time, and the population of the city stood at around 8000. The painting also shows an extraordinary atmospheric phenomenon, a solar reflection that creates the illusion of a double sun, which startled the people on 20 April 1535 (there's a 17th-century copy of the painting in Storkyrkan, p55).

Gustav Vasa's death in 1560 paved the way for his sons, Erik XIV, Johan III and Karl IX, to continue his nation-building work. They racked up taxation on the burghers to build up a military force and fund wars. Arms manufacturers did well, and the city's importance as a military headquarters increased. During the Thirty Years' War in particular, Sweden gained parts of German and Norwegian territory, and transcended Denmark as the primary power in northern Europe.

At the same time, the monarchy was cultivating Stockholm's high society, bringing in sophisticated artists and architects who had profound effects on Swedish culture.

By the end of the 16th century, Stockholm's population was 9000, and the city had steadily spread onto Norrmalm and Södermalm. (Norrmalm was briefly given town status in 1602, but that was withdrawn in 1635.)

In 1625 western parts of Gamla Stan were gutted by fire, and rebuilding took place on a grid pattern. At around the same time, the city's medieval wall began to be torn down to allow for expansion to the north and south. The first official city engineer, Anders Torstensson, planned the street grids in Norrmalm and Södermalm. Drottninggatan (Queen Street) was named for Queen Kristina, the daughter of Gustav II Adolf, who served as queen with Axel Oxenstierna as her regent; in 1654 she left the throne and moved to Rome to practise Catholicism and build a massive art collection. Her successor, Karl X Gustav, was responsible for the 1657 invasion of Denmark that resulted in the largest Swedish empire ever.

Stockholm had been proclaimed capital of Sweden in 1634, partly because of the prominence the city had gained after Gustav II Adolf and his chancellor Axel Oxenstierna moved the national assembly there in 1626. By 1650, the city had a typical grid-like Renaissance plan and a thriving artistic and intellectual culture; this was the time of Sweden's first poets and writers, as well as the two-man architectural renaissance that was the Tessins, who shaped the look of the city and built the impressive Drottningholms Slott in 1686. Stockholm had become an important European capital, supported by an expanding Swedish empire. The population soared from 15,000 in 1635 to 60,000 in 1685.

# RISING & FALLING FORTUNES

A string of disasters struck Sweden during the next couple of decades. Famine wiped out 100,000 people across Sweden during the harsh winter of 1696–97, and starving hordes descended on the capital. Also in 1697 the beloved old royal castle, Tre Kronor, burned down entirely save the new north wing. In 1709 Russia's Peter the Great trounced the Swedish troops under the adolescent King Karl XII during the battle of Poltava, vastly diminishing Sweden's empire. In 1711 plague arrived again – the death rate soared to 1200 per day, and a quarter of the population died. After a series of spectacular military defeats, loss of foreign possessions, and the death of Karl XII by assassination in Norway (1718), the country and its capital went into a serious slump. The king had no heir, and the limbo

| 1860s | 1863 | 1878 | 1891 |
|---|---|---|---|
| First railway line established | Stockholm's first sewerage system installed | University of Stockholm founded (as the Academy of Stockholm) | Skansen opens as part of a movement towards reviving traditional Swedish culture |

that occurred after his death weakened the role of the monarchy until it became essentially that of a figurehead; the real authority rested in the hands of the aristocracy. During this phase of scattered and weakened leadership, further Russian attacks in 1719 and the resulting one-sided peace treaty of 1721 finished off Sweden's military adventures.

The focus eventually turned inward, to industry and invention. Work on building the Kungliga Slott (the new Royal Palace) on the ruins of Tre Kronor began in 1727, but it wasn't completed until 1754. Many of the artisans who worked on the castle stayed in the city afterwards, helping to foster Stockholm's artistic environment. The Swedish Academy of Sciences was founded in 1739, and the observatory was opened in 1753. Widespread industrial awakening marked the 18th century – distilleries, breweries, porcelain works and glass factories commenced operations all over the country – and the invention of the tiled stove in 1767 revolutionised domestic heating. (Many of these beautiful stoves are still in use in some of Stockholm's older homes, cafés and restaurants.) In 1752 the first modern hospital (Serafimerlasarettet) opened. A stock exchange, Börsen (now the home of the Nobel Museum), was built at the edge of Stortorget in 1768, replacing the old town hall. The economic and industrial awakening was paralleled by an intellectual and scientific one; this was the era of Carl von Linné (see boxed text, below), the botanist who developed the template for the classification of plants and animals; Emmanuel Swedenborg (1688–1772), a radical and mystical philosopher who would have a profound influence on August Strindberg; and Anders Celsius (1701–44), who came up with the centigrade temperature scale.

In 1772 King Gustav III curtailed the powers of the *riksdag* (parliament); seven years later he assumed the role of absolute monarch. During his reign, Swedish science, architecture and arts blossomed, allowing the creation of institutions and fine buildings such as the original opera house (built in 1782 and architecturally an echo of the Arvfurstens Palats opposite, it was demolished 100 years later). The press also flourished during this time; several newspapers were established and enthusiastically adopted as a public forum. But Gustav III's increasing concentration of power in the hands of the monarchy didn't go over well with the general populace of Sweden nor, understandably, with the *riksdag*. In 1792, three years after the French Revolution, several members of the *riksdag* plotted to assassinate the king. During a masked ball in the Opera House, Jacob Johan Anckarström shot Gustav III in the back. The king died 13 days later, and Anckarström was executed for regicide (more specifically, he was beheaded after being flogged in several public squares).

A period of stagnation followed the death of the king, although it did result in parliamentary rule being restored. By 1810 Stockholm's population was around 65,000, but it was actually decreasing due to lack of confidence in the capital. Living conditions for the average person were spartan; the city had little running water, no sewerage system and – not

## Carl von Linné

Carl von Linné (1707–78), born Linnaeus (and usually called Carl Linnaeus in English), is known for his classification of minerals, plants and animals, as described in his work *Systema Naturae*. Linnaeus journeyed throughout Sweden to make his observations – his most famous journeys were to Lappland (1732), Dalarna (1734) and Skåne (1749). His pupils and colleagues also gathered information worldwide, from Australia (with Cook's expedition) to Central Asia and South America.

Linnaeus insisted on hard physical evidence before drawing any conclusions, and his rigorous research methods were thereafter absorbed by all the natural sciences. His theories of plant reproduction still hold today.

In 1739 Linnaeus became one of the founders of the Swedish Academy of Sciences in Stockholm. Among other achievements, he took Celsius' temperature scale and turned it upside down, giving us 0°C for freezing point and 100°C for boiling point, rather than the other way around.

| 1907 | 1914–18 | 1921 | 1930s |
| --- | --- | --- | --- |
| Men given the right to vote | Sweden neutral during WWI | Women given the right to vote | Sweden's welfare state begins to develop |

coincidentally – frequent epidemics. The government continually promised reforms which never arrived, and bloody street riots weren't unusual.

# INDUSTRIALISATION & EXPANSION

By the mid-19th century, the industrial revolution had gradually crept into Sweden, with the construction of factories, mills, a gasworks and a waterworks. Stockholm's long-awaited sewerage system was begun in 1863. In the same decade, railways were opened, and in 1871, the northern and southern lines were connected via Centralstationen (Stockholm's central train station) and Riddarholmen. This sparked a rapid catching-up in Sweden's industrialisation; by 1900 nearly a quarter of all Swedes lived and worked in cities. Stockholm expanded as rapidly as it industrialised – the capital city's population of 168,000 in 1880 had reached 245,000 just 10 years later.

Starting in the 1860s, further town planning, necessitated by the city's explosive growth, created many of the wide avenues and apartment blocks that can still be seen today, although a by-law in 1876 laid down strict rules limiting street widths and building heights. Östermalm was planned during the 1880s and Strandvägen was completed by 1897 – the same year Stockholm hosted the ambitious Art & Industry Exhibition in Djurgården. The 1890s also saw the arrival of various public utilities, including an electricity works in 1892. Other substantial buildings from this era include Operan (the current opera house), the central post office, Riksdagshuset Östra (the original parliament building) and Rosenbad (government offices).

In 1904 the city purchased land outside its borders, which it later employed when the city's residential areas expanded to the suburbs. By 1907, socialist power had grown to the point that the conservative government was pressured into giving the vote to all men over age 24. The government had hoped this would curb the influence of socialism, but it continued to gain power, and in 1909 a general strike was called, forcing major changes to workers' rights and salaries.

Sweden declared itself neutral in 1912, just before the outbreak of WWI. In that same year the summer Olympics were held in Stockholm at the newly built stadium in Östermalm. In 1915 some 364,000 people lived in Stockholm; the city centre continued on its way to becoming a thriving urban core, as symbolised by the opening of the NK department store. The construction of Kungsgatan, another major business street that was cut through the Brunkebergsåsen ridge, was completed in the 1920s.

Sweden again fell into crisis mode from 1914 to 1917 as a result of WWI; it refused to uphold a blockade against Germany, so Britain responded by attacking Sweden's supply lines, seizing goods and looting cargo ships and generally pulling the rug out from under the Swedish economy. The severe rationing brought on by food-supply shortages caused starving Stockholmers to riot in Gustav Adolfs torg, and protest demonstrations continued throughout 1917 and 1918.

Sweden was one of the first countries to give women the right to vote. To this day it's a leader in gender equality both in the workplace and in politics; at present, there are more women in the Swedish parliament than men. At around the same time as women got the vote, the Social Democrats gained control of the Swedish parliament, pushing through an agenda that includes many of the features people associate with Sweden today, most notably the famous Swedish welfare system, *folkhemmet* (the people's home). Also under the first Social Democratic prime minister, Hjalmar Branting, the government established Systembolaget (see boxed text, p122), the state-run alcohol monopoly that is still in operation today. It also introduced certain labour reforms, including the eight-hour workday. A meeting at Saltsjöbaden in 1938 between government officials and the country's main trade unions resulted in a precedent-setting system for resolving labour disputes that is still used today.

| 1939–40 | 1945 | 1973 | 1974 |
|---|---|---|---|
| Sweden neutral during WWII | Pippi Longstocking published | The current king, Carl XVI Gustav, inherits the throne | The monarchy's political power removed |

## Raoul Wallenberg

Of all the 'righteous gentiles' honoured by Jews around the world, one of the most famous is Swedish diplomat Raoul Wallenberg, known for his part in the rescue of as many as 35,000 Hungarian Jews during WWII.

His father died before Raoul Wallenberg was born into one of Sweden's most prominent families on Lidingö in 1912, and Raoul was subsequently raised by his mother. After leaving school, he studied in the US in 1931, then gained employment in Cape Town. From there, he moved to work for a Dutch bank in Haifa and came into contact with Jews who had escaped from Nazi Germany.

In 1944 Wallenberg was appointed first secretary at the Swedish legation in Budapest, which was then part of the Nazi empire. The American War Refugee Board financed a project to rescue the Hungarian Jews, which Wallenberg was to implement – with the full knowledge of the Swedish government. Wallenberg's office issued 'protection passes' to tens of thousands of Jews, who were moved to safe houses displaying the Swedish coat of arms before being taken to Sweden. Amazingly, the protection passes were actually completely worthless, but the Nazi authorities were easily influenced by such symbolism and failed to deal with what was happening. Even more incredible, Wallenberg threatened the German military commander, General Schmidthuber, with death by execution after the war if he massacred the remaining 97,000 Jews in Budapest – and the massacre plan was cancelled at the last minute.

After the Russians entered Budapest in 1945, however, Wallenberg was summoned by the Soviet authorities and disappeared without trace. The Russians claim he died in detention in Moscow in 1947, but rumours about Wallenberg being alive in the 1970s have surfaced, even quite recently. Claims that senior figures in the Swedish government washed their hands of Wallenberg and left him to his fate appear to be well supported.

Whatever happened to Wallenberg may always be a mystery, but he has become a worldwide symbol to victims of persecution. For more information, see the booklet *Swedish Portraits – Raoul Wallenberg*, available from the Swedish Institute.

The city's architecture reflected its politics during this period. Stadshuset (City Hall), which opened in 1923, instantly became a symbol of the city. The 1930 Stockholm Exhibition, which lasted more than four months and attracted 1.5 million visitors, highlighted the new functionalist styles of architecture and design that would come to dominate the city for years under socialist government.

Sweden remained rather uncomfortably neutral during WWII; the traditional Swedish enemy Russia was allied against Germany, and Sweden provided weapons to the Finns when the Soviet Union invaded in 1939. Sweden was also forced to supply raw materials to the Nazis and allow them to use its land and waterways to transport troops after Germany had invaded Denmark and Norway; the Swedish navy secretly fought Soviet submarines in 1942. But anti-German sentiment and resistance were common. Swedish businessman Raoul Wallenberg sheltered thousands of Jewish refugees (see boxed text, above), though it most likely cost him his life. Arrested as a spy, he vanished and is generally believed to have died in a Soviet prison.

Unlike during WWI, Sweden came through WWII in rather good shape economically, though at a high emotional and political cost. The desire for at least official neutrality has continued to be a goal of the Swedish government. When Denmark and Norway joined NATO in 1949, Sweden refused.

| 1986 | 1995 | 2002 | 2003 |
|---|---|---|---|
| Prime Minister Olof Palme assassinated | Sweden joins European Union | General election results in a coalition of the Greens, Left Party and Social Democrats | Foreign minister Anna Lindh murdered |

# Neighbourhoods

# Neighbourhoods

Stockholm is handily arranged on a series of 14 islands, so in most cases it's easy to tell when you move from one neighbourhood to the next – you cross water. The primary exceptions are the city centre neighbourhoods of Norrmalm, Vasastaden and Östermalm, which cling together on the main island. Smack in the middle of the city is the island of Gamla Stan, the historic Old Town, where the city of Stockholm was founded. Two smaller, satellite islands are linked to it by bridges – Riddarholmen (the Island of Knights) to the west; and Helgeandsholmen (the Island of the Holy Spirit) to the north, occupied by the Swedish parliament building.

To the north of Gamla Stan, beyond Helgeandsholmen, is the modern city centre. This core is composed of Norrmalm and Vasastaden – the boundaries between these two are debatable, but essentially Norrmalm stretches from the waterfront north to about Kammakargatan, and everything from there to the highway E4 and Sveaplan is Vasastaden. Birger Jarlsgatan serves as the eastern boundary for both neighbourhoods.

To the east of Gamla Stan is the island of Djurgården (the Animal Park), where many of Stockholm's better-known museums (Vasamuseet, Skansen) are located. The small island of Skeppsholmen sits between Djurgården and Gamla Stan; it's home to Moderna Museet, Arkitekturmuseet and the famous floating youth hostel *af Chapman* (p159). The little nub southeast of Skeppsholmen is Kastellholmen, a mostly symbolic seafaring fort.

Off the western edge of Norrmalm is the island of Kungsholmen, a mostly residential, formerly dreary part of town that's starting to become more interesting to visitors, with several new shops and restaurants cropping up.

Södermalm, the city's funky, bohemian area, inhabits the large island to the south of Gamla Stan. It's linked by the car-and-pedestrian bridge Centralbron as well as by the rather baffling traffic snarl called Slussen (the Lock). The park-like island to the west of Söder is Långholmen, historically a prison island; the prison is now a combination hotel, hostel and museum, and Långholmen boasts some of the city's nicer beaches.

## Stockholm for Children

Stockholm is an easy place to travel with children – they're welcome at restaurants, museums and anywhere their parents go. There are also several museums and activities that cater to children particularly. **Skansen** (p72) is an obvious choice; its open-air format, animal petting zoo and other hands-on exhibitions as well as dramatic features like the glassblowers' workshop consistently entrance wide-eyed youngsters. **Nordiska Museet** (p71) has a children's play area in a replica of a historic village, across from the café; children can ferry themselves across a 'river' or play medieval merchant, among other things. At **Junibacken** (p70), kids can visit the world of Pippi Longstocking. The **Teknorama** (p83) and **Naturhistoriska Riksmuseet** (p85) also have features that would appeal to kids, as does **Kungliga Myntkabinettet** (p52). For junior biologists, check out the wonderful **Aquaria Vattenmuseum** (p70), **Fågel- och Fjärilshuset** (p84) in Hagaparken and the quaint, timeworn **Biologiska Museet** (p70). **Gröna Lund** (p70) is an amusement park on the island of Djurgården, with all kinds of rides, carnival games and snacks. **Musikmuseet** in Östermalm (p82) has hands-on displays that kids will love. And the **Leksaksmuseet** (p78) is chock-full of toys.

Other than museums, there's **ice skating** in Kungsträdgården, a popular activity for kids and their keepers all winter long. **Kulturhuset** (p58) is a parent's dream – not only can you drop the little tykes at the Rum för Barn and run off on your own, you can also keep those moody teens entertained making crafts and artwork in the workshop attached to Lava. **Stadsteatern**, in the back of Kulturhuset, frequently stages children's plays. Similarly, **Dramaten** (p81) has a Teater för Barn (Theatre for Children).

Slightly further afield, there's **Tom Tits Experiment** (p171), a fantasia of hands-on scientific displays, including a planetarium. When the little nippers are hungry, take them to **Lasse i Parken** (p118), where they can scamper through a large open field that contains a playground. On the other hand, if you feel like having more grown-up food, you can still bring them along – virtually all restaurants in Stockholm, even the fanciest, welcome children.

The trendiest and historically the wealthiest part of town is Östermalm, on the main island to the east of Norrmalm and Vasastaden. It's bordered by Birger Jarlsgatan, Valhallavägen, Strandvägen and Oxenstiernasgatan. On the north side of Valhallavägen is Gärdet, and the green area to the east of Östermalm is Ladugårdsgärdet.

Some of the more interesting parts of Stockholm are to be found on the outskirts of town. In the north, Stockholms Universitetet has a thriving student culture, tons of parkland and great running trails. Its main visitor attractions are Naturhistoriska Riksmuseet and the Cosmonova Imax theatre, but it's worth spending some time wandering the easy trails at the fringes of the campus.

Rinkeby, a suburb most central Stockholmers once considered too dangerous or just too unappealing to visit, has recently

Street corner in Gamla Stan (p51)

gained a degree of cultural cachet. As a major nexus of several immigrant communities, it's steeped in traditions native Swedes find enticingly exotic, and its markets are full of unusual gifts and toys and hard-to-find foods.

# ITINERARIES

## TWO DAYS

Start your visit in Stockholm where the city itself began – Gamla Stan (p51), the Old Town. Peek into Storkyrkan (p55), then take a tour of Kungliga Slottet (p52), the Royal Palace – you might not have time to see it all, but try to be near the outdoor courtyard at midday for the Changing of the Guard. Spend the afternoon wandering the twisty, cobbled streets, stopping to *fika* (have coffee) in the city's oldest café, Sundbergs Konditori (p106). Then walk across Slussen to Södermalm (p75) – visit Stockholms Stadsmuseum (p79) if there's time – and hop the Katarinahissen (p78) for a spectacular evening view. Dine at Eriks Gondolen (p115 or prowl Södermalm for nightlife. The next day, visit Skansen (p69) and the Vasamuseet (p73) on Djurgården. Stop at Rosendals Trädgård (p113) for coffee, lunch or dinner.

## FOUR DAYS

Follow the two-day itinerary, then head to Östermalm to check out the Vikings exhibit at the Historiska museet (p81). Forage for lunch in Östermalms Saluhallen (p104), then get a grim lesson in military history at the nearby Armémuseum (p80) – or, if you're museumed-out, scope the goods at the boutiques lining Biblioteksgatan (p150). Dine on upscale *husmanskost* at Restaurant KB (p110), then join the queue waiting to get into Spy Bar (p134). The next day, take a sightseeing tour of Stockholm's waterways (p50). Stop for a drink or lunch at the historic and decadent Berns Salonger (p107), where Strindberg's first novel was inspired. Afterwards, wander over to Skeppsholmen for the three-way aesthetic treat of Moderna Museet (p73), Arkitekturmuseet (p73) and Svensk Form Design Centre (p74). The café at Moderna Museet serves excellent coffee, cakes and light meals.

## ONE WEEK

Follow the four-day itinerary, then do what Stockholmers love to do when they're on holiday: devote a couple of days to an excursion into Stockholm's archipelago (p171). On your last day, start with a visit to the world-class National Museum (p67). Afterwards, check out what's going on at the fringes of the Stockholm art world at **Magasin 3** (p81), then continue the theme by perusing the galleries and design shops in **Södermalm** (p75). Finish up with a distinctly unpretentious beer and mandatory Swedish meatballs at **Kvarnen** (p126) or **Pelikan** (p127).

# ORGANISED TOURS

## AIR

### BALLONGFLYG UPP OCH NER
☎ 695 01 00; www.uppner.se/indeng.htm; Hammarby vägen 37; 1hr trips from Skr995

An exciting way to see Stockholm is from a hot air balloon; it's one of the few cities where balloons are allowed to fly right over the city centre. This company offers trips of varying length, starting with a one-hour flight with champagne 'christening' for first-timers. Several other companies also offer flights, including **City Ballong** (☎ 34 54 64; www.cityballong.se; adult/child Skr1795/1050) and **Scandinavia Balloons** (☎ 10 95 95; www.balloons-sweden.se in Swedish; Skr1695). Contact the tourist office for details.

### STOCKHOLM HELICOPTER TOURS
☎ 656 90 70; www.helicoptertours.nu in Swedish; tours from Skr750

Get a bird's-eye view of the city with helicopter flights around Stockholm and the inner archipelago.

## BOAT

### STOCKHOLM SIGHTSEEING
Map pp236–8

☎ 58 71 40 20; www.stockholmsightseeing.com; Skeppsbron 22; Royal Canal Tour from Skr100, Stockholm Card free; 'Under the Bridges' tour from Skr160

The main source for sightseeing tours of the city by water, Stockholm Sightseeing runs interesting hourly cruises from early April to mid-December. The cruises leave from Strömkajen (near the Grand Hotel) or Nybroplan and take sightseers around the central bridges and canals. The one-hour 'Royal Canal' and 'Historical Canal' tours go to Kungsholmen and the archipelago (Fjäderholmarna), respectively. The 'Historical Canal' tour only runs from early June to mid-August. 'Under the Bridges of Stockholm' is an illuminating tour with entertaining commentary; it takes two hours and passes under 15 bridges on its way around Södermalm (May to October only). Several other tour options are available, all with commentary in English.

### STRÖMMA KANALBOLAGET
Map pp236–8

☎ 58 71 40 00; Skeppsbron 22; ☺ departures from Nybroplan once or twice hourly, 10am-11.30pm late Apr-early Sep; return Skr70

Kanalbolaget sails daily to Fjäderholmarna, a pair of small islands in the archipelago. 'Salmon & Shrimp' trips on Lake Mälaren depart every evening at 7.30pm (between late April and September) and take 3½ hours. For information on this company's other destinations, see p171

### SVEA VIKING
☎ 53 25 72 00; www.sveaviking.se; ☺ 5 daily departures, 10.45am-7.45pm, late Jun-late Aug; adult/student/child Skr150/120/50

This corny but fun Viking longship – complete with burly Viking warriors – runs 1¾-hour trips around the inner archipelago (Viking food and drinks included).

## BUS

### CITY SIGHTSEEING Map pp236–8
☎ 58 71 40 30; www.citysightseeing.com; Gustav Adolfs Torg; Stockholm Panorama tour Skr190

The other half of Stockholm Sightseeing, this outfit runs daily bus tours of the city, departing from the booth outside the Opera House at Gustav Adolfs Torg. Ask if free hotel pickup is available when you book. The 90-minute 'Stockholm Panorama' tour runs two to seven times daily all year; it's thorough and popular, but the commentary feels stale at times. 'Royal Stockholm' and 'Historical Stockholm' are more in-depth three-hour tours, but they only run from early April to mid-October (at 10am and 2pm respectively; from Skr275).

## OTHER TOURS

### AUTHORISED GUIDES OF STOCKHOLM
☎ 789 24 96; www.guidestockholm.com; 1hr; Skr50; 1.30pm Sat & Sun

This well-respected organisation does walking tours of Gamla Stan with an educational agenda that's heavy on the city's 750 years of history. Tours leave from the obelisk at Slottsbacken outside the Royal Palace.

## BIKE TOURS OF STOCKHOLM

☎ 58 71 40 30; www.citysightseeing.com; Skr190-270; ⊙ 2-3hr tours depart 9.30am & 2.30pm from Strömkajen in Sep

Another service of City Sightseeing, these bicycle tours get out to some of the city's most beautiful surrounding areas. They can also be booked for large groups.

## STOCKHOLM IN A NUTSHELL

☎ 58 71 40 30; www.citysightseeing.com; 2½hr; Skr280

The nutshell of the title refers to a coach tour of the city, plus a 1-hour boat trip to the cute little islands of Fjäderholmarna. The tour departs three to seven times daily, April to September.

## STOCKHOLM STORIES

☎ 0708 85 05 28; www.stockholmstories.com

In guided walks around Gamla Stan and Söder, historian and public speaker Maria Lindberg Howard tells interesting, quirky stories related to Stockholm buildings, streets and squares. Call to book a time.

# GAMLA STAN & RIDDARHOLMEN

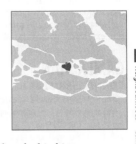

*Eating p104; Drinking p124; Shopping p143; Sleeping p155*

The oldest part of Stockholm, Gamla Stan (the Old Town) is a deeply atmospheric place, despite being crammed with tourists all summer long. Its contorted back alleys snake between cake-like rust- and mustard-coloured buildings sagging with fatigue after hundreds of years. From the enormous and impressive Kungliga Slott to Stockholm's tiniest alleyway (Mårten Trotzigs Gränd), it's a charming part of town that's drenched in history.

Most of the heavy tourism and souvenir hunting in Gamla Stan is concentrated along Västerlånggatan and Stora Nygatan, making it rather easy to avoid if you have no interest in miniature ceramic Vikings, Dalahäst key chains or Absolut Swede shot glasses. Venture into the smaller, back alleys and you'll find a city that seems almost unchanged since medieval times. Note the variously decorative iron anchors dotting the walls; many of them take patterns echoed today in everything from jewellery to saffron bread. Stortorget, the large square in the centre of the Old Town, was the site of the Stockholm Bloodbath that helped spark the Swedish people's rebellion against Danish rule in 1520 (see p41). These days it's the much more cheerful site of a Christmas market in the winter and café tables all summer. The large, pale yellow building facing the square is Börsen, the former stock exchange; it now houses the Nobelmuseet (p54). The tall, salmon-coloured building at No 20, now a café and a Stockholm landmark frequently photographed and depicted by artists, dates from 1650.

Riddarholmen, separated from Gamla Stan by a slender canal, feels even more like a village caught in a time warp, especially at night when it's almost completely deserted. Nobody lives on the island anymore; it's mostly used for government offices. Originally called Gråmunkeholmen (Grey Monks' Island), it started as the home of Franciscan monks. It took the name Riddarholmen, or The Island of Knights, because in the 17th century the knights who served in the Thirty Years' War were given palaces on the island. The most striking site on Riddarholmen is the iron-spired church, Riddarholmskyrkan (p56).

## Gamla Stan & Riddarholmen Top Five

- Kungliga Slottet (p52)
- Nobelmuseet (p54)
- Medeltidsmuseet (p54)
- Riksdagshuset (p55)
- Riddarholmskyrkan (p56)

The tiny speck of an island between Norrmalm and Gamla Stan is Helgeandsholmen, which houses the Swedish parliament building, Riksdagshuset. At the opposite end of the island, under Norrbro, is the moody, fascinating Medeltidsmuseet (p54).

## Orientation

Gamla Stan can be incredibly disorienting – in fact, the best approach is just to plan on getting yourself lost in its labyrinthine streets. It's a small island, after all; walk in any direction for a few blocks and you'll reach water. The island is connected to Norrmalm by five bridges – Strömbron, Norrbro and Riksgatan (which both cross Helgeandsholmen), Vasabron and Centralbron – and connected to Södermalm by the complicated street-and-waterway traffic system that is

## Transport

**Tunnelbana** T-Gamla Stan
**Bus** 43, 46, 55, 59, 76
**Car** Not recommended

Slussen. The Royal Palace (Kungliga Slottet) sits on the northernmost corner of Gamla Stan, just where the original Tre Kronor fortress and castle once stood. Skeppsbron edges the island's east side, while Slottskajen, Myntgatan and Munkbroleden wrap around its north, west and south sides. The main channels through the core of Old Town are Västerlånggatan, which is essentially a continuation of Norrmalm's Drottninggatan, and the parallel Stora Nygatan, both of which run vaguely northwest–southeast; and Österlånggatan, which runs north–south. The main square is Stortorget, just off Västerlånggatan toward the centre of the island. The *tunnelbana* (underground metro) station is off Munkbroleden on the southwest side of the island; one exit leads toward the island of Riddarholmen, the other into the heart of Old Town.

# GAMLA STAN

## CORNELISMUSEET Map pp239–41

☎ 667 73 65; Trångsund 8; adult/child Skr20/free; ✆ noon-4pm Sat & Sun; noon-4pm Mon-Sun 15 Jun-15 Aug; T-Gamla Stan

This small museum displays memorabilia, such as records, instruments, prizes and clothes, relating to the hugely popular (in Sweden) troubadour Cornelis Vreeswijk, who died in 1987. There's a guided tour every Wednesday at 8pm (Skr50).

## FINSKA KYRKAN Map pp239–41

☎ 20 61 40; Slottsbacken 2C; ✆ no set opening hrs; T-Gamla Stan

Though it's hard to imagine from looking at the diminutive yellow building, Finska Kyrkan (Finnish Church) was once an indoor tennis court that Fredrik I gave to Stockholm's Finnish community in the 1740s for use as a church. It's now used as a community centre and historical archive; it currently contains an early-18th-century inventory from a church near St Petersburg. Social events held at the church are posted on a sign near the walkway.

## KUNGLIGA MYNTKABINETTET
Map pp239–41

☎ 51 95 53 00; www.myntkabinettet.se; Slottsbacken 6; adult/senior/child Skr45/35/12, Sun free, Stockholm Card free; ✆ 10am-4pm; T-Gamla Stan, bus 43, 46, 55, 59, 76

Europe's first economic museum, Kungliga Myntkabinettet (Royal Coin Cabinet), is just across the square from the Royal Palace. The collection was initiated by Johan III in the 1570s. You'll find displays of coins (including

Viking silver) and banknotes covering the history of money over the past 2600 years. There are also replicas of bank offices, medal collections and a section designed for children.

The world's oldest coin (a Swedish copper plate weighing 19.7kg, from 625 BC) and the world's first banknote (issued in Sweden in 1661) can all be found here. The finest ancient coin on display shows a lion's head on one side and was minted by King Croesus of Greece in 550 BC. A sad example of hyperinflation can be seen on the lengthy German banknote 'Tausend Mark' – it's a mere DM1,000,000,000,000.

Information and floor plans are available in English. There's also a classy café and a souvenir shop.

## KUNGLIGA SLOTTET Map pp239–41

☎ 402 61 30; adult/child/under 7 Skr70/35/free, Stockholm Card free; ✆ 10am-4pm or 5pm summer, noon-3pm Tue-Sun winter; T-Gamla Stan, bus 43, 46, 55, 59, 76

Kungliga Slottet, the 'new' castle, was constructed on the site of the original fortress, Tre Kronor, which burned down in 1697. The walls of the north wing of the castle survived the fire and were incorporated in the palace, but the medieval designs are now concealed by a baroque exterior. *Designed* by the court architect Nicodemus Tessin the Younger, Kungliga Slottet took 57 years to complete. With 608 rooms, it's the world's largest royal castle still used for its original purpose.

The fascinating spectacle of the Changing of the Guard takes place in the outer courtyard at 12.10pm daily June to August (a more elaborate ceremony occurs at 1.10pm Sundays and public holidays); the rest of the year it's on Wednesday, Saturday and Sunday only. By the outer courtyard, there's a shop selling souvenir books and kitschy gifts. Indoor photography isn't permitted in Kungliga Slottet.

The **royal apartments** (free guided tours in English, 1.15pm daily) count as one unit and are open to the public except during state functions. A descriptive booklet with good colour photographs is available from the palace bookshop for Skr40. Originally, there were eight suites on the 1st and 2nd floors of Kungliga Slottet, with state rooms facing outward and smaller private rooms facing the inner courtyard. Allow at least an hour for viewing the royal apartments with their rococo and baroque designs, 18th- and 19th-century furnishings, portraits, porcelain and silverware. Highlights include the Bernadotte apartments, a suite of 13 rooms with uncomfortable-looking furniture and Lovisa Ulrika's audience chamber, throne and wall tapestries. Turning right leads you to the Hall of State, reminiscent of a Greek temple, where the Swedish parliament was opened by the monarch every year from 1755 to 1975. It contains Queen Kristina's silver throne, a gift from Magnus Gabriel de la Gardie in 1650. On the 2nd floor, there's a mosaic table in the guardroom – a gift from Pope Pius IX – and living quarters for the king and queen, though most monarchs have resided elsewhere. King

Gustav III died of gunshot wounds here in his neoclassical bedchamber (see p44).

**Slottskyrkan** (Royal Chapel), on the 1st floor of the south wing, has three ceiling paintings depicting Christ's ascension into heaven and an altarpiece featuring Christ in the Garden of Gethsemane. Parts of the pews were rescued from the Tre Kronor fire.

**Skattkammaren** (Royal Treasury; free guided tours in English 12.15pm daily), in the basement of the south wing, contains display cases of Swedish regalia, coronation cloaks, crowns, orbs, sceptres, keys and medals. Most impressive are Oskar II's ermine and velvet coronation cloak (1872), Karl XI's extraordinary silver-coated baptismal font and Gustav Vasa's sword of state, with a magnificently etched blade depicting Old Testament scenes from the burning bush to the drowning of the Egyptians in the Red Sea. In the basement of the north wing is **Gustav IIIs Antikmuseum**, which displays the marble Mediterranean sculptures acquired by that eccentric monarch during his Italian tour of 1784.

The **Museum Tre Kronor**, opened in 1999, was originally a 16th-century wood-storage cellar. Now it features the foundations of 13th-century defensive walls, exhibits rescued from the medieval castle during the fire of 1697, and a variety of mundane objects of medieval vintage; similar items are better presented at the Medeltidsmuseet (p54).

*Storkyrkan (p55) and Gamla Stan (p51) viewed from Riddarholmen island*

A combination ticket (adult/child Skr110/65) admits you to the Royal Apartments and Chapel, the Museum Tre Kronor, Gustav IIIs Antikmuseum and the Skattkammaren. Gustav IIIs Antikmuseum is open in summer only; the Royal Chapel is open between noon and 3pm Wednesday and Friday in summer and holds church services at 11am Sunday throughout the year.

## LIVRUSTKAMMAREN Map pp239–41

☎ 51 95 55 44; Slottsbacken 3, Kungliga Slottet; adult/senior/child/under 6 Skr65/50/20/free, Stockholm Card free; ⏰ 11am-5pm Tue-Sun, to 8pm Thu; T-Gamla Stan, bus 43, 46, 55, 59, 76

Though part of the palace grounds, Livrustkammaren (Royal Armoury) has a separate entrance and admission fee. Its displays cover 500 years of royal history, with a large collection of royal memorabilia that includes armour, weapons, ceremonial costumes and five colourful carriages. There's usually a large temporary exhibition in the upstairs section. Gustav II Adolf's horse, Streiff, stands proudly preserved in a glass case (its hide is fitted over a wooden frame). Look out for Karl XII's hat, complete with the assassin's bullet hole (1718), and the costume Gustav III was wearing at the masquerade ball when he was shot in 1792. One of the oddest displays is the jar holding the stomach contents of Baron Bielke (one of the men who conspired to kill Gustav III); he committed suicide by taking arsenic.

## MEDELTIDSMUSEET Map pp239–41

☎ 50 83 17 90; www.medeltidsmuseet.stockholm.se; Strömparterren; adult/student/under 17 Skr60/20/free, Stockholm Card free; ⏰ 11am-4pm Jul & Aug, to 6pm Wed; T-Gamla Stan, bus 43, 62, 65

Popular with adults and kids alike, Medeltidsmuseet (Medieval Museum) is located under the bridge at the eastern end of Helgeandsholmen. A 55m-long section of city wall dating from around AD 1530, plus 10 boats, 9000kg of human bones and 700 shoes, were discovered here in the late 1970s when an underground car park for Riksdagshuset was being excavated. The car park idea was abandoned, and you can now get a taste of medieval Stockholm by exploring faithful, on-site reconstructions of houses, sheds and workshops. The extraordinarily well-presented exhibits, complete with ambient music, are atmospheric almost to the point of being spooky; they include real skeletons, a secret 18th-century passage leading to Kungliga Slottet, medieval boats, weapons

and a grim hanging exhibit called Gallows Hill. Free guided tours in English start at 2pm daily in July and August.

## NOBELMUSEET Map pp228–9

☎ 23 25 06; www.nobel.se/nobel/nobelmuseum/; Börshuset, Stortorget; adult/student/child/under 7 Skr50/40/20/free, Stockholm Card free; ⏰ 11am-8pm Tue, 11am-5pm Wed-Sun; T-Gamla Stan, bus 3, 43, 46, 53, 55, 59, 76

Though it's not a huge place, there's a lot to absorb at this museum, housed in the Swedish Academy building (the former stock exchange). Video screens display the milieus of several Nobel Prize winners; portraits of each winner hang from a constantly moving rack that snakes across the building's ceiling. There's an audio archive where you can hear acceptance speeches, interviews and readings from Nobel Prize winners including Ernest Hemingway, William Faulkner and Isaac Bashevis Singer. Two film rooms show short documentaries about the nature of creativity and the conditions under which it tends to thrive; subjects include DNA detectives Watson & Crick and Japanese author Yasunari Kawabata.

## POSTMUSEUM Map pp239–41

☎ 781 17 55; www.posten.se/museum; Lilla Nygatan 6; adult/student/child/under 12 Skr50/40/25/free, Stockholm Card free; ⏰ 11am-4pm Tue-Sun, to 7pm Wed; T-Gamla Stan, bus 3, 53

The Postmuseum features temporary and permanent exhibits about the 360-year-long history of the Swedish postal service, which includes post office reconstructions and displays of Swedish stamps from 1855 to the present day. One recently added section outlines the fairly dramatic structural changes the postal service has undergone in the past few years. The knowledge centre, Post F@ktum, contains 220,000 documents, including books on stamps and postal history. There's also a miniature post office for children, a café/bistro and a shop.

## RIDDARHUSET Map pp239–41

☎ 723 39 90; Riddarhustorget 10; adult/child Skr40/10, Stockholm Card free; ⏰ 11.30am-12.30pm Mon-Fri; T-Gamla Stan

One of the loveliest buildings in Sweden is this 17th-century palace, The House of Nobility, built by Jean de la Vallee and Joost Vingboons. The Swedish parliament met here until 1865. The walls of the impressive Great Hall are plastered with 2345 coats of arms belonging to Sweden's nobility; some of the insignias are richly symbolic, others more perplexing. Look out for the precious Land Marshall's chair, carved in ivory and dating from at least 1650. It is still used by the chairman during the Assembly of Nobles, which takes place every third year. In the chancellery there's a unique collection of 525 pieces of heraldic porcelain displaying 170 different Swedish coats of arms. There's also a display of around 1600 signets, each with a family crest, and portraits of historically important Swedes. A colour booklet is available, in English, for Skr40.

## RIKSDAGSHUSET Map pp239–41

☎ 786 40 00; Riksgatan 3A; free; ☾ 1hr guided tours in English, 1.30pm Sat & Sun; T-Kungsträdgården, bus 43, 62

The little island of Helgeandsholmen, in the middle of Norrström, is home to Riksdagshuset, the Swedish parliament building. Though it may not sound like the most exciting way to spend an hour, tours of the building are in fact fascinating to anyone interested in how government works or doesn't. The rather dreamy Swedish system of consensus-building, as presented by knowledgeable tour guides, has been known to elicit astounded chuckles of disbelief from more than one visitor. Tours move through both the older front building (facing downstream), which dates from 1905 and includes an impressive central stairwell with pillars and a glass roof, and the more modern section, a former bank building that contains the debating chamber, the MP's club, a post office and restaurants. The system is very open; anyone can visit the public gallery and listen to the parliament's debates (in Swedish).

## STORKYRKAN Map pp239–41

☎ 723 30 00; Trångsund; May-Aug Skr10, Sep-Apr free, floor plan Skr5; ☾ 9am-6pm Jun-Sep, 9am-4pm Oct-May; T-Gamla Stan, bus 3, 43, 46, 53, 55, 59, 76

Sweden's monarchs used to be crowned in Stockholm's impressive cathedral, which lies next to Kungliga Slottet. This brick-built church was consecrated in 1306, replacing a smaller church on the same site which was gutted by fire. Within the baroque exterior, the ornate space features medieval paintings on the ceiling – notably work by Albertus Pictor in the Chapel of the Souls cross vault – and a life-sized statue of St George and his horse confronting

Neighbourhoods – Gamla Stan & Riddarholmen

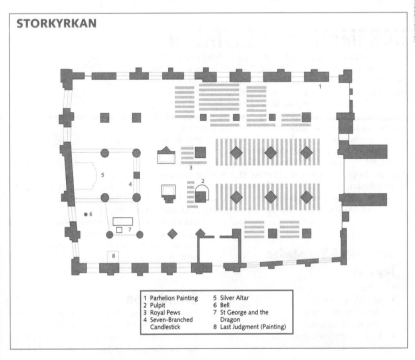

STORKYRKAN

| | |
|---|---|
| 1 Parhelion Painting | 5 Silver Altar |
| 2 Pulpit | 6 Bell |
| 3 Royal Pews | 7 St George and the Dragon |
| 4 Seven-Branched Candlestick | 8 Last Judgment (Painting) |

the mythical dragon, commissioned by Sten Sture the Elder to symbolise Sweden's freedom from Danish rule and sculpted by the German Berndt Notke in 1494. The extravagant pulpit is from 1700 (written on it is the Hebrew word Yahweh, meaning 'God'). Note also the two large royal-box pews with crown-shaped canopies, and the 350-year-old silver altar. Left of the altar sits a 2m-high bell, dating from 1493. The *Parhelion Painting (Vädersolstavlan)*, actually a 1630s copy of the original, depicts Stockholm during a spectacular display of atmospheric optics in 1535; it's on the southern wall, near the entrance. The Sunday service (in Swedish) is at 11am. Classical music concerts are held frequently; tickets cost from Skr70 to Skr400 depending on the performers. Call ☎ 723 30 09 for details.

### TYSKA KYRKAN Map pp239–41

☎ 411 11 88; Svartmangatan 16; admission free; ☺ noon-4pm early May-late Sep, noon-4pm Sat & Sun late Sep-early May; T-Gamla Stan, bus 3, 53

Tyska Kyrkan (the German Church) is one of Stockholm's finest churches. It dates from the 1570s, but was enlarged to its current size between 1638 and 1642. All the church windows are stained glass and there are 119 unique

gallery paintings (1660–65). The finest parts of the interior include the royal gallery (1672), the gold-painted altar and the astonishing ebony and alabaster pulpit (1660).

## RIDDARHOLMEN

### RIDDARHOLMSKYRKAN Map pp239–41

☎ 402 61 30; Birger Jarls Torg; adult/child Skr20/10; ☺ 10am-4pm mid-May–mid-Aug, noon-3pm Sat & Sun Sep; T-Gamla Stan, bus 3, 53

With its dramatic iron spire stabbing at the sky, Riddarholmskyrkan is visible from all over town. It was built by Franciscan monks in the late-13th century and was expanded in the mid-15th century. The church has been the royal necropolis since the burial of Magnus Ladulås in 1290. Along with the bodies of many faithful knights and nobles, it's home to the armorial glory of the Serafim order. The last regular church service was held in 1807 but funeral services still take place here. To the right of the altar is the Gustavian chapel, with the marble sarcophagus of Gustav II, Sweden's mightiest monarch. Directly opposite is the Carolean chapel, with the black marble sarcophagus of Karl XII. Look out for the massed wall-plates displaying the arms of the knights.

# NORRMALM & VASASTADEN

*Eating p106; Drinking p124; Shopping p144; Sleeping p156*

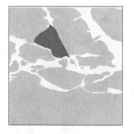

The modern heart of Stockholm, Norrmalm is as enthusiastically contemporary as Gamla Stan is antiquated. This bustling part of town is the home of Centralstationen, where all lines of transport throughout the city converge. Next to the station is Sergels Torg, a severely modern public square (though it's actually round) bordered on one side by the imposing glass Kulturhuset. Norrmalm is also the home of signature Scandinavian department store NK (Nordiska Kompaniet), and the beloved public park Kungsträdgården, where locals gather in all weather to picnic, ice skate, browse at a market or enjoy a cultural fair.

Vasastaden, or Vasastan, is the somewhat quieter, more residential area that extends to the north of Norrmalm. It is home to a couple of large parks, Observatoriemuseet (p68), the Jewish Museum and the Blå Tornet, where August Strindberg spent the last years of his life (now the Strindberg Museum). It's also where you'll find some of the best restaurants in Stockholm, from casual neighbourhood joints to Asian vegetarian places to ultra-fine dining.

## Norrmalm & Vasastaden Top Five

- Kulturhuset (p58)
- Konstakademien (p58)
- Medelhavsmuseet (p67)
- National Museum (p67)
- Vin & Sprithistoriska Museet (p69)

## Orientation

The boundaries between Norrmalm and Vasastaden are vague, but generally, Norrmalm stretches from the waterfront north to Kammakargatan or Tegnérgatan, and everything from there to the highway (E4) to the west and Sveaplan to the north is Vasastaden. Birger Jarlsgatan serves as the eastern boundary for both neighbourhoods.

## APOTEKSMUSEET Map pp236–8

☎ 723 50 00; Wallingatan 26A; Skr500 for group of 10; ⊗ by arrangement; T-Hötorget

The low-profile pharmacy museum, in the Swedish Academy of Pharmaceutical Sciences building, is well worth a visit if you can get at least 10 people together. Much of the enjoyment arises from the entertaining explanations given during the 90-minute guided tour in English. The museum describes the history of pharmacy, from primitive potions to modern medicine and includes collections of pharmacy signs and mixing jars, laboratory equipment for drug preparation, reconstructions of pharmacies and an exhibit about the famous Swedish chemist CW Scheele.

## BIOGRAFEN SKANDIA Map pp236–8

☎ 077 170 70 70 (Biljett Direkt); Drottninggatan 82; ⊗ for films (check local schedules); T-Hötorget

In 1923 the cinema Biografen Skandia was added to Warodellska House, one of the earliest apartment buildings in Stockholm (1850s). The interior, designed by architect Gunnar Asplund to meld seamlessly with the building's façade, is an absolutely stunning, warm-red rectangle with a deep blue vanishing ceiling and echoes of the wall paintings of Pompeii decorating its balconies. The cinema is constantly threatening to close due to financial difficulties, but at the time of writing it was still in operation, showing art-house films; if it's open during your visit, don't miss the chance to take a peek inside.

## BOLAGSMUSEET Map pp236–8

☎ 789 35 00; Kungsträdgårdsgatan 14; Skr20; ⊗ 1hr tours 10am & 2pm Wed; T-Kungsträdgården

One of the city's lesser-known museums, Bolagsmuseet, located in Systembolaget's head office, traces the fascinating history of alcohol, drunkenness and state control in Sweden. In 1467 *brännvin* (burnt wine) was first imported for use in gunpowder; later it was spooned out of tiny silver bowls as a medicine. But its true nature became clear in the late 16th century, when it was brought home in the form of vodka by Swedish troops who had fought in Russia. Serious boozing quickly became a national pastime. By the early 19th century, Swedes were consuming 46L of pure

## Transport

**Tunnelbana** T-Centralen, T-Kungsträdgården, T-Hötorget, T-Odenplan, T-Rådmansgatan, T-St Eriksplan
**Bus** Nearly every bus passes by Centralstationen on its route
**Train** City Terminalen is the main surface train station; it's connected to T-Centralen, the hub of the *tunnelbana* (underground metro) system
**Car** Not recommended

alcohol per person annually, and drunkenness was rife. Naturally the temperance movement gained popularity, and in 1849 King Oskar I asked parliament to consider controls on opening hours and age limits. Regulations became stricter and put most alcohol-sales premises out of business. (See also the boxed text, p122). The museum displays lots of reconstructions, including a noisy 19th-century pub, and alcohol-monopoly shops from 1907 to 1991. Text is in Swedish, but there's a detailed handout in English. Tours can be arranged at other times (between 9am and 5pm Monday to Friday, minimum five people, Skr20 per person) by calling ☎ 789 36 42.

## DANSMUSEET Map pp236–8

☎ 441 76 50; www.dansmuseet.nu; Gustav Adolfs Torg 22-24; adult/student/under 12 Skr50/30/free, Stockholm Card free; ⊗ 11am-4pm Mon-Fri, noon-4pm Sat & Sun Jun-Aug, closed Mon Sep-May; T-Kungsträdgården, bus 3, 43, 62, 65

Located in a neoclassical former bank building, the Dance Museum covers all aspects of staging and costume and has a high standard of exhibits. The Tibetan, Indian and African masks and costumes are particularly fine. There are also displays of Chinese and Japanese puppets, a Russian ballet exhibit and a summary of European dance history. You can also watch videos of dancers in action. The café serves hot meals and snacks and the friendly staff can advise on dance classes.

## GUSTAF VASA KYRKAN Map p230

☎ 736 03 35; Odenplan; admission free; ⊗ 11am-6pm Mon-Thu & 11am-3pm Fri-Sun; T-Odenplan, bus 4, 40, 42, 47, 53

This magnificent church has a 1731 baroque high altar sculpted in plaster, a marble pulpit, and a 60m-high cupola with ceiling frescoes. The creepy *columbarium* (crypt; ☎ 32 49 20; admission free; ⊗ 11am-3pm Wed, Fri-Sun,

11am-6pm Tue & Thu) has places for around 35,000 burial urns; enter from the Västmanna-gatan side of the church.

## JUDISKA MUSEET Map p230

☎ 31 01 43; Hälsingegatan 2; adult/senior/student Skr60/40/20, under 12 free; ☿ noon-4pm Mon-Thu & Sun, noon-2pm Fri; T-Odenplan, bus 4, 42, 47, 72

The small but very interesting Judiska Museet (Jewish Museum) describes the lives of Swedish Jewry from 1774. Topics covered include Nazi death camps, Raoul Wallenberg (see the boxed text, p46), Torah silverware and accessories, ceremonial items relating to the Sabbath and Passover (including a fine collection of silver spice boxes), and a cast featuring the Menorah, a unique seven-branched candlestick that was looted from Jerusalem by the Romans in AD 70. Male visitors may want to look out for the circumcision knives – or not! Leaflets giving descriptions in English, and coffee, tea and biscuits are available.

## KLARA KYRKA Map pp236–8

☎ 723 30 00; Klara Västra Kyrkogatan; free; ☿ 10am-5pm; T-Centralen

After King Gustav Vasa's death, his son Johan III ordered the reconstruction of several of the churches, convents and monasteries his father had looted and demolished. Among them was Klara Kyrka, a convent destroyed in 1527. The replacement was completed in 1590, but the church was badly damaged by fire in 1751 and has been rebuilt and renovated several times since. It is noted for its fine ceiling paintings; the central four are Old Testament scenes. Four wall paintings depict church history. Famed Swedish bard Carl Michael Bellman is interred in the churchyard.

Free lunch concerts, usually organ but sometimes choir, start at noon on weekdays and last up to 45 minutes.

## KONSERTHUSET Map pp236–8

☎ 786 02 00; www.konserthuset.se; Hötorget 8; admission Skr30; ☿ 1hr tours in Swedish 11.30am Sat monthly Sep-May; T-Hötorget

The design competition for the neoclassical and Art Deco Konserthuset was won by Ivar Tengbom. Originally completed in 1926, the main hall was rebuilt in the 1970s to improve the acoustics (which cost it its illusion of depth). The blue façade, with 10 enormous faux classical columns, hides a fairly mundane interior. The smaller, neo-Renaissance hall, however, features renowned murals and ceiling paintings by the famous Swedish artist Isaac Grünewald. The statues in the entrance hall and the sculpture of Orpheus with his lyre (in Hötorget) are by Carl Milles. Though the building is open for visits, a better way to see it is to attend a concert here; pick up a schedule at the office inside Konserthuset (entrance on Kungsgatan).

## KONSTAKADEMIEN Map pp236–8

☎ 23 29 45; Fredsgatan 12; admission free; ☿ 11am-5pm Tue-Fri, noon-4pm Sat & Sun; T-Centralen, bus 3, 53, 62, 65

Konstakademien (the Royal Academy of Fine Arts) inhabits a regal mansion designed by Nicodemus Tessin the Elder and originally constructed in 1672, though it has actually been rebuilt several times. The building is worth a look by itself, but the academy also has a couple of small galleries where it presents rotating exhibitions of work by new and established artists, sculptors and architects. In the ground floor of the same building is the temporary location of the Architecture Museum, as well as the noted restaurant Fredsgatan 12.

## KULTURHUSET Map pp236–8

☎ 50 83 15 08; Sergels Torg 3; admission free, exhibitions up to Skr50 (under 18 free); ☿ 10am-7pm Tue-Fri, 11am-5pm Sat & Sun; T-Centralen

The glass-fronted box that is Kulturhuset, designed by Peter Celsing after he won a competition, has taken nothing but abuse since its completion in 1974. The building, like the square it faces, was reviled as a symbol of demolished history and soulless, commerce-driven modern architecture. Lately, though, young Swedish architects have begun to champion the building as a rare adventure in Stockholm's stodgy urban milieu. Like it or hate it, Kulturhuset is a valuable institution; it hosts frequent art exhibitions and literary readings, and is the temporary home of Stockholm's tourist office. There's a bookshop, a design co-op, several cafés, a media centre and comics library, an Internet café and a crafts/clubhouse area where teens can hang out, drink coffee and express themselves with art supplies and sewing machines. Parents can drop their kids (under 12) at Rum för Barn to play in an educational environment. Stadsteatern is also here, and in the back of the building is a late-night salsa club (Red Square). Some activities and events have special opening hours; for details, check the programme booklets that are issued several times yearly.

*(Continued on page 67)*

1 The waterfront west of Stadshuset 2 Bandy player at Zinkensdamms Idrottsplats (p137) 3 Walkers in Hagaparken (p85) 4 Café life in Stortorget, Gamla Stan (p51)

**1** *Riddarholmen and Riddarholms-kyrkan (p56)* **2** *Stortorget and Storkyrkan at night (p55)* **3** *Traditional house at Skansen open-air museum (p72)* **4** *Nordiska Museet (p71)*

textilgalleriet
NORDISKA MUSEET

1 *Grand Hôtel Stockholm (p156)*
2 *Guard at Kungliga Slottet (p52)*
3 *Ekotemplet, Hagaparken (p85)*
4 *Figurehead of a Viking longboat*

1 *Kungliga Operan (p133)*
2 *Castor och Pollux, 2004, by Carl Anders Thorheim in Galleri Sveriges Allmänna Konstförening, Konstakademien (p58)*
3 *Dramatiska Teatern (p81)*
4 *Statue of Orpheus outside Konserthuset (p58)*

1

4

1 *Nordiska Kompaniet department store (p145)* 2 *Part of Alexander Calder's Four Elements at Moderna Museet (p73)* 3 *Examples of the famous Swedish glassware (p34)* 4 *Statues in Millesgården (p85)*

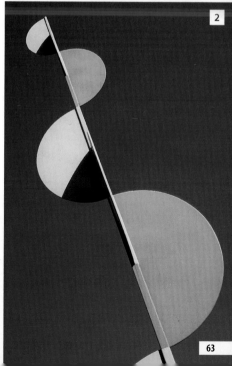

2

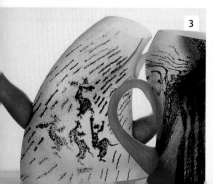

3

1 *Birger Jarl hotel (p163)* 2 *Vodka in ice at Icebar (p125)* 3 *Jazzclub Fasching (p136)* 4 *Handbags at the ready on Biblioteksgatan*

1 Eyubi (p108) 2 Bonden (p134)
3 Café Opera (p124) 4 A Stockholm chef holding a plate of
gravad lax (p101)

1 *Wooden buildings on Hamngatan, Vaxholm (p169)* 2 *Detail of a fountain in the grounds of Drottningholms Slott (p177)* 3 *Typical view of Stockholm archipelago (p171)* 4 *A floating restaurant on Lake Mälaren near Sigtuna*

*(Continued from page 58)*

## MARIONETTMUSEET Map pp236–8

☎ 50 62 01 00; www.marionetteatern.com in Swedish; Stockholms Stadsteater, Sergels Torg; adult/child Skr30/15, English CD tour Skr15; ☉ 1-4pm Tue-Sun; T-Centralen

The friendly and privately funded Marionett-museet (Puppet Theatre Museum) is moving from its former location to the Kulturhuset building, joining Stockholms Stadsteater, opening in its new premises in autumn 2004. The museum covers both Swedish and international puppet theatre. There's a lot to see, including anatomically correct Burmese puppets, horsemen and elephants from India, wild-looking red-faced puppets from Indonesia, and some magnificent Nepalese puppets. The theatre and museum put on puppet shows from September to April (tickets Skr30 to Skr100).

## MEDELHAVSMUSEET Map pp236–8

☎ 51 95 53 80; Fredsgatan 2; adult/under 21 Skr50/free, Stockholm Card free; ☉ 11am-8pm Tue, 11am-4pm Wed-Fri, noon-5pm Sat & Sun; T-Kungsträdgården, bus 3, 43, 62, 65

Often unjustly overlooked by tourists, the Museum of Mediterranean Antiquities hides a wealth of secret treasures. In a palatial former bank building with a chequerboard floor edged with Italianate marbled arcades, the collection includes beautiful Egyptian, Greek, Cypriot and Roman artefacts. Some of the displays are rather off-beat, such as the stone body parts that had been donated to an Etruscan temple (in hopes of curing whatever ailed the part represented). Most striking is the oddly lifelike crowd of terracotta figures Sweden excavated from a previously undisturbed temple in northern Cyprus. A magnificent limestone Assyrian palace relief from Nimrud (now in Iraq) dates from around 870 BC. Stolen by English adventurers who sawed it into six parts and shipped it to Britain, it was later sent as a present to the Swedish Queen Josephine. The tiny Gold Room, only open between 12.30pm and 1pm, and 2.30pm and 3pm daily, has displays of gold Greek burial wreaths and an extremely rare Hittite gold jug.

## MUSEET LEKSAKSLAND Map pp231–3

☎ 30 34 03; www.leksaksland.se; Hagagränd 2; adult/child Skr50/30; ☉ 10am-4pm Wed-Fri & noon-4pm Sat & Sun; T-Odenplan, bus 4, 42, 46, 52, 72

Appealing mainly to kids, Museet Leksaksland, formerly Stockholms Miniatyrmuseum, has mechanical models depicting scenes from prehistoric times to the Wild West to the futuristic colonisation of a distant planet. There are exhibits of vintage model cars, McDonald's collectables, a doll's house (complete with Barbie and friends), and an exhibit of dolls in national costumes from around the world.

Neighbourhoods – Normalm & Vasastaden

*National Museum (p68)*

# Adolf Erik Nordenskiöld

The great Swedish explorer and scientist Adolf Erik Nordenskiöld (1832–1901) is best known for the first successful sailing through the Northeast Passage.

After settling in Stockholm in 1858, Nordenskiöld became curator of mineralogy at Naturhistoriska Riksmuseet and later led a series of successful expeditions to Svalbard, the group of Arctic islands between Norway and the North Pole. In 1870 he visited Greenland, but five years later his interest switched to the east and he sailed as far as the Yenisey River, which flows into the Kara Sea. In 1878 Nordenskiöld's steamship *Vega* sailed from Tromsø in Norway and reached Cape Chelyuskin, the northernmost point of Siberia, just one month later. The ship became trapped in pack ice near the Bering Strait and the crew had to stay the winter there, from September 1878 to July 1879. After the break up of the ice, *Vega* continued to Alaska, then returned to Europe via China, Ceylon (now Sri Lanka) and the Suez Canal.

When the explorers returned to Stockholm in April 1880, they were given a rapturous welcome and Nordenskiöld was created a baron by King Oskar, in recognition of his impressive achievement.

## NATIONAL MUSEUM Map pp236–8

☎ 51 95 43 00; www.nationalmuseum.se; Södra Blasie-holmshamnen; adult/student/under 17 Skr75/60/free, Wed adults Skr60, Stockholm Card free; ⏰ 11am-5pm Mon, Wed, Fri-Sun, 11am-8pm Tue & Thu; T-Kungs-trädgården, bus 46, 55, 59, 62, 65, 76

The National Museum is Sweden's largest art museum and houses the main national collection of painting, sculpture, drawings, decorative arts and graphics, ranging from the Middle Ages to the 20th century. The seeds of the collection became state property in 1792 on the death of Gustav III, making this one of the earliest public museums in the world. Completed in 1866, the museum has been enlarged, rebuilt and restored several times. In January 2001 the museum gained unwanted notoriety when thieves made off in a boat with a Rembrandt self-portrait (still missing) and two Renoirs. Some 16,000 paintings and sculptures are on display, including magnificent works by artists such as Cézanne, Goya and Rubens. Design 1900–2000 describes the history of Swedish design and exhibits feature furniture and glassware. The staircase fresco *Midwinter Sacrifice* by Carl Larsson was commissioned but rejected by the museum, which devastated the artist. The painting spent several years in Japan before the National Museum brought it back for a Larsson retrospective and eventually bought it to hang in its intended place.

## OBSERVATORIEMUSEET Map pp231–3

☎ 31 58 10; www.observatoriet.kva.se; Drottning-gatan 120; adult/child Skr50/25; ⏰ 1hr guided tours (in English if requested in advance) at 1 & 2pm Sun, 6pm Tue & Thu; T-Rådmansgatan, bus 40, 52, 53, 69

Gamla observatoriet (the Old Observatory) contains the Observatory Museum. The ob-servatory, which was commissioned by the Royal Swedish Academy of Sciences in 1748, promoted studies of astronomy, geography and meteorology. The museum, open since 1991, houses the study used by Pehr Wilhelm Wargentin, Secretary General of the Royal Swedish Academy of Sciences, who lived here with his family from 1753 to 1783. Other exhibits include continuous weather records since 1756; the old meridian room with a clock from 1748 and a transit instrument (used to measure the movements of various celestial bodies); the observation room, which contains three 18th-century telescopes; and the Vega Room, which has with details about Nordenskiöld's journey through the Northeast Passage from 1878 to 1880 (see the boxed text, above). The Tuesday evening tour is followed by an hour at the telescope, observing the night sky.

## ST JAKOBS KYRKA Map pp236–8

☎ 723 30 00; St Jakobs torg; admission free; ⏰ 11am-3pm Sep-May, 9am-6pm Jun-Aug; T-Kungsträdgården, bus 43, 46, 55, 59, 65

St Jakobs kyrka was completed in 1643 and features both Renaissance and Gothic archi-tecture with a magnificent vaulted ceiling. Of particular note are the ornate pulpit (1828), high altarpiece (1937), heraldic shields, stained-glass windows and elaborate southern entrance. There's a colour brochure in English (Skr5) and an English service at 6pm every Sunday.

## STOCKHOLMS LÄNSMUSEUM Map p230

☎ 690 69 70; www.lansmuseum.a.se; Sabbatsbergs-vägen 6; admission free; ⏰ noon-4pm Tue-Thu & Sun; T-St Eriksplan

The Stockholm County Museum is a small, one-room exhibit that deals with such subjects as archaeology, cultural heritage, history and art in Stockholm's *län* (county). There is also a continually changing program of temporary exhibitions.

## STRINDBERGSMUSEET Map pp236–8

☎ 411 53 54; www.strindbergsmuseet.se; Drottninggatan 85; adult/senior/under 16 Skr40/25/free, Stockholm Card free; ☾ noon-7pm Tue, noon-4pm Wed-Sun; T-Rådmansgatan, bus 52, 69

Strindbergsmuseet is in the Blå Tornet apartment where August Strindberg spent his final four years; the rooms are preserved as if he had just stepped out for tea. You'll see his dining room, bedroom, study and interesting library. On the table in the study are Strindberg's spectacles and other personal belongings, such as his camera, flute, guitar, some of his paintings, programme sheets from his time as a director, and a copy of his *Ockulta Dagboken* (*The Occult Diary*, 1896–1908). For more information about the author, see the boxed text on p28.

## VIN & SPRITHISTORISKA MUSEET

Map p230

☎ 744 70 70; www.vinosprithistoriska.a.se; Dalagatan 100; adult/student/under 12 Skr40/30/free, Stockholm Card free; ☾ 10am-7pm Tue, 10am-4pm Wed-Fri, noon-4pm Sat & Sun, tours in Swedish 2pm Wed & Sun; bus 69

Looking at history through a *snapps* glass, the Vin & Sprithistoriska Museet (Wine & Spirits History Museum) explains the weird stories behind *brännvin*, *punsch* (a sweet, strong, arrack-and-rum-based drink) and the birth of the conservative Swedish alcohol policy. It's housed in the former headquarters of Vin- och Spritcentralen (from 1920), the former state alcohol import monopoly. Among the most interesting exhibits is the multimedia presentation of Swedish drinking habits (available in English); stills, pumps and the control room from the former Reimersholme distillery; a spice organ with 55 different spices; and a 1920s bottling plant that you can start up by pushing a button (see the boxed text, p123). There's also an 'educational' wine bar.

# DJURGÅRDEN & SKEPPSHOLMEN

*Eating p112; Shopping p147; Sleeping p159*

Djurgården, originally set aside as the private hunting grounds of the monarchy, makes an idyllic setting for some of Stockholm's best museums. The unbeatable Skansen is located here, as are the Vasamuseet, Nordiska Museet and Astrid Lindgren's Junibacken. Most of the island is still wide-open green parkland; a large portion of Ekoparken, the National City Park, is on Djurgården. This is also where the Stockholm Expo was held in 1897; some of the buildings are still in use. Complementing the great museums here are some of the city's prettiest garden-setting cafés.

Skeppsholmen is a small, tree-covered island that's home to the famous floating *af Chapman* youth hostel, as well as Moderna Museet, Arkitekturmuseet and the Svensk Form Design Centre.

## Djurgården & Skeppsholmen Top Five

- Skansen (p72)
- Nordiska Museet (p71)
- Thielska Galleriet (p73)
- Prins Eugens Waldemarsudde (p71)
- Moderna Museet (p73)

## Orientation

Djurgården is connected to the city centre by Djurgårdsbron, at the end of Strandvägen; it's an easy and pleasant stroll from Norrmalmstorg or T-Centralen. The main road circling the island is Djurgårdsvägen. There's no *tunnelbana* connection to the island, but there is a vintage tram that runs to Skansen and buses that go to all the various attractions. Cycling is the best way to get around, but if you're just visiting for the attractions, take bus 47 from Centralstationen at Vasagatan, or the summer Djurgården ferry services from Nybroplan, Skeppsholmen or Slussen. You can also go by vintage tram from Norrmalmstorg. Parking is limited during the week and prohibited on summer weekends, when Djurgårdsvägen is closed to traffic.

Skeppsholmen, to the west of Djurgården, is linked to Norrmalm by the Skeppsholmsbron (Skeppsholmen Bridge), which starts near the National Museum.

# DJURGÅRDEN

## AQUARIA VATTENMUSEUM
Map pp231–3

☎ 660 49 40; www.aquaria.se; Falkenbergsgatan 2; adult/senior/child Skr65/55/35, Stockholm Card free; ☽ 10am-6pm Jun-Aug, 10am-4.30pm Tue-Sun Sep-May; bus 44, 47, tram 7

The excellent Aquaria Vattenmuseum (Aquaria Water Museum) has a waterfall on either side of its entrance. The museum features a hot and steamy tropical forest complete with thunderstorm, rain torrents and a bridge over a pool of piranhas. You'll also see huge redtail catfish, mudskippers (which come out of the water), angler fish that spit at their prey, and a colourful coral reef. Aquariums hold dozens of bright, jewel-like fish; there's even a moray eel and a seahorse. There's a sewer kids can explore, a mountain pool with trout and arctic char, and a salmon ladder where wild Baltic salmon come and go between the museum and the sea. The café offers fine views and a special guest in the pond.

## BIOLOGISKA MUSEET Map pp231–3

☎ 442 82 15; www.biologiskamuseet.com; Hazeliusporten; adult/child/under 5 Skr30/10/free, Stockholm Card free; ☽ 10am-4pm Apr-Sep, noon-3pm Mon-Fri, 10am-3pm Sat & Sun Oct-Mar; bus 44, 47, tram 7

The design of the endearingly antiquated Biologiska Museet (Museum of Biology) is based on Norwegian stave churches, but the double spiral staircase is curiously reminiscent of DNA. Admission is included in the price of Skansen admission, but only if you visit Biologiska Museet first. There are two dioramas of stuffed creatures – High Arctic wildlife and Swedish wildlife. The latter is illuminated by natural light. Look out for the amusing *skvader*, a stuffed combination of a capercaillie hen and a mountain hare.

## GRÖNA LUND Map pp231–3

☎ 58 75 01 00; www.gronalund.com in Swedish; adult/under 7 Skr50/free, 72hr SL Tourist Pass free;

☽ noon-11pm Mon-Sat, noon-10pm Sun mid-Jun–mid-Aug, hours vary Sep-May; bus 44, 47, tram 7

The crowded Gröna Lund fun park has 28 rides, ranging from the easy circus carousel to the terrifying 'Free Fall', where you drop from a height of 80m in two seconds (although the brief view from the top is stellar), and 'Extreme', where you get whirled around and subjected to high G-forces. The most thrilling ride is 'Drop 'n' Shot', where you're shot 60m upwards at 3.5G, then downwards at –1G. There are lots of places to eat and drink in the park, but whether you could keep anything down is another matter. All rides except the Haunted House (Skr25) are covered by Gröna Lund's ride coupon scheme (Skr10 per coupon); individual rides range from one to four coupons each. The Grönakortet season pass gives free admission to the park (Skr100). There are lots of easy rides for small children but some of the other rides have minimum height restrictions.

## JUNIBACKEN Map pp231–3

☎ 58 72 30 00; Djurgården; adult/student/child/under 2 Skr95/75/85/free; ☽ 9am-6pm Jun-Nov, 10am-5pm Tue-Sun Dec-May; bus 44, 47, tram 7

Junibacken recreates the fantasy scenes of Astrid Lindgren's children's books, which will stir the imaginations of children and the memories of adults familiar with her characters. You'll go on a 10-minute train journey past miniature landscapes, you'll fly over Stockholm, observe Swedish historical scenes and traditions, and pass through houses. It's a very professional and rather unusual form of entertainment. In Villekulla cottage, kids can shout and squeal and dress up like Pippi (complete with wigs!). The average age of visiting children is around five years.

The Stockholm Card allows Skr20 discount from 9am to 11am June to August and 10am to noon September to May. There's also a café and a well-stocked children's bookshop (see p147).

# Astrid & Pippi

Astrid Lindgren was born in 1907. Upon leaving school she went to Stockholm and trained to be a secretary, got a job in an office, married and had two children.

In 1941, when Lindgren's daughter Karin was ill, she wanted to be told a story. Lindgren asked her if she'd like to hear about a little girl called Pippi Longstocking. Pippi was a hit with Karin and her friends and the story was told over and over again.

In 1944 Lindgren sprained her ankle, and to pass the time she started writing down the Pippi stories in shorthand. She sent a copy to a publisher but it was rejected. However, she had written a second book, which she sent to another publisher and this won second prize in a girls' story competition. The next year, the same publisher organised a children's book competition and Lindgren entered a revised Pippi manuscript, which won first prize. In 1946 her publisher announced a new competition for detective stories for young people and she entered *Bill Bergson Master Detective*, and this won a shared first prize.

Lindgren's impressive output includes picture books, plays and songs and her books have been translated into more than 50 languages. She has worked in radio, television and films, was head of the Children's Book Department at her publishers for four years and has received numerous honours and awards from around the world. Lindgren died at her home in Stockholm in 2002.

## LILJEVALCHS KONSTHALL Map pp231–3

☎ 50 83 13 41; Djurgårdsvägen 60; adult/student/senior/under 17 Skr50/30/30/free, Stockholm Card free; 🕙 11am-5pm Mon, Wed, Fri-Sun, 11am-8pm Tue & Thu; bus 44, 47

Liljevalchs Konsthall (Liljevalchs Art Gallery) is a marvellous building, its design the result of an architectural competition in 1913. It's partly neoclassical, with cast-iron pillars on the south-facing façade. The statues by the entrance (an archer and wolves) are by Carl Milles. The main hall has interesting windows placed high up, allowing natural light to illuminate the contents to best advantage. It's an ideal place to view art exhibits. The gallery shows 20th-century international art in temporary exhibitions of video, photography, painting, sculpture, drawings and etchings. There are four to six major exhibitions per year. In February and March there's an art show where everything is for sale. Guided tours (in Swedish) start at 2pm daily except Monday.

## NORDISKA MUSEET Map pp231–3

☎ 51 95 60 00; www.nordiskamuseet.se; Djurgårdsvägen 6-16; adult/senior/student/under 17 Skr75/50/30/free, Stockholm Card free; 🕙 10am-5pm Fri-Wed 10am-7pm Thu Jun-Aug, 10am-4pm Mon-Fri, 10am-5pm Sat & Sun Sep-May; bus 44, 47, tram 7

Nordiska Museet (the National Museum of Cultural History) was founded by Skansen creator Artur Hazelius. At 126.5m long and 24m high, the museum is the second-largest indoor space in Sweden, and it's housed in an enormous, eclectic, four-storey Renaissance-style castle. The gigantic seated statue of Gustav Vasa, in the Great Hall, was created by Carl Milles. Free guided tours in English run at 1.30pm every day in summer (June to August) except Monday. There are also architectural tours of the building at 11am in summer.

There are notable temporary exhibitions (changing annually) and endless Swedish collections from 1520 to the present day. Of greatest interest is the superb Sami exhibition in the basement, which includes a shaman's drum and an extraordinary 1767 drawing of a rather cool-looking reindeer being castrated by a Sami using his teeth! The Strindberg painting exhibition indicates the depth of this man's tortured soul, and the intriguing 'small object exhibition' includes previously ordinary items that have now become rare and valuable. On the 4th-floor gallery, the Swedish Home exhibition allows a peek into the lives of both rich and poor in times past. Other exhibitions include fashion from the 17th to 20th centuries, the 'table settings' exhibition (running continuously since 1955), Swedish traditions and national costume, and furniture.

## PRINS EUGENS WALDEMARSUDDE Map pp228–9

☎ 54 58 37 00; www.waldemarsudde.com; Prins Eugens väg 6; adult/senior/student/under 18 Skr75/55/55/free, Stockholm Card free; 🕙 11am-5pm Tue-Sun, to 8pm Thu; bus 47, tram 7

Prins Eugens Waldemarsudde, at the southern tip of Djurgården, was the private palace of the painter-prince who preferred art to royal pleasures. The palace now holds his large collection of Nordic art, including fine works by Zorn and

Larsson and the prince's own oil paintings of landscapes in Sweden and Italy. There are also temporary exhibitions in the gallery space, and occasionally in the cottage building. The several buildings that make up the museum, including an old windmill, are surrounded by picturesque gardens.

## ROSENDALS SLOTT Map pp231–3

☎ 402 61 30; www.royalcourt.se; Rosendalsvägen; adult/child Skr50/25; ⏰ tours in English hourly, noon-3pm Tue-Sun Jun-Aug, Sat & Sun Sep; bus 47, 69, tram 7

On the northern side of Djurgården, the prefabricated wooden Rosendals Slott was built as a retreat for Karl XIV Johan and his family in the 1820s. It features sumptuous furnishings and is the finest example in the city of the so-called Empire style. The furnishings from Karl XIV Johan's bed chamber at Kungliga Slott were moved to Rosendals Slott in the 20th century to make this palace museum more complete. Take bus 47 from Centralstationen to the Djurgården terminus, then walk 700m.

## SKANSEN Map pp231–3

☎ 442 80 00; www.skansen.se; Djurgården; adult/child Skr70/30, Stockholm Card free; ⏰ 10am-10pm Jun-Aug, 10am-8pm May, 10am-5pm Sep, 10am-4pm Oct-Apr; bus 44, 47, tram 7

Skansen, the world's first open-air museum, was founded in 1891 by Artur Hazelius to let visitors see how Swedes lived in previous times. Around 150 traditional houses (inhabited by staff in period costume) and other exhibits from all over Sweden occupy this attractive hilltop. It's a spectacular 'Sweden in miniature'; you could easily spend all day here. There are 46 buildings from rural areas around the country, including a Sami camp (with reindeer), farmsteads representing several regions, a manor house and a school. There's also a fascinating glass-blowing exhibit, a zoo full of Nordic animals, and an aquatic section with the requisite playful otters. The **Bergbana** (Mountain Railway; adult/child under 6 Skr20/free) climbs from the northern entrance to the top of the hill. Near the upper station, look out for the Forestry Information Centre and Älvros Gården, a quaint farmstead arranged around a courtyard.

Daily activities take place on Skansen's stages, including folk dancing and music. A map of the park (Skr5) and an excellent 24-page booklet (Skr30) are available (in English and other languages).

## SKANSEN AKVARIET Map pp231–3

☎ 660 10 82; Djurgårdsslätten; adult/child/under 5 Skr65/35/free; ⏰ 10am-4pm Mon-Fri, 10am-5pm Sat & Sun Jul, Sep-May, 10am-6pm Mon-Fri, 10am-7pm Sat & Sun Jun & Aug; bus 44, 47, tram 7

*Farmstead at Skansen open-air museum (above)*

The Skansen Aquarium is also a must. En route to the fish (including piranhas and sharks) you'll walk among lemurs, snakes, spiders and bats and see pygmy marmosets – the smallest monkeys in the world. The display of rats running around a house is less exotic but quite memorable.

## THIELSKA GALLERIET Map pp228–9
☎ 662 58 84; Sjötullsbacken 6; adult/child Skr50/30; ⏰ noon-4pm Mon-Sat, 1pm-4pm Sun; bus 69

An unmissable museum for anyone interested in Scandinavian art, Thielska Galleriet perches on the eastern end of Djurgården. The mint-green and white mansion, completed in 1907, was purpose-built for the tycoon Ernest Thiel, a patron and friend of several Swedish artists. It now contains Thiel's notable collection of late-19th- and early-20th-century Nordic art on three floors, including Anders Zorn's portraits and nudes, Carl Larsson's portraits, Bruno Liljefors' precisely rendered wildlife paintings and August Strindberg's wild landscapes. The highlight is a substantial collection of Edvard Munch paintings and sketches, including his enormous portrait of Strindberg (and one of Thiel).

From the grounds, you can watch huge ferries sailing by. About 400m east of the gallery, at Blockhusudden, there's **Stora Sjötullen**, a former customs station from 1727, which kept an eye on ships sailing into the harbour.

## TOBACCO & MATCH MUSEUM
Map pp231–3
☎ 442 80 26; Gubbhyllan, Skansen; admission free for Skansen visitors; ⏰ 11am-3pm; bus 44, 47, tram 7

Trace the unhealthy history of smoking on three floors at the Tobacco & Match Museum. This fascinating building, near the main southern entrance to Skansen, was built in 1816 and moved to its current location in 1864. It contains a working tobacco factory, an extensive matchbox collection (including the bizarre Kali Safety Match box, which shows a beheading) and a display of some of the 300,000 clay pipes found at Slussen in 1984.

## VASAMUSEET Map pp231–3
☎ 51 95 48 00; Galärvarvsvägen 14; www.vasamuseet .se; adult/student/child/under 7 Skr70/40/10/free, adults after 5pm Wed Skr50, Stockholm Card free; ⏰ 9.30am-7pm mid-Jun–mid-Aug, 10am-5pm Thu-Tue, 10am-8pm Wed mid-Aug–mid-Jun; bus 44, 47, tram 7

In a purpose-built museum whose shape gives away its contents, the ill-fated flagship Vasa

rests in a carefully controlled environment. The museum, behind Nordiska Museet on the western shore of Djurgården, allows you simultaneously to look into the lives of 17th-century sailors and to appreciate a brilliant achievement in marine archaeology. Guided tours in English run hourly from 10.30am in summer and at least twice daily at other times (25 minutes).

On 10 August 1628, the 69m-long top-heavy flagship Vasa overturned and went straight to the bottom of Saltsjön within minutes of its launching. After being painstakingly raised in 1961, the ship and its incredible wooden sculptures were pieced together like a giant 14,000-piece jigsaw – almost all of what you see today is original. Light levels are kept low and there are strict controls on temperature and humidity to protect the ship. There's a 25-minute film that supplements the tale and three levels of complementary exhibits.

Just outside are **Museifartygen** (Museum Ships; separate admission fee adult/child Skr30/10; ⏰ noon–5pm mid-Jun–mid-Aug, to 7pm Jul), Sweden's first sea-going icebreaker Sankt Erik (launched in 1915) and the characteristic red-and-white lightship Finngrundet (1903), which had a crew of eight until it was decommissioned in 1969.

# SKEPPSHOLMEN

## ARKITEKTURMUSEET Map pp239–41
☎ 58 72 70 00; www.arkitekturmuseet.se; Exercisplan 4; admission free; ⏰ 10am-8pm Tue-Wed, 10am-6pm Thu-Sun; bus 65

Arkitekturmuseet, attached to the Modern Museum, is equally interesting. It's in an extraordinary building and has displays on Swedish and international architecture, with a permanent exhibition covering 1000 years of Swedish architecture, from cabins to castles, and an archive of 2.5 million documents, photographs, plans, drawings and models. There's also a seasonal program of temporary exhibitions, and the museum arranges seminars (in Swedish) and architectural walks.

## MODERNA MUSEET Map pp239–41
☎ 51 95 52 00; www.modernamuseet.se; Exercisplan 4; free; ⏰ 10am-8pm Tue-Wed, 10am-6pm Thu-Sun; bus 65

Moderna Museet is back in its Rafael Moneo-designed building after a year-long renovation to counter problems with mould; among the improvements is that the newly reopened museum has free admission. The world-class collection of modern art, sculpture and installation includes all the big names of the era, from Duchamp to Dali to Picasso to Robert Rauschenberg's pre–Damien Hirst sheep-in-a-tyre creation *Monogram*. There are also temporary exhibitions several times a year. The outdoor sculpture garden holds colourful dancing figures created by Jean Tinguely and Niki de Saint Phalle. The gift shop stocks an eye-popping selection of art books and monographs, and the upper-level café with its panoramic windows offers a beautiful view over the water.

### SVENSK FORM DESIGN CENTRE
Map pp239–41
☎ 463 31 36; www.svenskform.se in Swedish; Holmamiralens väg 2; Skr20; ✆ noon-7pm Tue-Thu, noon-5pm Fri-Sun; bus 65

Svensk Form Design Centre, run by the Swedish Society of Crafts & Design, features temporary exhibitions on Swedish and international design and has a bookshop and sales outlet. The centre also publishes the excellent design magazine *Form*.

### ÖSTASIATISKA MUSEET Map pp239–41
☎ 51 95 57 50; www.ostasiatiska.se; Tyghusplan; bus 65

Across the bridge on Skeppsholmen, up on the hill and by the church, Östasiatiska Museet (Museum of Far Eastern Antiquities) displays ancient and contemporary ceramics, paintings and sculpture in temporary and permanent exhibitions. Reopening in autumn 2004 after extensive renovations, the museum has one of the best collections of Chinese art, stoneware and porcelain in the world (mainly from the Song, Ming and Qing dynasties). There's also a fine exhibit of Hindu and Buddhist sculptures.

# KUNGSHOLMEN

*Eating p113; Drinking p125; Shopping p147; Sleeping p160*

The main visitor sight on Kungsholmen is Stadshuset, Stockholm's city hall, a landmark building that has come to symbolise the city. But this quiet little island neighbourhood also contains some of the city's more interesting museums, including Polishistoriska Museet (Police History Museum) and Tullmuseet (Customs Museum).

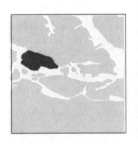

## Orientation

To reach Stadshuset from Norrmalm, walk across Stadshusbron (Stadshus Bridge) – you'll have to wend your way through a confusion of pedestrian crosswalks and underpasses. The main street leading into Kungsholmen from Stadshuset is Hantverkargatan, which passes by Kungsholms Kyrka and its lovely grounds. Parallel to Hantverkargatan is Scheelegatan, one of the island's main thoroughfares. The main business streets on Kungsholmen are St Eriksgatan and Flemminggatan. Where they meet is the new shopping centre, Västermalmsgallerian. Kungsholmen is connected to Södermalm by the bridge Västerbron.

### Transport
**Tunnelbana** T-Rådhuset, T-Fridhemsplan
**Bus** 1, 3, 4, 40, 52, 57, 62

### KARLBERGS SLOTT Map p230
☎ 56 28 13 05; Karlbergsstrand; ✆ by arrangement, groups only; bus 42, 72

Karlbergs Slott, situated on the lake Karlbergssjön, was commissioned by Magnus Gabriel de la Gardie in the 1670s; it swallowed up a smaller, early-17th-century building. The substantial palace was extended in the 18th century and in 1792 became a training school for military officers.

### LANDSTINGSHUSET Map p230
Hantverkargatan 45; ✆ not open to the public; T-Rådhuset

The Stockholm County Council convenes in Landstingshuset, formerly the military hospital Garnisonssjukhuset (1816–34) and extended in 1970. The neoclassical building, featuring a temple-style gable, large columns and a south-facing external semicircular staircase with a double stair and cornice, is quite distinctive.

### POLISHISTORISKA MUSEET Map p230
☎ 401 90 53; Polhemsgatan 30; adult/child Skr60/40, under 16 not allowed; ☼ 2hr guided tours in Swedish 2.30pm Tue-Fri, in English by arrangement; T-Rådhuset, bus 40, 52, 62

Although it's another relatively unknown museum, Polishistoriska Museet (Police History Museum) has some of the finest and most unusual exhibits in the city. You'll see displays covering police history from the 1720s, including displays about spies, forgery, fingerprinting, uniforms, illegal stills and insurance swindles. The most extraordinary exhibits include events connected to the terrorist attack on the West German Embassy in 1975 (look out for pages from the Red Army Faction terrorist handbook) and the murder room, which covers some particularly disturbing crimes. There's also a reconstruction of a bank vault as it was during a bizarre five-day robbery and siege at Norrmalmstorg in 1973. When the police used tear gas to clear out the robber, his accomplice and the four hostages, the hostages sided with the robber in the first known case of what's now called 'Stockholm Syndrome'. At the time of research, the museum was closed for renovations; it was scheduled to reopen in late 2004, but call first to make sure.

### ROYAL MINT Map pp236–8
Hantverkargatan & Samuel Owens Gata; ☼ not open to the public

The Royal Mint is housed in the former Samuel Owens foundry and engineering workshop from 1809. It isn't open to the public, but the spectacular gateway is worth a look.

### STADSHUSET Map pp236–8
☎ 50 82 90 58; Hantverkargatan 1; adult/under 12 Skr50/free, Stockholm Card free; ☼ 45min guided tours in English 10am, noon, 1, 2 & 3pm Jun-Aug; T-Centralen, bus 3, 62

Stadshuset (the city hall) looks like a large church, but its size is deceptive – it has two internal courtyards. Climb its dominant, square, brown-brick **tower** (adult/under 12 Skr15/free; ☼ 10am-4.30pm May-Sep) for a good view of Gamla Stan. The tower is topped with a golden spire and the symbol of Swedish power, the three royal crowns.

Inside the building you'll find the beautiful mosaic-lined Gyllene salen (Golden hall, made with 10kg of gold), the impressive council meeting chamber (with a roof like an overturned boat), Prins Eugen's own fresco re-creation of the lake view from the gallery, and the Blue Hall, where the annual Nobel Prize banquet is held. The terrace outside by the lake features sculptures by Carl Eldh. The tour is informative and entertaining, and you get to walk down the steps as if you'd just won a Nobel Prize.

### TULLMUSEET Map p230
☎ 653 05 03; Alströmergatan 39; admission free; ☼ 11am-4pm Tue-Sun; T-Fridhemsplan, bus 1, 3, 4, 57

Tullmuseet (the Customs Museum) explains the history behind Stockholm's inland customs stations (Skanstull, Hornstull, Norrtull and Roslagstull), which operated from 1622 to 1810 and taxed agricultural goods. There's also a section on the coast guard service and a reconstruction of a 1920s customs warehouse and office. The main part of the exhibition deals with the smuggling of animals, alcohol, guns, cigarettes and drugs, and how it has been controlled. Some rather startling dioramas illustrate the stories. Unfortunately the exhibits are only described in Swedish, but there is a little leaflet with some English text.

# SÖDERMALM & LÅNGHOLMEN
*Eating p115; Drinking p125; Shopping p148; Sleeping p160*

Södermalm is quite possibly Stockholm's most interesting neighbourhood. Historically home to many of the city's artists, Söder (as locals affectionately call it) has a slightly raw, bohemian feel, though it's certainly more stylish and hipster-friendly than dangerous. Alternative youth culture scarcely ever ventures beyond the borders of this island; in the classic pattern of gentrification, the 'cool' parts of town change frequently as once-grubby areas are adopted by scene-makers, tamed down for the mainstream and then abandoned for a more out-there part of town. At the moment, the area around Hornstull is taking over from 'SoFo' (South of Folkungagatan – an ironic-but-sincere pet name that invokes New York) as *the* neighbourhood.

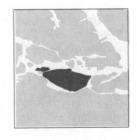

## Södermalm & Långholmen Top Five

- Stockholms Stadsmuseum (p79)
- Katarinahissen (p78)
- Långholmens Fängelsemuseum (p79)
- Spårvägsmuseet (p78)
- Katarina Kyrka (opposite)

Other than the very informative, well-arranged Stadsmuseum, the sights in Söder are mostly offbeat smaller museums and churches. The primary sight of interest to visitors may, in fact, be the view of the rest of the city – it's unbeatable from Monteliusvägen, the little pedestrian lane that skirts the cliffs of Söder Heights, or from just about anywhere else up there (see the Eastern Södermalm walk, p92).

Other than its funky shops and art galleries, Södermalm is primarily known as the capital of Stockholm's nightlife – or, at any rate, a more relaxed hub of bar-hopping than you'll find around Stureplan. For more information, see p125 and p133.

Långholmen, an island in Lake Mälaren, once housed the notorious Kronohäktet prison, which in its day was the largest prison in Sweden. It is now mostly a recreational island, with beaches lining its shores and forest trails crisscrossing the sparsely populated bulk of the island.

## Orientation

Södermalm is connected to Gamla Stan via Slussen, a complicated transportation nexus based around a system of locks and a mousetrap traffic interchange. Walking across Slussen to Söder from the Old Town is easy, but there are also several *tunnelbana* stops on the island. Götgatan is the main north–south thoroughfare, with Hornsgatan plunging off to the west, Folkungagatan zigzagging to the east and Ringvagen circling the island's nether regions. The main squares include Mosebacketorg on the hill just south of Slussen, Medborgarplatsen (the Citizens' Square) further south off Götgatan, and Mariatorget off Hornsgatan.

To get to Långholmen, take the metro to Hornstull, then walk north along Långholmsgatan and turn left onto Högalidsgatan.

### Transport

**Tunnelbana** T-Slussen, T-Medborgarplatsen, T-Mariatorget, T-Skanstull, T-Hornstull
**Train** *Pendeltåg* (commuter train) J-Stockholm södra, J-Slussen
**Bus** 3, 4, 40, 46, 53, 55, 59, 66, 74, 76

## SÖDERMALM

### ALMGRENS SIDENVÄVERI MUSEUM
Map pp239–41

☎ 642 56 16; www.kasiden.se; Repslagargatan 15; adult/under 12 Skr55/free, Stockholm Card free; 🕑 9am-5pm Mon-Thu, 9am-4pm Fri, 11am-3pm Sat; T-Slussen, bus 59

The unique Almgren's Silk Weaving Mill & Museum is the only full-time silk mill still operating in Scandinavia. KA Almgren started the place as a factory in 1833 after studying the secrets of Jacquard loom weaving in France – essentially an industrial spy, Almgren posed as a Frenchman in order to be allowed to learn the craft. He then smuggled the parts of a Jacquard loom back to Sweden hidden in barrels of cognac and crates of prunes. The handful of weavers here still use the ancient equipment to hand-weave traditional patterns.

The factory moved to its current location in 1846 and produced up to 90,000 silk scarves per year; it was closed from 1974 to 1991, until Almgren's grandson revived it as a working museum. You can see a warping machine, watch the workers using the Jacquard looms (weekdays only), see displays of silk (including patterns ordered by royalty) and watch a slide show and video (in English). The museum shop is the best place in Stockholm for high-quality hand-woven products.

The opening hours can vary a bit on Saturdays, so it's advisable to call first.

### BELLMANHUSET Map pp239–41
☎ 640 22 29; Urvädergränd 3; Skr60; 🕑 guided tours 1pm, 1st Sun of the month; T-Slussen, bus 3, 46, 53, 59, 76

During one of the most productive periods of his life (1770–74), the Swedish poet and songwriter Carl Michael Bellman lived in this house, which is now a museum. Guided tours, with music or singing, are also given during Bellmansveckan, which is usually the last week in July (except Monday). For an events program, contact the museum directly.

## ERSTA DIAKONIMUSEET Map pp239–41
☎ 714 63 48; Erstagatan 1M; adult/child Skr10/free; ⏲ 9am-4pm Mon-Fri & 1 Sun per month Jun-Aug, 1-3pm Tue & Thu Sep-May; T-Slussen

Run by the Ersta Society for Parish Welfare, a Christian charity which provides medical and geriatric care, support for the poor and homeless, and further education, Ersta Diakonimuseet (Ersta Parish Welfare Museum) provides an interesting insight into the development of Swedish nursing. Across the road, Ersta Hospital now specialises in gastroenterology. The museum building has, in the past, been a soup kitchen for the homeless and there was once an orphanage for 20 children upstairs. You'll see an *oblatmaskin*, which makes communion bread, and an unusual collection of bedpans on the staircase. Upstairs, you'll find out about the orphanage and see original children's beds. There's also a nursing display, blood transfusion equipment and surgical equipment from the 19th century (look out for the amputation saw) to the present day.

## FOLKSAMHUSET Map pp234–5
☎ 772 60 00; www.folksam.se; Bohusgatan 14; ⏲ not open to the public

This 27-storey landmark is a strange-looking structure with narrow rectangular windows, was built in 1959. It's the headquarters of Folksam, one of Sweden's largest insurance companies.

## IVAR LO-MUSEET Map pp239–41
☎ 658 25 84; Bastugatan 21; adult/child Skr55/free; open by appointment; T-Mariatorget

This museum, in the former apartment of the proletarian writer Karl Ivar Lo-Johansson (see p23), remains as it was when he died in 1990. It features his clothing and furniture, including a writing table. Unfortunately members of staff don't speak English. Tours can be arranged through your hotel, hostel or the tourist office.

## KAPELL ERSTA DIAKONISSANSTALT
Map pp239–41
Erstagatan 1M; Admission free; ⏲ 8am-6pm; T-Slussen

Ersta Chapel is a wonderful octagonal church. The text surrounding the congregation (on the balcony) is 1 Timothy 2: 4-6. Prayers are held at 8.15am and noon daily, with services at 6pm on Wednesday and 11am on Sunday. Nearby, there's a monument to the victims of the *Estonia* ferry disaster (see the boxed text, below).

## KATARINA KYRKA Map pp239–41
☎ 743 68 00; Högbergsgatan; admission free; ⏲ 9am-5pm Mon-Fri, 10am-5pm Sat & Sun Apr-Sep, to 4pm Oct-Mar; T-Medborgarplatsen, bus 3, 46, 53, 59, 76

The beautiful Katarina Kyrka (Katarina Church) is on the site of a former late-14th-century chapel. The church was badly damaged by fire in 1723 and was rebuilt in the form of a Greek cross with a central altar. A more serious fire in 1990 caused the cupola to collapse and the interior was completely gutted. The church was rebuilt in its original style for Skr270 million, despite the lack of original plans, and was reconsecrated in 1995.

## The *Estonia* Ferry Disaster

On 28 September 1994, the passenger and car ferry MS *Estonia* capsized and sank off the Finnish coast, with a loss of 852 lives. Most of the victims were Swedish or Estonian and there were only 137 survivors, making this Europe's worst ferry disaster since WWII.

At 1am, the ship was 35km southeast of Utö, an island in the outer reaches of the Turku archipelago. Despite the stormy weather and waves up to 5m, the ship was sailing at full speed, directly from Tallinn towards Stockholm. It has since been found that the bow visor was torn off by the waves, then the hydraulic latches on the forward ramp opened, allowing water onto the car deck leading to rapid loss of stability and a severe list. To make matters worse, the ship's officers reacted badly – the *Estonia* didn't initially slow down and the alarm wasn't raised for five minutes, by which time the list was so severe it would have been virtually impossible to escape. There was also difficulty using life-saving equipment and no information was forwarded to the terrified passengers.

The monument at Galärkyrkogården in Stockholm has been vandalised with text saying that the sinking wasn't an accident and the Swedish government is lying. There's also a memorial cross at Ersta Diakoni, the hospital where some survivors went for counselling.

## KATARINAHISSEN Map pp239–41

☎ 743 13 95; Slussen; Skr5; ⊕ 7.30am-10pm Mon-Sat, 10am-10pm Sun; T-Slussen, bus 3, 46, 53, 76

You'll get great views from the bridge at the top of Katarinahissen, a lift dating from 1936 that replaced a previous lift from 1881. The lift itself is windowless, but it takes you 38m up to the magnificently located Gondolen restaurant and the hills above Slussen. The lift inside the adjacent Cooperative Association office building is free and takes you to the other end of the elevated 'bridge'.

## LEKSAKSMUSEET Map pp239–41

☎ 641 61 00; Tegelviksgatan 22; adult/child Skr50/30, Stockholm Card free; ⊕ 10am-4pm Tue-Fri, noon-4pm Sat & Sun; bus 46, 55, 66

Leksaksmuseet (Hobby & Toy Museum) is an oversized fantasy nursery full of everything you probably ever wanted as a child (and may still hanker after as an adult). There are four floors with model railways (ancient and modern), planes, cars, boats, fire engines, clockwork animals, a toy zoo, dolls, excellent miniature room scenes and old board games. There's also an accordion display, polyphones, musical clocks, early phonographs (from 1890) and a bizarre birdcage with three singing toy birds. In the attic, don't miss the superb dioramas of historical and fictional events, including Greek mythology, and Roman and ancient Egyptian scenes. Children will enjoy themselves in the

*Katarinahissen (above)*

playroom (with Lego) and at the daily children's theatre (Skr50, including museum admission).

The museum is moving to join forces with Spårvägsmuseet (below) and should be open in its new premises late 2004.

## LILLA BLECKTORNET Map pp234–5

Lilla Blecktornsparken; ⊕ not open to the public; T-Skanstull

Lilla Blecktornet is a distinctly odd little neo-classical mansion from 1781 with octagonal towers at either end. The park is always open and the building is definitely worth a look.

## MARIA MAGDALENA KYRKA

Map pp239–41

☎ 640 53 34; Hornsgatan 21; admission free; ⊕ 11am-5pm Thu-Mon, 11am-8pm Wed; T-Slussen, bus 4, 43, 55, 59, 66

The cruciform Church of St Mary Magdalene was consecrated in 1634 and was later re-stored by both Nicodemus Tessin the Elder and the Younger. In 1759, most of the church was destroyed by fire but was rebuilt in 1763 and has remained basically the same since. Of greatest interest are the *Adoration of the Shepherds* altarpiece painting (dating from around 1800) and the rococo-style pulpit, placed in the church in 1763 and featuring a medallion of Mary Magdalene. A free leaflet describing the church inventory is available in English. Free lunchtime concerts are held from 12.15pm to 12.35pm on Thursday.

## MÅLERIYRKETS MUSEUM Map pp234–5

☎ 668 66 19; Brännkyrkagatan 71; admission free; ⊕ 3-6pm Thu Sep-Apr; T-Zinkensdamm

The Building Painters' Museum features impressive oak panelling, stone floors and furniture, including a magnificent marble desk. The exhibits include equipment such as brushes and tubs of different colours of paint. The historical information is carefully presented and the accoutrements of the painting trade well preserved.

## SPÅRVÄGSMUSEET Map pp234–5

☎ 462 55 31; Tegelviksgatan 22; adult/student/under 6 Skr30/15/free, Stockholm Card free; ⊕ 10am-5pm Mon-Fri, 11am-4pm Sat & Sun; bus 46, 55, 66

Spårvägsmuseet (Stockholm Transport Museum) is in the Söderhallen bus depot and near the Viking Line terminal. It covers public transport in the city from rowing boats c 1700 to the latest innovations in bus, train and metro travel. There are nearly 60 vehicles, including horse-drawn carriages, Stockholm metro trains, vintage trams and buses. There's a horse-drawn tram from 1877 (used for the museum logo), a two-compartment motor bus from 1928 (in working order), and a red-painted city bus from 1938, which you can board. Also look out for the restored kiosk from Ängbyplan, which dates from the 1930s; the centrally placed exhibit on metro art; the 'tunnel trams'; and the videos showing the development of the metro (in Swedish). You can also create your own computer-generated public transport network.

In spring and autumn, the museum organises one-hour tours of the city in a double-decker bus twice daily on weekends. Contact the museum for times and ticket prices.

### STOCKHOLMS STADSMUSEUM

Map pp239–41

☎ 508 316 00; www.stadsmuseum.stockholm.se; Ryssgården, Slussen; adult/senior/child/under 6 Skr60/40/10/free, Stockholm Card free; ◷ 11am-5pm Tue-Sun, 11am-9pm Thu Sep-May, 11am-7pm Thu Jun-Aug; T-Slussen, bus 3, 4, 46, 53, 55, 59

Stockholms Stadsmuseum (Stockholm City Museum) is housed in an impressive late-17th-century building called Ryssgården, designed by Nicodemus Tessin the Elder and one of the more visible elements in the approach to Södermalm from Gamla Stan. Exhibits in the very well-presented museum include a 'time-travel' exhibit developed in conjunction with the city's 750th anniversary. It's an entertaining way to learn about the growth and culture of Stockholm quickly.

The 2nd floor has some interesting local archaeological finds, an exhibit on the metro and a good reconstruction of a cottage from the 1940s. The 3rd floor has more reconstructions – a registry office, a primary school from around 1900 and a factory worker's home life in 1897. Temporary exhibitions change several times yearly; a recent one focussed on restaurant culture in Stockholm, with miniature reproductions of Operakällaren, Berns etc. There's also a museum shop and a romantic little café.

## LÅNGHOLMEN

### BELLMANMUSEET Map pp234–5

☎ 669 69 69; Stora Henriksvik; adult/child Skr30/free; ◷ noon-6pm Jun-Aug, noon-4pm Sat & Sun May & Sep, closed Oct-Apr; T-Hornstull, bus 4, 40, 66, 74

The tiny Bellmanmuseet commemorates Carl Michael Bellman, the 18th-century composer of daring drinking songs. It's mostly of local interest, but guided tours for groups are available all year on request.

### LÅNGHOLMENS FÄNGELSEMUSEUM

Map pp234–5

☎ 668 05 00; www.langholmen.com; adult/child/under 7 Skr25/20/free; ◷ 11am-4pm; T-Hornstull, bus 4, 66

Displays at this museum, inside the prison building that now operates as a youth hostel, cover 250 years of prison history and the curious story of how, in the 19th century, the formerly barren island was transformed into a park after the prisoners had covered it in mud from the lake. You'll also see a reconstructed guard's office and find out about escapees, the prison hospital, executions and chains weighing 40kg.

# ÖSTERMALM, GÄRDET & LADUGÅRDSGÄRDET

*Eating p118; Drinking p127; Shopping p150; Sleeping p163*
Östermalm contains some of Stockholm's most exclusive addresses; the mostly wealthy, residential area is composed of wide avenues lined with trees and stately apartment buildings. The centre of activity here is Stureplan, marked by the popular rendezvous point locals call 'Svampen' (the Mushroom), an odd, mod pavilion on a stem that looks like it belongs at

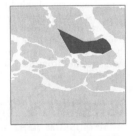

an airport. Surrounding Stureplan are the city's most highbrow nightclubs, including the queue-crazy Spy Bar and the hip Lydmar Hotel lobby bar. Similarly, the shops in this area are for big spenders in search of hot brands. Sturegallerian, the shopping mall that borders Stureplan, contains several exclusive boutiques, a gourmet cake shop and the Art Nouveau bathhouse Sturebadet (p139).

Two of the city's top museums – the Armémuseum and Historiska Museet – are also found here. Kungliga Biblioteket (the Royal Library) anchors the neighbourhood's main park, Humlegården, where outdoor theatre performances happen in the summer.

## Östermalm, Gärdet & Ladugårdsgärdet Top Five

- Armémuseum (below)
- Hallwylska Museet (opposite)
- Historiska Museet (opposite)
- Östermalms Saluhall (p82)
- Folkens Museum Etnografiska (p82)

At Östermalmstorg, the focus of activity is on Östermalms Saluhallen, a gorgeous building housing a gourmet food market full of fresh produce, hard-to-find delicacies from around Sweden and elsewhere, and cafés.

Bordering the water's edge to the south is the majestic avenue Strandvägen, a fabulous place for a stroll in the evening when the glimmering lights of Stockholm reflect in the water. There's a chance you'll catch a glimpse of the Royal Family on a leisurely promenade. This is also where you'll find the shop Svenskt Tenn (p152), a mainstay of Swedish interior design.

Gärdet is the park-heavy residential area to the northeast of Östermalm. Its most notable sight is Kaknästornet, the radio tower. There's also Filmhuset and, up in Frihamnen, the forward-thinking art gallery Magasin 3.

Below and to the east of Gärdet is the vast open parkland of Ladugårdsgärdet, where people walk their dogs across the street from three interesting and frequently neglected museums, the Etnografiska, Tekniska and Sjöhistoriska museums.

Ladugårdsgärdet was once the name for all the open land to the east of Norrmalm; it means, roughly, 'field of barns'. These days the name refers to the open parkland to the southeast of Gärdet.

## Orientation

Bordering Norrmalm to the east, Östermalm is a vaguely wedge-shaped area bounded by Birger Jarlsgatan, Strandvägen and Valhallavägen, with Gärdet to the northeast and Ladugårdsgärdet sprawling out directly east. Its two focus points are Östermalmstorg and Stureplan, both of which are reached via the Östermalmstorg *tunnelbana* stop. Stureplan is a major public transit hub, so most buses come through here. It can be confusing to find your way around Östermalm, as the streets seem oddly skewed in relation to the water's edge. Nybrogatan runs from Östermalmstorg into Strandvägen right behind Dramatiska Teatern, whereas Storgatan hits Strandvägen further east, just beyond Djurgårdsbron.

### Transport

**Tunnelbana** T-Östermalmstorg, T-Stadion, T-Karlaplan, T-Gärdet
**Bus** 44, 46, 47, 55, 56, 62, 69, 76, 91; for Ladugårdsgärdet, take bus 69 from Centralstationen or Sergels Torg

North of Djurgården is a huge open paddock for the royal sheep – Ladugårdsgärdet. It's a bit of a wasteland, but the museums are interesting. Ladugårdsgärdet is part of Ekoparken (www.ekoparken.com), the first National City Park in the world. Ekoparken is 14km long and stretches from the Fjäderholmarna islands all the way to Ulriksdal, in the northern suburbs of Stockholm.

## ÖSTERMALM & GÄRDET

### ARMÉMUSEUM Map pp236–8

☎ 788 95 60; www.armemuseum.org; Riddargatan 13; adult/student/child Skr60/40/30, Stockholm Card free; ⏰ 11am-8pm Tue, 11am-4pm Wed-Sun; T-Östermalmstorg, bus 46, 47, 55, 62, 69, 76, 91

The Armémuseum contains striking, graphic depictions of the horrors of war – it's enthralling for adults, but definitely isn't suitable for children or people of a nervous disposition.

Comprehensive information sheets in English are available from the admission desk. There are three floors, with medieval and Renaissance times on the top floor. Look out for the grim medieval representation of a city being invaded by an army of skeletons and the rows of human skulls on the floor. There are fascinating model armies and incredibly lifelike dioramas of charging horsemen, starving civilians and the frozen corpses left behind by Armfeldt's retreating army at New Year 1719.

On the 1st floor, highlights include films of the Finnish winter war (1939–40) and a reconstruction of a mid-1960s barracks. A display on medieval torture devices includes a hands-on replica of the 'sawhorse' that visitors can try for themselves. The ground floor has a shop with some rather expensive models, a cafeteria, and a display of artillery from a medieval cannon (1400) to the latest laser-guided missile technology.

## DRAMATISKA TEATERN Map pp236–8

☎ 665 61 00; Nybroplan; guided tour Skr40; 🕑 guided tours in English 3pm Sat, Jul & Aug; T-Östermalmstorg, Kungsträdgården, bus 46, 47, 55, 62, 69, 76, 91

Dramaten, as the royal theatre is often called, has impressive marble halls and stairways, gilded stucco, and wonderful painted ceilings in the theatre restaurant. Some of the interior can be seen without taking the tour and it's well worth a look.

## HALLWYLSKA MUSEET pp236–8

☎ 51 95 55 99; www.lsh.se; Hamngatan 4; adult/child/under 7 Skr65/30/free, Stockholm Card free; 🕑 1hr tours in English 1pm Sun, 1pm Mon-Sun 24 Jun-18 Aug; T-Östermalmstorg, bus 42, 62, 69, 91

The delightful Hallwylska Museet is a private palace that was already wired for electricity when completed in 1898. From the age of 10, Wilhelmina von Hallwyl collected items as diverse as kitchen utensils, Chinese pottery, 17th-century paintings, silverware, sculpture, weapons (Swedish, German and some Oriental guns, crossbows, swords and suits of armour), jewellery and even her children's teeth. In 1920 she and her husband donated their entire house (including contents) to the nation. The ornate baroque-style great drawing room is particularly impressive with a gilded stucco ceiling and a rare, playable grand piano. The ladies salon has rococo furniture, late-16th-century tapestries and ceiling paintings. It's also possible to join one of the more regular tours (in Swedish).

## HISTORISKA MUSEET Map pp231–3

☎ 51 95 56 00; www.historiska.se in Swedish; Narvavägen 13-17; adult/senior/child/under 13 Skr60/50/35/free, Stockholm Card free; 🕑 10am-5pm mid-May–mid-Sep, 11am-5pm Tue-Sun, to 8pm Thu mid-Sep–mid-May; T-Karlaplan, bus 44, 47, 56, 69, 76

The main national historical collection is at Historiska Museet. It covers nearly 14,000 years of Swedish history and culture (up to 1520),

including arrowheads from around 12,000 BC, the oldest skeleton found in Sweden (8730 years old) and archaeological finds from the Viking town of Birka. There's also a model of a Stone Age cult community, which lived in a swamp 3000 years ago.

Don't miss the incredible Gold Room in the basement, with its rare treasures in gold, silver and iron. The most astonishing artefact is the 5th-century, seven-ringed gold collar with 458 carved figures, which weighs 823g. It was found in Västergötland in the 19th century and was probably used by pagan priests in ritualistic ceremonies.

Also, look out for the medieval triptychs, altar screens and textiles (including a 15th-century coffin pall and the 11th-century Kyrkås coverlet) on the 1st floor. The Iron Age exhibit has a pair of cow-bone ice skates and a picture stone from Gotland. A new Viking Age exhibition opened in 2001, but don't look for helmets with horns – they didn't exist. The excellent website includes a virtual tour of the museum.

## KUNGLIGA HOVSTALLET Map pp236–8

☎ 402 61 06; www.royalcourt.se; Väpnargatan 1; adult/child/under 12 Skr30/10/free, Stockholm Card free; 🕑 1hr guided tours in English 2pm Mon-Fri mid-Jun–mid-Aug, 2pm Sat & Sun mid-Aug–mid-Jun; T-Östermalmstorg, bus 46, 47, 55, 62, 69, 76, 91

At Kungliga Hovstallet (the Royal Mews) you'll see stables, horses, ceremonial coaches, harnesses and uniforms. The current building was commissioned by King Oskar II in 1894, but Kungliga Hovstallet had been kept in various quarters around Stockholm since it was founded by Gustav Vasa in 1535. There are now 11 cars and 40 coaches dating from the mid-19th century, including the Seven-Glass coach used during state visits. The royal family also stables 14 horses here.

## MAGASIN 3 Map pp231–3

☎ 54 56 80 40; www.magasin3.com; Frihamnen; adult/under 15 Skr25/free; 🕑 noon-7pm Thu, noon-5pm Fri-Sun; closed Jun-Aug & during Christmas holidays; bus 1, 76

This impressive gallery in a vast warehouse space has been hosting gutsy, impeccably executed art shows since it opened in 1987. Its exhibitions of hot young international and Swedish artists in a variety of media rotate three or four times a year; the excellent website has an archive with photos of past shows. See the Arts chapter (p19) for more.

## MUSIKMUSEET Map pp236–8

☎ 51 95 54 90; http://stockholm.music.museum/;
Sibyllegatan 2; adult/child/under 6 Skr50/25/free,
Stockholm Card free; ◷ noon-7pm Tue, noon-4pm
Wed-Sun; T-Östermalmstorg, bus 46, 47, 55, 62, 69,
76, 91

Musikmuseet – in the austerely beautiful Krono-
bagariet (Crown Bakery), where bread was
baked for the admiralty from 1645 to 1958 –
is a well-presented and child-friendly collection. You can handle and play some of the
musical instruments and see original ABBA
paraphernalia. The 2nd-floor exhibit, Tutti, has
an incredible range of 500 instruments from
around the world, from Madagascan zithers to
Sami shaman drums. Children enjoy the music
workshop in the basement and there are also
regular children's activities. Concerts are held
in the King's Hall on the 2nd floor up to three
times weekly (Skr80 to Skr250, depending on
the status of the performer), and rock, pop and
jazz musicians play frequently in the museum's
Cafe Mix.

## ÖSTERMALMS SALUHALL Map pp236–8

Nybrogatan 26-28; Östermalmstorg; admission free;
◷ 9.30am-6pm Mon-Thu, 9.30am-6.30pm Fri,
9.30am-4pm Sat, to 2pm Sat in summer; T-Östermalmstorg, bus 46, 47, 55, 62, 69, 76, 91

The impressive Östermalms saluhall is constructed of brick on a cast-iron frame, with
turrets and pinnacles, vaulted windows and
considerable decorative detail. It was completed in 1889 and is still used for its original
purpose as a market hall. Inside, you'll find
lots of shops selling meat, fish, cheese, fruit,
vegetables and traditional Swedish foods.
There are also several restaurants; see p118
for details.

# LADUGÅRDSGÄRDET
## FOLKENS MUSEUM ETNOGRAFISKA

Map pp231–3

☎ 51 95 50 00; www.etnografiska.se; Djurgårdsbrunnsvägen 34; adult/under 21 Skr50/free, Stockholm
Card free; ◷ 10am-5pm daily, to 8pm Wed; bus 69

The excellent Folkens Museum Etnografiska
(National Museum of Ethnography) covers
non-European races and cultures and has
interesting temporary exhibitions, usually imported from national libraries or other sophisticated institutions; one such display detailed
the origins and progression of Chinese writing.
There are exhibitions of cultural artefacts from
native people all over the globe, including

North America, Greenland and Australia.
Among the Asian collections from the explorer Sven Hedin there's a Mongolian tent
with an exquisite interior. You'll see some
interesting masks from Africa (look out for
the crocodile mask from Mali). On the ground
floor, there's a section about the religious cities
of the world.

In the grounds of the museum is a good
café serving Indian and Asian meals, dozens
of exotic bottled beers and imported teas. A
Japanese teahouse opens at 5.30pm Wednesday and Sunday. Guided tours (in Swedish) are
available at 2pm on Sunday.

## KAKNÄSTORNET Map pp231–3

☎ 667 21 05; Ladugårdsgärdet; adult/child/under 7
Skr35/15/free, Stockholm Card free; ◷ 10am-9pm,
9am-10pm May-Aug; bus 69

About 500m from Sjöhistoriska Museet,
Folkens Museum Etnografiska, and Tekniska
Museet, Teknorama Science Centre & Telemuseum is the 155m-high Kaknästornet (Kaknäs
Tower), opened in 1967 and still the tallest
building in the city. It's the automatic operations centre for radio and TV broadcasting in
Sweden, but most people visit it for the stunning 360-degree views. The top two floors are
square and aligned at 45-degree angles to
each other, creating a startling star shape at
the top of the tower. Here you'll find an observation deck and a restaurant. The restaurant's
windows are made from gold-coated glass,
which reflects 75% of the sun's heat.

## SJÖHISTORISKA MUSEET Map p231–3

☎ 51 95 50 00; www.sjohistoriska.se; Djurgårdsbrunnsvägen 24; adult/student/senior/child/under 7
Skr50/50/50/20/free, Stockholm Card free;
◷ 10am-5pm; bus 69

The Sjöhistoriska Museet (National Maritime
Museum) exhibits an extensive range of maritime memorabilia. It's in a beautiful, curved
neoclassical building with a round central
tower and a copper roof. Purpose built and
opened in 1935, the museum houses more
than 1500 model ships, including Swedish
boats from AD 300, ferries, freighters, liners,
sailing ships, naval vessels, tankers and tugs.
The oldest model ship dates from the mid-
17th century (the votive ship *Solen* was built
in Lübeck in 1669) but the most extraordinary
model is the fantasy galleon which bristles
with cannons. There's also a model oil rig,
a lighthouse and full-size reconstructions of
living quarters on board a freighter and a

barquentine, the *Hoppet*. Information in English is available on plastic-coated cards.

As well as the permanent exhibit, there's usually a temporary exhibition. There's also a kids' playroom, a shop and a café on site. Drivers should note that the car park costs Skr12 per hour or Skr25 for a three-hour pass.

### TEKNISKA MUSEET, TEKNORAMA SCIENCE CENTRE & TELEMUSEUM

Map pp231–3

☎ 450 56 00; www.tekniskamuseet.se; Museivägen 7; adult/senior/child/under 6 Skr60/40/30/free, Stockholm Card free; ☉ 10am-5pm Mon-Fri, to 9pm Wed, 11am-5pm Sat & Sun; bus 69

The vast Tekniska Museet & Teknorama Science Centre (Museum of Science & Technology) is just around the corner from Sjöhistoriska Museet, and you'll need at least two hours to appreciate it. There are exhaustive exhibits on technology, machinery and transport, including

Swedish inventions and their applications. Information sheets are available in English. There's a café and a museum shop in the complex.

Tekniska Museet's machinery hall is packed with cars, bicycles, motorcycles and aircraft, including the first motor car in Sweden (from 1897). There's also a fascinating steam-powered fire engine from 1878. Downstairs in the artificial mine, Ferrum, you'll see mining dioramas, read about the miners' strike in 1969, and find out about mining in Sweden today. At the far end of the southern corridor, you'll find the interesting history of electric power exhibition.

The Teknorama Science Centre (at the rear of the complex) has 'hands-on' displays on topics such as the basic principles of physics.

The two-storey Telemuseum covers radio, television, the telegraph and telephone. Part of the same science and technology complex, it keeps the same hours and admission is included with the Tekniska Museet ticket.

# OUTLYING AREAS

*Eating p120; Shopping p152; Sleeping p165*

Several of the more interesting sights and attractions in Stockholm are just outside the city's central core. Up north is Stockholms Universitet, which is situated in the midst of lovely parkland full of good walking trails. Its main tourist draw is the Naturhistoriska Riksmuseet and Bergianska Trädgård. Also to the north is famed sculptor Carl Eldh's studio museum and Ulriksdals Slott. On Liljeholmen you'll find the progressive arts institution Färgfabriken, while Lidingö houses the palatial Carl Millesgården and a giant statue of Raoul Wallenberg.

Closer in, Haga Parken is home to the fascinating Fågel- och Fjärilshuset (Bird and Butterfly House), and on the grounds

### Top Five in the Outlying Areas

- Skogskyrkogården (p86)
- Millesgården (p85)
- Medicinhistoriska museet (p85)
- Naturhistoriska Riksmuseet (p85)
- Fågel- och Fjärilshuset (p84)

of the Karolinska Sjukhus you'll find the morbid but tremendously appealing Medicinhistoriska Museum. Speaking of morbid, one of the most strangely beautiful places to visit in Stockholm is the Unesco World Heritage–listed graveyard Skogskyrkogården, which, among other things, is where Greta Garbo finally got her wish to be left alone.

### BERGIANSKA TRÄDGÅRDEN

Map pp228–9

☎ 54 59 17 00; www.bergianska.se in Swedish; Frescati; conservatory Skr40, Stockholm Card free; Victoriahuset Skr15; ☉ conservatory 11am-5pm, park 8am-9pm, Victoriahuset 11am-4pm, to 5pm Sat & Sun; guided tour of Bergianska in Swedish 1pm Tue; T-Universitetet, J-Universitetet, bus 40, 540

Situated just across the road from Naturhistoriska Riksmuseet and located on the shores of

Brunnsviken, the pleasant garden Bergianska Trädgården was donated to the Swedish Academy of Sciences in 1791. It's now Stockholm University's botanic garden and has more than 9000 plant species. The garden contains trees and shrubs from around Europe, America and Asia. In addition, there are beds of Nordic and Mediterranean flowers, as well as a Japanese garden with a pond. A special environmental trail describes environmental problems and research.

Don't miss the spectacular **Victoriahuset**, a tropical greenhouse with giant water lilies (Victoria cruziana) and tropical crops (banana plants, rice, yams etc). The other must-see is Edvard Andersons Växthus, which opened in 1995. This attractive building contains a winter garden of Mediterranean flora, but there are also many other flowering plants from areas around the world with a Mediterranean climate. Look out for the flesh-eating plants in the tropical rooms.

## CARL ELDHS ATELJÉMUSEUM
Map pp228–9

☎ 612 65 60; Lögebodavägen 10; adult/child Skr40/20; ☺ guided tours in English 1pm Tue-Sun Jun-Aug, 1pm Sat & Sun May & Sep, 1pm Apr & Oct; bus 40, 46, 52, 73

This sculpture museum is the former home and studio of Carl Eldh (1873–1954) and features more than 400 of his works, plus his moulds and personal belongings. You'll see many bronze statues by Eldh around the city, notably the dramatic statue of Strindberg in Tegnérlunden Park. The studio is a curious building, with rustic tarred vertical weatherboards and an attached circular house complete with cupola. It was specially designed to allow the best possible natural light conditions inside and was used by Eldh from 1919 to 1954.

Guided tours in Swedish are frequent; contact the museum or the tourist office for details. To get to the museum, take bus 46 to Sveaplan, then it's a short walk through Bellevueparken. Motorists can park at the distinctive Wenner-Gren Center, on the north side of Sveaplan.

## COSMONOVA Map pp228–9

☎ 51 95 51 30; www.nrm.se; adult/child Skr75/50, no children under 5; ☺ shows hourly 10am-7pm Tue-Sun

In the same complex as Naturhistoriska Riksmuseet is Cosmonova, a combined planetarium and Imax theatre, which shows films in the world's largest format using seven projectors and a 760-sq-metre hemispherical screen. Films are entertaining, informative and impressive, and English sound is available on request. The diverse topics covered include the Arctic, dolphins and UFOs.

## FRISÖRMUSEET Map pp228–9

☎ 87 04 30; Per Ekströms väg 3, Bromma; admission by donation; ☺ by arrangement; T-Islandstorget

One of the oddest museums in Stockholm is Frisörmuseet (Museum of Hairdressing). It describes the work of hairdressers from 1896 to the present day.

## FÅGEL- OCH FJÄRILSHUSET
Map pp228–9

☎ 730 39 81; www.fjarilshuset.se; Hagaparken; adult/senior/child Skr70/50/30, Stockholm Card free; ☺ 10am-3pm Tue-Fri (to 4pm mid-Jun–Aug), 11am-4pm Sat & Sun (to 5.30pm mid-Jun–Aug); T-Odenplan, then bus 515 to Haga Norra

In Hagaparken (a former royal kitchen garden dating from 1785), is the warm (literally and figuratively), friendly Fågel- och Fjärilshuset (Bird & Butterfly House), with free-flying birds and butterflies in giant greenhouses. Some birds, such as parrots, are in cages. There are around 35 species with a total of 400 mainly tropical butterflies; to see them at their best, visit on a sunny day (or a sunny day with snow in winter). There are also Japanese fish and birds, cactuses, spectacular long-tailed finches and comical, diminutive, Chinese quail. The café serves good sandwiches and drinks.

## FÄRGFABRIKEN

☎ 645 07 07; Lövholmsbrinken 1, Liljeholmen; adult/child Skr40/free, Stockholm Card free; ☺ noon-6pm Thu-Sun during exhibitions; T-Liljeholmen

Färgfabriken (the Centre for Contemporary Art & Architecture), is a powerful cultural force and an experimental centre for art, architecture, design and installations of various types. Its exhibitions are held at semi-regular times throughout the year; check local listings or call first to see what's on, and don't miss the chance to go to an opening party.

## GUSTAV IIIS PAVILJONG Map pp228–9

☎ 402 61 30; www.royalcourt.se; Hagaparken; Skr50; ☺ hourly guided tours in Swedish noon-3pm Tue-Sun Jun-Aug, Sat & Sun Sep

Also located in Hagaparken, Gustav IIIs Paviljong is a superb example of neoclassical style, one of the finest such buildings in Europe. The mainly original furnishings and décor reflect Gustav III's interest in things Roman after his Italian tour in 1782. Beyond the pavilion, a trail leads south alongside Brunnsviken; it splits then reconverges at Haga Södra (the southern entrance to the park). Between the eastern trail and Brunnsviken, you'll see the ornate **Kinesiska paviljongen** (Chinese Pavilion; 1787). The western route passes near **Turkiska paviljongen** (Turkish Pavilion) another of Gustav III's architectural wonders.

## HAGAPARKEN Map pp228–9

🕐 24hr; bus 3, 52, or T-Odenplan then bus 515 to Haga Norra

King Gustav III, who was interested in country pursuits as well as French and Italian culture, organised the development of Haga as an English-style park but with a palace similar to Versailles. Although work on the palace started in 1786, it was halted when the king was assassinated in 1792. Near the incomplete structure (called Slottsruinen, but not a ruin at all) lies another royal palace, **Haga Slott**, which was built 1802–04. It's an official Swedish government residence and isn't open to the public.

A few minutes' walk from the Haga Norra bus stop brings you to the amazing, brightly painted **Koppartälten** (Copper Tent; 🕐 11am-4pm, 10am-5pm Jun-Aug), which was built in 1787 as a stable and barracks for Gustav III's personal guard. It now contains a café, an inn and Haga Parkmuseum, which contains displays about the park, its pavilions and Haga Slott. **Ekotemplet** (Echo Temple; admission free; 🕐 24hr) was designed as a summer dining room for Gustav III. Take special note of its ceiling paintings.

## MEDECINHISTORISKA MUSEET
Map p230

☎ 54 54 51 50; www.medhm.se in Swedish, Karolinska Sjukhuset Eugenia T-3; adult/student Skr40/30; 🕐 11am-4pm Tue, Thu & Fri, 11am-7pm Wed, noon-4pm Sun, closed Sat & Mon; bus 3, 52, 73

The grim and enthralling Medicinhistoriska museet (Medical History Museum), in a former school and living quarters for disabled children, features medical and dental equipment, documents, art, and well-curated temporary exhibitions that change every few months. The staff here are enthusiastic and pleasant. A descriptive colour booklet is available in English for Skr10, or you can borrow a pamphlet from the front desk.

Among the morbidly fascinating exhibits are cases of wax casts from syphilis victims and various unpleasant skin conditions. If that doesn't put you off, proceed upstairs to see excellent displays including reconstructions of a 19th-century dental practice, operating theatres and hospital ward. Some of the old traction equipment in the orthopaedics room and the horrors in the psychiatry room are reminiscent of medieval torture chambers. Look out for the X-ray of the footballer Thomas Brolin's broken fibula (Sweden–Hungary match, 1994). There's also an interesting treatment of folk medicine and the history of medical practices.

## MILLESGÅRDEN Map pp228–9

☎ 446 75 90; www.millesgarden.se in Swedish; Carl Milles Väg 2, Lidingö; adult/student Skr75/60, senior/child/under 6 Skr60/20/free, Stockholm Card free; 🕐 noon-4pm Tue-Fri, 11am-5pm Sat & Sun Oct-Apr, 10am-5pm Mon-Sun May-Sep; T-Ropsten, then bus 207 direct or bus 201, 202, 204, 205, 206, 207, 212 to Torsvik plus 5min walk

The superb sculpture garden and museum Millesgården is on the island of Lidingö and has great views across to the mainland. There's only very basic free information in English, though you can buy a detailed 32-page catalogue and map (Skr15). The house, a stately, Italian-style palazzo with sprawling multilevel gardens, was sculptor Carl Milles' home and studio. The gardens are decorated with his outdoor sculptures (some with fountains), including a replica of his enormous Poseidon statue in Gothenburg (1930). The Little Studio contains a respectable art collection, including pieces by Milles' wife and elder sister. In the music room, you'll see an organ reputedly played by Mozart's father, a tapestry and medieval church sculptures. There's also Milles' beautifully displayed indoor collection of ancient Egyptian, Greek, Etruscan and Roman items, including sculpture, coins and rings. Temporary exhibitions occupy the main gallery.

## NATURHISTORISKA RIKSMUSEET
Map pp228–9

☎ 51 95 40 00; www.nrm.se; Frescativägen 40; adult/child/under 5 Skr75/50/free, Stockholm Card free; 🕐 10am-7pm Tue-Sun; T-Universitetet, bus 40, 540

The extensive three-storey Naturhistoriska Riksmuseet (National Museum of Natural History) was founded by Carl von Linné in 1739. It's now Sweden's largest museum and includes reliably interesting biology displays of prehistoric life, sea life and the fauna of the polar regions. Many are dioramas; one of the best of these shows baby dinosaurs breaking out of eggs. The volcano video is quite impressive. On the 1st floor, 'Life in Water' is supported by models, charts and videos. The tour around the human body has hands-on exhibits (!) and computerised features with English text. There are also temporary exhibitions and a restaurant.

## OLLE OLSSON-HUSET Map pp228–9

☎ 83 97 44; Hagalundsgatan 50; Skr30; ☽ noon-4pm Sun-Thu; bus 515 from T-Odenplan to Kolonnvägen or take the metro to T-Solna Centrum

The original residence of artist Olle Olsson Hagalund, who painted with knives, is now a gallery of modern art. It is a traditional house with temporary exhibitions that change every month.

## POLISTEKNISKA MUSEET Map pp228–9

☎ 401 90 53; Polishögskolan, Sörentorp; groups of 10 Skr500, per extra person Skr50, min age 16; ☽ by appointment

The Police Technical Museum is in the grounds of the police academy. It displays vehicles from 1903 (including a fine collection of BMW motorcycles, all in working order) and other things such as radio equipment. There isn't any convenient public transport, apart from taxis.

## RAOUL WALLENBERG STATUE

Map pp228–9

Bus 205 or 225 from T-Ropsten to Lidingö Stadshus, on Lejonvägen

This intriguing 4m-high bronze statue was erected in 1999 and shows Wallenberg holding out protection passes towards Jews trying to escape Nazi tyranny. It's located in Stadshusparken on Lidingö. See also the boxed text, p46.

## SKOGSKYRKOGÅRDEN Map pp228–9

☎ 50 83 01 93; Sockenvägen 492, Enskede; free, guided tours Skr50; ☽ 24hr, tours in English 5pm Mon, May-Sep; T-Skogskyrkogården

---

### Underground Art

The artwork featured in over 90 tunnelbana stations along 110km of track is considered to be the longest art exhibition in the world. Originally presented to the city council in 1955 as a motion designed to improve the aesthetics of bleak metro stations, around 130 artists have contributed paintings, engravings, reliefs, sculptures and mosaics to the metro art project. Restoration is continuous and the SL Art Council spends Skr2.5 million annually on improvements and additions. Displays well worth a look include the metro stations at Kungsträdgården (Map pp236-8; classical pieces, ferns and dripping water), Fridhemsplan (Map p230; terracotta tiles celebrating Carl von Linné) and Östermalmstorg (Map pp236-8; women's rights and peace and environmental movements). For more information, visit www.sl.se/english.

---

The Unesco World Heritage–listed graveyard Skogskyrkogården has a pine woodland setting and features several functionalist and neoclassical buildings, including an astoundingly elegant crematorium and several chapels. Designed by Gunnar Asplund and Sigurd Lewerentz, the grounds are dominated by a massive granite cross. It's also known as the final resting place of Hollywood actress Greta Garbo (1905–90), who hailed from Stockholm. Her ashes were interred in Skogskyrkogården in 1999.

## SPÅNGA KYRKA Map pp228–9

☎ 36 26 50; Spånga Kyrka väg; admission free; ☽ by arrangement; T-Tensta plus 15min walk

The stone-built Spånga kyrka is one of Stockholm's oldest and most architecturally interesting churches. The nave dates from the end of the 12th century and has impressive 15th-century wall and ceiling frescoes featuring biblical scenes. Some earlier works have been dated to the mid-14th century. Look out for St George and the dragon, God holding Christ on his cross and a lion painting, all from the 1460s. The porch also has impressive artwork. Among the inventory is a pulpit from 1759 and a communion plate from around 1500. In the grounds there are three spectacular rune stones from the 11th century. A segment of another rune stone is located in the southern wall. A colour booklet (in Swedish only) is available for Skr10.

## ULRIKSDALS SLOTT Map pp228–9

☎ 402 61 30; www.royalcourt.se; adult Skr55, plus Orangery & coronation carriage adult/child Skr80/40, free under 7; ☽ 10am-4pm Tue-Sun 15 May-31 Aug, Sat & Sun Sep; T-Bergshamra, then bus 540

The yellow-painted royal Ulriksdals Slott (Ulriksdal Palace) sits in Ulriksdals Park on the waterfront at Edsviken. This large, early-17th-century building was home to King Gustav VI Adolf and his family until 1973. You can visit several attractive apartments on two floors. The living room is one of the finest 20th-century interiors in Sweden. Gustaf VI Adolf's drawing room, which dates from 1923, contains part of his art collection as well as furniture designed by Carl Malmsten. In the northern wing you'll see rooms from the time of Karl XV; the southern wing contains the offices of the World Wide Fund for Nature.

The nearby **Orangery** ( ☎ 402 61 30; Skr50; ☽ 10am-4pm Tue-Sun 15 May-31 Aug, Sat & Sun Sep) contains Swedish sculpture and Mediterranean plants. You can also see **Queen Kristina's coronation carriage** ( ☎ 402 61 30; Skr20; ☽ guided tours in English 1.40pm & 3.40pm Tue-Sun May-Aug).

# Walking Tours

# Walking Tours

Stockholm is compact and lends itself to sightseeing on foot. Set out in any direction from Centralstationen and you'll end up wandering through trendy neighbourhoods, past historical buildings and through wild parks on your way to an attractive waterfront. The six routes described here will each take a few hours to complete, and longer if you decide to make some of our suggested stops for refreshments. For details of commercial walking tours, see p50.

## CITY CENTRE & GAMLA STAN

This walk takes you through the core of Stockholm – old and new. You'll see some of the most historic architecture in the city and, just a bridge away, some of the most modern. If you have limited time in Stockholm, this is a good way to get a feel for the city.

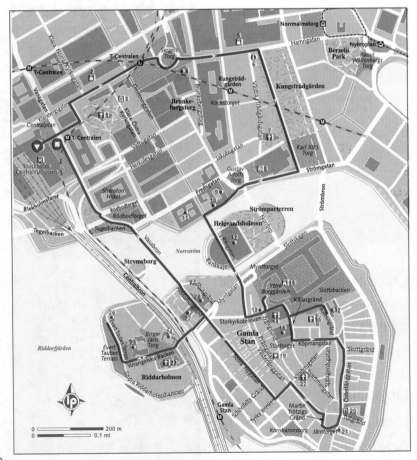

## Walk Facts

**Start** Centralstationen
**Finish** Centralstationen
**Distance** 3.5 km
**Duration** 2–3 hours
**Transport** *Tunnelbana* to T-Centralen

Start your walk at **Centralstationen**, the main railway station, which dates from 1867 but has been altered many times since. Cross Vasagatan and enter the side street Vattugränd. Turn left onto Klara Västra Kyrkogatan, past **Klara Kyrka** 1 (p58), then turn right onto Klarabergsgatan. This is one of Stockholm's main modern shopping streets, with designer shops, expensive boutiques and the **Åhléns** 2 (p146) department store. Looking down Klara Östra Kyrkogatan, you'll see **Läkaresällskapets hus** 3, a fine brick building dating from 1906, built in National Romantic style but with Art Nouveau windows and interior.

**Sergels Torg**, named after the local 18th-century sculptor Johan Tobias Sergel, was controversial when it was built and still is today. It was designed to fill the aesthetic void created when builders flattened several blocks of the historic Old Klara neighbourhood to put up modern office buildings, something the city immediately regretted. Generally deemed an aesthetic failure and haunted by dodgy characters, the square nevertheless has its appeal; it's an important public forum for demonstrations and seasonal activities (there's a big Christmas market here). Anchoring Sergels Torg is **Kulturhuset** 4 (p58), The Culture House, a sleek and equally controversial modern building designed by Peter Celsing in 1968. Abhorred by the mainstream, it has become the darling of the city's younger architects, who are bored out of their skulls by Stockholm's conservative approach to architecture.

Continue a short way along Hamngatan, passing the landmark 1915 department store **NK** 5 (p145) on your left. Turn right after **Sverigehuset** 6, the tourist office, into wide-open **Kungsträdgården**. This park, originally Gustav Vasa's kitchen garden and later an orchard, was opened to the public in 1763; people ice skate here in winter, and there are festivals all year. If you're ready for an espresso, pop into **Piccolino** (p112). Don't miss the 17th-century **St Jakobs kyrka** 7, and, just behind it, the always-provocative Wetterling Gallery.

Walk through the park to its southern end at **Karl XII's Torg**, where there's a statue of the warmongering king. On your right there's **Operan** 8 (p132), the Royal Opera House (opened in 1896), and across the road you'll see the narrow strait **Norrström**, which is the freshwater outflow from Lake Mälaren.

Continue along the waterfront past **Gustav Adolfs Torg** to the grandiose **Arvfurstens palats** 9, now housing the foreign ministry, and the adjacent small white house, **Sagerhus** 10, the prime minister's official residence. Beyond Drottninggatan is **Rosenbad** 11, originally a 17th-century steam bath that now contains government offices.

Turn left over the bridge Riksbron, at the foot of Drottninggatan. The route continues across **Helgeandsholmen** (Island of the Holy Spirit), between the two parts of Sweden's parliament building, **Riksdagshuset** 12 (p55). Cross a short bridge and you'll arrive on **Stadsholmen** (City Island), the medieval core of Stockholm.

Cross Mynttorget and follow Västerlånggatan for one block, then turn left into Storkyrkobrinken, where you'll see the lovely rouge **Oxenstiernas palats** 13, a mansion built in 1653 by Jean de la Valleé for a famous 17th-century chancellor, and **Storkyrkan** 14 (p55), the city's cathedral and the oldest building in Gamla Stan. Facing the cathedral across

*Sergels Torg (p100)*

the cobbled square is **Kungliga Slottet** 15 (p52), the 'new' Royal Palace. Behind the cathedral lies **Slottsbacken**, a large open area with a central **obelisk**; this is where the entertaining Changing of the Guard ceremonies take place. On the southern side of Slottsbacken is **Finska Kyrkan** 16 (p52), the Finnish church (now a cultural centre), and **Tessinska palatset** 17, a late 17th-century palace used by the Stockholm county governor.

The lane Källargränd leads southwards from Slottsbacken to the square Stortorget, where the Stockholm Bloodbath took place in 1520. Three sides of the square are formed by quaint tenements painted in complementary colours. On the fourth side of the square there's **Börsen** 18, the Swedish Academy building, completed in 1778; it now houses **Nobelmuseet** (p54), a worthwhile stop if you have time. Stortorget has a charming Christmas market in December. If you're hungry, grab an outdoor table at **Chokladkoppen** 19 (p124).

The narrow streets of the eastern half of Gamla Stan still feel medieval, winding along their 14th-century lines and linked by a fantasy of lanes, arches and stairways. Walk down Köpmangatan to the small square **Köpmantorget**, where there's a statue of St George and the dragon. Turn right into **Österlånggatan**, where you'll find antique shops, art galleries, handicraft outlets and **Den Gyldene Freden** 20 (p105), which has been serving food since 1722.

Follow Österlånggatan as far as **Järntorget** (Iron Square), where metals were bought and sold in days long past. On the southeastern side of the square stands **Gamla Riksbankhuset** 21 – completed in 1682, it's the oldest national bank building in the world. From Järntorget, keep right and turn into Västerlånggatan, looking out for **Mårten Trotzigs Gränd** by No 81; at less than 1m wide this is Stockholm's narrowest lane. Follow Mårten Trotzigs Gränd to Prästgatan to the lavishly decorated German church, **Tyska Kyrkan** 22 (p56).

Västerlånggatan is crammed with souvenir shops and wide-eyed tourists, so unless you want to feel like a human pinball, follow the quieter parallel street Stora Nygatan instead. On reaching Riddarhustorget, turn left and cross the short bridge Riddarholmsbron to **Riddarholmen** (Island of Knights). The large **Riddarholmskyrkan** 23 (p56) has a grimly impressive modern spire and the corpses of dozens of knights stored deep in its crevices. Across Birger Jarls torg, **Stenbockska palatset** 24 dates from the 1640s and is one of Nicodemus Tessin the Elder's best-preserved mansions; it now houses the supreme court. Beyond Riddarholmskyrkan, you'll come to the far side of the island; on your right is the southern tower of the **Wrangelska palatset** 25, part of the medieval city wall (1530s). Further north, **Birger Jarls torn** 26 is another brick watchtower built around 1530 from the remains of the demolished Klara monastery.

Retrace your steps to Riddarhustorget, then turn left into Vasabron and pass between **Riddarhuset** 27 (House of Nobility; p54) and **Bondeska palatset** 28, another of Tessin the Elder's 17th-century mansions, now used by the appeals court. Continue across Vasabron and along Vasagatan back to Centralstationen.

# SKEPPSHOLMEN, DJURGÅRDEN & ÖSTERMALM

This tour takes you past some of the most imposing buildings in Stockholm, including the city's main synagogue, the enormous but lovely Grand Hôtel Stockholm and the impressive National Museum, onto the park-like island of Djurgården, past the astounding Vasa museum and through Stureplan, the city's trendiest area, where you'll find top-of-the-line fashion boutiques as well as clubs full of people in top-of-the-line fashion.

Start this walk at **Sverigehuset** (Sweden House), the tourist office. Heading east on Hamngatan, turn right onto Kungsträdgårdsgatan, a street lined on one side with large buildings facing Kungsträdgården. The head office of System-

## Walk Facts

**Start** Sverigehuset
**Finish** Sverigehuset
**Distance** 4km
**Duration** 2–3 hours
**Transport** Tunnelbana to T-Centralen or T-Kungsträdgården

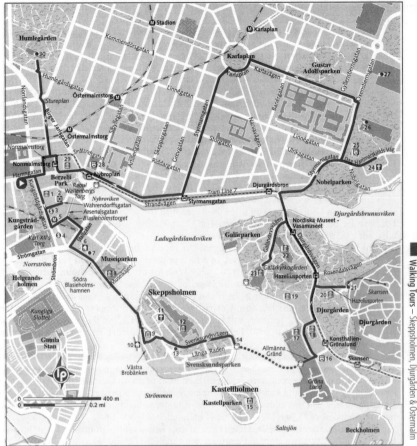

bolaget, at No 14, contains **Bolagsmuseet 1** (p57), which has an entertaining description of the history of alcohol in Sweden.

If you go a short way along Wahrendorffsgatan, you'll find **Synagogan 2**, the 1867 synagogue, with a magnificent interior. At Kungsträdgårdsgatan 8, there's **Stockholms Enskilda Bank 3**, with a neoclassical façade and Carl Milles sculptures by the entrance. **Handelsbanken 4**, at Kungsträdgårdsgatan 2, is another magnificent building, open during regular banking hours.

Just north of Handelsbanken, turn into Arsenalsgatan for the eastern entrance to the metro station **T-Kungsträdgården 5**. This station is known for its fine public art, based on casts from the ruins of the Makalös Palace, the former Royal Dramatic Theatre, which was destroyed by fire in 1825 (you'll need a valid metro ticket to see the art). From Arsenalsgatan, turn right into **Blasieholmstorget**, a cobbled square with two bronze horses cast from the four at San Marco in Venice.

Turn right again, onto Stallgatan, then left along Södra Blasieholmshamnen. The large building on the left is the **Grand Hôtel Stockholm 6** (p156), originally built in 1874 with an internal carriageway (now the glass-roofed Winter Garden). The hotel's **Hall of Mirrors**, with its gilded stucco, classical columns, chandeliers and mirrors, was once used for Nobel Prize dinners. The hotel has absorbed the next building, **Bolinderska huset 7**; its particularly fine interior was restored in the 1990s. On your right is the quay **Strömkajen**, popular with anglers and a departure point for boats to the archipelago. The next large building on your left is the impressive **National Museum** 8 (p67); its café, the **Atrium**, is an excellent stop for lunch or to *fika* (have coffee and cake).

Cross the bridge to the island **Skeppsholmen**. Straight ahead you'll see the impressive **Gamla Amiralitetshuset** 9, the original headquarters of the Swedish admiralty (1650); it was rebuilt as a barracks in 1846, when the spectacular turrets and gables were added. It's now used by Svenska Turistföreningen (STF; Swedish Touring Club). Keep right, walk past some cannons, and you'll reach **Vandrarhem af Chapman** 10 (p159).

Go up the steps opposite *af Chapman* and pass the rear of Gamla Amiralitetshuset. On the hill ahead of you is the octagonal neoclassical church **Skeppsholms kyrkan** 11, with an original interior from 1842; unfortunately, it's not open to the public. Turn right when you reach the roadway (Svensksundsvägen), passing **Arkitekturmuseet** (p73) and **Moderna Museet** 12 (p73) on your left and the colourful **modern sculpture garden** 13 on your right. Continue to the Djurgårdsfärjan **boat terminal** 14, where you can catch a boat to the Gröna Lund terminal on Djurgården (Skr20; the boat goes via Slussen from autumn to spring).

If you have time, you can first pay a quick visit to **Kastellet** 15 on the island of Kastellholmen, reached by bridge from Skeppsholmen. This strange little structure replaces a fort which blew up in the 1840s due to a botched gunpowder experiment.

On arrival in Djurgården, you'll see **Gröna Lund Tivoli** 16 (p70) on the right. Take the first left, wander between the **Aquaria Vattenmuseum** 17 (p70) and **Liljevalchs konsthall** 18 (p71); the adjacent café **Blå Porten** (p113) is highly recommended.

Turn left onto tree-lined Djurgårdsvägen. On your left between the road and the water is **Dykhusmuseet** 19, the Diving Museum, in a former marina building. On your right is the extraordinary-looking **Biologiska Museet** 20 (p70), built for the 1897 Stockholm Exhibition in 'Nordic dragon style'; just beyond is the Hazelius entrance to **Skansen** 21 (p72).

Continuing north on Djurgårdsvägen and passing the grandiose **Nordiska Museet** 22 (p71) on your left, take the next left onto Galärvarvsvägen, toward **Vasamuseet** 23 (p73) and the rear of the naval officers' cemetery **Galärkyrkogården**, where you'll find the controversial **Estonia monument** (see the boxed text, p77). Return to Djurgårdsvägen, turn left and cross the bridge to the mainland.

Turn right into Strändvägen, which becomes Strändvägen, passing **Nobelparken** on your right, and continue on Dag Hammarskjölds väg as far as **Engelska Kyrkan** 24, the obviously English-looking church. Retrace your steps by 200m, then head north on Oxenstiernasgatan, passing **Berwaldhallen** 25 (p135) and **Radiohuset** 26, national Swedish radio headquarters. Turn left onto Karlavägen, one of Östermalm's impressively wide, tree-lined boulevards, from where you have a good view of **TV-huset** 27, the home of national Swedish television in all its glory.

Follow Karlavägen to **Karlaplan**, a large circular area with a central pond and fountain, then take a left into Styrmansgatan and continue onto majestic Strandvägen, a wide waterfront boulevard lined with Art Nouveau hotels and the city's most exclusive addresses. At its western end, opposite Nybroplan, is the ornate **Dramatiska Teatern** 28 (p81).

Beyond the major artery Birger Jarlsgatan lies **Hallwylska Museet** 29 (p81) and the square Norrmalmstorg. Turn right and follow the pedestrian street Biblioteksgatan through the heart of the trendy part of town, to **Stureplan** and **Kungliga Biblioteket** 30 (The Royal Library), set in quiet **Humlegården** park. Stop in for a drink or a meal at the chic Lydmar Hotel (p118) before returning to Norrmalmstorg and taking a right on Hamngatan to end your walk at Sverigehuset.

# EASTERN SÖDERMALM

The steep climbs along this walk are rewarded by phenomenal vistas over Gamla Stan and central Stockholm – and innumerable chances to repair to a pub with a beer. Don't worry, the pink elephants you see are not hallucinations – they're part of Stockholm's public art.

This walk begins at the Slussen *tunnelbana* station. Leave via the main upper-level exit onto Södermalmstorg and turn immediately left into the steep, cobbled lane Peter Myndes backen, between **Stockholms Stadsmuseum** 1 (p79), the city museum, and **Hotell Anno 1647** 2 (p161). Take the first street on your left, **Götgatan**, the main shopping street in Södermalm. The second lane on your left is Klevgränd; take the next left after Klevgränd and ascend

## Walk Facts

**Start** T-Slussen
**Finish** T-Slussen
**Distance** 3.2km
**Duration** 1–2 hours, minus pub stops
**Transport** *Tunnelbana* to T-Slussen

the stairs to Urvädergränd, which climbs steeply past **Bellmanhuset** 3, a small yellow house where Sweden's well-known bard Carl Michael Bellman lived from 1770 to 1774.

You'll get the best view of the **Slussen clover-leaf junction**, built in 1935 for the switch to right-hand-drive traffic, by following the mesh-covered walkway on the left out to the upper entrance to **Katarinahissen** 4 (p78); there's a stellar view of the entire city. If you want to save your legs, you could always take the lift up (Skr5) and start the tour here. Parched already? Grab a drink or a nice meal at **Eriks Gondolen** 5 (p115), the bar/restaurant perched atop the Katarina lift.

Return to the top of Urvädergränd, where you'll find **Södrateatern** 6, a theatre dating from the 1850s. It faces **Mosebacketorg**, a cobblestone, tree-lined square containing the Nils Sjögren statue **Systrarna** (The Sisters).

Follow Östgötagatan south from Mosebacketorg for one block, then turn left into Hög-bergsgatan. On your right, you'll see the church **Katarina Kyrka** 7 (p77), a faithful replica of the 17th-century original, which was gutted by fire in 1990. It's surrounded by a serene park. Beyond the church, continue along Mäster Mikaels Gata, lined with small, wooden, 19th-century houses.

Cross Katarinavägen and follow Fjällgatan, and be sure to stop at the spectacular **cliff-top viewpoint** 8 on the left. Further along the street, Fjällgatan makes a sharp right turn and becomes Erstagatan, separating the specialist hospital **Ersta sjukhus** and **Ersta diakonisällskap**, both run by a charitable religious foundation. If you turn left into the latter, you'll find the interesting **Ersta Diakonimuseet** 9, hotel and café – another fine place to stop for sustenance – and **Kapell Ersta diakonissanstalt** 10 (p77), an octagonal chapel with a pointed roof.

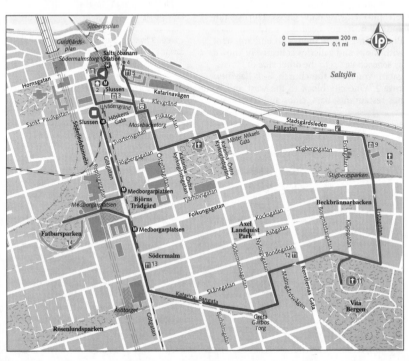

Return to Erstagatan and follow it for about 400m south to Skånegatan; turn right for 150m, then cross the street and climb up to **Sofia kyrka** 11, an early 20th-century church on top of the hill Vita Bergen. You'll be able to see the **Globen** dome far to the south. Return to Skånegatan and follow it west toward Södermannagatan; you'll pass **Folkhemmet** 12 (p116), a socialist-run restaurant with great food and a cool bar. Then turn left for 150m to reach **Greta Garbos Torg**, where three pink elephants frolic – a rather strange street sculpture.

From Greta Garbos Torg, follow Katarina Bangata northwestwards; at its junction with Skånegatan there's another odd sculpture, this one a woman with a pram. Continue to the main drag, Götgatan – if you're famished, duck into **Jerusalem Royal Kebab** 13 (p118) – then turn right to Södermalm's central square, **Medborgarplatsen**. There's a food court in the market hall, bars and restaurants (Snaps, Mondo, Kvarnen) clustered around the square, and a couple of hotdog/kebab stands in the middle – you can hardly go wrong.

From the square, the narrow street Bangårdsgatan leads west into **Fatbursparken**, a park dominated by the immense, semicircular, Vatican-goes-Blade Runner apartment building **Bofills Båge** 14, part of a planned 'urban block city' collaborative design by some of Stockholm's top architecture firms. Retrace your steps to Götgatan and follow it north back to T-Slussen.

# WESTERN SÖDERMALM & LÅNGHOLMEN

This tour takes you through art galleries, churches, parks and a prison. You'll see one of the city's best vistas from the Söder cliffs, some fine examples of early industrial architecture, a park-like island that once housed prisoners and now has some of Stockholm's finest beaches, and the southern island's major sports arena. At the end – sushi!

This walk also starts from T-Slussen. Head north, past Stadsmuseum, then turn left into Hornsgatan. Cross Hornsgatan and follow its northern side until you reach Pustegränd, where there's an embankment with shops and galleries collectively known as **Hornspuckeln** 1. On the other side of Hornsgatan, you'll see the church **Maria Magdalena**

**kyrka** 2. One city block to the west and lying south of Hornsgatan, the square **Mariatorget** has restaurants, bars, clubs and **Leksaksmuseet** 3 (p78), a museum dedicated to hobbies and

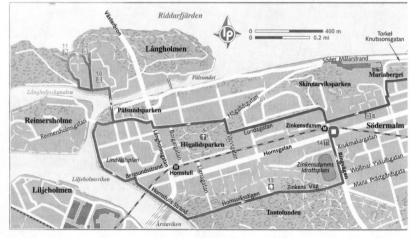

*Långholmens Fängelsemuseum (p79)*

toys. Also right on the square is the fiercely retro **Rival Hotel** 4 (p162), which has a good café attached.

From the northern side of Hornsgatan, turn into Blektornsgränd, then left into Bastugatan. About 200m to the west is **Ivar Lo's Park**, named after Ivar Lo-Johansson, a well-known author whose apartment on Bastugatan is now the **Ivar Lo-museet** 5 (p77). There are fine views across Riddarfjärden from the top of the cliff **Mariaberget** 6.

Near the western end of Bastugatan, on Torkel Knutssonsgatan, the former foundry and engineering works **Ludvigsberg** 7 is the city's best surviving example of 19th-century industrial architecture; adjacent is the owner's mansion with an octagonal tower. Cross Torkel Knutssonsgatan and follow Brännkyrkagatan; on your left you'll see the **Måleriyrkets Museum** 8 (p78). Continue walking along Brännkyrkagatan, then turn right onto Lundagatan. Ahead you'll see **Högalidskyrkan** 9, completed in 1923 and the only twin-spired church in Stockholm.

Turn right at the end of Lundagatan, then left onto Högalidsgatan, which terminates at the busy Långholmsgatan. Cross this street using the pedestrian crossing and walk downhill, skirting **Pålsundsparken**; turn right and cross the **Pålsundet** strait on a road bridge to reach the quiet suburban island of **Långholmen**. Keep left and walk around the former **Långholmen prison** 10 (p162), now a hotel, hostel and restaurant; there's also an interesting **prison museum** (Långholmens Fängelsemuseum; p79) here. **Långholmens strandbad** 11, on the northern shore of the island, is a pleasant beach for swimming in Mariebergsfjärden. The nearby **Bellmanmuseet** 12 (p79) is located in a 17th-century wooden customs house.

Return to Pålsundet and re-cross the bridge to Södermalm, then turn right along the shore and pass under the Liljeholmsbron. About 1km ahead, crossing Årstaviken, you'll see **Årstabron**, a railway bridge from 1929, which looks like a Roman aqueduct. Well before you reach it, turn left onto Hornviksstigen, with the huts of **Tantolunden Park** on your right. You'll pass the quietly located **Zinkensdamm Hotell & Vandrarhem** 13 (p163) on your left as the roadway becomes Zinkensväg. Continue to the main road, Ringvägen, then turn left, passing the sports field **Zinkensdamms Idrottsplats** (p137) on your left. The tour ends at T-Zinkensdamm, on the north side of Hornsgatan. If you've worked up an appetite, stop in at **Sushi Bar Sone** 14 (p117) before you catch the train; it's the tiny shopfront right by the station entrance.

# LOWER DJURGÅRDEN

This walk along the lower edge of Djurgården takes you through some of the island's natural beauty, as well as including stops at two of the most interesting galleries in Stockholm, both of which highlight particularly Nordic artwork that isn't easy to see in other, more mainstream galleries.

This is a fairly long walk, and it doesn't have many stops, so you'll need to plan ahead and make sure that you allow yourself enough time to visit each of the museums properly. Start your walk at the fun park **Gröna Lunds Tivoli** 1 (p70). Take Djurgårdsvägen west and continue walking along it as it becomes Ryssviksvägen, and then as it becomes Prins Eugens vägen. Following the signs, take a right to **Prins Eugens Waldemarsudde** 2 (p71), a sprawl-

## Walk Facts

**Start** Gröna Lund
**Finish** Thielska Galleriet
**Distance** 3km
**Duration** 3–5 hours depending on time spent at museums
**Transport** Djurgården ferry from terminal 41 to Gröna Lund, bus 69 back from Thielska Galleriet to Sergels Torg

ing museum that incorporates the beloved Prince Eugene's mansion and attached gallery as well as a separate lodge and cottage. There's quite a good little café on the 1st floor

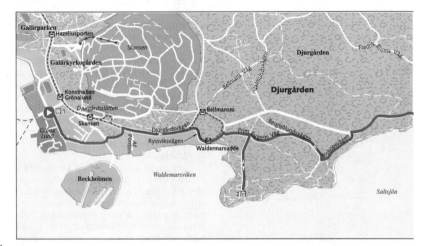

*Looking east from Kaknästornet (p82)*

of the museum's main building, and the museum grounds offer a number of fantastic views out over the water.

After your visit, continue heading east – either by retracing your steps up to Djurgårds-vägen and taking a right, or by following the edge of the water (along Biskopsvägen) until it meets the main road. Keep going east – it's a fairly long walk covering hilly, tree-

strewn parkland on the lower fringes of the former royal animal park, and it feels quite remote from the bustling city – until you reach **Thielska Galleriet** 3 (p73). This cake-like white-and-green mansion was designed by Ferdinand Boberg, who created Waldemarsudde at around the same time. The museum grounds are ideal for taking short strolls, and the building itself is jam-packed with important pieces of Nordic art, including Edvard Munch's portraits of August Strindberg and Friedrich Nietzsche, as well as several drawings by Carl Larsson and a darkly enchanting group portrait by Vilhelm Hammershöi.

Bus 69 stops directly in front of the museum to take you back to Sergels Torg – or if you've still got plenty of energy, you can make your way back by doing the walk in reverse.

# DJURGÅRDSBRUNNSVIKEN

This is a pleasant stroll around the channel separating Djurgården from Gärdet, past a cluster of frequently overlooked museums and up to Kaknästornet, a radio tower with spectacular 360-degree views.

Start your walk on the north side of **Djurgårdsbron 1**, the bridge that links Djurgården with the city centre. Head east along Strandvägen through **Nobelparken 2** until the road becomes Nobelgatan; it more or less runs parallel to the water's edge. This area is home to most of the embassies in Stockholm. At the far end of Nobelparken the road becomes Djurgårdsbrunnsvägen; continue east on this road to the **Sjöhistoriska Museet 3** (p82). From here you can tackle several nearby museums – the **Tekniska Museet, Teknorama Science Centre & Telemuseum 4** (p83) and **Folkens Museum Etnografiska 5** (p82) – or head back toward the waterline and follow the slender Folke Bernadottes Väg east. Where it meets Lidovägen, head north, following signs to the radio tower **Kaknästornet 6** (p82). The views from this tower are unbeatable on a clear day. There's also a café and restaurant in the tower.

Retrace your steps to Lidovägen and continue east toward Djurbrunnsbron. Nearby is one of Stockholm's most exciting venues for art installations, **Projekt Djurgårdsbrunn 7** (p25) where, in the summer months, you'll find rotating fine-art exhibitions geared toward pushing boundaries. You'll also see the interesting **Judiska Teatern 8**.

From **Djurbrunnsbron 9** you can choose whether to catch bus 69 back to the city centre (Sergels Torg), or to cross the bridge and walk back along the other side of the water. The latter makes for a bit of a hike but it takes you through lovely natural scenery. Follow the edge of the water along the upper fringes of Djurgården, the former royal animal park, and you'll see a few small fishing boats and occasional wildlife; strolling this quiet area makes you feel as if you're in the middle of nowhere, rather

> ## Walk Facts
>
> **Start** Djurgårdsbron, at the end of Strandvägen
> **Finish** Djurgårdsbron
> **Distance** 4km
> **Duration** 2–3 hours, longer depending on museum stops
> **Transport** Bus 47 to Djurgårdsbron; optional short cut: bus 69 back from Djurbrunnsbron to Sergels Torg

than a only short walk from one of Europe's most vibrant urban centres. It's an excellent 'getaway' within the city. About halfway back, **Rosendals slott 10** (p72) with its **Trädgård café** (p113) is a wonderful place to stop for a drink or a snack. Following the waterline westward will bring you back to Djurgårdsbron.

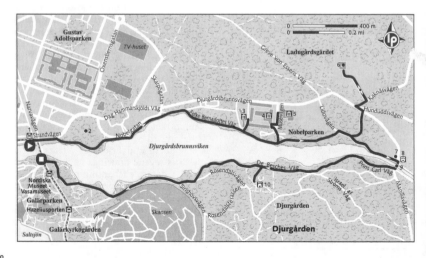

# Eating

# Eating

The restaurant scene in Stockholm, like nearly every other aspect of life in the city, constantly seeks to be at the forefront of fashion; if there's a food trend happening, you can bet that all the hot restaurants in town are offering their own takes on it. Stockholmers are serious about food as a cultural medium; a meal in an upmarket restaurant is treated as a culinary adventure. Most restaurants in the city lean towards providing the dinnertime crowd with a unique experience – not just filling hungry bellies.

This makes for some outstanding evenings of adventurous dining, but it also means that finding a casual place to grab a quick bite can be a challenge. If you want a fast meal without much fanfare, your best bet is to visit one of Stockholm's many small cafés (most are listed under Cheap Eats). Aside from the beloved Swedish ritual of *fika* (coffee and cakes), these cafés also serve filling lunches – seafood salads, ham-and-cheese pies (quiches), baguettes filled with salami and brie, and the trademark Swedish sandwiches *(smörgåsar)*, which are open-faced, frequently elaborate arrangements of shrimp or salmon, lettuce, boiled egg, mustard sauce and garnishing.

The typical Stockholm breakfast *(frukost)* is simply coffee and a pastry *(wienerbröd or kanelbulle)* in a café, or cereal with yogurt or *fil*, a type of buttermilk. Most hotels and hostels provide extensive breakfast buffets laden with all of the above plus fresh fruit, cold cuts, liver paté, cheese, Swedish hardbread and the like.

Cafés and restaurants usually serve a weekday lunch special (or a choice of several) called *dagens rätt* at a fixed price (typically Skr65 to Skr85) between 11.30am and 2pm Monday to Friday. It's a practice originally supported and subsidised by the Swedish government with the goal of keeping workers happy and efficient all day, and it's still one of the most economical ways to sample upmarket Swedish cooking. The bistro Tysta Mari inside Östermalms Saluhall (p104) has a particularly tasty and varied *dagens rätt* menu that leans heavily on fresh seafood.

For a quick, inexpensive snack, it's hard to beat a *grillad korv med bröd* – your basic grilled hotdog on a bun, available for around Skr15 from thousands of stands and carts all over the city. Variations include *kokt korv* (boiled hotdog) and several types of *rulle*, which are hotdogs wrapped up with mashed potatoes, onions, shrimp salad and other unlikely things in pita-style bread.

The more traditional restaurants in Stockholm specialise in *husmanskost*, or classic Swedish 'plain food', but many other places also include a *husmanskost* section on the menu. Typical dishes are *pytt i panna*, a meat-and-potato hash served with pickled beetroots and a fried egg; fried or pickled herring, called *sill* or *strömming* depending on which coast it comes from, and prepared in various ways according to the season; *lax* (salmon) in several forms, from grilled to smoked to salt-and-sugar cured *(gravad)*; *kåldolmar*, stuffed cabbage rolls reminiscent of Mediterranean dolmades; game such as elk, and reindeer, particularly delicious when cured and then boiled *(rimmad)*; and of course the requisite Swedish meatballs, eaten with lingonberry sauce. There's

## Top Five Eat Streets

- **Götgatan & around, Södermalm** – Everything from old-fashioned *husmanskost* to vegan and vegetarian places cling to this channel through Söder.
- **Luntmakargatan, Vasastan** – Extraordinary Asian restaurants, including the all-veg Lao Wai, line this street.
- **Österlånggatan, Gamla Stan** – This winding old shopping street in the Old Town is full of classy joints, including the historic Den Gyldene Freden.
- **Kungsgatan, Norrmalm** – A major thoroughfare in the city centre, Kungsgatan has innumerable places to nosh.
- **Scheelegatan, Kungsholmen** – Two tapas bars anchor this busy eating street in Kungsholmen.

# Traditional Swedish Foods

If your experiences in Stockholm's restaurants inspire you to try your hand at *husmanskost* at home, these basic recipes will get you started. For more recipes, as well as details about the traditions behind many Swedish foods, check out the entertaining *Maypoles, Crayfish and Lucia: Swedish Holidays and Traditions* by Jan-Öjvind Swahn, published by the **Swedish Institute** (www.si.se). Also recommended are *Scandinavian Feasts: Celebrating Traditions throughout the Year* by Beatrice A Ojakangas; *Scandinavian Holiday Recipes* by Michelle Nagle Spencer; and *Splendid Swedish Recipes* by Kerstin O Van Guilder.

For a taste of what's going on at the forefront of Swedish cooking, check out *Aquavit and the New Scandinavian Cuisine* by Marcus Samuelsson (Houghton Mifflin Co, October 2003), the celebrated young Ethiopian-Swedish chef of Aquavit restaurant in New York.

## Gravad Lax (Cured Salmon)

Marinated and cured salmon can be served *smörgåsbord*-style or it can be enjoyed along with dill-stewed potatoes.

### Ingredients

1kg fresh or well-thawed salmon
   in two equal size fillets
4 tbsp sugar
4 tbsp salt

2 tsp coarse pepper
1 posy of dill, finely chopped
1 lemon

### Method

Clean and dry the salmon, leaving the skin intact. Mix the sugar, salt and pepper, then rub the mixture into both salmon fillets. Place the fillets together, nose-to-tail, with the skin facing outward. Pop the fillets in a sealed plastic bag and place in a fridge for around 36 hours, turning the bag over after 18 hours. Remove the seasoning and thinly slice the salmon. Serve with sliced lemon and chopped dill garnish.

## Köttbullar (Swedish Meatballs)

Meatballs are best eaten along with boiled or steamed vegetables such as potatoes, carrots and peas, and they're traditionally paired with lingonberries.

### Ingredients

3½ tbsp breadcrumbs
300g beef mince
1 tbsp grated onion
1 egg

butter or margarine suitable for frying
100mL water
pinch salt
pinch pepper

### Method

Place the breadcrumbs in a bowl and add the water. Leave standing until the water is absorbed. Add the mince, onion, egg, salt and pepper, and work until you have a rubbery-feeling paste. Roll sections of paste into balls around 2cm in diameter. Fry the meatballs over a moderate heat until they're suitably brown.

## Janssons Frestelse (Jansson's Temptation)

### Ingredients

7 big potatoes
2 big onions
7 anchovy fillets
50g butter

150mL double cream
100mL milk (3% fat)
2 tbsp breadcrumbs

### Method

Peel the potatoes and cut into matchsticks. Peel the onions cut into thin slices. Fry in butter until soft and golden brown. Grease an oven-proof dish with butter. Layer the potatoes, onions and anchovy fillets; begin and end with the potatoes. Pour some the anchovy brine over the top and then add the cream and milk. Bake for about 30 minutes at 200°C. Sprinkle with breadcrumbs and shaved butter. Cook for another 20 minutes, until the top is browned and the potatoes cooked through.

also the infamous jiggly white *lutfisk*, which is dried cod preserved – unlikely as it may sound – in lye, then reconstituted and usually served with potatoes, peas and a béchamel sauce. In keeping with Sweden's tendency to schedule everything, split-pea and ham soup is traditionally eaten on Thursdays, especially in winter, and followed up with potato pancakes and jam.

Leading up to the Christmas holidays – and year-round at a few places – the justifiably famous Swedish *smörgåsbord* or *julbord* (Christmas table) is served. To navigate a *smörgåsbord* successfully, start with a plate of pickled herring, red onions and crispy hardbread, then move on to the more substantial fare – ham, sausages, thick, fried shortribs, meatballs, potatoes, roasted game, *gravad lax* and *Janssons frestelse* (Jansson's Temptation), a potato-and-onion casserole made with heavy cream and anchovies. (You're expected to make several trips to the *bord*, so don't overload your plate – taking more than you can eat and leaving it behind is not the done thing.) *Snaps* (aquavit) and *punsch* (a strong arrack- and rum-based drink), naturally, are *de rigueur* accompaniments to the feast. Also around the holidays you'll find fragrant saffron rolls, called *lussekatt*, in bakeries and cafés everywhere. Don't miss the chance to try these, preferably while browsing at an outdoor Christmas market accompanied by a steaming mug of *glögg* (mulled wine). For more about what Swedes drink to keep out the cold, see Drinking, p121.

August and Midsummer bring two other beloved Swedish specialities to the table: *surströmming* and crayfish *(kräftor)*. The former, which is Baltic herring that's been tinned and fermented for up to a year, is decidedly an acquired taste; the smell of a tin of *surströmming* being opened will quickly separate the seasoned Swedish-food veteran from the rank amateur. Crayfish parties happen just after Midsummer; thanks to disease and overfishing, most of the crayfish eaten in Sweden these days are imported, but that hardly dampens the locals' enthusiasm for sucking the guts out of the little things at moonlit parties throughout August.

In addition to restaurants serving *husmanskost* and other traditional Swedish foods, there are plenty of ambitious, boundary-pushing kitchens in Stockholm. It's a rather food-obsessed city (see City Life, p14), and diners pounce on standout places like Bon Lloc (p107), whose star chef Mathias Dahlgren combines Swedish ingredients with Mediterranean influences, and Eyubi (p108), a chic Kurdish-Persian place inhabiting a former parking garage. There are also countless eateries throughout the city serving authentic Thai, Turkish, Greek, Spanish, Lebanese, Indian, Italian and Chinese food, among others.

## Opening Hours

Breakfast, usually just a coffee and pastry, runs anywhere from 7am to 10am. Bakeries, cafés and coffee shops usually serve breakfast as well as lunch. Most restaurants serve lunch and dinner and are open from 11am to 10pm or 11pm. The lunch special *(dagens rätt)* at most restaurants is served between 11.30am and 2pm; this is the main meal out for many locals, so the best places will be crowded. Most people eat dinner around 7pm or 8pm. Places serving dinner only typically open at 5pm. Kitchens usually close by 11pm even in places with a bar area that stays open later.

## How Much?

Expect to pay Skr25 to Skr35 for a coffee and pastry in a café; sandwiches and salads à la carte cost around Skr35 to Skr50. In restaurants and some full-service cafés, look for *dagens rätt* (the daily special), a set lunch menu that normally includes a main course (meat, fish or vegetarian), salad, drink (juice or light beer), bread and butter and coffee. It's almost always filling and affordable (Skr65 to Skr85 in most places).

At dinner, *husmanskost* plates and other main dishes can cost anywhere from Skr85 to Skr285, depending on the meal itself and the exclusivity of the setting. Most fine restaurants have multicourse set menus that cost Skr225 to Skr450 and up depending on the number of courses.

Keep in mind that many places charge a cloakroom fee of around Skr15 at the door.

# Booking Tables

Reservations are recommended, particularly on Friday and Saturday evenings and at popular restaurants. Bars and restaurants are doubly crowded on and just after the 25th of each month, when Stockholmers get their paychecks. Many good restaurants close entirely in July for summer holidays, so it's important to call in advance.

# Tipping

Service charges are figured into the bill in Stockholm, but most restaurant diners leave a 10% to 20% tip unless they're unhappy with the service. In bars and coffee shops, locals tend not to tip much, if at all, usually just rounding up the bill to the nearest Skr5.

# Self-Catering

Shopping in grocery shops is one of the joys of visiting Stockholm. Where else can you get reindeer meat, rice pudding, caviar, jam and gravy all in aerodynamic little tubes? It's easy – though not particularly cheap – to put together an interesting picnic or a hostel meal with a few local specialities, such as Wasa hardbread, *gravad lax*, jars of pickled herring in dozens of different sauces, hunks of *Västerbottens ost* (a hard, crumbly cheese) and elk sausage. Supplement it with produce and fresh pastries from one of the city's vibrant market halls (p103).

The main supermarket chains in Stockholm are ICA, Konsum and Hemköp. By law, shops must display both the item price and the comparative price per kilogram. Plastic carrier bags must be purchased at the checkout (usually Skr1). Most supermarket employees speak English.

### BAKERIES

In addition to the cafés listed in this chapter, many of which have a bakery section, Stockholm has several traditional bakeries where you can pick up cakes to take away. Recommended bakeries include **Gunnarssons Specialkonditori** (Map pp234-5; ☎ 641 91 11; Götgatan 92; ✆ closed Sun); **Konditori Ritorno** (Map p230; ☎ 32 01 06; Odengatan 80), which is the bakery side of a charming old café; **Munken Konditori** (Map pp234-5; ☎ 57 15 49 10; Renstiernas Gata 19; ✆ closed Sun); **Sturekatten** (Map pp236-8; ☎ 611 16 12; Riddargatan 4), there's a great bakery on the first floor of this dolls house coffee shop; and **Tösse** (Map pp231-3; ☎ 662 24 30; Karlavägen 77), which is beloved by the grand dames of Östermalm.

### MARKET HALLS

Stockholm's colourful market halls are excellent places to sample local and exotic tastes while window shopping and people watching.

Located in the basement below Filmstaden cinema, **Hötorgshallen** (Map pp236-8; Hötorget; www.hotorgshallen.se; ✆ 10am-6pm Mon-Thu, 10am-6.30pm Fri, 10am-4pm Sat Jun-Aug, 10am-6pm Mon-Fri, 10am-3pm Sat Sep-May; T-Hötorget) has several fine specialist food shops selling meat, fish, cheese, groceries, coffee and tea, plus Asian fast-food stands selling kebabs and the like. At lunch time locals cram themselves into a galley-themed dining nook of Kajsas Fiskrestaurang for huge bowls of fish stew with mussels and aioli (*fisksoppa*; Skr75) – a treat not to be

Östermalms Saluhall (p104)

missed. Outside in the square there's a daily street market with stalls selling flowers, fruit, vegetables and knick-knacks.

More upmarket than Hötorgshallen, **Östermalms Saluhall** (Map pp234-5; Östermalmstorg; ✆ 9.30am-6pm Mon-Thu, 9.30am-6.30pm Fri, 9.30am-4pm Sat, to 2pm Sat Jun-Aug; T-Östermalmstorg) is excellent for fresh fish and meat as well as hard-to-find cheeses. The building itself is a Stockholm landmark, designed as a Romanesque cathedral of food in 1885. For a quick lunch, belly up to the bar at Depå Sushi; for more substantial fare, check the extensive *dagens rätt* board at the classy Tysta Mari (Skr60 to Skr85). The pastries at Amandas Brödbod are gorgeous. There's a clean, well-hidden – and free – WC in the far corner opposite the entrance.

**Söderhallarna** (Map pp234-5; Medborgarplatsen 3; ✆ 10am-6pm Mon-Wed, 10am-7pm Thu & Fri, 10am-4pm Sat; T-Medborgarplatsen), a more modern food hall, includes a great vegetarian restaurant, deli, cheese shop, an Asian supermarket and a pub that has live jazz most nights. It's not the most atmospheric place, so plan on enjoying your lunch outdoors on Medborgarplatsen.

### SUPERMARKETS

Picking up food for self-catering meals in Stockholm's supermarkets is convenient and surprisingly entertaining. The shops listed here are major ones, but these chains also have smaller branches throughout the city.

**Coop Konsum** (Map pp239-41; Katarinavägen 3-7; ✆ 7am-9pm Mon-Fri, 9am-9pm Sat & Sun; T-Slussen)

**Hemköp** (Map pp236-8; Åhléns basement, Mäster Samuelsgatan 57; ✆ 8am-9pm Mon-Fri, 10am-9pm Sat & Sun; T-Centralen)

**ICA Baronen** (Map pp231-3; Odengatan 40; ✆ 8am-10pm; T-Odenplan)

**Vivo T-Jarlen** (Map pp236-8; ✆ 7am-9pm Mon-Fri, 10am-7pm Sat, noon-6pm Sun) Inside the Östermalmstorg *tunnelbana* station (Grev Turegatan entrance).

# GAMLA STAN & RIDDARHOLMEN

The Old Town is the place to go for atmospheric old restaurants with vaulted brick cellars serving traditional *husmanskost* meals. It also has some of Stockholm's best cafés and lunch spots.

### ARDBEG ROOM

Map pp239–41          *International*
☎ 791 90 90; www.theardbegroom.com; Västerlång-gatan 68; starters Skr75-105, oysters Skr23 each, bar menu Skr105-145, mains Skr129-295; ✆ 4-11pm Mon, 4pm-1am Tue-Thu, 3pm-1am Fri, noon-1am Sat, 1-11pm Sun; T-Gamla Stan

In this sunken, white-walled room suffused with honey-coloured light, diners pack the golden, wooden tables for fine grilled meats and seafood. Starters include single oysters and smoked salmon on toast with horseradish cream. The focus is keenly on the grill, from barbecued beef to salmon with garlic-hollandaise sauce. A comfort-food bar menu includes cheeseburgers and fish and chips; these might go nicely with one of the Ardbeg's

### Gamla Stan Top Five

- **Den Gyldene Freden** (opposite)
- **Pontus in the Greenhouse** (p106)
- **Mandus** (p106)
- **Zum Franziskaner** (p106)
- **Fem Små Hus** (opposite)

200-plus types of single-malt scotch. It also has the widest selection of Swedish microbrewed beer in town, including Nils Oscar's trappist ales and the popular Heaven, Hell and Fallen Angel from Jämtlands Bryggeri.

### BISTRO RUBY & GRILL RUBY

Map pp239–41          *American*
☎ 20 60 15; Österlånggatan 14; mains Skr170-279 bistro, Skr129-255 grill; ✆ dinner, bar until 1am; T-Gamla Stan

On the grill side of this pair of Texas-via-the-Continent eateries, you choose a hunk of meat and a variety of accompanying tapas. On the bistro side, things feel a bit more grown-up, with simply prepared, classic French and Mediterranean dishes.

### CAFÉ ART Map pp239–41 *Café*

☎ 411 76 61; Västerlånggatan 60; sandwiches from Skr35; ⊗ lunch & dinner; T-Gamla Stan

This barrel-vaulted and brick-lined cellar, trendy when it first opened, has recently relaxed into a more low-key role as an atmospheric retreat from the Old Town shopping mayhem. Nestle in for coffee and cakes, shrimp salad or a salami-and-brie baguette.

### CATTELIN Map pp239–41 *Swedish*

☎ 20 18 18; Storkyrkobrinken 9; weekday lunch buffet Skr75, mains Skr90-185; ⊗ Mon-Sun Jun-Aug, Mon-Fri Sep-May; T-Gamla Stan

Cattelin, an old favourite with atmospheric décor and popular garden seating in summer, serves reasonably priced Swedish dishes and specialises in fish.

### DEN GYLDENE FREDEN

Map pp239–41 *Swedish*

☎ 10 90 46; Österlånggatan 51; mains from Skr250, 2-/3-course menu Skr418/468, husmanskost Skr96-185; ⊗ dinner Mon-Fri, lunch & dinner Sat until midnight; T-Gamla Stan

Once owned by famed Swedish painter Anders Zorn, and now run by the Swedish Academy, Den Gyldene Freden (The Golden Peace) is a keystone in Stockholm's history. Its three barrel-vaulted cellar dining rooms (two with plasterwork paintings) have been open continuously since 1722. There are few better places in town for classic *husmanskost*, particularly the plate of pickled herring with *Västerbottens ost*.

### FEM SMÅ HUS Map pp239–41 *Swedish*

☎ 10 04 82; Nygränd 10; menu Skr365-460, mains Skr205-265; ⊗ dinner until midnight Tue-Sat, to 11pm Sun & Mon; T-Gamla Stan

Located in a series of brick-vaulted cellars, this cosy, long-standing favourite specialises in reindeer, salmon, beef and veal cooked using traditional Swedish techniques.

### KÄLLAREN DIANA *Swedish*

☎ 10 73 10; www.kallarendiana.com; Brunnsgränd 2-4; starters Skr85-185, mains Skr185-285; ⊗ dinner; T-Gamla Stan

One of the best ways to brush up on your knowledge of Swedish herring in all its forms is to hit the herring boat (fondly nicknamed the 'Skiff of the Archipelago') in Diana's vaulted cellar rooms. Offered as an appetiser, the ship-shaped *sill* and *strömming* buffet – with dozens

## Top Five Romantic Restaurants

- Sabai Sabai (p110)
- Den Gyldene Freden (below)
- Operakällaren (p109)
- Spisa Hos Helena (p114)
- La Habana (p109)

of varieties – easily makes a meal, especially with a finger or two of *snaps* to wash it down. The cured reindeer salad (Skr85) is uniquely pungent and satisfying. Diana's turns into a late-night disco at weekends.

### KÄLLARE RESTAURANG MOVITZ

Map pp239–41 *Swedish-Italian*

☎ 20 99 79; Tyska brinken 34; 2-/3-course meals from Skr225/285; ⊗ lunch & dinner (to midnight Fri-Sun); T-Gamla Stan

This pleasant, 17th-century, white-painted and brick-arched cellar is a busy place, serving traditional Swedish fare with an Italian twist. The clientele are usually expense-accounters looking to close a deal or celebrate one. The classy menus include fish, lobster, beef with gorgonzola, veal and pork. Meals are also served upstairs in the pub, where there's often live music.

### LEIJONTORNET

Map pp239–41 *Swedish-Italian*

☎ 14 23 55; Lilla Nygatan 5; starters Skr165-195, mains Skr275-320; 3-/5-course menus Skr420/675; ⊗ 6-10.30pm Mon-Sat; T-Gamla Stan

Leijontornet's basement dining room includes the foundations of a 14th-century tower. The brick-vaulted ceilings and candlelight add to the atmosphere, but the furnishings feature modern design. The superb menu, one of the city's finest, includes fish, duck, game and vegetarian dishes. There's also a cheaper mid-range Italian-style *bakfickan* (literally 'back pocket', a less fancy dining room in the back of the restaurant) menu.

### MAHARAJAH Map pp239–41 *Indian*

☎ 21 04 04; Stora Nygatan 20; mains Skr70-90, clay oven tandoori dishes Skr75-119; ⊗ dinner; T-Gamla Stan

This long and narrow, warmly decorated Indian restaurant, with appropriate music and an open fire in winter, serves excellent food at keen prices. The Swedish songwriter Carl Michael Bellman lived here from 1787 to 1789.

Eating – Gamla Stan & Riddarholmen

## MANDUS Map pp239–41 *Eclectic*

☎ 20 60 55; Österlånggatan 7; mains Skr130-200;
🕒 5pm-midnight; T-Gamla Stan

This small, wildly decorated, gay-friendly place has a manic pace, a simple menu and a welcoming feel. The core of the menu is composed of Swedish staples – reindeer steaks, salmon, potatoes and the like – but with nice augmentation by Mediterranean and Asian dishes, such as lemongrass-sautéed tiger shrimp. But the charm of this place is really the vibe.

## MICHELANGELO Map pp239–41 *Italian*

☎ 20 93 91; Västerlånggatan 62; pizzas Skr80-110, mains Skr85-200; 🕒 lunch & dinner; T-Gamla Stan

Always packed, this Italian restaurant located on Gamla Stan's main drag has a fantastic classical-style atmosphere, paraffin lamps, painted ceilings and Roman statues. Good luck trying to walk past it when all the delicious cooking smells reach through the windows and tickle your nose.

## PONTUS IN THE GREENHOUSE

Map pp239–41 *Swedish*

☎ 23 85 00; Österlånggatan 17; starters Skr215-400, mains Skr295 and up; 🕒 11.30am-3pm & 6-11pm Mon-Fri, noon-4pm & 5.30-11pm Sat; T-Gamla Stan

Just across from the St George monument, this stylish modern restaurant with greenish décor has been declared the best in Sweden and it deserves the fine reputation. You can eat while seated at a central bar or at regular tables. Courses, including beluga caviar and Greenhouse canapés, are exceedingly well presented.

## SIAM THAI RESTAURANT

Map pp239–41 *Thai*

☎ 20 02 33; Stora Nygatan 25; dagens rätt from Skr65, mains Skr95-165; 🕒 lunch & dinner, closed Sun; T-Gamla Stan

A friendly, accommodating restaurant in a brick cellar, this vividly decorated place offers a range of authentic mild to spicy Thai dishes. The food is excellent, portions are large and the service is great.

## ZUM FRANZISKANER

Map pp239–41 *Swedish-german*

☎ 411 83 30; Skeppsbron 44; dagens rätt Skr65, husmanskost Skr92-225; 🕒 lunch & dinner, closed Sun; T-Gamla Stan

Founded in 1421 by German monks and claiming to be the oldest restaurant in the city,

Zum Franziskaner serves German and Austrian beers (bottled) and sausages as well as simply enormous Swedish *husmanskost* meals. The herring plate with *Västerbottens ost* claims to be an appetiser but is easily meal-size; the delicious *isterband*, a savoury Swedish country sausage, comes on a vast bed of potatoes in cream sauce. Although the current building dates from 1906, it looks like a museum inside, with its well-preserved wooden stalls, ornate cabinets and ceiling artwork.

# CHEAP EATS

## HERMITAGE Map pp239–41 *Vegetarian*

☎ 411 95 00; Stora Nygatan 11; dagens rätt Skr65-85, salads Skr65; 🕒 lunch & dinner; T-Gamla Stan

A modern café in a 17th-century building, Hermitage rustles up fine vegetarian fare from around the world. Two daily specials are offered at lunch (11.30am-2pm).

## SUNDBERGS KONDITORI

Map pp239–41 *Café*

☎ 10 67 35; Järntorget 83; lunch specials Skr59; 🕒 breakfast, lunch & dinner; T-Gamla Stan

Sundbergs is the oldest bakery-café in Stockholm, dating from 1785, and has a fine early-20th-century-style interior, complete with a copper samovar full of self-serve coffee. The café serves delicious hot sandwiches, pies, omelettes, lasagne and an assortment of to-die-for pastries.

# NORRMALM & VASASTADEN

This large swath of downtown Stockholm unsurprisingly has a tremendous variety of dining options. You'll find everything from Stockholm's most exclusive restaurants (whether old favourites like Operan and the Grand Hotel or new stars like Eyubi

### Norrmalm & Vasastaden Top Five

- Bon Lloc (opposite)
- Eyubi (p108)
- Narknoi Bar & Restaurang (p109)
- Sabai Sabai (p110)
- Café Tranan (p108)

and Bon Lloc) to the humblest kebab stand. Some of the city's best Asian restaurants are here, most notably along Luntmakargatan, as are some of the nicest cafés. In short, there's something in this area to suit every budget and taste.

### ATRIUM CAFÉ Map pp236–8 *Café*
☎ 611 34 30; Södra Blasieholmshamnen inside the National Museum; coffee Skr25, pastries Skr15-30, sandwiches Skr55; ⏰ lunch & dinner; T-Kungsträd-gården, bus 65

The café inside the National Museum, which you can visit without paying for admission to the museum, is among the nicest of Stockholm's many great museum cafés. It's in a cool inner courtyard reminiscent of an Italian piazza, and the walls are adorned with castings from the frieze-illustrated battle narrative on Trajan's Column in Rome. The food, from pastries to healthy sandwiches to hot *husmanskost* meals, is excellent.

### BAKFICKAN Map pp236–8 *Swedish*
☎ 676 58 09; Karl XII's Torg; mains Skr85-125; ⏰ 11.30am-midnight Mon-Sat; T-Kungsträdgården, bus 46, 55, 59, 62, 76

With superb service, Art Nouveau décor, stools around the bar and opera-related photos, this little restaurant – the 'back pocket' of Opera-källaren – serves gourmet-quality Swedish *husmanskost* at moderate prices. Try the assorted herring, boiled potatoes and crispbread. Look out for opera singers, who tend to eat here after a performance.

### BERNS SALONGER
Map pp236–8 *International*
☎ 56 63 22 22; Berzelii Park; mains from Skr245, set menu Skr345; ⏰ lunch & dinner (lunch only Sun & Mon); T-Kungsträdgården, bus 46, 47, 55, 69, 76

Looking like an ornate theatre with gilded stucco, immense chandeliers and paintings of composers, this magnificent place was thoroughly – but sensitively – renovated by Sir Terence Conran in 1999. August Strindberg named his satirical novel *Röda rummet* (Red Room) after a Berns salon that now functions as a private meeting room. The international menus have good choices of meat and fish, but not many vegetarian dishes. Dinner reservations should be made at least a week in advance. The huge building's many bars are popular and crowded, and there's occasional live music.

### BISTRO BOHEME
Map pp236–8 *Swedish-Czech*
☎ 411 90 41; Drottninggatan 71A; mains Skr65-175; T-Hötorget

This place has weird designer furniture (like gigantic chairs), as well as a tiled bar with loud music, and a beer garden that's open in summer. The menu includes Czech goulash soup and vegetarian lasagne. You can drink *storstark* beer (a large, strong beer) from enormous mugs, or try the unusually flavoured Swedish *punsch*.

### BON LLOC
Map pp231–3 *Swedish-International*
☎ 660 60 60; Regeringsgatan 111A; mains Skr105-325, set menus Skr635-1050; ⏰ dinner Mon-Sat, bar until 1am, closed Jul; T-Rådmansgatan, bus 42, 43, 44, 46, 52

Chef Matthias Dahlgren, the darling of culinary Stockholm, has developed something he has christened 'Estilo Nuevo Euro-Latino', a cooking philosophy that melds traditional Swedish *husmanskost* with inventive French and Catalan cooking techniques. For the set menus, each course is paired with a particular wine. Bon Lloc has been awarded one star in the well-known Guide Rouge and *Gourmet* magazine named it as the best restaurant in Sweden for 2002.

### BRONCOS BAR Map pp231–3 *Swedish*
☎ 16 02 15; Tegnérgatan 16; mains Skr65-125; ⏰ dinner; T-Rådmansgatan, bus 43, 52

The bright and airy Broncos Bar is renowned for its fast service and good, filling *husmanskost*. It also has its own beer and is run by a former weightlifter. The extensive menu includes classics like meatballs, *falukorv* (a type of sausage that is generally fried) and *pytt i panna*.

### CAFÉ PIASTOWSKA Map pp231–3 *Polish*
☎ 21 25 08; Tegnérgatan 5; menu from Skr150; ⏰ 6-11pm Mon-Sat, lunch Tue-Fri; T-Rådmansgatan, bus 43, 52

This is an extraordinarily quaint place with unusual décor, a vaulted cellar and genuine Polish cooking. There is a different soup on offer every day, as well as sausages, blinis (thin buckwheat pancakes) and steak with 'Pommes Polonaises' (Polish Potatoes, potatoes served with hard-boiled egg, parsley and butter – it might sound odd but it's really good). It's a small place, so you should consider booking ahead.

## CAFÉ TRANAN Map p230 *Swedish-Italian*

☎ 52 72 81 00; Karlbergsvägen 14; starters Skr55-125, mains Skr95-265; 🕑 dinner until 1am; T-Odenplan

This stylish, busy place on Odenplan looks like a classic French bistro, with its rustic furniture and checked tablecloths. It's one of the most popular neighbourhood restaurants in Stockholm, and is constantly recommended by devoted locals. It has an excellent and comprehensive international menu, including a traditional Swedish herring platter. Don't miss the basement bar, called simply Tranan (see p135).

## DJINGIS KHAN Map pp236–8 *Chinese*

☎ 21 63 85; Sveavägen 36; Mongolian buffet Skr140; 🕑 dinner; T-Hötorget

Djingis Khan is an outrageously ornate restaurant serving Chinese à la carte but better known for its vast buffet, which includes soup, bread, seven main courses, a salad bar and dessert.

## EYUBI Map pp231–3 *Kurdish-Persian*

☎ 673 52 36; Döbelnsgatan 45; mains Skr60-195, meze platter Skr180; 🕑 5pm-midnight Tue-Thu, to 1am Fri & Sat; closed Midsummer-Aug; T-Rådmansgatan

Dramatically situated in a former carpark at the end of a long concrete hallway lined with photos by cutting-edge Stockholm artists, Eyubi makes it clear straightaway that it is no ordinary Mediterranean restaurant. Its classy industrial style and sophisticated menu – where hummus and tabouleh rub shoulders with saffron-marinated chicken, scampi and lime-orange salmon – draw the trendy and arty from all over the city.

## FRANSKA MATSALEN

Map pp236–8 *French*

☎ 679 35 84; Grand Hôtel Stockholm, Södra Blasieholmshamnen 8; mains Skr195-485, set menu (including vegetarian) Skr895-1300; 🕑 lunch & dinner Mon-Fri, dinner only Sat; T-Kungsträdgården, bus 46, 55, 59, 62, 65

The ornate French restaurant at the Grand Hôtel fairly wallows in decadence, with its elaborate chandeliers, lots of dark wood and deep red carpets. It has been called the best restaurant in Sweden, and the food is certainly spectacular. A twist on beef Wallenberg made with pheasant, a cheese plate with chanterelle-lingonberry chutney, port-braised foie gras with figs, sage-beetroot ravioli, curry apple scallops – are you salivating yet? There's also

an extensive French wine list. A *smörgåsbord* lunch is available between 11.30am and 3pm weekdays in the hotel's Grand Veranda.

## FREDSGATAN 12 Map pp236–8 *Swedish*

☎ 24 80 52; Fredsgatan 12; starters Skr135-250, mains Skr245-345; 🕑 lunch & dinner, closed Sun; T-Centralen, bus 3, 53, 62, 65

With minimalist modern décor and classical touches, this fine restaurant – in star chef Melker Andersson's stable – has a menu divided into taste categories (light, nature, ocean, meat, sweet) and a waterside setting that's unbeatable, especially in summer when the terrace is open.

## GRILL Map pp236–8 *International*

☎ 31 45 30; Drottninggatan 89; starters Skr95-195, mains Skr135-285; 🕑 lunch & dinner until 1am (10pm Sun); T-Rådmansgatan

This oddly homey restaurant, started by renowned chefs Melker Andersson (of Fredsgatan 12) and Danyel Couet, inhabits a sprawling space that looks like a furniture shop, with 10 small dining areas that are set up like demonstration living rooms. The menu is arranged by grill type: rotisserie, charcoal, barbecue etc. Mix and match dishes with choices like Asian table-grilled tuna, barbecued beef brisket, blackened salmon, wood-fired duck, scrumptious desserts –

*Eyubi (above)*

and don't neglect the extensive wine list, which is also conveniently organised by flavour. The restaurant's service is both casual and accommodating.

## HAGA RESTAURANG & DELIKATESSER
Map pp231–3                                    *Italian*

☎ 31 96 95; Hagagatan 18; pizzas Skr79-89, pasta Skr94-129, mains Skr139-179; ⓨ lunch & dinner; T-Rådmansgatan

This cosy and friendly Italian-style family restaurant includes an old-fashioned tiled deli section. Italian wines are served. Antipasti and desserts feature on the menu, and the pizzas are particularly good.

## LA HABANA Map pp231–3                         *Cuban*

☎ 16 64 65; Sveavägen 108; mains Skr100-150; ⓨ dinner, to 1am; T-Rådmansgatan

Though better known as a salsa dance club, La Habana is also a good Cuban restaurant with friendly staff and a great atmosphere. Cuban cigars, beer and excellent rum-based drinks are available, and afterwards you can work off your dinner dancing to salsa music in the basement.

## LAO WAI Map pp231–3          *Vegetarian-Chinese*

☎ 673 78 00; Luntmakargatan 74; mains Skr100-185; ⓨ dinner Tue-Sat; T-Rådmansgatan

This strictly vegetarian restaurant is heavy on philosophy (the menu is more of a manifesto) and simple in presentation. In a small white room with simple wooden tables, spices coax miraculous flavours out of various tofu and vegetable combinations.

## LE BISTROT DE WASAHOF
Map p230                                        *Seafood*

☎ 32 34 40; Dalagatan 46; mains Skr140-220; ⓨ dinner, bar until 1am, closed Sun; T-Odenplan

Here you'll find a genuine bistro milieu, including wooden tables and lamps, a huge range of seafood (from oysters to lobsters to whelks) and an extensive wine list. Meals are beautifully presented and the service is exemplary, but you'll need to reserve a table up to three days in advance. The same menu is available at Musslan, the hipper, more club-like bar next door.

## LEONARDO Map pp231–3                          *Italian*

☎ 30 40 21; Sveavägen 55; pasta Skr90-125, pizza Skr75-100, mains Skr155-190; ⓨ lunch & dinner; T-Rådmansgatan

There's a huge menu at this excellent, cosy Italian restaurant, where the house speciality is wood-fired oven pizza (also available for takeaway).

## MOONCAKE Map pp231–3                           *Asian*

☎ 16 99 28; www.mooncake.se; Luntmakargatan 95; mains Skr190-275; ⓨ dinner Mon-Sat; T-Rådmansgatan, bus 4, 42, 43, 46, 52, 72

The menu of modern Chinese and Vietnamese cuisine at always-crowded MoonCake features inventive takes on traditional meat and fish dishes, including monkfish and Peking duck, as well as Vietnamese spring rolls and an impressive range of vegetarian options.

## NARKNOI BAR & RESTAURANG
Map p230                                          *Thai*

☎ 30 70 70; Odengatan 94; mains Skr121-184; ⓨ lunch & dinner, Sat & Sun dinner only; T-St Eriksplan, bus 3, 4, 47, 72

This award-winning, friendly and unpretentious restaurant is fairly small, with minimalist styles. The mild to hot dishes on the menu include many types of meat and fish and a less expensive vegetarian selection. Book well in advance.

## OPERAKÄLLAREN Map pp236–8                     *French*

☎ 676 58 00; Karl XII's Torg; starters Skr275-310, mains Skr380-410, tasting menus from Skr895 (Skr550 vegetarian); ⓨ 5-10pm; T-Kungsträdgården

The finest place within the Opera House is the century-old Operakällaren (the Opera Cellar), with fantastic décor (it has to be seen to be believed), deep red carpets, paintings and extravagant furnishings. The gourmet menu, printed in French, includes caviar, fish, hare and pigeon. Try the chocolate soufflé with liquorice ice-cream for dessert. It's also known as the place to go for the ultimate traditional *julbord* (Christmas *smörgåsbord*). Men must wear a suit and tie in order to be admitted. To get a table here on weekends, you'll need to make reservations a fortnight in advance.

## ORIENTEXPRESSEN RESTAURANG
& BAR Map pp236–8                             *Swedish*

☎ 20 20 49; Centralstationen; starters Skr70-135, mains Skr89-225, 2-course lunch/dinner Skr185/275; ⓨ breakfast, lunch & dinner, until late; T-Centralen

This place inside Central Station is an old Stockholm favourite, serving certified organic meals in authentic reproductions of railway carriages. The food is great value; try the braised char in butter sauce or the fried root vegetables and Västerbotten cheese in a creamy basil sauce.

### RABARBER Map p230 *Swedish*
☎ 31 17 75; Karlbergsvägen 52; mains Skr85-100; ☾ 4pm-1am; T-St Eriksplan

The bar in this friendly neighbourhood restaurant is popular with an after-work crowd and serves tasty traditional Swedish meals. It doubles as an art gallery, with some fairly wild stuff.

### RESTAURANG MALAYSIA
Map pp231–3 *Malaysian*
☎ 633 56 69; Luntmakargatan 98; mains Skr125-185; ☾ lunch & dinner; T-Rådmansgatan

The excellent food in this tropical-style restaurant has been recommended by Asian visitors to Stockholm. It includes noodle and rice dishes as well as beef, lamb, duck, fish and cuttlefish.

### RESTAURANG PATPONG
Map pp231–3 *Thai*
☎ 458 95 67; Luntmakargatan 63; 4-course lunch buffet Skr65-85, soups Skr35-55, mains Skr85-135; T-Rådmansgatan

This fine Thai restaurant has minimalist décor but a luxurious atmosphere. Try the Thai-style fondue, with marinated meat and seafood.

### RESTAURANG SPICE HOUSE
Map pp236–8 *Indian*
☎ 14 10 32; Upplandsgatan 6; lunch from Skr65, mains from Skr80; ☾ lunch & dinner

At this uncluttered, neighbourhood Indian restaurant the food is authentic, portions are large and the vegetarian dishes are highly recommended.

### RESTAURANT ANNA RELLA
Map pp236–8 *International*
☎ 51 72 63 00; Scandic Hotel Sergel Plaza, Brunkebergstorg 9; mains Skr95-230, lunch husmanskost from Skr120; ☾ 11.30am-2pm Mon-Fri & 6pm-late; T-Centralen

This fine restaurant's discreet alcoves are popular with Swedish politicians for lunchtime conversations, so you need to make sure you book well in advance. The restaurant has a heavy 1980s style with an emphasis on blue, and it becomes a piano bar at night. It has competitive prices and an international-style

menu that caters to most tastes and includes salads, fish, meat and vegetarian options.

### RESTAURANT KB Map pp236–8 *Swedish*
☎ 679 60 32; Smålandsgatan 7; starters Skr95, dagens husmanskost Skr120-150, mains Skr180-250, bar menu Skr75-125; ☾ 11.30am-midnight Mon-Fri, 5pm-midnight Sat; T-Centralen

KB stands for 'Konstnärs Bar' – the Artists' Bar. On the ground floor of Konstnärs Huset, which provides housing, studio space and classes for artists, the restaurant serves traditional Swedish cuisine in arrangements that, as you might expect, highlight each plate's visual beauty. The assorted herring and anything vegetarian or fish-based are highly recommended. The attached bar has wall paintings that date from 1931.

### ROLFS KÖK Map pp236–8 *Eclectic*
☎ 10 16 96; Tegnérgatan 41; mains Skr165-250; ☾ 11-1am Mon-Fri, 5pm-1am Sat & Sun; T-Rådmansgatan

At this friendly, '90s-style fusion restaurant, you can either get table service or sit at the central bar. The unusual décor, by noted designers Thomas Sandell and Jonas Bohlin, includes chairs hanging from the walls. Fish, duck and lamb are on the menu, and the wine list describes which wines should be paired with each course.

### SABAI SABAI Map pp236–8 *Thai*
☎ 790 09 13; Kammakargatan 44; mains Skr85-179; ☾ dinner; T-Rådmansgatan

Friendly and laid-back Sabai Sabai, frequently named as Stockholm's best Thai restaurant, serves great food in an ornate tropical-style interior. The extensive menu includes wok, noodle, curry, fish and seafood dishes. Reservations are recommended.

### STADSHUSKÄLLAREN
Map pp236–8 *Swedish*
☎ 650 54 54; Stadshuset, Hantverkargatan 1; mains Skr185-270, Nobel Menu Skr1350 including wine; ☾ 11.30am-11pm Mon-Fri & 2-11pm Sat; T-Centralen, bus 3, 62

This chic restaurant, where the Nobel Prize Banquet is prepared, has two main rooms with impressive paintings on the walls and vaulted ceilings. The seasonal à la carte menu always has a variety of well-presented meat and fish dishes, and you can choose to eat the Nobel Banquet menu (see the boxed text, p111) from any year it was served, starting in

## The Nobel Banquet – A Prize Feast

The conventional wisdom that Alfred Nobel created the Nobel Prize to appease his conscience after inventing dynamite makes for a nice story, but the facts don't quite bear it out. Nobel (1833–96), a Swedish chemist, engineer and industrialist, made his name and fortune partly by inventing and patenting weapons technology, long after the destructive nature of dynamite had become clear.

Nobel had moved to St Petersberg with his family when he was nine years old. While studying abroad he met the inventor of nitroglycerine, Ascanio Sobrero; later, back in Russia, he played around with ways to control the substance. In 1862 he patented a detonator for it. Four years later, having moved back to Sweden in 1863, he made the remarkable discovery that the chalky material kieselguhr could absorb nitroglycerine safely while remaining an explosive substance. This combination became known as dynamite.

It didn't take long, of course, for the practical uses of a stable, transportable, extremely powerful explosive to become apparent. Nobel's factories expanded enormously to cope with demand, increasing their output 6000-fold over the next 30 years.

By then a very wealthy industrialist, Nobel continued his work as an inventor throughout his life; he owned 355 patents by the time he died. His will created the annual Nobel Prizes (starting in 1901) in physics, chemistry, medicine/physiology, literature and peace, to be awarded to those who had benefited mankind the most in the preceding year. A sixth prize, for economics, was added in 1969, sponsored by the Swedish National Bank.

Each year on 10 December, the anniversary of Nobel's death, the prizes are awarded by the king of Sweden at Konserthuset; the Peace Prize is given simultaneously in Oslo. After the ceremony, the Nobel Banquet is held in the Blue Hall at Stadshuset. There are about 1350 guests including prizewinners and their families, international guests representing science and literature, members of the royal family, representatives from the government and MPs.

The banquet, covered by Swedish and international media, is a vast affair. Laying the tables takes 30 people six hours, and there's a serving staff of 240. The 25 chefs produce three different menus; 340 bottles of champagne are consumed during the first course and 340 bottles of wine wash down the main course. The after-dinner drink is a mere 330L of coffee!

You don't have to wait until you receive your Nobel Prize to eat the Nobel Banquet, however. Visitors to Stockholm can enjoy the previous year's Nobel Menu at Stadshuskällaren, the restaurant in the basement of Stadshuset (see opposite). Sure, it's not quite like dining in the Blue Hall, but the food is spectacular nonetheless.

1901. (Nobel menus from all but the previous year are available only to groups of eight or more, and you must reserve in advance.)

### STORSTAD Map pp231–3 *Swedish*
☎ 673 38 00; Odengatan 41; mains Skr150-225; ☽ dinner; T-Odenplan

You'll get a good meal and excellent service in this design-heavy but unpretentious restaurant. The international menu includes a reasonable range of meat and fish dishes. At night it's one of the city's most energetic bars (see p125).

### TENNSTOPET Map p230 *Swedish*
☎ 32 25 18; Dalagatan 50; mains Skr114-267; ☽ 4pm-1am Mon-Fri, 1pm-1am Sat & Sun; T-Odenplan, T-St Eriksplan

This traditional and laid-back bar/restaurant, the oldest pub in Stockholm, has a very pleasant, comfortable atmosphere, with paintings, mirrors and padded chairs. There's a wide seasonal range of *husmanskost*; specials start at Skr90.

## CHEAP EATS

### 11350 CAFÉ & DELI Map pp231–3 *Café*
☎ 15 74 45; Sveavägen 98; sandwiches/salads from Skr35/48; ☽ 9am-9pm Mon-Fri, 11am-5pm Sat, noon-6pm Sun; T-Odenplan

This trendy place just off Odenplan appeals to the 18 to 30 set, with its picture windows, loud music, hearty sandwiches and filling pasta salads.

### CAFÉ PANORAMA Map pp236–8 *Café*
☎ 21 10 35; 5th floor Kulturhuset, Sergels Torg 3; coffee & pastries Skr35, sandwiches from Skr55; ☽ lunch & dinner; T-Centralen

This vast cafeteria on the 5th floor of Kulturhuset offers affordable meals and fabulous views over the city. If all the window seats are full, there's a larger café with more seating one level down, which also serves affordable and filling meals and has almost as good a view.

### CAFE SIRAP Map pp231–3 *Café*
☎ 642 94 19; Surbrunnsgatan 31A; breakfast & lunch from Skr55; ☽ 9am-7pm; T-Rådmansgatan

This small, pleasant, no-frills brunch place serves a full eggs-and-bacon breakfast that's popular at the weekend (vegetarian options available). The huge menu also includes American pancakes and various sandwiches. If you want a leisurely meal, come on a weekday; the weekends are crowded and can feel rushed.

### CAFÉ VIVELS Map pp236–8 *Café*
☎ 20 01 57; Kungsgatan 7; husmanskost Skr65-85; ⓨ 8am-10pm Mon-Thu, 8am-1am Fri, 11am-1am Sat, 1pm-10pm Sun; T-Östermalmstorg or T-Hötorget

Vivels is a large and bright – though smoky – café serving hot breakfast, salads, wok dishes, good club sandwiches and desserts.

### KONDITORI RITORNO Map p230 *Café*
☎ 32 01 06; Odengatan 80-82; coffee & pastries from Skr25; ⓨ 7am-10pm Mon-Fri, 8am-6pm Sat, 10am-6pm Sun; T-St Eriksplan

Serving scrumptious pastries and with a sweet back room that looks just like the lobby of an antique movie house that has fallen on hard times, Konditori Ritorno is one of the most comfortable cafés in Stockholm. Miniature jukeboxes grace each table (and they actually work!), smoking students glare into textbooks, and punks and pensioners commingle with families.

### KUNGSHALLEN Map pp236–8 *Food Hall*
☎ 21 80 05; Kungsgatan 44; ⓨ 9am-11pm Mon-Fri, 11am-11pm Sat, noon-11pm Sun; T-Östermalmstorg or T-Hötorget

Kungshallen is a vast food court across the street from Hötorget where you can eat anything from Tex-Mex to Indian at budget prices; things change quickly and the quality at some places is dubious, so sniff around before you decide. The American-style coffee shop Robert's Coffee serves ice cream, milk shakes and a good range of speciality coffees (Skr17 to Skr32). The upstairs sushi bar Ikki has good food and a nice atmosphere (daily sushi lunch special Skr65). A range of fast food bars in the basement churns out kebabs, pasta, wok dishes, curries and tacos.

### LUNDBERG Map p230 *International*
☎ 30 57 47; Rörstrandgatan 14; mains Skr65-95; ⓨ 11am-11pm Mon-Sat; T-St Eriksplan

At small, quiet Lundberg, you'll find brick walls, a modern-design bar and an international menu with good food and friendly service.

### PICCOLINO Map pp236–8 *Café*
Kungsträdgården; sandwiches Skr35-65; ⓨ breakfast, lunch & dinner

Popular as much for its setting and the building itself as for the food, Piccolino is a glassed-in café at the edge of Kungsträdgården, the ideal spot to see and be seen – which makes it popular with models and voyeurs alike. Some say it was the first espresso bar in Stockholm.

### SOSTA Map pp231–3 *Café*
☎ 612 13 49; Sveavägen 84; coffee from Skr15; ⓨ 8am-7pm Mon-Fri, 10am-5pm Sat, 11am-4pm Sun; T-Rådmansgatan

If you're craving Italian espresso the way they serve it in Italy, here is where you go. Elbow your way up to the counter – no tables in this tiny shop – and bellow your order in the least Swedish way you can manage. Cornetti, gelato and focaccia are recommended.

### VETEKATTEN Map pp236–8 *Café*
☎ 21 84 54; Kungsgatan 55; tea, coffee & snacks from Skr25; ⓨ 7.30am-8pm Mon-Fri, 9am-5pm Sat, noon-5pm Sun; T-Hötorget

Popular with shoppers and families, the labyrinthine Vetekatten is one of the city's most traditional cafés, with lots of small rooms and a great atmosphere. You can also buy baked goods, large sandwiches and cakes to take away.

### ÅHLÉNS CAFÉ Map pp236–8 *Café*
☎ 676 60 00; Klarabergsgatan 50, top floor of Åhléns; husmanskost from Skr65, sandwiches from Skr55; ⓨ 10am-6.30pm Mon-Fri, 10am-5.30pm Sat, noon-3.30pm Sun; T-Centralen

This vaguely Italian cafeteria in the Åhléns department store also has a large weekday vegetarian buffet and offers 25% discount on takeaways. The seating area is large and pleasant, with a nice view over the city from some of the window tables. The *dagens rätt* meals are recommended.

# DJURGÅRDEN & SKEPPSHOLMEN

The museum-laden park island of Djurgården is home to some of the most pleasant places to eat in Stockholm, thanks to its sprawling, garden setting and relaxed atmosphere. In fine weather, few things are nicer than taking a leisurely stroll then lingering over lunch in a backyard garden full of flowers.

## BLÅ PORTEN CAFE Map pp231–3 *Café*
☎ 663 87 59; Djurgårdsvägen 64; pastries from Skr15, mains Skr65-105; ☙ 11am-7pm (to 9pm Tue & Thu), longer hours Jun-Aug; bus 44, 47, tram 7
Best on a sunny day, when you can linger over lunch in the garden, this café next to Liljevalchs Konsthall offers an amazing display of baked goods. The Swedish and international meals are particularly recommended.

## KROGKONST Map pp239–41 *Swedish*
☎ 611 99 89; Amiralitetsbacken 3, Skeppsholmen; lunch from Skr90, salad buffet Skr60; ☙ 11.30am-2.30pm Mon-Fri; bus 44, 47, tram 7
A bright and airy restaurant on Skeppsholmen with a vast patio, Krogkonst – formerly Normans Mat & Form – has gone a little more upmarket but preserved the tradition of combining good food and interesting art; it features small, temporary exhibits of painting, sculpture and modern design. Food servings are generous – at lunch you choose from a fish, meat or vegetarian dish, plus soup and salad. Service is very friendly and the wine list is surprisingly good. Patio service is open on sunny days 'until the sun sets over *af Chapman*'.

## RESTAURANG HASSELBACKEN
Map pp231–3 *Swedish*
☎ 51 73 43 07; www.restauranghasselbacken.com; Hazeliusbacken 20; 2-/3-course menu Skr325/375; ☙ 10am-2pm & 5-10pm Mon-Fri, 1-10pm Sat & 1-9pm Sun; 1-10pm Mon-Sat late Jun–mid-Aug (restricted menu); bus 44, 47, tram 7
This restaurant, in Scandic Hotel Hasselbacken, serves fine classical Swedish meals with foreign influences in a wonderful jewel-box dining room dating from 1923. The menu includes such twists on *husmanskost* as reindeer fillet with *Västerbottens ost*, potatoes and morel-currant gravy. There is an intricately carved ceiling and a raised dining area with alcoves and sofas.

## VÄRDSHUSET ULLA WINBLADH
Map pp231–3 *Swedish*
☎ 663 05 71; www.ullawinbladh.se; Rosendalsvägen 8; starters Skr95-140, mains Skr195-290, daily lunch Skr80; ☙ lunch & dinner; bus 44, 47, tram 7
Named after one of Carl Michael Bellman's lovers, this villa was built as a steam bakery for the Stockholm World's Fair (1897) and now

serves fine food in an early-20th-century-style restaurant with a garden setting. The menu features international dishes and traditional Swedish meals, including meatballs and crayfish tails, and it's known for an outstanding herring *smörgåsbord*.

## WÄRDSHUSET GODTHEM
Map pp231–3 *Swedish*
☎ 661 07 22; Rosendalsvägen 9; 2-/3-course menu Skr185/225; ☙ 11.30am-midnight Mon-Fri, noon-midnight Sat & Sun; bus 44, 47
Just across the road from Värdshuset Ulla Winbladh, this strange-looking grey building with an octagonal tower and spire is another early-20th-century-style restaurant. The rows of light bulbs don't inspire confidence, but the food, largely steak- and salmon-based, is high quality. Other main courses include smoked salmon, smoked reindeer and braised monkfish (anglerfish).

# CHEAP EATS
## ROSENDALS TRÄDGÅRD
Map pp231–3 *Café*
☎ 54 58 12 70; Rosendalsterrassen 12; cakes & pies from Skr35; ☙ winter 11am-4pm Tue-Sun, summer 11am-5pm daily; bus 47 (15 min walk from Djurgårdsbron)
Rosendals is an idyllic spot for a fruit pastry and coffee in the summer or a warm cup of *glögg* and a *lussekatte* (saffron roll) in winter. If the weather is ugly, skulk around the gardens and greenhouses, look moody and pretend you're Strindberg.

# KUNGSHOLMEN
There are a number of great neighbourhood eateries in this part of town, including one of the city's most authentic Chinese restaurants, a stylish Cuban bar, a Hare Krishna–run vegetarian buffet and a homey *konditori*. Prices and pretension levels are low.

## Kungsholmen Top Five
- Spisa Hos Helena (p114)
- El Cubanito (p114)
- Hong Kong (p114)
- Govindas (p114)
- Salzer Restaurant & Bar (p114)

## EL CUBANITO Map p230 *Cuban*

☎ 650 12 38; Scheelegatan 3; starters Skr60-70, mains Skr125-195; 🕑 dinner, bar until late; T-Rådhuset

This tiny Cuban bar and restaurant's luscious dark wooden floor, pressed-tin bar and decorative ceramic tiles give it the lived-in feel of a stylish old bodega. On the menu are favourites like *ropa vieja* (shredded beef; literally 'old clothes'), fried plantains, tropical chicken and flan for dessert, plus specialities such as *arroz a la Hemingway*, red snapper marinated in cardamom, and Cuban approaches to Swedish ingredients, like fillet of venison in lingon and guava. You can also, of course, get Cuban cigars and a wide selection of rum drinks (see p125).

## HONG KONG Map p230 *Chinese*

☎ 653 77 20; Kungsbro Strand 23; starters Skr75-90, mains Skr115-200, Peking duck Skr1460; 🕑 lunch & dinner; bus 1, 40, 59

Restaurang Hong Kong serves a good range of authentic Chinese dishes, but what brings people here to celebrate special occasions is the Peking duck, which serves four and must be ordered two days in advance.

## HOT WOK CAFÉ Map p230 *Asian*

☎ 654 42 02; Hantverkargatan 78; lunch Skr65-95, mains Skr120-180; 🕑 11am-midnight Mon-Fri, 1pm-midnight Sat & Sun

Contemporary art and trendy music feature strongly in this busy place, where you order one of a handful of cutely named dishes at the counter. The staff are friendly, the service is fast, and the pan-Asian, noodle- and veg-based meals are enormous.

## MAMAS & TAPAS Map p230 *Spanish*

☎ 653 53 90; Scheelegatan 3; tapas Skr35, mains Skr75-150; 🕑 4pm-1am Mon-Fri & noon-1am Sat & Sun; T-Rådhuset

Mamas & Tapas is a bustling tapas joint; it isn't spectacularly authentic, but it makes a fun stop for pre-clubbing drinks and snacks. A couple of Spanish sandwiches are also available, if you want something more substantial. Kitschier than El Cubanito next door, the bar here sports brightly coloured tiles and effusive Spanish-style art.

## SALZER RESTAURANT & BAR

Map p230 *Swedish*

☎ 650 30 28; John Ericssonsgatan 6; starters Skr12-150, mains Skr160-220, Sunday brunch buffet Skr150; 🕑 5pm-midnight Mon-Sat, noon-8pm Sun; T-Rådhuset, bus 3, 40, 52, 62

The menu at this well-liked *kvarterskrog* (neighbourhood pub) features Swedish and continental choices, including vegetarian. The Swedish country sausage called *isterband*, served over potatoes in a cream sauce, is a favourite dish here. You can also try the local Kungsholmen brew, Lundbergs lager. Prices are lower in the 'Propeller *bakfickan*', so called because John Ericsson, after whom the street is named, invented the propeller.

## SPISA HOS HELENA Map p230 *Eclectic*

☎ 654 49 26; www.spisahoshelena.se; Scheelegatan 18; starters Skr75-100, mains Skr130-200; 🕑 lunch & dinner, to midnight Sat, closed Sun; T-Rådhuset, bus 1, 3, 40, 52, 62

This tiny, atmospheric bar and restaurant, with rich red walls and low candlelight, emphasises grilled fish and seafood, as well as offering new twists on traditional meals like beef Rydberg or Swedish meatballs with pickles, lingon and potatoes. The small bar area up front is a warm, cosy place to meet for a drink or a coffee and one of Helena's homemade truffles (Skr22).

# CHEAP EATS

## CAFÉ JULIA Map p230 *Café*

☎ 651 45 15; St Eriksgatan 15; dagens rätt Skr65, soup special Skr55; 🕑 10.30am-9pm Mon-Thu & 10.30am-7pm Fri-Sun; T-Fridhemsplan, bus 3, 52, 94

The attractive art and minimalist style in this airy café complement the food perfectly. Try one of the home-made soft cheeses, from a fiercely guarded secret recipe that started in the café owners' small apartment.

## GELATERIA ITALIANA Map p230 *Ice Cream*

☎ 653 01 40; Drottningholmsvägen 22; sandwiches from Skr35, ice cream scoop Skr12; T-Fridhemsplan

A small coffee shop serving excellent toasted sandwiches and home-made ice cream, this gelateria is known as a haunt of SL bus drivers.

## GOVINDAS Map p230 *Vegetarian*

☎ 654 90 04; Fridhemsgatan 22; small/large lunch menu Skr65/85; 🕑 11am-7pm Mon-Fri, 12-7pm Sat; T-Fridhemsplan

The authentically decorated, Hare Krishna–run Govindas restaurant is cafeteria-style and offers an imaginative vegetarian menu in two sizes, both enormous; the offerings change daily but are always interesting and unusual. Don't miss the mini pancakes if they're available.

### INDIAN CURRY HOUSE Map p230    *Indian*
☎ 650 20 24; Scheelegatan 6; lunch from Skr50, specials Skr65-120; ☺ lunch; T-Rådhuset
The food in this small, basic restaurant, often referred to as Stockholm's cheapest Indian restaurant, is delicious and includes samosas, curries, thali and murgh dishes. Takeaways are possible.

### R.O.O.M. Map p230    *Café*
☎ 692 50 00; www.room.se; Alströmergatan 20; coffee & pastries from Skr35; ☺ 10am-6.30pm Mon-Fri, 10am-5pm Sat, 11am-5pm Sun; T-Fridhemsplan
The café at this design shop (see p147) serves great coffee, sandwiches, salads, and healthful desserts to weary shoppers. There are also occasional DJ gigs in the evenings.

### THELINS KONDITORI Map p230    *Café*
☎ 651 19 00; St Eriksgatan 43; coffee & cakes from Skr35; ☺ 7.30am-7pm Mon-Fri, 9am-5pm Sat & Sun
A traditional, old-fashioned *konditori* with red-velvet-covered theatre-style furniture, faux-Parisian white streetlamps sticking up in the middle of the dining area and curtained-off booths in the large back room, Thelins is all charm. Its display case contains some of the best and most beautiful cakes and pastries in Stockholm.

# SÖDERMALM & LÅNGHOLMEN

The food options in Söder, like everything else in this artsy part of town, are just a little edgier, a little more individualistic and a little more off-beat than in the rest of Stockholm. Diners can choose among old-school Swedish beer halls like Pelikan, neo-retro design havens like Metro, vegan hang-outs like Chutney or a busy hole-in-the-wall run by one of the most renowned sushi chefs in the city.

### CHUTNEY Map pp234–5    *Vegetarian*
☎ 640 30 10; www.chutney.se; Katarina Bangata 19; salads Skr85-95, mains Skr110-125; ☺ lunch & dinner until midnight, closes 11pm Sun; T-Skanstull or T-Medborgarplatsen
This trendy, always-hopping vegetarian restaurant dishes out complex soups and stews

## Södermalm & Långholmen Top Five
- Pelikan (p117)
- Östgötakällaren (p117)
- Matkultur (p116)
- Koh Phangan (p116)
- Crêperie Fyra Knop (p118)

for lunch and really inventive vegetarian or vegan cuisine for dinner, including potato pancakes with sour cream and beets, a rich mushroom ravioli, and a silken roasted pumpkin and coconut stew. There are also good versions of vegan standards – sautéed tofu and vegetables, meatless burrito – and organic wine. Outdoor dining is available in summer.

### DIONYSOS Map pp234–5    *Greek*
☎ 641 91 13; Bondegatan 56; lunch Skr65-95, set menus Skr165-240; T-Medborgarplatsen
Dionysos is a charming and friendly place that opened in 1974 – the first Greek restaurant in Stockholm. The menu includes tzatziki, moussaka and a vegetarian dish. Greek wines, ouzo and a long list of cocktails are available. Nuovo, a new 'sister inn' next door, is now open during lunch.

### ERIKS GONDOLEN Map pp239–41    *Swedish*
☎ 641 70 90; Stadsgården 6; 2-/3-course menu Skr320/395, weekday lunch Skr95-295, dinner Skr255-450; ☺ lunch & dinner until 1am; T-Slussen
With perhaps the most unusual location in Stockholm – at the top of Katarinahissen, the Slussen elevator built in 1883 – Gondolen offers fantastic views, a dizzyingly patterned wood floor, comfortable armchairs in the bar and fine food. The herring and warm cloudberries with ice cream are particularly recommended. The bar has a lower-priced bistro menu.

### FENIX Map pp239–41    *Eclectic*
☎ 640 45 06; Götgatan 40; starters Skr7-90, mains Skr142-187; ☺ lunch & dinner, bar until 1am; T-Slussen
This modern, colourful international-style restaurant/bar, jammed from checkerboard floor to moulded ceiling with eclectic art and designer furniture, is a busy place serving bar-friendly snacks such as nachos, wok dishes, Cajun tortillas and sushi.

Eating – Södermalm & Långholmen

Eriks Gondolen (p115)

## FOLKHEMMET

Map pp234–5        *Swedish-Crossover*

☎ 640 55 95; Renstiernas Gata 30; mains Skr120-198, set menus Skr85/125/215; ☯ dinner, bar until 1am; bus 46, 53, 59, 66, 76

Filed under 'only in Sweden' is this madly popular socialist-run bar and restaurant, named after the Social Democratic Party's conception of a welfare state (The People's Home). But the food is nowhere near as proletarian as that might imply. The ambitious menu, which changes eight to 10 times a year, features such combinations as redbeet tartlets and asparagus salad with truffle vinaigrette.

## INDIRA INDISK RESTAURANG & BAR

Map pp234–5        *Indian*

☎ 641 40 46; Bondegatan 3B; mains Skr95-135, vegetarian Skr75-90; ☯ 5-11pm Mon, 3-11pm Tue-Fri, 1-11pm Sat & Sun; T-Medborgarplatsen

The opulent Indian-style décor at this popular restaurant includes an aquarium; the huge menu features good authentic food. Don't miss the uniquely sweet saffron ice cream for dessert.

## KOH PHANGAN Map pp234–5      *Thai*

☎ 642 68 65; Skånegatan 57; mains Skr125-265; ☯ dinner until 1am; T-Medborgarplatsen or T-Skanstull, bus 59

This outrageously kitsch Thai restaurant has to be seen to be believed. It's best at night, when you can enjoy your meal in a real tuk-tuk to the accompanying racket of crickets and a tropical thunderstorm. The food is good, but service tends to be sluggish. There's a DJ after 10pm, Tuesday to Sunday.

## LITTLE PERSIA Map pp234–5     *Persian*

☎ 644 85 69; Östgötagatan 32; salads Skr75-90, mains Skr1120-195; T-Medborgarplatsen, bus 59, 66

Expect the best in Persian home cooking here, but you'll need to relax among the huge cushions and the pleasant atmosphere, since your dinner will take most of the evening to be served. The menu includes vegetarian and kebab dishes.

## LO SCUDETTO Map pp234–5      *Italian*

☎ 640 42 15; Åsögatan 163; pasta from Skr95, mains Skr175-225; ☯ dinner, closed Sun; bus 46, 59, 66, 76, 53

Lo Scudetto, named after an Italian football trophy, is a pleasant, minimalist-style restaurant serving some of the best Italian food in town, with a notable wine list and good friendly service.

## MATKULTUR Map pp234–5      *Eclectic*

☎ 642 03 53; Erstagatan 21; mains Skr135-200; ☯ lunch & dinner, closed Sun; bus 3, 46, 53, 66, 76

This is a bright, arty restaurant dedicated to exploring international food. The frequently changing menu includes things like Cambodian beef with lemongrass jasmine rice, achiote-marinated chicken baked in banana leaves, and a curry burger. Its Turkish-influenced lamb dishes are always popular. At the attached bar, El Mundo, DJs play world music for media types and mega hipsters.

## MEST Map pp234–5      *International*

☎ 641 36 53; Götgatan 46; mains Skr98-198; T-Slussen or T-Medborgarplatsen

You'll get good food and good service in this large, modern-style bar. Check the daily specials menu, which usually includes a grilled fish and at least one vegetarian option – dishes include a vegetarian lasagne, grilled salmon with pepper aioli, and a Lebanese-style penne pasta served with kebab meat and yogurt sauce.

## METRÓ Map pp234–5 *Swedish*
☎ 442 03 20; www.metrosthlm.com; Götgatan 93; mains Skr135-230; ⏰ dinner until 1am, to 2am Fri & Sat; T-Skanstull

A sprawling, multilevel space with gorgeous, over-the-top '60s-influenced design, Metró was opened by chef Kim Bjälvenäs, who spent some time in the kitchen of New York's famed Swedish restaurant Aquavit. Items like tournedos with truffle-and-cognac sauce, swordfish, and a shellfish cannelloni with mussel gravy grace the menu. The hopping, Moulin Rouge–style bar has DJ music most nights.

## PELIKAN Map pp234–5 *Swedish*
☎ 55 60 90 90; Blekingegatan 40; mains Skr75-185; ⏰ dinner daily & lunch Sat & Sun; minimum age 23; T-Skanstull, bus 3, 55, 59, 74

This well-established place has a unique atmosphere with rooms in three different styles, including a German-style beer hall (see p127) with monkeys painted on the pillars and ceiling. The food is good – the menu is classic *husmanskost*, and there's usually a vegetarian special on the blackboard.

## RESTAURANG HO'S Map pp234–5 *Chinese*
☎ 84 44 20; www.restauranghos.com; Hornsgatan 151; mains from Skr150; ⏰ closed Mon, lunch & dinner Tue-Fri, dinner only Sat & Sun; T-Hornstull, bus 4, 74

One of the most authentic Chinese restaurants in Stockholm, Ho's has none of the kitsch but all of the quality. It's sparsely decorated, and atmosphere is created with soft Chinese music. Dumplings are recommended, as are the mussels with black beans and paprika and the shellfish in hot pepper sauce.

## RESTAURANG MING PALACE
Map pp239–41 *Chinese*
☎ 640 86 86; Mariatorget 2; lunch from Skr60, mains Skr95-145; ⏰ lunch & dinner; T-Mariatorget

Ming Palace is an authentic Chinese restaurant, with elegant black-and-white décor, a goldfish pond and a waterfall. Particularly recommended are the four-course special and the ice cream with preserved ginger.

## SODA Map pp239–41 *Café*
☎ 462 00 75; Bellmansgatan 26; snacks Skr20-30; ⏰ 8am-8pm Mon-Fri, 10am-7pm Sat & Sun; T-Slussen

A smoky café that's full of moody teens and 20-somethings mooning over their diaries and stealing secret glances at each other, Soda serves coffee American-style in huge green and yellow mugs. It has endearingly indie-rock artwork on the walls, and best of all it'll let you read its diaries.

## SONJAS GREK Map pp234–5 *Greek*
☎ 702 22 29; Bondegatan 54; lunch from Skr85, mains Skr85-195; ⏰ lunch & dinner; T-Medborgarplatsen

Close to Dionysos, this restaurant offers stylish dining, fine examples of the usual Greek dishes, friendly staff and an ouzo bar.

## SUSHI BAR SONE Map pp234–5 *Sushi*
☎ 668 29 88; Ringvägen 8; mains Skr65-145; ⏰ lunch & dinner Mon-Fri, 3-9pm Sat; T-Zinkensdamm

This tiny shopfront right outside the Zinkensdamm *tunnelbana* station could be the best sushi place in town. Go for whatever Mr Sone has as a special; it'll be squirmingly fresh. Handrolls (the big cone-shaped ones) are particularly recommended.

## ÖSTGÖTAKÄLLAREN
Map pp234–5 *Swedish*
☎ 643 22 40; Östgötagatan 41; mains Skr80-180; ⏰ dinner until midnight; T-Medborgarplatsen

This place has everything to recommend it – a dimly lit romantic atmosphere, friendly service and unpretentious *husmanskost* like Swedish meatballs, *pytt i panna* and all sorts of fish. It's a nice place to linger over a beer or glass of wine.

# CHEAP EATS
## AH'S GLASSBAR Map pp234–5 *Ice Cream*
Skånegatan 85; cone (2 scoops) Skr15, sandwiches from Skr35; ⏰ lunch & dinner; T-Medborgarplatsen

You'll get the best ice cream in town at this little ice-cream parlour.

## CAFÉ STRING Map pp234–5 *Café*
☎ 714 85 14; Nytorgsgatan 38; mains from Skr55; ⏰ breakfast, lunch & dinner; T-Medborgarplatsen, bus 3, 59, 66

Café String is a hugely popular and atmospheric place that looks like a second-hand shop, and almost everything actually is for sale – you can buy your cup or even your chair. Besides coffee and cakes, there are lunch pies, baked potatoes and other affordable hot food choices.

Eating – Södermalm & Långholmen

117

## CRÊPERIE FYRA KNOP

Map pp239–41                                    *French*

☎ 640 77 27; Svartensgatan 4; crepes from Skr35, mains Skr60-80; 🕑 dinner Mon-Fri, lunch & dinner weekends; T-Slussen

Crêperie Fyra Knop serves excellent crepes in an intimate, romantic little building, with plenty of small rooms tucked away just off the main drag in Söder. A good place for a quiet chat before you hit the clubs down the street.

## HERMANS TRÄDGÅRDSCAFÉ

Map pp239–41                                *Vegetarian*

☎ 643 94 80; Fjällgatan 23A; lunch/dinner Skr85/125; 🕑 lunch & dinner to 9pm (to 11pm Jun-Aug); T-Slussen

At this place you'll get gigantic portions of excellent vegetarian food, served on tables in two barrel-vaulted basement rooms, or at the summer veranda seating with a five-star view. There's also a lunch buffet and home-made snacks are available as well.

## JERUSALEM ROYAL KEBAB

Map pp234–5                                 *Fast Food*

Götgatan 61; from Skr15; 🕑 24hr; T-Slussen or T-Medborgarplatsen

This rather unprepossessing kebab place is actually quite popular, and the kebabs and felafel sandwiches explain why. Of course, it doesn't hurt that it's open all night in the city's main bar-hopping neighbourhood; you should expect long queues around 3am, when clubbers get the munchies.

## LASSE I PARKEN Map pp234–5           *Café*

☎ 658 33 95; Högalidsgatan 56; coffee & pastries Skr20-40; 🕑 11am-4.30pm Tue-Sat May-Aug, 11am-5pm Sat & Sun Sep-Apr; T-Hornstull, bus 4, 66

Your coffee break can't get any cuter than at this adorably dilapidated little cottage in the middle of a park. The cheesecake's divine, there's a playground for the kids, and there are outdoor theatrical performances during the summer.

## NYSTEKT STRÖMMING

Map pp239–41                                  *Swedish*

Södermalmstorg; herring with potatoes about Skr30; 🕑 lunch & dinner; T-Slussen

As you'd expect from its name (Newly Fried Herring) you'll get some of the best fried herring in Stockholm from this little caravan located outside the *tunnelbana* station at Slussen.

### Östermalm Top Five

- Sturehof (opposite)
- Lydmar Hotel (below)
- Sturekatten (opposite)
- Örtagården (opposite)
- Grodan Grev Ture (below)

# ÖSTERMALM

Though better known for its clubs and nightlife, Östermalm is also home to some of the city's classiest restaurants. The common theme in this part of town is 'see and be seen', so dress like a film star and sit near the window.

## GRODAN GREV TURE

Map pp236–8                           *French-Italian*

☎ 679 61 00; Grev Turegatan 16; lunch Skr95, mains Skr97-202, dinner mains Skr127- 219; 🕑 11.30am-1am Mon-Thu, 11.30am-2am Fri & Sat; T-Östermalmstorg

This huge, sophisticated place includes modern dining areas, a raging cocktail bar and a picture-windowed 18th-century-style room with ornate plasterwork, antique paintings and lighting worthy of Rembrandt. The French-leaning menu, including venison, pike and vegetarian lasagne, is popular with young professional types.

## KHARMA RESTAURANT &
## NIGHTCLUB Map pp236–8                *Indian*

☎ 662 04 56; Sturegatan 10; 3-course menus Skr385-415; 🕑 dinner, closed Sun; T-Östermalmstorg

This classy and ultrahip dinner restaurant has an attractive modern Indian-style ambience and an even more attractive waiting staff. The menu features innovative takes on classic Swedish cuisine. There's also a swanky bar and nightclub.

## LYDMAR HOTEL Map pp236–8       *International*

☎ 56 61 13 00; www.lydmar.se; Sturegatan 10; mains from Skr95 lunch, from Skr150 dinner; 🕑 11.30-1am Mon-Thu, 11.30-2am Fri, 1pm-2am Sat, 1pm-1am Sun; minimum age 25; T-Östermalmstorg

In the wide-open restaurant section at the back of this chic hotel lobby/bar, a kind of rigorous simplicity reigns. Plates arrive clean and uncluttered, with nothing on them but one perfect-looking lamb shank, for example, or a beautifully cooked piece of fish. Diners can create their own meals by combining items from various parts of the menu; the number and amount of each item depends on how hungry you are. The dining room makes for great eye-candy, too – its picture windows, sporting huge etched-in fingerprints, put the hungry and beautiful people of Stockholm on fabulous display.

### RESTAURANT RICHE Map pp236–8 *French*
☎ 679 68 40; Birger Jarlsgatan 4; 3-course lunch Skr295, mains Skr110-265; ❧ lunch & dinner until 3am, closed Sun; T-Östermalmstorg

Restaurant Riche is a stylish establishment with a glass-fronted veranda and classical décor; one room deep in the interior of the restaurant displays statues and wigs. It's perfect for diners who like to be seen – Madonna reportedly ate here when she visited Stockholm. The fine menu has a French touch and includes steak, fish, veal and duck.

### STUREHOF Map pp236–8 *Swedish*
☎ 440 57 30; Stureplan 2; mains Skr95-330; ❧ 9-2am Mon-Fri, noon-2am Sat, 1pm-2am Sun (kitchen closes 1am); T-Östermalmstorg

One of Stockholm's busiest restaurants, particularly in summer when the terrace is perpetually hopping, Sturehof has a modern menu vast enough to satisfy just about everyone's taste. The seafood dishes are recommended, as is the popular and tiny O-baren in the basement (see p128).

*Sturehof (above)*

### TURES Map pp236–8 *Swedish*
☎ 611 02 10; Sturegallerian 10; mains Skr88-165; ❧ breakfast, lunch & dinner; T-Östermalmstorg

Highly recommended, this pleasantly dark, red-and-black decorated café sits in the middle of the highbrow Sturegallerian shopping centre. Try the excellent fried herring and *Västerbottens ost*. It's a great place to have coffee and cake, or to have a beer break if your knees get weak while shopping in the mall's exclusive boutiques.

### ÖRTAGÅRDEN Map pp236–8 *Vegetarian*
☎ 662 17 28; Nybrogatan 31 (1st fl, Östermalms Saluhall building); dagens lunch Skr70, lunch buffet Skr75; ❧ 10.30am-9.30pm Mon-Fri, 11am-8.30pm Sat, noon-8.30pm Sun; T-Östermalmstorg

Perched unobtrusively above the food market in Östermalms Saluhall, this vegetarian restaurant offers an extensive buffet at lunch and dinner. The setting, as you'd expect from the name (the Herb Garden), is reminiscent of a courtyard garden, with fountains and ferns galore.

# CHEAP EATS
## CAFE RESTAURANT AUSTRIA
Map pp236–8 *Café*
☎ 667 76 24; Strandvägen 1; cakes Skr15-45; ❧ breakfast, lunch & dinner; T-Östermalmstorg or Kungsträdgården

If you want to feel like part of the royal family – and perhaps even see them promenading along the Strand – grab a table at the window of this plush, red-walled café. The prices are a bit high but it oozes class and luxury, and the cakes and sandwiches are divine.

### GATEAU Map pp236–8 *Café*
☎ 611 75 54; Sturegallerian, Stureplan; pastries Skr15-35; ❧ 8am-6pm Mon-Fri, 10am-4pm Sat, noon-4pm Sun; T-Östermalmstorg

The pastries and cakes at this sprawling café in the plush Sturegallerian shopping centre are serious stuff. This is no great surprise, considering that Gateau's chief baker, Tony Olsson, competes on Sweden's national cooking team.

### STUREKATTEN Map pp236–8 *Café*
☎ 611 16 12; Riddargatan 4; cakes & pies Skr15-70, baguettes Skr65; ❧ 8am-8pm Mon-Fri, 10am-6pm Sat, 11am-6pm Sun; T-Östermalmstorg

Sturekatten looks like a life-size dolls house, built over three levels and featuring a quaint late-19th-century ambience, with antique chairs, paintings and lamps. This is where those ladies-who-lunch take their mothers-in-law. In summer, if there's room, you can indulge in coffee and cake in the restaurant's lovely little courtyard.

## TILT                                              *Café*
☎ 678 04 24; Grev Turegatan 8; snacks & meals Skr35-65, smoothies Skr32-45; ⏰ 10.30am-11pm Mon-Thu, 10.30am-midnight Fri, 1pm-midnight Sat, 1-9pm Sun; T-Östermalmstorg

Coffee, low-fat snacks, healthy fruit-and-herb smoothies, Internet games and pinball – what more could you want? The music is loud and the vibe chaotic at this café/rec centre, located just outside the Grev Turegatan exit of the Östermalmstorg *tunnelbana* station.

# OUTLYING AREAS
## EDSBACKA KROG          *French-Swedish*
☎ 96 33 00; www.edsbackakrog.se; Sollentunavägen 220, Sollentuna; mains lunch Skr175-400, dinner Skr300-425, lunch/dinner/vegetarian menus Skr335/720/495; ⏰ dinner (closed Jul); J-train to Sollentuna Centrum, then bus 525, 527, 607

Sweden's only Michelin two-star restaurant, Edsbacka Krog has been turning out French-influenced Swedish cuisine under the steady hand of chef Christer Lingström (Sweden's first Food Ambassador) for two decades now. The menu changes with the seasons to reflect the chef's reverence for working with what nature provides. Just reading it will send shivers up the spine of any true gourmand – the things Lingström does to salmon, scallops, lobster, lamb and rabbit are almost criminally good.

# Drinking

# Drinking

The best thing about drinking in Stockholm bars is the way you order your beer. Rather than asking for a particular brand, since the mass-market Swedish beers are virtually indistinguishable from one another by flavour, you order by grade; the usual order is a *storstark* – which translates to a 'big strong'. (If you're not feeling up to a big strong, you can also order a *mellanöl*, or medium beer.) Beer in Sweden is regulated by alcohol content. *Starköl* is anything over 4.5% alcohol; *mellanöl* has between 3.5% and 4.5% alcohol, and *folköl* (literally, people's beer) has between 2.25% to 3.5% alcohol.

*Folköl* and *lättöl* (light beer; more of a 'near beer' at less than 2.25% alcohol) are available in supermarkets and account for about two-thirds of all beer sales in Sweden. *Mellanöl* and *starköl* can only be bought at the state-owned alcohol shops (Systembolaget; see Systembolaget, below) and, of course, in bars.

The worst thing about drinking in Stockholm bars is the expense. Buying a round, even for good friends, is not a matter to be undertaken lightly. A *storstark* – typically an Imperial pint of one of the cheap and uninspiring local mega-brew lagers, such as Spendrups, Pripps or Falcon – costs anywhere from Skr35 to Skr52, and imported beer or mixed drinks can be twice that amount.

It's no wonder, then, that Swedes want their bar time to be quality time. There are very few – if any – genuinely styleless dive bars in Stockholm. You can drink in ornate mansions, monastic cellars, candlelit beer halls or sleek bars with designer lighting, but you'll have some trouble finding a truly boring bar in this city.

The main drinking areas in town are the liver-destruction zone around Medborgarplatsen and down Tjärhovsgatan in Södermalm; the crescent of class in Norrmalm that connects

## Systembolaget

The goal of Swedish alcohol policy, as stipulated by the Swedish parliament, is to reduce alcohol consumption and therefore alcohol-related illness. This seems to work, since Sweden has one of the lowest death rates from cirrhosis of the liver in Europe.

Limiting private profit from alcohol sales is an integral part of the Swedish alcohol policy, since private profit and competition increase both sales and the negative effects of too much alcohol consumption. Sweden, along with a majority of Nordic countries, operates a government monopoly on the sale of alcohol.

The Swedish Alcohol Retailing Monopoly, *Systembolaget*, is responsible for selling strong beer, wine and spirits to the general public. The wholly state-owned company, which has 411 shops and 580 local agents throughout Sweden, employs 3246 people and has annual sales of around Skr23 billion. Due to EU trading regulations, changes to the system are likely, although the government has dragged its feet in facing the issue. It seems likely that the monopoly will be split up and sold off – much to the benefit of big business.

Systembolaget doesn't favour any particular brand nor does it promote Swedish products over imported brands; as a result, the choice available from the company's catalogue is impressive. Supermarket-style outlets are rapidly replacing the former queue-by-number shops, and extended hours (for evenings and on Saturday) are under trial.

In central Stockholm, you'll find 23 outlets of Systembolaget; we've listed some below, but for a complete listing check out the back of the Systembolaget price list or the Internet at www.systembolaget.se (in Swedish).

**Klarabergsgatan** ☎ 21 47 44; Klarabergsgatan 62; ⏰ 10am-8pm Mon-Fri, 10am-3pm Sat

**Regeringsgatan** ☎ 796 98 10; Regeringsgatan 44; ⏰ 10am-7pm Mon-Fri, 10am-2pm Sat

**Grev Turegatan** ☎ 611 22 70; Grev Turegatan 3; ⏰ 10am-6pm Mon-Wed, 10am-7pm Thu, 10am-6.30pm Fri, 10am-2pm Sat

**Fleminggatan** ☎ 653 10 58; Fleminggatan 56; ⏰ 10am-6pm Mon-Wed, 10am-7pm Thu & Fri, 10am-2pm Sat

**Långholmsgatan** ☎ 669 71 05; Långholmsgatan 21; ⏰ 10am-6pm Mon-Wed, 10am-7pm Thu & Fri, 10am-2pm Sat

## Brännvin Distilleries

In the mid-17th century, after grain took over from wine as the raw material for *brännvin* (also called *aquavit* or *snaps*), stills were no longer found only in the homes of the rich. In fact, most of the population was distilling at home and imbibing the drink on a daily basis. The amounts of alcohol consumed were incredible, and state control was only a matter of time. In 1756 there was a temporary ban on home distilling and around 180,000 household stills were confiscated. In 1775 King Gustav III introduced the first of 60 crown distilleries and again made home distilling illegal, but the people defied the law and the last crown distillery was closed in 1824.

In 1830 there were around 175,000 private distilleries in Sweden, but potato-based distillation, which required larger production units, gradually took over and the number of home-based stills dwindled. State control reasserted itself in 1855 and the number of legal distilleries fell to 591 by 1861. In 1910 the distillers amalgamated into one company, which became Vin och Spritcentralen in 1917. By 1970 only one of the distilleries remained open – Gärdsbränneriet, in Nöbbelöv (Skåne) – the others were closed to maximise efficiency, even the distillery on Reimersholme, which pioneered new techniques back in the 1860s. Rectification (the purifying process) now takes place in Åhus (Skåne) and in Stockholm, but all Vin och Spritcentralen spiced aquavit is produced in Skåne.

Berns, Operabaren and Fredsgatan 12; the swank Stureplan district of posh discos; and the Scheelegatan–Fleminggatan–St Eriksgatan route on Kungsholmen.

The legal drinking age in Sweden is 18 years, but many bars and restaurants impose significantly higher age limits – and these usually differ for men and women, which incidentally flouts the European Union (EU) sex discrimination laws.

Sweden's largest breweries, including Spendrups, Pripps, Kopparbergs, Falcon and Åbro, produce a wide range of drinks from cider to light and dark lagers, porter and stout. Apple or pear cider is usually less than 3.5% alcohol; there is also a wide range of alcohol-free ciders. Popular strong Swedish beers include Norrlands Guld Export, Mariestads Export and Pripps Extra Strong.

Wines and spirits can only be purchased at Systembolaget, where – as in the bars and restaurants – alcohol prices are kept high as a matter of policy (for details see Systembolaget, opposite). Pick up a free copy of the price list (with an extensive range of mainly imported products), updated every two months.

Vin och Spritcentralen (also known as Vin och Sprit, or V&S; www.vinsprit.se) produce some fruit wines and *glögg* (hot mulled wine). Sweden produces its own spirit, a form of vodka called variously *brännvin*, *snaps* or *aquavit*; it's a fiery and strongly flavoured drink, usually distilled from potatoes. Renat Brännvin (the classic purified, unspiced Swedish vodka, 39% alcohol by volume) still ranks at the top of the liquor league in annual home sales.

Drinking at home is something of a ritualised affair, particularly at formal meals. It's considered impolite to sip your drink before the host or hostess has lifted his or her glass in a toast to the table (*skål!*, which you should repeat back). Make eye contact with whoever offered the toast as you're sipping; before you set your glass back down, it's polite to nod at each person sitting at the table.

Beer or wine is usually drunk with dinner; at lunch, *lättöl* or *folköl* is fairly standard. Snaps tends to be reserved for special occasions, but it's almost a requirement with pickled herring or with any *smörgåsbord* (Swedish buffet). During winter, tiny mugs of *glögg* become indispensable for fending off the cold. This is also the time of year when you'll see a few more interesting seasonal beers produced by the local breweries. Marked '*Jul-öl*', these dark beers are sweet and heavily spiced with wintery flavours like cinnamon and cardamom. After-dinner drinks, such as port wine or cognac, are not uncommon, particularly at formal dinners and holiday celebrations. The infamous Swedish *punsch*, a rum-based drink made with the liqueur arrack, is served warm with the traditional Thursday meal of split-pea-and-ham soup, or chilled as an after-dinner *digestif*.

## Top Five Historical Places to Drink

- Kvarnen (p126)
- Pelikan (p127)
- Berns Salonger (p124)
- Mosebacke (p126)
- Dovas (p125)

# GAMLA STAN & RIDDARHOLMEN

If what you want is to nestle into a vaulted, brick-lined cellar drenched in candlelight and history, Gamla Stan won't disappoint. The golden rule here is: always go downstairs. What might seem like your average, strictly functional drinkery above ground often hides labyrinthine wonders in its basement rooms.

### CHOKLADKOPPEN & KAFFEKOPPEN
Map pp239–41

☎ 20 31 70; Stortorget 18 & 20; ☼ 9am-11pm Mon-Thu & Sun, to midnight Fri & Sat; T-Gamla Stan

In a pair of gorgeous Renaissance buildings from the 1650s, the gay-friendly Chokladkoppen and its next-door sibling, Kaffekoppen, are among the best hang-outs in Old Town. The atmosphere improves even more during nice weather, when the outdoor terrace tables fill up and bring life to Stortorget.

### MANDUS Map pp239–41

☎ 20 60 55; Österlånggatan 7; mains Skr130-200; ☼ 5pm-midnight

The small, wildly decorated, gay-friendly Mandus has a manic pace, a simple menu and friendly, welcoming bartenders.

*Café Opera (above)*

### WIRSTRÖMS IRISH PUB Map pp239–41

☎ 21 28 74; Stora Nygatan 13; ☼ to midnight Mon-Fri, to 1am Sat & Sun

This place feels more like a medieval dungeon than an Irish pub – its dark, mysterious, brick-vaulted cellar goes on forever. Arrive early to find a candlelit corner and snuggle in with a pint of Guinness (Skr52). Bar meals and sandwiches (including vegetarian) are available for Skr75 to Skr95. There's live music in the evening Wednesday to Saturday.

# NORRMALM & VASASTADEN

Some of the city's coolest bars are here in the city centre, from the decadent Berns Salonger to the epitome of the chic Stockholm pickup bar that is Storstad to the down-to-earth Loft.

### BERNS SALONGER Map pp236–8

☎ 56 63 20 00; www.berns.se; Berzelii Park; ☼ to 1am Mon & Tue, to 3am Wed & Thu, to 4am Fri & Sat, to midnight Sun

With half a dozen bars spread across three levels, this grand mansion is drenched in history but buzzing with contemporary energy. On the basement level is a popular disco; there's also a wine bar, a cocktail bar, a mirrored bar and a terrace.

### CAFÉ OPERA Map pp236–8

☎ 676 58 07; Operahuset, Karl XII:s Torg; ☼ to 3am

Inside one of the most impressive buildings in Stockholm, the baroque interior of Café Opera gives it an unmistakably luxurious feel. A highly regarded restaurant by day, the Café turns into one of the liveliest, swankiest and most popular bars in Stockholm in the evening.

### CLIFF BARNES Map p230

☎ 31 80 70; Norrtullsgatan 45; ☼ to 1am Mon-Sat

People come here to sing along to popular tunes, dance on the tables and get inebriated. It's a hugely popular beerhall-type place with an outdoor bar in summer.

### FREDSGATAN 12 Map pp236–8

☎ 411 73 48; Fredsgatan 12; ☼ to 3am Tue-Sun

This bar on the ground floor of the Royal Art Academy, also a gourmet restaurant by day, is popular as a hip DJ bar and in particular for its outdoor terrace in summer. Its sleek, serious design will appeal to those who think 'quirky' is a naughty word.

### ICEBAR Map pp236–8
☎ 50 56 30 00; www.nordichotels.se; inside the Nordic Sea Hotel, Vasaplan 4; admission Skr125; ⏰ to midnight Mon-Sat, closed Sun

Of course, it's silly, but you're intrigued, admit it: a bar built entirely out of ice, where you drink from glasses carved of ice at tables made of ice. The admission price gets you warm booties, mittens, a parka and one drink; refills cost Skr85 extra, but you'll probably be too cold to want one anyway.

### KARLSSON & CO Map pp236–8
☎ 54 51 21 40; Kungsgatan 56; admission free Mon & Tue, Skr40 after 9pm Wed & Thur, Skr80 Fri & Sat; ⏰ to 3am Mon-Sat

Karlsson & Co is a kitschy dance restaurant and nightclub with an extensive crossover menu, a fairly comfortable pub-like seating area and a disco renowned as a pick-up joint. There's a dress code (no jeans or trainers on weekends).

### LOFT Map pp236–8
☎ 411 19 91; Regeringsgatan 66; ⏰ to 1am, to 3am on busy weekends

The Loft is a totally unpretentious, unaffected Irish pub with wooden beams, Irish beers and whiskeys, and a full restaurant menu with table service in the back rooms. The mostly Irish staff are everyone's best friend, and you can't go in without meeting 10 new people – essential qualities in an Irish pub.

### MUSSLAN BAR Map p230
☎ 34 64 10; Dalagatan 46; ⏰ to 1am Mon-Sat

This small, dark DJ bar next door to the Bistro de Wasahof is a relaxed place where you can settle into a cushy couch and sip a drink under the stars (they're painted on the blue ceiling).

### STORSTAD Map pp231–3
☎ 673 38 00; Odengatan 41; ⏰ to 1am Mon & Tue, to 3am Wed-Sat

This super-trendy bar is the definition of Stockholm style, with its bright-white walls, L-shaped bar and enormous picture windows. It has a more relaxed vibe than usual, though – this is one of the few places in town where someone might noticeably try to pick you up. DJs play most nights.

**Top Five Design Bars**

- Metró (p126)
- Lydmar Hotel (p128)
- Fredsgatan 12 (opposite)
- East (p128)
- Storstad (below)

# KUNGSHOLMEN

If there's any bar that defies the stereotypical Stockholm starkness, it is here in Kungsholmen and its name is Dovas. Other hang-outs in this neighbourhood include the cute El Cubanito and – representing the classic Swedish bar aesthetic – the sparsely decorated Lokal.

### DOVAS Map p230
☎ 650 80 49; St Eriksgatan 53A; ⏰ to 1am

This is the kind of place where you could straggle in at 8am and order a whiskey with a beerback and nobody would look at you strangely. This Kungsholmen *kvarterskrog* (neighbourhood pub) has been here forever, and so have many of its patrons. It's dark, cheap and unintentionally charming.

### EL CUBANITO Map p230
☎ 650 12 38; Scheelegatan 3; ⏰ to 1am

The rum-based drinks at this cosy, authentic Cuban bar and restaurant – from a classic *mojito* cocktail full of fragrant mint leaves to a dozen other rum creations, including a *cuba libre* and a 'Fidel' – are impeccably poured and delicious enough to make you forget it's grey and snowing just outside the door. See also p114.

### LOKAL Map p230
☎ 650 98 09; Scheelegatan 8; ⏰ to 1am Mon, Tue, Sun, to 2am Wed & Thu, to 3am Fri & Sat

A relatively new bar, this clean-lined, airy corner space serves tapas-style food in beautiful but slightly over-starched surroundings; it's very similar to Storstad, but with fewer hipsters (so far).

# SÖDERMALM & LÅNGHOLMEN

Söder is Stockholm's undisputed capital of alcohol consumption. The bars here range from the punkish basement hang-out

Drinking – Kungsholmen

(Söderkällaren) to above-it-all grace (Eriks Gondolen) to traditional beer hall (Pelikan, Kvarnen). The crowds are enthusiastic about having a good time.

### AKKURAT Map pp239–41
☎ 644 00 15; Hornsgatan 18; ☽ to 1am Mon-Sat
Fans of beer should make a point of visiting Akkurat; it has a huge selection of Belgian ales as well as a good range of Swedish-made microbrews, notably the semi-divine Jämtlands Bryggeri trio Heaven, Hell and Fallen Angel. There's also a vast wall of whiskey, and there are mussels on the menu.

### AUGUST BAR BISTRO Map pp234–5
☎ 644 87 00; Folkungagatan 59; ☽ to 1am
Comfortable, classy and laid-back, August Bar Bistro has slowly become the haven of the Medborgarplatsen area's hipsters who have outgrown Söderkällaren but are tired of waiting to get into Kvarnen. It serves beer and wine along with affordable bar food.

### BONDEN MAT & BAR Map pp234–5
☎ 641 86 79; Bondegatan 1C; ☽ to 1am
In this small bar, easily located by a cow sign outside the door, you'll find a strangely curved ceiling with 19th-century-style light bulbs. It's a nice place to sit and have a quiet chat, but it fills up fast. Next door is the larger, more rock-oriented Bonden Club; see p134.

### CARMEN Map pp234–5
☎ 641 24 70; Tjärhovsgatan 14; ☽ to 1am Mon-Sat, to 11pm Sun
Carmen is a large, busy '70s-style pub that's trying to head upmarket; the front room is full of grizzled old regulars, while the vast back room is jammed with hipsters chattering and smoking their heads off. Storstark is cheap, at around Skr25/30 before/after 8pm.

### ERIKS GONDOLEN Map pp239–41
☎ 641 70 90; Stadsgården 6; ☽ to 1am Mon-Sat
It's hard to beat the view from up here – you can sip a cocktail and pretend to be king or queen of all you survey, which amounts to most of Stockholm. Hint: if you don't want to spend the Skr5 on Katarinahissen, there's a free lift between Gondolen and the Konsum/Coop building. See also p115.

### FENIX Map pp239–41
☎ 640 45 06; Götgatan 40; ☽ to 1am Mon-Sat, to midnight Sun

This eclectically decorated bar/restaurant has a dizzying checkerboard floor, crazy art and an auburn-painted, decoratively moulded ceiling; grab a seat at the window and watch the action on Götgatan.

### FOLKHEMMET Map pp234–5
☎ 640 55 95; Renstiernas Gata 30; ☽ to 1am
This friendly, popular place, run by socialists and named after the Swedish welfare state, doesn't have a doorman or an admission charge. Although the place is better known as a restaurant (see p116), in the evenings the pillow-strewn benches of the cosy bar section fill up with hipsters, while DJs spin alternative rock, hip hop, reggae and electronica.

### KVARNEN Map pp234–5
☎ 643 03 80; Tjärhovsgatan 4; ☽ to 3am
A cheerful mixture of Hammarby football fans and Left Party former communists regularly packs Kvarnen, one of the best bars in Söder. The vast traditional beer hall dates from 1907 and seeps tradition; beyond the scruffy old beerhounds and college boys, though, there's a hot dance party in the back room featuring some of the city's best DJs. Queues are fairly constant but, for once, justifiable.

### METRÓ Map pp234–5
☎ 442 03 20; Götgatan 93; ☽ to 1am, to 2am Fri & Sat
This vast, multi-level restaurant/bar space, with brilliant red über-'60s design, has a hopping, Moulin Rouge-style bar with DJ's playing music most nights. Dress your best so as not to be completely outshined by the bar's décor.

### MOSEBACKE ETABLISSEMENT
Map pp239–41
☎ 55 60 98 90; Mosebacketorg 3; ☽ to 1 am Jun-Aug, to 2am Fri & Sat Sep-May
Even if you're not partaking of Mosebacke's many cool club nights, in summer its terrace bar is an absolutely fantastic place to relax with

---

## Top Five Spots for Outdoor Drinking
- **Mosebacke** (above)
- **Chokladkoppen** (p124)
- **Fredsgatan 12** (p124)
- **Sturehof/O-baren** (p128)
- **Cliff Barnes** (p124)

*Czech beer mats at Soldaten Svejk (below)*

a drink and gaze out over Gamla Stan from the heights of Söder.

### PELIKAN Map pp234–5
☎ 55 60 90 90; Blekingegatan 40; ☽ to 1am

Similar to Kvarnen with its steeped-in-history feeling, but with a much quieter, more placid vibe and no disco in the back, Pelikan is a great place to drink a beer. There's Guinness and Staropramen on tap; the large glass is *really* big. Simple sandwiches and *husmanskost* (traditional Swedish fare) meals are served, and the staff are gracious and helpful. On the left side of the entry is an attached cocktail bar, Kristallen, with a dark blue Oriental motif.

### SNAPS Map pp234–5
☎ 640 28 68; www.snaps.org; Götgatan 48;
☽ to 1am Mon-Fri, to 3am Fri & Sat

Snaps is housed in one of Söder's coolest buildings, across from Mondo on Medborgar-platsen. With its clusters of candles, brick walls and rustic exposed-beam ceiling, it's one of the most popular bars in the area. Downstairs is Rangus Tangus, a lounge and dance-bar with a dangerously low curved ceiling.

### SOLDATEN SVEJK Map pp234–5
☎ 641 33 66; Östgötagatan 35; ☽ 5pm-midnight
Sun-Thu, 5pm-1am Fri-Sat

In this crowded, amber-windowed, wooden-floored pub decorated with heraldic shields, you can get great Czech beer, including the massively popular Staropramen on tap. There are also simple and solid Czech meals (Skr75 to Skr115); try some of the excellent smoked cheese along with your beer. Be sure to arrive early – there are often long queues for tables.

### SÖDERKÄLLAREN Map pp234–5
☎ 55 69 55 57; Tjärhovsgatan 12; ☽ to midnight

Formerly the Indian Star Restaurang, this budget eatery has become much better known for its cellar beer hall, where the dirtier end of the hipster spectrum slurps cheap beer for around Skr29. There's still a huge range of meals, most around Skr70 – the ultra-strong vindaloo curry should soak up many a storstark.

### WC
☎ 644 19 81; Skånegatan 51; ☽ to 1am

The gimmick here is a fairly understated one: the barstools are made with toilet seats (get it? WC?). Nothing else about the place is terribly silly, though; it's a narrow, L-shaped bar slightly below ground – you can look down into the place from the huge street-level windows. It has a pleasant atmosphere and friendly bartenders in a happening section of town.

### ZOMBIE BAR Map pp234–5
☎ 640 18 07; Ringvägen 151; ☽ to 1am

The beer is cheap and the rock is loud at this small, wild bar on the edge of Södermalm. DJs play a variety of '70s and '80s punk rock and modern alt-rock most nights of the week. The booths are a little worse for wear, but you probably won't be sitting down anyway.

### ÖSTGÖTAKÄLLAREN Map pp234–5
☎ 643 22 40; Östgötagatan 41; ☽ to 1am

With brick-lined and wood-panelled walls and a lovely old-fashioned, dramatically candlelit atmosphere, the ÖK invites serious lingering over a pint or a glass of wine. The hearty menu of traditional Swedish food is full of bargains. For a whole different scene, slink down to the Goth-swank Vampire Lounge in the basement.

# ÖSTERMALM, GÄRDET & LADUGÅRDSGÄRDET

The bars in Östermalm tend to be dance clubs more than places to sit and have a drink; the few listed here, however, are excellent and stylish places to do just that.

# The Vodka King

The gloomy residential island of Reimersholme was once the setting for a dramatic tale that, as so often happens, had its start with vodka. In the 19th century, prisoners from Långholmen built a textile factory on Reimersholme; it was later used to make paraffin, but when wealthy young industrialist Lars Olsson Smith took over the building, he quickly converted it into a distillery. Smith was a visionary, and he'd seen a way to get rich by giving the people what they couldn't refuse.

In 1879 Smith developed a way to get rid of the terrible taste of pure ethanol created during the production of strong liquor. The filtering method, called rectification, is used to this day; with it, Smith created a new kind of vodka he called 'Absolut Rent Brännvin' (absolute pure vodka), the obvious ancestor to today's Absolut Vodka. (Before settling on the name Absolut, however, marketers considered several more amusing options, including 'Swedish Blonde Vodka', 'Swedish Black Vodka' and 'Damn Swede', the latter featuring an illustration of a modern-day Viking strutting across the bottle.)

Smith, an ambitious chap, wasn't happy with having made a better-tasting vodka; he also wanted to break the city of Stockholm's monopoly on selling the stuff. He refused to apply for a permit to sell his product in Stockholm, instead undercutting the city at a retail store he opened next to his distillery, which happened to be just outside the city limits. Adding insult to injury, he offered Stockholmers a free shuttle-boat ride to the island so they could buy his booze. It was a brilliant marketing plan, and it worked.

The zealous quest to control the region's alcohol market won Smith the dubious title 'The King of Vodka'. There's still a variety of Swedish *snaps* called Reimersholme, but it's no longer made on the island.

## EAST Map pp236–8
☎ 611 49 59; Stureplan 13; ⌚ to 3am

The dance floor at East gets seriously hopping late at night. If dancing's not your thing, there are always a few quiet seats near the bar where you can relax over cocktails, or maybe sake and sushi.

## HALV TRAPPA PLUS GÅRD Map pp234–5
☎ 611 02 75; Lästmakargatan 3; ⌚ to 3am, to 1am Mon & Tue

The back patio here has its own bar and heaters, making it a popular summer hang-out – if you can get in, that is. The classy, labyrinthine bar and chill-out lounges are notoriously well protected from anything that might seem to be less than the height of fashion. If you want to get in, make sure you dress like the mannequins in the Filippa K windows and try to arrive by 10pm.

## LYDMAR HOTEL Map pp236–8
☎ 56 61 13 00; www.lydmar.se; Sturegatan 10; ⌚ to 1am Sun-Thu, to 2am Fri & Sat

If it's not absurdly crowded with attractive young business types, Lydmar's lounge is a great place to relax with a cocktail and feel incredibly swank.

## O-BAREN Map pp236–8
☎ 440 57 30; Stureplan 2; ⌚ to 2am

This bar deep inside Sturehof restaurant is a popular late-night, last-call stop; it's less manic at other times, and a nice place to hang out. The white-tiled standing-room-only bar at the front of the restaurant, facing Stureplan, is also good for a drink and to watch the rendezvous action under Svampen (the mushroom in the centre of Stureplan). In fine weather, the bar's expansive terrace on Stureplan is always packed and perfect for people-watching.

# Entertainment

# Entertainment

So what do people do for fun in this town, other than visit museums, meet for cakes and coffee and shop till they drop (and, of course, drink – see p121)? The answer depends on which you'd prefer – being a spectator or a participant. In the former category, there are cinemas galore, from the divine Biografen Skandia to the warehousey Filmstaden Sergel. You can also take in a ballet, a dramatic performance, or any number of sporting events, depending on the time of year. On the other hand, you can strap on skates and play some ice hockey yourself; salsa dance your way across a packed floor; shoot some pool; take a dip; rent a kayak; or go for a run in the park. The options are legion; we've listed some of the best here.

*Playing ice hockey (p138)*

There's no shortage of local sources for up-to-date entertainment options in town. The free *Metro* tabloid, available on *tunnelbana* trains, has a few nightlife events listings. A more thorough source, also in Swedish, is *På Stan*, the Friday entertainment supplement in *Dagens Nyheter*; you can pick it up free at the tourist information office in Kulturhuset, along with queer-friendly tabloid *QX* and the monthly magazine *What's On – Stockholm*, published by the tourist office. Other good resources include: www.alltomstockholm.se (in Swedish), which is affiliated with Citysearch and has a good searchable database of cultural events; **Aftonbladet** (☎ 725 20 00; www.aftonbladet.se in Swedish), an evening tabloid full of gossip, with some events listings; **Expressen** (☎ 738 30 00), which is similar to *Aftonbladet*; *Kalendarium*, a monthly pocket-sized glossy guide to clubs and DJ nights, available free at coffee shops and bars – an excellent source for nightlife options; **Nöjesguiden** (www.nojesguiden.se in Swedish), a free monthly music-focused entertainment paper with feature articles and extensive club listings, available free at most record shops, newsstands and coffee shops.

## Gay & Lesbian Stockholm

Stockholm is a very gay-friendly city, and the entertainment scene here is not as segregated – particularly not between gays and lesbians – as it can be in other big cities. Listings and descriptions of gay-friendly bars, restaurants cafés, discos, nightclubs and cultural events can be found in the free monthly tabloid newspaper **QX** (www.qx.se/english/). Lesbians can find tourist information (for clubs, bars, coffee shops and restaurants) at www.corky.nu.

**Mandus** (p106) is a cute and energetic gay-friendly restaurant/bar in Gamla Stan, as is **Chokladkoppen** (p124). The **Bitch Girl Club** (Map pp239-41; ☎ 720 52 05; Kolingsborg, Södermalmstorg 2) stages parties every other Saturday; check the website for details. The battleship **Patricia** (Map pp239-41; ☎ 743 05 70; www.ladypatricia.se; Stadsgårds-kajen 152), now a hopping DJ/rock club, is known for its excellent queer nights – complete with drag show – that draw partiers of all persuasions every Sunday. **Tip Top** (Map pp231-3; ☎ 32 98 00; Sveavägen 57) is a long-running gay disco with a lesbian lounge; the queer weekday crowd inevitably gets invaded by straights at the weekend. **Häcktet** (Map pp234-5; ☎ 84 59 10; Restaurang Bysis, Hornsgatan 82) is a comfortable, check-flannel-lesbian hangout in an old country manor.

Please note that unlike other chapters, the listings in this chapter are organised by category, rather than by neighbourhood.

## Tickets & Reservations

Most venues listed in this chapter sell tickets in advance through **Biljett Direkt** ( ☎ 077 170 70 70 in Sweden only; www.ticnet.se in Swedish).

# THEATRE

Stockholm is a theatre city, with outstanding performances in a variety of styles nearly every night of the week during theatre season, which runs most of the year but peaks in autumn and winter. Pick up a free copy of *Teater Guide* from the tourist office for an overview. For tickets, contact the tourist office (which charges a fee), theatre box offices or **Biljett Direkt** ( ☎ 077 170 70 70; www.ticnet.se in Swedish). Prices depend on your seat position, the length of performance, and various other factors. Saturday shows are often sold out. Shows are nearly always in Swedish and many theatres are closed in July and August. Operas are performed in their original language (usually Italian or German), or in Swedish.

### DRAMATISKA TEATERN Map pp236–8

☎ 667 06 80; www.dramaten.se; Nybroplan; tickets Skr120-260; T-Östermalmstorg, Kungsträdgården, bus 46, 47, 55, 62, 69, 76, 91

Quite easily the most impressive theatre in Stockholm, Dramatiska Teatern (also called Dramaten) presents a range of plays from Shakespeare to Strindberg in a fantastic Art Nouveau environment. This is *chez* Bergman, where the famous director has been a driving force since the 1960s as well as a frequent beret-clad sight since he retired from film some years ago. There's a new experimental stage affiliated with Dramaten, called **Elverket** (Linnégatan 69; same contact info). Unsold tickets are offered an hour before shows at a 35% discount.

### ENGLISH THEATRE COMPANY

Map pp236–8

☎ 662 41 33; www.englishtheatre.se; Nybrogatan 35; tickets Skr220-300

This company consists entirely of native English-speakers performing fairly standard, conservative fare at Vasa Teatern (Vasagatan 19–21), Södrateatern (at Slussen) and other places.

### HAMBURGER BÖRS Map pp236–8

☎ 787 85 00; Jakobsgatan 6; tickets from Skr175; ☺ 9.30pm, meals from 7.30pm

The outlandishly decorated Hamburger Börs has a cabaret restaurant with a stage that hosts stand-up comedy, song and dance. Occasionally you can see international artists performing here.

### OSCARS TEATERN Map pp236–8

☎ 20 50 00; Kungsgatan 64; tickets Skr150-400; ☺ Tue-Sat

The classic 960-seat Oscars Teatern runs 'Broadway' musicals and occasional comedies, all in Swedish.

### STOCKHOLMS STADSTEATERN

Map pp236–8

☎ 50 62 01 00; Kulturhuset, Sergels Torg; tickets around Skr200, lunch theatre Skr120 Tue-Sat; ☺ closed Mon

At Stockholms Stadsteatern, there are regular performances of Swedish plays and Swedish versions of international plays on six stages. There are also guest appearances by foreign theatre companies. The hour-long Swedish-language lunch-time performance (reservation compulsory) includes soup, bread and butter.

### VASA TEATERN Map pp236–8

☎ 24 82 40; www.operan.se; Vasagatan 19-21; tickets Skr55-260; ☺ closed Sun & Mon

Some plays in English are staged here by various companies around town, as well as operas, ballet and musicals.

# DANCE

Stockholm's Kungliga Balett (Royal Ballet), founded in 1733, is among the oldest dance companies in the world. However, its young choreographers seem to be the ones doing really provocative, vibrant dance work. Names to look out for include favourite son Mats Ek, Jens Östberg, Christina Caprioli and Margaretha Åsberg. For up-to-date listings of dance performances and events, get hold of the magazine *Danstidningen* (www.danstidningen.se).

### DANSENS HUS Map pp236–8

☎ 50 89 90 90; 12-14 Barnhusgatan; tickets Skr160-270; ☻ noon-6pm Mon-Sat Jun-Aug only; T-Hötorget, T-Centralen, bus 1, 47, 53, 69

The stomping ground of Mats Ek's Culberg Ballet, Dansens Hus has a large main auditorium as well as the diminutive 'Blue Box' (Blå Lådan). It presents new choreography and dance.

### KUNGLIGA OPERAN Map pp236–8

☎ 24 82 40; Gustav Adolfs torg; tickets Skr40-450; ☻ noon-6pm Mon-Fri, noon-3pm Sat, closed Jun-Aug; T-Kungsträdgården, bus 43, 46, 55, 59, 62, 76

The Royal Opera houses Stockholm's classical Royal Ballet Company, whose work incorporates both the old favourites and some new, modern material.

### MODERNA DANSTEATERN Map pp239–41

☎ 611 32 33; Slupskjulsvägen 32; tickets Skr150; bus 65

Moderna Dansteatern is a small theatre that's home base for local freelance choreographers. It's the place to go to see postmodern dance in Stockholm.

# CINEMAS

Friday to Sunday are the big movie-going days in Stockholm; if you want to see a film on a weekend, make sure you buy your tickets in advance. The same goes for top new releases. Foreign films are almost always screened in their original language (usually English), with Swedish subtitles; some animated children's features are dubbed, which is indicated by '*Svenskt tal*' or '*sv tal*' on advertisements. Most of the big cinemas in Stockholm show mainstream Hollywood fare, but there are some smaller alternative cinemas (where 25% to 35% of movies are in English).

The two big cinema chains are Sandrews (☎ 10 13 00) and SF (☎ 56 26 00 00); you can buy tickets for any cinema in a chain at any of its other cinemas. The daily newspapers have comprehensive cinema listings. Tickets usually cost between Skr75 and Skr85 (they're sometimes cheaper early in the week); ask about child/student/senior discounts. Some art-house cinemas are closed in July.

### ASTORIA Map pp236–8

☎ 660 00 25; www.sandrewmetronome.se in Swedish; Nybrogatan 15; T-Östermalmstorg

Built in 1928, this single-screen theatre has a great sound system and is one of Stockholm's primary, first-run theatres.

### BIOGRAFEN SKANDIA Map pp236–8

☎ 56 26 00 00; www.sf.se; Drottninggatan 82; T-Hötorget, bus 1, 47, 52, 53, 69

The stunning interior of this 1923 movie house, designed by Gunnar Asplund, threatens to outshine any film shown here (see p57). It shows art-house films.

### BIOGRAFEN STURE Map pp236–8

☎ 678 85 48; www.biosture.se in Swedish; Birger Jarlsgatan 41; T-Östermalmstorg, bus 1, 46, 55, 56

This cinema shows well-chosen art films. It also has Baby-bio screenings for parents with children.

### COSMONOVA Map pp228–9

☎ 51 95 51 30; www.nrm.se/cosmonova; Naturistoriska Riksmuseet, Frescativägen; tickets Skr75; T-Universitetet, bus 40, 540

This Imax theatre, next to Naturhistoriska Riksmuseet, shows giant-format Imax nature films such as *Everest*, *Under the Sea* and *The Grand Canyon*. If you're at all susceptible to motion sickness, you might want to make sure you sit near an exit because the films can be nauseatingly realistic.

### FILMHUSET Map pp231–3

☎ 665 11 00; www.sfi.se; Borgvägen; T-Gärdet, bus 56, 72, 76

Filmhuset, a building designed by Peter Celsing's, houses the Swedish Film Institute and a film-club-only cinema.

### GRAND Map pp231–3

☎ 411 24 00; www.sandrewmetronome.se in Swedish; Sveavägen 45; T-Rådmansgatan, bus 43, 52

The Grand is notable mostly for its historical interest; this is the cinema Olof Palme visited before he was shot.

### RÖDA KVARN Map pp236–8

☎ 56 26 00 00; www.sf.se in Swedish; Biblioteksgatan 5; T-Östermalmstorg, bus 46, 47, 55, 59, 62

First-run and some art-house films show in this smallish theatre, whose name is a literal translation of Moulin Rouge.

## ZITA Map pp236–8
☎ 23 20 20; www.folketsbio.se/zita; Birger Jarlsgatan 37; T-Östermalmstorg, bus 1, 46, 55, 56

Stockholm's only cinema with its own bar, Zita is owned by the nonprofit Folkets Bio. The three-screen cinema opened in 1913 and is Stockholm's oldest cinema still in operation.

# OPERA

## FOLKOPERAN Map pp234–5
☎ 616 07 50; Hornsgatan 72; tickets Skr270-350; ☽ early Sep-early May

Known internationally for its unconventional productions, Folkoperan brings opera to ordinary people five or six days weekly. You can also catch some modern ballet and concerts here. The intimate bar/restaurant is a beloved hangout for artists.

## KUNGLIGA OPERAN Map pp236–8
☎ 24 82 40; www.operan.se; Gustav Adolfs torg; tickets Skr130-380, no view Skr40; ☽ closed Sun

Operan, the Royal Opera house, is the place to go for serious opera in Stockholm. The main theatre has three tiers of impressively ornate balconies reached via marble staircases. Classical concerts are held in the smaller halls. The cheapest tickets are for *lyssnarplats*, seats from

where you can only hear but not see the stage, so make sure you check the seating plan when purchasing tickets.

# CLUBBING

Every night of the week, people are dancing their feet off somewhere in Stockholm. Club culture here is a finely honed instrument that detects and magnifies trends to the nth degree, then broadcasts them all over town. The hottest clubs are constantly jammed, with queues out the door; even at less popular places, it's not at all uncommon for people to wait in line for 20 to 40 minutes before getting in. Club doormen are notoriously difficult to get past; you're much more likely to be allowed into a packed club if you're female, white, well-dressed and English-speaking. (If you're not, try to stand next to someone who is, and follow them in nonchalantly.) The longer the queue, the more prestigious the bar and the higher the drink prices.

Stureplan in Östermalm is the pinnacle of chic, trendy clubs in Stockholm, and the Spy Bar (p134) is its crown jewel. Capping off a night of clubbing by standing in line at the Spy Bar spotting local celebrities is a favourite activity; actually being admitted to the bar is icing on the cake.

*Kungliga Operan (above)*

## Top Five Stockholm Clubs

- Spy Bar (below)
- Berns Salonger (below)
- East (below)
- Mondo (below)
- Tranan (opposite)

Most clubs charge a cloakroom fee at the door of Skr10 to Skr20. There is also frequently an age limit, often higher for men than women, but these tend to be enforced loosely and at the doorman's discretion; carry a piece of photo ID, just in case. While most bars close at 1am, a few clubs in Södermalm stay open until 3am, and most of the nightlife spots around Stureplan are open until 4am or 5am. Covers for dance clubs and DJ nights can range from nothing to Skr150.

Listed in this section are some of the city's main dance clubs and DJ clubs. Places where drinking takes precedence over dancing are listed in the Drinking chapter (p121), and bars or clubs that primarily feature live music are listed under Music (opposite).

### BERNS SALONGER Map pp236–8
☎ 56 63 22 22; Berzelii Park; ☽ to 3am or 4am, to midnight

The many bars and dance floors in this decadent old manse ensure you'll find something to suit your tastes. The music styles vary, but the atmosphere in all the rooms is consistently decadent.

### BONDEN Map pp234–5
☎ 641 86 79; Bondegatan 1; ☽ to midnight

The casual basement club at Bonden Bar hosts an eclectic mix of DJ nights, from indie-rock to house to hip-hop.

### DAILY NEWS CAFE Map pp236–8
☎ 21 56 55; Kungsträdgården; ☽ to 3am, closed Sun

A sprawling club with many levels, the Daily can be a little bit sleazy but it's fun to roam around and check out the scene in the various rooms. Occasional live bands perform music in a variety of styles, from hip-hop to alt-rock.

### EAST Map pp236–8
☎ 611 49 59; Stureplan 13; ☽ to 3am

This sleek Asian restaurant turns into a swank hip-hop bar at night.

### KVARNEN Map pp234–5
☎ 643 03 80; Tjärhovsgatan 4; ☽ to 3am

Beyond the scruffy beer hounds in this traditional Swedish beer hall is a hot dance party, with DJ nights that range from reggae to house. The queues are constant. See also p126.

### LA HABANA Map pp231–3
☎ 16 64 65; Sveavägen 108; ☽ to 1am

This Cuban restaurant turns into a crowded salsa bar at night, with limber-legged Swedes and Latinos intermingling over *mojitos* and *cuba libres* in the basement.

### MONDO Map pp234–5
☎ 673 10 32; Medborgarplatsen 8; ☽ to 3am

This newly opened club and cultural centre, in a former school building, puts on unusual, top-notch events every night of the week. It has a bar/restaurant, a large dance floor and music hall, and a tinier club upstairs, as well as a gallery and a small movie theatre. The music ranges from some of Sweden's biggest singer-songwriters to the DJ next door, but for the most part you'll find hip-hop, techno and indie-rock bands both local and international.

### MOSEBACKE ETABLISSEMENT
Map pp239–41
☎ 55 60 98 90; Mosebacketorg 3; ☽ to 1am Sun-Thu, to 2am Fri & Sat; T-Slussen, bus 3, 46, 53, 76

Noted for a couple of outstanding, long-standing club nights – the occasional Re: Orient, which focuses on Eastern sounds, and Blacknuss, the Friday jazz and soul night – Mosebacke also has frequent live music performances and a popular outdoor terrace bar in summer.

### SPY BAR Map pp236–8
☎ 54 50 37 01; www.thespybar.com; Birger Jarlsgatan 20; admission Skr125; ☽ 10pm-5am Wed-Sat

Felicitously nicknamed 'the Puke' (because *spy* in Swedish means 'vomit'), this bar is the ice queen of the club scene – you can't help wanting to get in, but you hate it because it won't let you. Waiting in the queue is almost as much fun as going in, as you get to see local stars dissed by bouncers. Those who do breach the threshold will find several well-designed levels of gorgeous people in shiny clothes dancing and drinking very expensive drinks.

## STACY Map pp236-8

☎ 411 59 00; Regeringsgatan 61; ◷ to 3am (to midnight Mon-Tue)

This high-class, crisply styled hip-hop bar hosts some wildly popular dance-hall, R&B and reggae nights.

## STURECOMPAGNIET Map pp236-8

☎ 611 78 00; Sturegatan 4; admission Skr120 after 10pm Fri & Sat; ◷ 10pm-5am Wed-Sat

One of the more welcoming clubs in Stureplan, this ornate, high-ceilinged, red-velvet-curtained bar also serves decent food.

## TRANAN Map p230

☎ 52 72 81 00; Karlbergsvägen 14; ◷ to 1am; T-Odenplan

The basement-bar counterpart to locally revered Café Tranan, this is a classic DJ dance club with frequent guest spots, occasional big names at weekends, and a tiny stage.

# MUSIC

The live rock- and pop-music scene in Stockholm is something local scenesters and media types love to complain about, but in fact the number of small venues and bands has been on the upswing lately. Mondo, Alcazar, Debaser and Öst 100 are among the best new places to hear bands. As for classical music, it continues

### From Warship to Nightclub

The *Patricia* was launched in 1938 at Smith's shipyard in Middlesbrough, England, with the intention of serving as a lightship off the British coast. However, when WWII broke out in September 1939, it was hastily rebuilt as a warship and pressed into service with the Royal Navy. The *Patricia* was attacked by the Luftwaffe during the evacuation of Allied troops at Dunkirk in 1940, but didn't suffer serious damage. The ship was also involved in naval operations relating to the D-day landings in Normandy during June 1944.

After WWII, the *Patricia* was rebuilt once more, this time as a luxury royal yacht, and it sailed to Helsinki with Princess Elizabeth (now Queen Elizabeth II) on board in 1952. The ship ultimately came to Stockholm in 1986 and was berthed near Slussen, where it has been used as a novel restaurant and nightclub known as Lady Patricia ever since.

to thrive. The opera season runs from September to May; classical music concerts run from August through June. In summer, outdoor courtyards and parks all over town become music venues. For up-to-date schedules, check the monthly *What's On - Stockholm*, produced by the tourist office, or the *På Stan* section of Friday's *Dagens Nyheter*. The website www.konsertguiden.nu (in Swedish) is a good source of current classical music schedules and upcoming events.

Most of the venues listed in this chapter sell tickets in advance through **Biljett Direkt** ( ☎ 077 170 70 70 in Sweden only; www.ticnet.se).

# CLASSICAL

## BERWALDHALLEN Map pp231-3

☎ 784 18 00; Dag Hammarskjölds Väg 3; tickets Skr50-350; ◷ box office noon-6pm Mon-Fri, closed midsummer-Aug; bus 56, 69, 76

Almost as interesting to look at as it is to sit in, this building was designed in the 1970s for Radio Sweden with an eye towards it blending into the surrounding Djurgården. Built mostly underground, and finished in 1979, the hall centres on a hexagonal auditorium that offers brilliant acoustics. It's named after Swedish composer Franz Berwald. The Swedish Radio Symphony Orchestra performs contemporary, frequently Swedish music. The Radiokören based here is considered to be one of the best choirs in the world.

## KONSERTHUSET Map pp236-8

☎ 50 66 77 88; www.konserthuset.se; Hötorget; tickets Skr65-400; ◷ 11am-6pm Mon-Fri, 11am-3pm Sat; T-Hötorget, bus 1, 43, 52, 56

The large, blue-fronted auditorium on Hötorget holds concerts and events throughout the year; pick up a schedule in its office off Kungsgatan.

## NYBROKAJEN 11 Map pp236-8

☎ 407 17 00; www.nybrokajen11.rikskonserter.se; Nybrokajen 11; tickets Skr150-200; ◷ noon-5pm Mon-Fri, closed mid-Jun–mid-Aug; T-Kungsträdgården

This venue for classical music is connected to the smaller Stallet, home of folk music from Sweden and elsewhere in the world. It's an extremely graceful, gold, pink and grey hall with killer acoustics and good sightlines from the 600-plus seats.

# JAZZ

## FYLKINGEN Map pp234–5

☎ 84 54 43; www.fylkingen.se; Münchenbryggeriet, Torkel Knutssonsgatan 2; tickets free-Skr85; ☺ box office 10am-5pm Mon-Fri; T-Mariatorget, bus 4, 43, 55, 66

Together with **EMS** (Elektroakustisk Musik i Sverige; www.ems.rikskonserter.se), and housed in the same building, Fylkingen is *the* centre for experimental music in Sweden. Started in 1933, it has hosted the likes of John Cage and Swedish provocateur Karl-Erik Welin (known for hacking his leg apart while performing with a chainsaw on a grand piano). Anyone interested in the bleeding edge of music shouldn't miss it. Fylkingen also has a record label and produces multimedia events with the fringe arts group Nursery.

## GLENN MILLER CAFE Map pp236–8

☎ 10 03 22; Brunnsgatan 21A; ☺ 5pm-midnight Mon-Thu, 5pm-1am Fri & Sat; T-Hötorget, bus 1, 43, 52, 56

This tiny jazz and blues bar draws a faithful, fun-loving crowd to its performances. It's also known for serving excellent, affordable *husmanskost* meals.

## JAZZCLUB FASCHING Map pp236–8

☎ 21 62 67; Kungsgatan 63; tickets Skr20-200; ☺ to 1am Mon-Thu, to 4am Fri-Sat; T-Centralen, bus 1, 47, 53, 69

*Jazzclub Fasching (above)*

A world-renowned jazz club, Fasching hosts local artists and unknowns as well as big names in the international jazz world. It's a small, cosy place with a great view from the balcony but limited standing room.

## LYDMAR HOTEL Map pp236–8

☎ 56 61 13 00; www.lydmar.se; Sturegatan 10; entry free to hotel guests, minimum age 25; ☺ 11.30am-1am Mon-Thu, 11.30am-2am Fri, 1pm-2am Sat, 1pm-1am Sun; T-Östermalmstorg

The swanky Lydmar Hotel (see also p164) hosts unannounced concerts from internationally known names in jazz and hip-hop a few nights a week.

## NALEN Map pp236–8

☎ 453 34 00; Regeringsgatan 74; tickets free-Skr250; ☺ box office noon-4pm Mon-Fri; T-Hötorget, bus 1, 43, 46, 56

Nalen has been around almost as long as live music has been played in Stockholm; the height of its popularity occurred between the 1930s and the 1960s, when big bands and jazz acts came from all over.

## STAMPEN Map pp239–41

☎ 20 57 93; www.stampen.se; Stora Nygatan 5; tickets Skr100-150; ☺ 8pm-1am Mon-Wed, to 2am Thu-Sat; T-Gamla Stan, bus 3, 53, 55, 59, 76

This well-known club in Gamla Stan, with timeworn, quirky décor and a friendly vibe, has blues and some jazz concerts every night; there's also a free blues jam featuring local musicians at 2pm on Saturday afternoons.

# ROCK & POP

## ALCAZAR Map pp236–8

☎ 453 34 00; Regeringsgatan 74 (entrance on David Bagaresgatan); admission Skr150, Wed free

This cool little basement bar underneath historic jazz club Nalen has been showcasing up-and-coming Stockholm rock and indie bands and drawing a devoted following – especially to its Wednesday-night 'Come Out and Play', a new-band night with no cover charge.

## CIRKUS Map pp231–3

☎ 660 10 20; www.cirkus.se; Djurgårdsslätten 43-45; tickets Skr200-600; ☺ box office 10am-6pm Mon & Tue, 10am-7.30pm Wed-Fri, noon-7pm Sat, 1-3pm Sun; bus 47

Big-name touring rock bands play at this bizarre-looking stadium on Djurgården.

## GLOBEN Map pp234–5
☎ 077 131 00 00; www.globen.se; Arenavägen, Johanneshov; tickets Skr100-600; ⏰ 9am-6pm Mon, until 4pm Tue-Fri (box office); T-Globen, bus 4, 150, 164
Even bigger-name touring rock bands – KISS and the like – play at the Globe, Stockholm's famous oversized golf ball that's visible from miles away.

## GÖTA KÄLLARE Map pp234–5
☎ 57 86 79 00; Folkungagatan 45; concert tickets Skr100-250; ⏰ 9pm-3am Thu-Sat; T-Medborgarplatsen, bus 55, 59, 66
This friendly, comfortable bar – behind a wall of corrugated tin at one entrance to the Medborgarplatsen subway station – often has DJs spinning records, but it hosts live indie-rock bands on a weekly basis.

## KAFÉ 44 Map pp234–5
☎ 644 53 12; Tjärhovsgatan 44; tickets Skr40-100; ⏰ 2-3 times a week for concerts; T-Medborgarplatsen, bus 3, 46, 53, 59, 66
This alcohol-free, politically oriented, all-ages anarchist club hosts the kind of bands you'd expect from a politically oriented, all-ages anarchist club – loud, earnest, vegan and fiercely obscure. It's definitely worth checking out to see what Stockholm's plugged-in kids are up to.

## MONDO Map pp234–5
☎ 673 10 32; Medborgarplatsen 8; tickets free-Skr150; ⏰ to 3am; T-Medborgarplatsen, bus 55, 59, 66
This giant, new, music complex has live bands most nights, often on all three stages at once. The top-floor lounge usually offers free shows from local bands.

## MOSEBACKE ETABLISSEMENT
Map pp239–41
☎ 55 60 98 90; Mosebacketorg 3; tickets Skr80-250; ⏰ 4pm-1am Mon-Thu, Sun, to 2am Fri & Sat; T-Slussen, bus 3, 46, 53, 76
Well-known acts of all genres play at the historic Mosebacke, where the sophisticated, regal atmosphere augments any style of music.

## MÜNCHENBRYGGERIET Map pp234–5
☎ 658 00 20; www.munchen-bryggeriet.com/engelsk; Söder Mälarstrand 29 (entrance); tickets Skr100-250; T-Mariatorget, bus 43, 55, 66

This genre-jumping venue is in an old brewery that also houses Fylkingen and EMS (see p136).

## ÖST 100 Map pp234–5
☎ 55 69 76 70; Östgötagatan 100; admission free-Skr150
This large, open-plan, modern club at the tail end of Östgötagatan, overlooking the Hammarby channel, has a large bar and tons of seating, plus a good-sized stage for bands and frequent DJ nights. Big picture windows mean you can investigate the scene before going in.

# SPORT & FITNESS
In Stockholm it's just as easy – and as entertaining – to pick up a bandy stick and hit the ice yourself as it is to grab a thermos of something warm and watch from the bleachers. The city lends itself to winter sports, not surprisingly, but there are also plenty of warm-weather pursuits available, from swimming to sailing, as well as year-round indoor activities like billiards and badminton.

## BADMINTON
In case you get the urge to whack that birdie, Stockholm is home to an enormous badminton hall.

### BADMINTONSTADION Map pp234–5
☎ 642 70 02; Hammarby slussväg 4; courts per hr Skr100-120; T-Skanstull
Stockholm's largest badminton hall is a vast cathedral of sport where locals in spandex and T-shirts gather to worship the 'feather ball'.

## BANDY
*Bandy* matches, a uniquely Scandinavian phenomenon, take place all winter at Stockholm's ice arenas. Impromptu matches are played in the square at Medborgarplatsen; official games are scheduled at Zinkensdamms Idrottsplats.

### ZINKENSDAMMS IDROTTSPLATS
Map pp234–5
☎ 668 93 31; Ringvägen 12-14; ⏰ 8am-2pm Tue-Thu, 8am-11pm Sat, 1-4pm Sun Nov-Feb; T-Zinkensdamm

Watching a *bandy* match at Zinkensdamm Idrottsplats is great fun. The sport, which was a precursor to ice hockey but with more players (11 to a side) and less fighting, has become massively popular since the late-1990s rise of the Hammarby team. There's a round vinyl ball instead of a puck, and the rules are similar to football, except that you hit the ball with a stick instead of kicking it. The season lasts from November to March, which means it's absolutely vital to bring your own thermos of *kaffekask* – a warming mix of coffee and booze. You can also bring your own stick and ask to join in.

## BILLIARDS

### STOCKHOLMS BILJARDSALONG
☎ 31 32 50; Gyldéngatan 2; per table Skr115; T-Odenplan

You can find pool and billiards at a number of bars and pubs, but this is one of the few clubs dedicated solely to the pursuit of the pockets. There are 20 billiard tables plus darts and blackjack.

## FOOTBALL

Football matches take place weekly between April and October at Söder Stadion (home to Hammarby football club), adjacent to Globen (same contact details and prices; see below).

### RÅSUNDA STADION Map pp228–9
☎ 735 09 35; Solnavägen 51; tickets around Skr200; T-Solna Centrum

Råsunda is Sweden's national football stadium and you can see the national team or AIK (Allmänna Idrottsklubben) play here.

### STADION Map pp231–3
☎ 50 82 83 62; Lidingövägen 1; tickets Skr150–200; T-Stadion

Premier League (Allsvenskan) football matches take place here once weekly between April and October. There are also occasional track and field events in summer, as well as the sports festival DN Galan (www.dngalan.com) in mid-July.

## GYMS

You don't have to break your work-out routine while you're on holiday. There are a couple of Stockholm gyms that are open to the public.

### FRISKIS & SVETTIS Map pp230
☎ 429 70 00; Mäster Samuelsgatan 20; nonmembers Skr80; ☺ 6.30am-9pm Mon-Thu, 6.30am-7pm Fri, 10am-12.30pm Sat, 3.30-6.30pm Sun; T-Hötorget

This gym, 'Healthy and Sweaty', is a relaxed place with a crowd that's not too focussed on checking out each other's buff pecs. There's another outlet at St Eriksgatan 54 (same phone number).

## HORSE RACING

Horse racing combines two leisure pursuits into one – watching sports and betting on them. The main draw in Stockholm is trotting races.

### SOLVALLA TRAVBANA Map pp228–9
☎ 635 90 00; Travbaneplan, Sundbyberg; tickets usually Skr20; T-Rissne

At Solvalla Travbana you'll see trotting, a sport in which horses pull sulkies, each with a driver. It's a popular spectator sport and it's closely connected to gambling. Races take place several times weekly.

## ICE HOCKEY

It's no accident that Stockholmers love ice hockey – it's cold here more than half the year, and the amount of water in the city means there's an abundance of frozen surfaces on which to play the game. Swedes are internationally competitive in hockey, and that's part of the reason it's such a popular spectator sport.

### GLOBEN Map pp234–5
☎ 600 34 00; www.globen.se; Arenavägen, Johanneshov; tickets Skr150-200; T-Globen, bus 4, 150, 164

Ice hockey matches take place at Globen two or three times weekly from October to April. This is the most popular sport in Sweden during the winter; the two main teams, AIK and Djurgården, draw huge crowds with fierce (by Swedish standards) rivalries. If you're interested in spectator sports at all, don't miss the chance to watch an ice-hockey derby at Globen.

## ICE SKATING

Impromptu public skating areas spring up during the winter at **Kungsträdgården** in Norrmalm and in **Medborgarplatsen** in Södermalm. Skate-rental booths next to

## Ice Hockey

In Sweden ice hockey is the second-biggest sport after football. The sport originated in North America and European settlers added rules to the original native American game in 1875. Ice hockey then spread rapidly throughout Canada, the USA and Scandinavia and became an official sport at the Winter Olympics in 1920.

There are only five active players plus a goalkeeper per side. Ice hockey is extremely fast and aggressive and it's the only major sport where unlimited substitution is possible during play – active players are drawn and returned from the full team of 20 to 25 players every few minutes.

Most Swedish communities have amateur teams and an *ishall*, where ice hockey matches are played during winter. There are 15 professional teams in the Premier League and important games are shown on television. Strong rivalry exists between the national teams of Sweden and Finland; some Swedish players play abroad, notably in the Canadian league.

For further details on the sport in Sweden, contact **Svenska Ishockeyförbundet** ( ☎ 449 04 00, fax 91 00 35; Bolidenvägen 22, Box 5204, SE-12116 Johanneshov).

the rinks rent equipment for Skr35/10 for adults/children.

# KAYAKING, CANOEING & BOATING

Seeing Stockholm by water is fantastic, and it's something every visitor should do if time permits. Rent small boats from **Segelfartygsrederiet** (Map pp234-5; ☎ 702 02 02; Hammarby vägen 3; ☉ 9am-9pm phone info). Sail boats and motorboats of all sizes can be rented from **Blue Water Cruising Club** (Map pp231-3; ☎ 717 68 00; Galärvarvsvägen 2; ☉ 9am-9pm). **Djurgårdsbrons Sjöcafe** (Map pp231-3; ☎ 660 57 57; Galärvarvsvägen 2; ☉ 9am-9pm) rents out canoes, kayaks, rowboats and pedal boats, and **Tvillingarnas Båtuthyrning** (Map pp236-8; ☎ 663 37 39; Strandvägskajen 27; ☉ 9am-7pm, closed Nov-May) hires out small sail boats and motorboats of all sizes.

# RUNNING

Paths around the parks on Långholmen and Djurgården and through Hagaparken are great for jogging. If you're more serious about running, the **Midnattsloppet** (Midnight Race; ☎ 649 71 71) is a 10km street race that takes place in Södermalm in August. The **Stockholm Marathon** ( ☎ 54 56 64 40; www.marathon.se), which attracts some 14,000 runners to the city in mid-June, is famed for its lovely route, which starts at Stadion and goes along Strandvägen, Norrmälarstrand and Skeppsbron.

# SWIMMING

There are plenty of unofficial swimming spots throughout the city, including the terrace next to **Stadshuset**, **Evert Taubes Terass** on Riddarholmen, and best of all the beach at **Långholmen**.

### CENTRALBADET Map pp236–8

☎ 24 24 02; www.centralbadet.se; Drottninggatan 88; tickets Skr90-120; minimum age women/men 18/23; ☉ 6am-9pm Mon-Fri, 8am-9pm Sat & Sun; T-Hötorget

More accessible to visitors and less posh than Östermalm's Sturebadet, Centralbadet has a lovely garden courtyard with a good café, plus various types of spas and saunas, swimming pools, herbal soaks and, of course, Swedish massages.

### ERIKSDALSBADET Map pp234–5

☎ 50 84 02 50; Hammarby slussväg 8; T-Skanstull
This outdoor pool is open from May to August, with a toddler pool, water gymnastics classes and a beach volleyball court. Look out for year-round swimming competitions in the indoor arena.

### STUREBADET Map pp236–8

☎ 54 50 15 00; www.sturebadet.se; Sturegallerian, Stureplan; day membership Skr295, minimum age 18; ☉ 6.30am-10pm Mon-Fri (to 9pm mid-May–mid-Aug), 9am-7pm Sat & Sun (to 6pm in mid-May–mid-Aug); T-Östermalmstorg
This plushly appointed spa in the centre of Sturegallerian shopping centre has all the services you'd expect, plus appropriately snobby service and an exclusive clientele.

# TENNIS

Mention the words 'Sweden' and 'tennis' together and the next thing you'll hear is 'Bjorn Borg'. The tennis star is still big news in Stockholm, though more for fashion than sports these days. The game where he made his name is popular both with spectators and participants.

## KUNGLIGA TENNISHALLEN Map pp231-3
☎ 459 15 00; www.kungl.tennishallen.com; Lidingövägen 75; per hr Skr235-255; ☻ 7am-11pm Mon-Thu, 7am-9pm Fri, 8am-8pm Sat, 8am-10pm Sun; bus 73
The Royal Tennis Hall is open to the public, and this is where the Stockholm Open is played each autumn. The cost of court hire varies depending both on the court and on the time of day that you want to play.

# Shopping

# Shopping

Stockholm is a shopper's dream – the city's fascination with cutting-edge style and design means there are endless opportunities to pick up clothing and interior-design items from top-notch names. Swedish-made crafts tend to be of a uniformly high quality. Among the best souvenirs are Sweden's internationally renowned glassware (whether practical – bowls, jugs, glasses, *glögg* (hot mulled wine) mugs – or decorative, like Orrefors' mysterious glass faces – or both, like the ubiquitous crystal snowball candleholder); trademark red- or blue-painted wooden horses from Dalarna; intricately carved woodwork in the form of toys, serving trays or kitchen utensils; linen tablecloths and hand towels; and beautiful amber and silver jewellery.

Uniquely Swedish foods, such as cloudberry jam, *lingonsylt* (lingonberry jam) or pickled herring in *brännvin* (aquavit) sauce, are also well worth taking home – although keep in mind that some foods, particularly produce and any kind of meat product, are restricted or prohibited by customs officials in most countries. You might also consider inflicting the joys of Swedish *snaps*, *punsch*, *brännvin* (forms of vodka) or even stranger drinks like cloudberry liqueur on your loved ones back home.

Handicrafts carrying the round token *Svensk slöjd* (hammer and shuttle emblem) are endorsed by Svenska hemslöjdsföreningarnas riksförbund, the national handicrafts organisation whose symbol is found on affiliated handicraft shops. Look out for signs reading 'Hemslöjd', indicating handicraft sales outlets.

Sami handicrafts from Lappland, typically made with materials such as reindeer bone, reindeer hide, birchwood, silver and tin, include intricately carved knives and sheaths, drums, cups and bowls, colourful textiles and jewellery ornately embroidered with silver thread. Look for the *Duodji* label (a round coloured token of authenticity), and be aware that fakes are fairly common in souvenir shops along major tourist thoroughfares.

A tip for those visiting Stockholm in the winter: nearly all the shops in town have massive end-of-year sales during the three days immediately after Annandag Jul, the day after Christmas – in other words, hold off from buying gifts to take home until 27 to 29 December.

## OPENING HOURS

Shops are generally open from 10am to 6pm Monday to Friday, 10am to 5pm Saturday and noon to 4pm Sunday, although smaller shops have limited hours on Saturday and are often closed on Sunday. Department stores are generally open from 10am to 7pm Monday to Saturday and 10am to 6pm Sunday. Exceptions to these general guidelines are noted in the reviews in this chapter.

### Tax-Free Shopping

If you intend to do a lot of shopping and you're not a citizen of the European Union (EU), check whether the outlet is part of the Tax Free Shopping network when making a single purchase of more than Skr200, as you're entitled to a refund of 15% to 18% on your purchase. (Look for a 'Tax Free' sticker on the door or by the cash register. If you don't see one, ask anyway – some shops don't advertise that they're part of the network.) Show your passport at the checkout and ask for a Global Refund Cheque.

The purchased goods will be sealed and mustn't be opened until after you leave Sweden (or the last EU country you visit on your trip). At that point, you can cash your Global Refund Cheques at any Global Refund office (there are two at Stockholm's Arlanda Airport, one in Terminal 5 and one at the Forex counter in Terminal 2; see www.globalrefund.com for other locations).

For a list of shops in the network, ask the tourist office for a free copy of the *Tax Free Shopping Guide to Sweden*, updated annually. Most shops included are on a fairly well-trodden tourist circuit and should be easy to find.

The monthly magazine *What's On – Stockholm*, produced by the tourist office in both English and Swedish, also has information for shoppers. For more details, see Taxes & Refunds, p202.

Suprisingly, a lot of shops, mainly specialty boutiques, close during July, when Stockholm collectively goes on holiday; if you visit during this time, the first Swedish word you'll learn is likely to be '*stängt*' (closed).

# GAMLA STAN

It's easy to be swept into the frenzy of souvenir shops hawking miniature Vikings, woollen hats and 'Absolut Swede' T-shirts along Gamla Stan's main shopping thoroughfare, Västerlånggatan. Worse things could happen – but if you'd like to avoid the crush, veer off onto almost any side street and you'll find more interesting, out-of-the-way shops in a much more atmospheric setting.

### CARL WENNBERG

Map pp239–41                             *Handicrafts*
☎ 20 17 21; Svartmangatan 11; ◷ closed Sun; T-Gamla Stan
This is the place for superb Sami art and handicrafts, including knives, silver and tin jewellery, drums, clothes and ceramics; almost everything sold here is made by Sami people.

### FLODINS Map pp239–41            *Antiques*
☎ 20 48 81; www.flodins.aos.se; Västerlånggatan 37; ◷ closed Sun; T-Gamla Stan
Flodins sells gorgeous antique maps and prints, architectural drawings, and old encyclopedia-style illustrations of plants and animals, both framed and unframed; prices range from Skr250 to Skr6000.

### GAMLA STANS TE & KAFFEHANDEL

Map pp239–41                             *Tea & Coffee*
☎ 20 70 47; Stora Nygatan 14; ◷ 11am-6pm Mon-Fri, noon-4pm Sat; T-Gamla Stan
Follow your nose into this haven of tea and coffee, full of antique tins, china tea sets and an interesting stash of unusual gift items (decorative wooden chickens etc).

### GRAY'S AMERICAN FOOD STORE

Map pp239–41                             *Food & Gifts*
☎ 21 95 00; Västerlånggatan 14; ◷ 10.30am-7pm Mon-Fri, 11am-7pm Sat, noon-6pm Sun; T-Gamla Stan
Homesick yanks and curious Swedes can find cornflakes, marshmallows and *The Simpsons* keyrings here. The shop's shelves provide an eye-opening perspective on just what is considered 'American food'.

### JACKSON'S Map pp239–41           *Design*
☎ 411 95 87; Tyskabrinken 20; ◷ closed Sun; T-Gamla Sta

## Clothing Sizes
**Measurements approximate only, try before you buy**

**Women's Clothing**

| Aus/UK | 8 | 10 | 12 | 14 | 16 | 18 |
|---|---|---|---|---|---|---|
| Europe | 36 | 38 | 40 | 42 | 44 | 46 |
| Japan | 5 | 7 | 9 | 11 | 13 | 15 |
| USA | 6 | 8 | 10 | 12 | 14 | 16 |

**Women's Shoes**

| Aus/USA | 5 | 6 | 7 | 8 | 9 | 10 |
|---|---|---|---|---|---|---|
| Europe | 35 | 36 | 37 | 38 | 39 | 40 |
| France only | 35 | 36 | 38 | 39 | 40 | 42 |
| Japan | 22 | 23 | 24 | 25 | 26 | 27 |
| UK | 3½ | 4½ | 5½ | 6½ | 7½ | 8½ |

**Men's Clothing**

| Aus | 92 | 96 | 100 | 104 | 108 | 112 |
|---|---|---|---|---|---|---|
| Europe | 46 | 48 | 50 | 52 | 54 | 56 |
| Japan | S | | M | M | | L |
| UK/USA | 35 | 36 | 37 | 38 | 39 | 40 |

**Men's Shirts (Collar Sizes)**

| Aus/Japan | 38 | 39 | 40 | 41 | 42 | 43 |
|---|---|---|---|---|---|---|
| Europe | 38 | 39 | 40 | 41 | 42 | 43 |
| UK/USA | 15 | 15½ | 16 | 16½ | 17 | 17½ |

**Men's Shoes**

| Aus/UK | 7 | 8 | 9 | 10 | 11 | 12 |
|---|---|---|---|---|---|---|
| Europe | 41 | 42 | 43 | 44½ | 46 | 47 |
| Japan | 26 | 27 | 27½ | 28 | 29 | 30 |
| USA | 7½ | 8½ | 9½ | 10½ | 11½ | 12½ |

Jackson's specialises in modern design, particularly museum-quality Swedish glassware and ceramics with intimidating prices (up to Skr20,000) that make you watch where you put your elbows.

### KALIKÅ Map pp239–41              *Toys*
☎ 20 52 19; Österlånggatan 18; T-Gamla Stan
This wholesome children's gift shop sells old-fashioned stuffed animals and wooden toys with unique designs. You can also buy toy-making kits to put together with your kids.

### KÖPMANGATAN 3 ANTIQUE SHOP

Map pp239–41                             *Antiques*
☎ 21 02 39; Köpmangatan 3; ◷ noon-6pm Mon-Fri, 11am-4pm Sat; T-Gamla Stan
This shop, in a fascinating old building, specialises in antique porcelain, fine art, maps, glassware, silverware and cutlery.

## SWEDEN BOOKSHOP Map pp239–41 _Books_
☎ 789 21 31; bookshop@si.se; Slottsbacken 10;
🕐 10am-6pm Mon-Fri, 11am-3pm Sat, also 10am-3pm Sun Jul & Aug; T-Gamla Stan

This is the place for books about Sweden and Stockholm in English and other languages. The Swedish Institute publishes high-quality, scholarly books and brochures on various aspects of Swedish life, from economics to pop culture to historical figures; they're not cheap, but they're well done and the translations are generally excellent. Mail order is available. The shop is usually on the 1st floor of Sverigehuset, Hamngatan 27; it's scheduled to reopen there in November 2004. The Swedish Institute's headquarters will stay at Slottsbacken.

## TOMTAR & TROLL Map pp239–41 _Gifts_
☎ 10 56 29; www.tomtar-troll.com; Österlånggatan 45; T-Gamla Stan

If you want to pick up cute little _tomtar_ (elves) and trolls as souvenirs, this cosy shop is a good place to get them – they're well crafted and look traditional, rather than corny and colourful.

# NORRMALM & VASASTADEN

The city centre houses the main shopping malls and department stores, including the landmark Nordiska Kompaniet (NK), as well as always-busy pedestrian shopping street Drottninggatan.

There's a large concentration of antique shops at the northern end of Upplandsgatan (T-Odenplan), each with a different specialty. Besides those listed below, several of these shops – such as **Antikt Evensen Nött & Nytt** ( ☎ 34 61 66; Upplandsgatan 48); **Bacchus Antik** ( ☎ 30 54 80; Upplandsgatan 46); **Carléns Antik** ( ☎ 31 34 01; Upplandsgatan 40); **Lady Lisabeth Dream** ( ☎ 32 41 45; Upplandsgatan 45); **Odens Antik** ( ☎ 34 65 22; Upplandsgatan 41); **St Eriks Antik** ( ☎ 34 89 00; Upplandsgatan 51); and **Trädkronan Antik** ( ☎ 31 72 10; Upplandsgatan 43) – carry an impressive variety of unusual items, from elaborate lamps to heirloom decorations, antique paintings and glassware. You could easily spend hours window shopping.

## AKADEMIBOKHANDELN
Map pp236–8 _Books_
☎ 613 61 00; Mäster Samuelsgatan 32; 🕐 closed Sun; T-Centralen

This enormous shop carries the widest range of new books in Stockholm; the lower levels are mostly textbooks and academic studies in Swedish, but there's a huge stash of English paperbacks on the top floor.

## ANTIKT & MODERNT Map p230 _Antiques_
☎ 30 31 44; Upplandsgatan 44; 🕐 closed Sun; T-Odenplan

This shop stocks antique glassware, ceramics, wooden figures, silver and some nice pieces of china.

## ANTIKVARIAT MIMER Map pp231–3 _Books_
☎ 612 05 00; Tegnérgatan 4; T-Rådmansgatan

The second-hand and antiquarian books sold here are mostly philosophy and history titles.

## BLUE FOX Map pp236–8 _Fetish Clothing_
☎ 20 32 41; Gamla Brogatan 27; 🕐 closed Sun; T-Centralen

The source for latex clubwear, piercings, tattoos, hair dye in vivid primary colours, Goth-friendly jewellery, fetishy footwear, and assorted mesh and feathered things.

## BUKOWSKI'S Map pp236–8 _Auctions_
☎ 614 08 00; www.bukowskis.se; Arsenalsgatan 4; 🕐 9am-5pm Mon-Fri; T-Kungsträdgården

Sweden's primary auction house, Bukowski's specialises in valuable antique furnishings, jewellery and artwork.

## CENTRALANTIKVARIATET
Map pp236–8 _Books_
☎ 411 91 36; Drottninggatan 73B; 🕐 noon-6pm Tue-Fri, 11am-3pm Sat

This shop sells a wide range of second-hand books covering music, travel and history, including lots of titles in English.

## DUKA _Homewares_
☎ 20 60 41; Konserthuset, Kungsgatan; T-Hötorget

This impressive shop carries a prime selection of glassware from Småland (Orrefors, Kosta Boda etc), as well as kitchenware and crockery.

## EXPERT Map pp236–8 _Electronics_
☎ 24 93 20; Drottninggatan 53; T-Centralen

This chain shop sells a vast range of electronics, as well as still and video film and equipment.

## FRILUFTSBOLAGET
Map pp236–8 _Outdoor Gear_
☎ 24 19 96; www.friluftsbolaget.se in Swedish; Kungsgatan 26; 🕐 closed Sun

This outdoors shop stocks high-performance camping and hiking equipment, including boots, jackets, fleeces, sleeping bags, tents, stoves and backpacks.

### GALLERIAN Map pp236–8  *Shopping Centre*
☎ 791 24 45; www.gallerian.se; Hamngatan 37; T-Centralen

Across from NK, this large shopping mall contains around 50 shops – including Clas Ohlsson, which sells practically everything in randomly arranged bins, and Vero Moda, where you can get shimmery clothing in the three colours deemed fashionable each season – and a dozen places to eat.

### H&M Map pp236–8  *Clothing*
☎ 796 54 32; Hamngatan 22; T-Centralen or T-Kungsträdgården

Hennes & Mauritz, affectionately known as H&M, sells well-made knock offs of each season's trendiest fashions at cut-rate prices. What's not to like? There are branches all over town, but this is one of the larger and better-stocked shops.

### HALLÉNS ANTIKVARIAT
Map pp231–3  *Books*
☎ 20 02 70; Tegnérgatan 17; ☼ closed Sun; T-Rådmansgatan

One of the few places to find really inexpensive second-hand books (from Skr20), this bookseller stocks a huge range covering history, food and fiction, many of which are in English.

### JONES ANTIKVARIAT Map pp231–3  *Books*
☎ 30 76 97; Norrtullsgatan 3; ☼ closed Sun; T-Odenplan

This shop's selection includes books on art, medicine and science; there are also biographies, children's books and some titles in English.

### KARTBUTIKEN Map pp236–8  *Books & Maps*
☎ 20 23 03; Kungsgatan 74; ☼ closed Sun; T-Centralen

Kartbutiken has an excellent selection of low-priced travel books, as well as maps, cards and journals.

### KONSTHANTVERKARNA
Map pp236–8  *Handicrafts*
☎ 611 03 70; Mäster Samuelsgatan 2; ☼ closed Sun; T-Östermalmstorg

This shop is run by a craftsmen's co-op; it stocks glassware, ceramics, textiles, leather, silver and wood handicrafts, and there are rotating art exhibits featuring the work of local artists.

### KONST-IG Map pp236–8  *Books*
☎ 50 83 15 18; basement of Kulturhuset, Sergels Torg; ☼ 10am-7pm Mon-Sat, noon-4pm Sun; T-Centralen

This shop stocks a tantalising collection of luscious, beautiful books on fine-art, architecture and design in both Swedish and English, covering the national and international scenes.

### MELANDERS BLOMMOR
Map pp236–8  *Flowers*
☎ 611 28 59; www.melandersblommor.se; Hamngatan 2; ☼ closed Sun; T-Östermalmstorg

Melanders is a traditional, old-fashioned florist, but it's not behind the times – you can order flowers and chocolate delivered via the company's website (available in English).

### NATURKOMPANIET
Map pp236–8  *Outdoor Gear*
☎ 723 15 81; Kungsgatan 4A; ☼ closed Sun

Similar to Friluftsbolaget, this shop carries clothing and equipment for the outdoor explorer and weekend warrior – or just someone trying to cross Kungsträdgården in the middle of December. There's another branch in **Kungsholmen** (Map p230; ☎ 651 35 00; Hantverkargatan 38-40).

### NK Map pp236–8  *Department Store*
☎ 762 80 00; Hamngatan 18-20; ☼ 10am-7pm Mon-Fri, 10am-5pm Sat, noon-5pm Sun, noon-4pm Sun Jun & Jul, basement closes 1hr later; T-Centralen or T-Kungsträdgården

Nordiska Kompaniet, marked by the gigantic, rotating NK sign visible across half the city, is an enormous store with over 110 departments selling cosmetics, designer clothing, Swedish handicrafts, and its own-brand pastries and chocolates. The basement market sells some traditional foods, and there's also a health-food shop. The book department has a particularly good English-language section. It's a great place to pick up holiday decorations and souvenirs. There's a decent bar/restaurant on the top level.

### NORDISKA KRISTALL
Map pp236–8  *Glassware*
☎ 10 43 72; Kungsgatan 9; ☼ closed Sun

This shop carries Swedish glassware by Orrefors, Kosta Boda, Målerås and other big names in the Scandinavian glassmaking empire. Look

*Mannequins at NK (p145)*

Shopping – Normalm & Vasastaden

### ROTSPEL Map pp231–3 · *Music*
☎ 16 04 04; Tulegatan 37; ☾ closed Sun; T-Rådmansgatan
An unusually eclectic record shop, Rotspel sells albums and CDs of Scandinavian folk, Sami traditionals and world music.

### SERGEL FOTO Map pp236–8 · *Photography*
☎ 20 59 59; Slöjdgatan 1-5; ☾ closed Sun
This shop is the recommended sales outlet for Fuji films; it also develops slides and prints.

### SKOUNO Map pp236–8 · *Shoes*
☎ 20 64 58; Gamla Brogatan 34; ☾ closed Sun; T-Centralen
This is your main source for platform go-go boots, Doc Martens, creepers, Converse trainers and just about any other type of fashionable footwear imaginable, including stiletto snakeskin cowboy boots in colours nature never intended. And it's relatively cheap!

### STADIUM Map pp236–8 · *Clothing & Shoes*
☎ 723 08 75; Kungsgatan 8; T-Centralen
This clothing and shoe shop also sells general sporting goods, such as athletic shoes, various team-affiliation sweatshirts and ice-skating equipment.

### SVENSK HEMSLÖJD
Map pp236–8 · *Handicrafts*
☎ 23 21 15; Sveavägen 44; ☾ closed Sun
This specialty shop carries traditional Swedish handicrafts in wood, textiles, wool and glass, including large Dalarna wooden horses and chickens, carved or moulded serving trays and wicker baskets.

### SVENSKT HANTVERK
Map pp236–8 · *Handicrafts*
☎ 21 47 26; Kungsgatan 55; ☾ closed Sun
Handmade Swedish items are the specialty here, including classic Dalarna horses, kitchen and eating utensils, candelabras, jugs, bowls and fine linen tablecloths.

### ÅHLÉNS Map pp236–8 · *Department Store*
☎ 676 60 00; Klarabergsgatan 50; T-Centralen
A department store with moderate prices, Åhléns sells clothing (its own brand and designer labels), glassware, books, cosmetics, sportswear, photography, computers and music. There are other branches throughout Stockholm. The Hemköp supermarket in the basement sells ready-made vegetarian foods; there's also a good café (see p112) on the top floor and a WC (Skr5) on the 2nd level.

out for gritty, innovative glass creations by Orrefors wunderkind Per B Sundberg, such as plates shaped like Lego and partially frosted globes encasing dirty comic strips (see p34).

### PLAN ETT:1 Map pp231–3 · *Design*
☎ 55 52 97 07; Tegnérgatan 13; ☾ closed Sun; T-Rådmansgatan
This oddly named shop carries a variety of Swedish interior design, from glassware to furniture.

### PLATINA Map p230 · *Jewellery*
☎ 30 02 80; Odengatan 68; ☾ closed Sun; T-Odenplan
Platina sells metalwork and jewellery designed by Swedish and international artists.

### PUB Map pp236–8 · *Department Store*
☎ 402 16 11; Hötorget; T-Hötorget
This large department store, spread over two connected buildings bordering the Hötorget market square, has more than 50 departments, covering music, video, clothing, books, toys and cosmetics; there are also several brand-name boutiques within the store. Greta Garbo got her start as a salesgirl and hat model here.

### QRIOSA ANTIK Map p230 · *Antiques*
☎ 30 92 30; Odengatan 87; ☾ closed Sun; T-Odenplan
This antique shop sells furniture, chandeliers, silver, art, glassware, porcelain and candelabras.

# DJURGÅRDEN & SKEPPSHOLMEN

The main place to shop on Djurgården is, of course, the market at Skansen. Each of the island's excellent museums (see Neighbourhoods, p70) also has a good gift shop; a stand out is the children's books selection at Junibacken. If you're in Stockholm during December, don't miss the *julmarknad* (Christmas market) at Skansen.

### JUNIBACKEN                                      *Books*
☎ 58 72 30 00, Galärparken; ☽ 10am-5pm Tue-Sun, 9am-6pm Jun-Aug; bus 47
The bookshop at Astrid Lindgren's theme park (see p70) has a good selection of children's books, both in English and Swedish.

### SKANSEN SHOP Map pp231-3    *Handicrafts*
☎ 442 82 68; Djurgårdsslätten 49-51; ☽ daily except Christmas Eve; bus 47
At this old-fashioned market you'll find a wide range of quality traditional and modern handicrafts, artwork, souvenirs and food from around Sweden.

# KUNGSHOLMEN

The swank new shopping centre on the corner of St Eriksgatan and Flemminggatan has brought new vitality to this once-dodgy area.

Most of the shops on this residential, largely tourist-free island have a small, neighbourhood feel. This is also where you'll find some of the best second-hand record shops in town, clustered around St Eriksgatan. Besides those listed below, several include **The Beat Goes On** ( ☎ 31 27 17; St Eriksgatan 67); **Golden Oldies Shop** ( ☎ 32 22 40; St Eriksgatan 96); and **Masen's Rock Center** ( ☎ 34 32 00; St Eriksgatan 100).

### GOVINDAS BUTIK Map p230    *Food*
☎ 654 90 02; Fridhemsgatan 22; ☽ 11am-7pm Mon-Fri, noon-7pm Sat; T-Fridhemsplan
At this shop, affiliated with the Hare Krishna–run Govindas vegetarian buffet restaurant, you'll find lots of unusual spices, teas, and Indian and Nepali clothing, as well as vegetarian foods and cooking supplies.

### RECORD PALACE Map p230    *Music*
☎ 650 19 90; St Eriksgatan 56; ☽ closed Sun; T-Fridhemsplan
Calling itself the largest second-hand music shop in town, Record Palace carries everything from classical and jazz to pop and rock, though you'll need to dig around a bit to find what you want.

### R.O.O.M. Map p230    *Design*
☎ 692 50 00; www.room.se; Alströmergatan 20; ☽ closed Sun mid-May–mid-Aug; T-Fridhemsplan
Interior-design heaven for newlywed yuppies with cash to burn, R.O.O.M. is as entertaining

## To Market, to Market

There's nothing like whiling away an afternoon poring over assorted goods (and bads) at a really great neighbourhood market. Stockholm is known for the *julmarknad* (Christmas market) – there are excellent ones in Gamla Stan's Stortorget, Skansen on Djurgården and Sergels Torg in the city centre throughout December. The permanent stalls lining Kungsträdgården also fill up with goods throughout the year during various seasonal markets and events, and there are always a few tables of leather goods and woven things around T-Centralen, Östermalmstorg and Hötorget. For year-round markets, though, your best bet is to hit the suburbs.

There's a food-and-crafts market in Rinkeby just outside the highly recommended international food shop **Rinkeby Orientlivs** ( ☎ 761 36 61; Hinderstorpsgränd 24, Rinkeby; ☽ 9am-7pm Mon-Fri, 10am-6pm Sat & Sun; T-Rinkeby). The shop itself stocks food and cooking supplies from a vast array of sources; you can buy everything from Turkish rosewater to South American spices. Right outside, the market is known for its inexpensive produce, as well as unusual toys, gifts and imported knick-knacks.

The **Skärholmen flea market** ( ☎ 710 00 60; bottom floor of Skärholmen Centrum parking garage; admission Skr10; ☽ 11am-6pm Mon-Fri, 9am-3pm Sat, 10am-3pm Sun; T-Skärholmen) is a large and popular one, with vendors selling everything from typical accessories, clothing and jewellery to Indian and Pakistani videos; there's an African beauty shop that also stocks Eritrean and Ethiopian music, a fabric shop and a Caribbean tarot-card reader, all in a gigantic, unassuming basement.

For food markets, such as Hötorgshallen or Östermalms Saluhall, see p103.

when viewed as a furniture-trends museum. An in-house team of designers makes most of what's for sale, and it is undeniably cool – especially the inventive lighting fixtures and sleek wardrobe systems. If your knees go weak from looking at the price tags, you can always repair to the café and test those clean-lined Swedish chairs for yourself (see p115).

### SKIVBÖRSEN Map p230 · Music
☎ 32 03 17; St Eriksgatan 71; ⊙ closed Sun; T-St Eriksplan

Skivbörsen (the Disc Exchange) has lots of non-mainstream, second-hand LPs and CDs; it's just one in a cluster of great second-hand record shops on this street.

### VÄSTERMALMSGALLERIAN
Map p230 · Shopping Centre
☎ 737 20 00; St Eriksgatan at Flemingatan; ⊙ 10am-7pm Mon-Fri, 10am-5pm Sat, 11am-5pm Sun; T-Fridhemsplan, bus 1,3, 4, 57, 59

This new shopping centre in Kungsholmen contains a classy bar/café and several popular boutiques, including Ordning & Reda, H&M and DesignTorget.

# SÖDERMALM & LÅNGHOLMEN

In its role as the funkier, hipper part of town, Söder has the best vintage clothing shops, second-hand record shops, galleries and offbeat gadget shops. Many of these places rarely see tourists, so they're great options for picking up unusual souvenirs and gifts.

The conglomeration of well-established galleries and shops called Hornspuckeln, along Hornsgatan, has the best selection of fine art for sale. Many of the galleries here are members of Svenska Galleriförbundet, an association that produces a quarterly listing of exhibitions (you can pick one up at any of the galleries found along Hornsgatan or at the tourist office). Exhibitions change every three to four weeks. Items on display are usually for sale, with prices from Skr4000 to Skr20,000.

### AGATA Map pp234–5 · Design
☎ 643 09 80; Nytorgsgatan 36; ⊙ 11am-6pm Tue-Fri, 11am-4pm Sat; T-Medborgarplatsen

This shop deals in unique modern styles of ceramics, glassware and textiles.

### ALVGLANS Map pp234–5 · Comics
☎ 642 69 98; Folkungagatan 84; ⊙ closed Sun; T-Medborgarplatsen

A comic fan's nirvana, Alvglans is packed with animated videos and DVDs, toys, action figures and, of course, loads of comics and graphic novels. The stock covers everything from *The Sandman* to *The X-Men* and includes several purely Swedish titles.

### ANDREAS SKIVOR Map pp234–5 · Music
☎ 640 88 39; Skånegatan 90; ⊙ closed Sun; T-Medborgarplatsen

The knowledgeable staff can advise on the latest club music on CD. Fliers for shows all over town can be picked up here.

### BLÅS & KNÅDA Map pp239–41 · Handicrafts
☎ 642 77 67; www.blasknada.com; Hornsgatan 26; T-Slussen

This artists' and craftsmen's co-op has built a name for itself by producing and selling high-quality glassware and fine ceramics. It also acts as a gallery and can be fun just to look around.

### BOKMAGASINET Map pp234–5 · Books
☎ 668 05 80; Hornsgatan 80; ⊙ closed Sun; T-Mariatorget

Pick up new and second-hand books – some titles are in English – at this book warehouse.

### DESIGNTORGET Map pp239–41 · Design
☎ 462 35 20; Götgatan 31; T-Slussen

DesignTorget is an interesting concept: a consignment shop for artists, it collects the work of several independent up-and-comers and brings it to a much wider market. Browsing in any of the DesignTorget branches, you'll find new Swedish design of all types, from toys and textiles to furniture and storage systems,

## Top Five Stockholm Bookshops

- **Rönnells Antikvariat** (p151) Has a great selection of second-hand books.
- **Alvglans** (above) A comic fan's heaven.
- **Sweden Bookshop** (p144) Has highbrow books on Sweden in a variety of languages.
- **Hedengrens** (p151) Has a good selection of new books in English.
- **Akademibokhandeln** (p144) Has a great range of paperbacks in English.

created by the future stars of the Stockholm design scene. This branch also sells clothing and accessories. There are other outlets at **Kulturhuset** (☎ 50 83 15 20), in **Sturegallerian** (☎ 611 53 03), Stureplan, and in **Västermalmsgallerian** (☎ 33 11 53), Kungsholmen.

### EAST STREET TATTOO

Map pp234–5 *Tattoos*

☎ 702 06 54; www.east-street.com; Östgötagatan 77; T-Skanstull

Get your own genuine Swedish artwork to take home as a souvenir of your trip – East Street is the best-known tattoo shop in Stockholm, and its work is reliably high-quality. There's a piercing studio next door.

### EMMAUS PRAKTISK SOLIDARITET

Map pp239–41 *Second-Hand Wares*

☎ 644 85 86; Götgatan 14; ⊗ closed Sun; T-Slussen

This charity shop deals in second-hand clothing, books and designer wares; because it's in Södermalm the stock is a little funkier than usual.

### FILIPPA K Map pp239–41 *Clothing*

☎ 55 69 85 85; www.filippak.com; Götgatan 23; T-Slussen

The epitome of regulation Stockholm fashion, this local clothing label simply wouldn't produce anything that doesn't look just right; it's not the most exciting shop in the world, but if you want to blend in and look like a local, this is where you should get your costume. There's another outlet on **Grev Turegatan** (Map pp236-8; ☎ 54 58 88 88; Grev Turegatan 18).

### GRAFISKA SÄLLSKAPET

Map pp239–41 *Fine Arts*

☎ 643 88 04; Hornsgatan 6; ⊗ noon-6pm Tue-Thu, noon-4pm Fri-Sun; T-Slussen

One of the most interesting and energetic galleries in the *smörgåsbord* of art that lies in and around Hornspuckeln, Grafiska Sällskapet curates shows from seriously accomplished graphic art to whimsical and humorous paintings, drawings and constructs. Other galleries on this strip include **Galleri Hera** (Hornsgatan 6), **Galleri Puckeln** (Hornsgatan 26) and **Galleri Embla** (Hornsgatan 42), but the styles change so often that it's best to just browse and peek into any place that looks intriguing.

### GÖTGATSBACKENS HÄLSOKOST

Map pp239–41 *Food*

☎ 640 90 40; Götgatan 21; ⊗ closed Sun; T-Slussen

## Top Five Shopping Streets

- **Drottninggatan** (T-Centralen) A pedestrian mall full of the practical and the affordable.
- **Biblioteksgatan** (T-Östermalmstorg) Big-name designer boutiques.
- **Hamngatan** (T-Centralen, T-Kungsträdgården) NK on one side, Gallerian on the other.
- **Götgatan** (T-Slussen, T-Medborgarplatsen) The main artery through the heart of Södermalm has everything from art collectives to record shops to clothing boutiques.
- **Västerlånggatan** (T-Gamla Stan) Like the running of the bulls in Pamplona, but slower, narrower and with more souvenir keyrings.

This health-food shop stocks organic fruit and vegetables, dietary supplements, and vegetarian and vegan foods.

### HELLE KNUDSEN Map pp239–41 *Fine Arts*

☎ 644 40 72; Södermalmstorg 4; ⊗ 11.30am-5.30pm Tue-Thu, 11.30am-4pm Fri, noon-4pm Sat, 1-4pm Sun; T-Slussen

This gallery right on the square deals in modern art, graphic design and sculpture.

### JUDITS SECOND HAND

Map pp234–5 *Second-Hand Clothing*

☎ 84 45 10; Hornsgatan 75; T-Zinkensdamm

Judits specialises in high-quality second-hand goods; it's more vintage than thrift, and the styles are typically Söder-edgy.

### KAOLIN Map pp239–41 *Fine Arts*

☎ 644 46 00; Hornsgatan 50B; T-Slussen

Excellent porcelain is for sale in this gallery/shop owned by a collective of 20 artists.

### KLÄDD I KONST Map pp234–5 *Clothing*

☎ 668 88 12; Hornsgatan 43; ⊗ closed Sun; T-Mariatorget

This well-known shop carries unusual women's clothing and silver jewellery.

### KUS & KOMPANIET Map pp239–41 *Clothing*

St Paulsgatan 1; ⊗ closed Sun; T-Slussen

Swedish-made women's clothing is sold here.

### LISA LARSSONS SECONDHAND

Map pp234–5 *Second-Hand Clothing*

☎ 643 61 53; Bondegatan 48; ⊗ 1-5pm Tue-Fri, 11am-3pm Sat; bus 46, 53, 59, 66, 76

Shopping – Södermalm & Långholmen

149

This microscopic vintage clothing shop is packed to overflowing with great second-hand clothes, from frocks and skirts to cheongsams and sports coats. There's a whole wall of cool leather jackets, and the selection of footwear is small but well chosen.

### LUSH Map pp239–41      *Cosmetics*
☎ 642 00 89; Götgatan 26A; T-Slussen

A good place to pick up gifts, Lush sells luxurious handmade cosmetics, natural soaps, lotions and oils that look and smell good enough to eat.

### METALLUM Map pp239–41      *Fine Arts*
☎ 640 13 23; www.metallum.com; Hornsgatan 30; 
☽ 11am-6pm Tue-Fri, 11am-4pm Sat, noon-4pm Sun; T-Slussen

This gallery/shop carries modern art created from various metals, including gold and silver jewellery and sculptures.

### MULTIKULTI Map pp239–41      *Music*
☎ 643 61 29; St Paulsgatan 3; ☽ 11am-6.30pm Mon & Tue, 11am-7pm Wed-Fri, 11am-4pm Sat; T-Slussen

This tiny shop front sells a huge variety of world music, jazz, salsa, reggae, African pop, and Asian and Middle Eastern dance music. It's also a ticket outlet for world-music concerts at several of Stockholm's major clubs.

### MYRORNA
Map pp234–5      *Second-Hand Clothing*
☎ 55 60 59 82; Hornsgatan 96; T-Zinkensdamm

This cute little shop sells vintage clothes for men and women, plus some other second-hand goods (accessories, jewellery, handbags etc).

### ODENLAB Map pp234–5      *Photography*
☎ 54 54 17 41; Timmermansgatan 32; T-Mariatorget

OdenLab develops film and provides high-quality prints; there are branches throughout the city but this is among the most conveniently located.

### ORDNING & REDA      *Paper*
☎ 728 20 60; www.ordning-reda.com; Götgatan 32; T-Slussen

Besides being a defining phrase in the Swedish psyche, Ordning & Reda is a ubiquitous stationery retailer. Sweden is known for its paper, and the brightly coloured journals and creamy-paged diaries here are great representatives. The chain's many outlets, with their displays arranged to look like sweet shops, are hard to miss.

### PET SOUNDS Map pp234–5      *Music*
☎ 702 97 98; Skånegatan 53; T-Medborgarplatsen

One of Söder's best-known record shops, Pet Sounds stocks indie and alt-rock, pop, rock and dance music. The knowledgeable staff can offer advice, and you can also pick up fliers and concert tickets here.

### PRESS STOP Map pp239–41      *Newsstand*
☎ 644 35 10; Götgatan 31; T-Slussen

The best newsstand in Stockholm, Press Stop sells an impressive selection of English-language paperbacks and magazines, as well as Swedish and EU-produced newspapers and glossies. This location is attached to a Wayne's Coffee shop and DesignTorget; other Press Stop shops are located at Sergels Torg, Gallerian and Sky City (at Arlanda airport). There's another branch in **Norrmalm** (Map pp236-8; ☎ 411 11 93; Drottninggatan 35).

### 10 SWEDISH DESIGNERS
Map pp239–41      *Design*
☎ 643 25 04; www.tiogruppen.com; Götgatan 25; ☽ closed Sat; T-Slussen

Started in 1970 by a group of then-maverick textile artists, Tiogruppen is now on the level of Svenskt Tenn in terms of being classic Swedish design. This shop front is a great place to browse for small gifts or household items, including kitchen towels, handbags, distinctively patterned serving trays, and draperies.

# ÖSTERMALM, GÄRDET & LADUGÅRDSGÄRDET

Östermalm is the city's high-class shopping district, with outlets for top Swedish designers as well as all the biggest names in fashion and accessories. The swank shopping mall Sturegallerian alone could keep a serious shopaholic entertained all day, but there's also the red-carpeted Biblioteksgatan and a number of exclusive boutiques on the side streets.

### ANNA HOLTBLAD Map pp236-8      *Clothing*
☎ 54 50 22 20; Grev Turegatan 13; ☽ closed Sun; T-Östermalmstorg

This small boutique is the shop front for Anna Holtblad, one of the top designers in the country. Her classic clothes are well made from top-notch materials; they're not cheap, but they'll far outlast your bargain-basement purchases and look great doing it.

## CARL MALMSTEN INREDNING

Map pp236–8 *Interior Design*

☎ 23 33 80; www.c.malmsten.se; Strandvägen 5B; 🕑 closed Sun; T-Östermalmstorg

Next door to Svenskt Tenn and similarly revered for its classic designs, this shop sells the creations of Carl Malmsten and his school of interior designers. The chandeliers are particularly out there, and the vibrantly coloured chairs and rugs combine retro '50s cool with avant-garde flair.

## DIS INREDNING

Map pp236–8 *Interior Design*

☎ 611 29 07; Humlegårdsgatan 19; 🕑 closed Sun

Another interesting interior-design shop, this one sells Swedish furnishings, decorative items, porcelain, glassware, baskets etc.

## FACE STOCKHOLM

Map pp236–8 *Cosmetics*

☎ 611 00 74; www.facestockholm.com; Sturegallerian; T-Östermalmstorg

One of several outlets selling this internationally coveted line of cosmetics, this branch's clean lines and crisp organisation make its products resemble precious gems in a jewellery shop.

## HEDENGRENS Map pp236–8 *Books*

☎ 611 51 28; Sturegallerian; T-Östermalmstorg

One of Stockholm's better bookshops, Hedengrens has a great variety of hardcover and paperback fiction in English on its lower level. There's also a small rack of travel guides and maps near the door, and a decent stock of books on Swedish art and design. Don't miss the central atrium with its cylindrical shelves of sci-fi, crime and mystery novels.

## MONROE Map pp236–8 *Clothing*

☎ 611 80 15; Sturegallerian; T-Östermalmstorg

Considering its diminutive size, the number of outrageously cute tops and frocks in this shop is amazing. This is the place to splurge on a really funky dress that no one else will own but everyone will want.

## NANSO Map pp236–8 *Clothing*

☎ 679 70 85; Stureplan 13; T-Östermalmstorg

This boutique specialises in comfortable clothes for women, made in Finland.

## NORDISKA GALLERIET

Map pp236–8 *Design*

☎ 442 83 60; Nybrogatan 11; 🕑 closed Sun; T-Östermalmstorg

Set up like a museum of modern interior design, Nordiska Galleriet is worth a peek even if you've no interest in buying anything. With chairs, couches, lamps and shelves designed by big names like Alvar Aalto and Philippe Starck, as well as lesser known artists, it's an eye-opening place. Pick up a copy of the Swedish design magazine *Form* here for even more ideas.

## NUTIDA SVENSKT SILVER

Map pp236–8 *Jewellery*

☎ 611 67 18; Arsenalsgatan 3; 🕑 closed Sun & Jul; T-Östermalmstorg

At this gallery/shop, you'll find exhibitions and items for sale by 50 modern Swedish silversmiths and goldsmiths, including jewellery and silverware.

## RÖNNELLS ANTIKVARIAT

Map pp236–8 *Books*

☎ 679 75 50; www.ronnells.se; Birger Jarlsgatan 32; T-Östermalmstorg

Possibly the best second-hand bookshop in Stockholm, Rönnells has around 100,000 books on three levels – many in English – from art and literature to travel. It has a sales rack that rewards a bit of foraging, and a great collection of valuable antiquarian books in several languages.

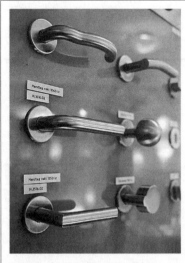

*Designer door handles at Nordiska Galleriet (above)*

## Top Five Swedish Design Shops

- **Svenskt Tenn** (below) An old-school standard setter, shaped by Josef Frank.
- **Nordiska Galleriet** (p151) Like a museum of hot design trends.
- **DesignTorget** (p148) Where known and upcoming designers hawk their wares.
- **10 Swedish Designers** (p150) Söder's funky collective, now well established.
- **Ikea** (below) Bringing high design to the masses.

**SVENSK SLÖJD** Map pp236–8 *Handicrafts*
☎ 663 66 50; Nybrogatan 23; ☺ closed Sun; T-Östermalmstorg

Run by the Association of Swedish Handicraft, this shop carries strictly authentic arts and crafts – it's a great place to explore Swedish artisanship or pick up genuinely worthwhile souvenirs. You'll find textiles, glassware, woodwork, ceramics, clothing and traditional Sami handicrafts by over 150 artists.

**SVENSKT TENN** Map pp236–8 *Design*
☎ 670 16 00; Strandvägen 5; ☺ closed Sun

Founded in 1924 and famous as the decades-long home of Josef Frank, whose abstract flower patterns and other designs have become emblematic of Swedish interior design, Svenskt Tenn is as much a museum as a shop (with nearly museum-level prices to boot). Its stock of furniture, lighting, glassware, dishes and textiles represents the pinnacle of modern interior design.

# OUTLYING AREAS

**IKEA** Map pp228–9 *Design/Furniture*
☎ 744 83 00; www.ikea.se; Kungens Kurva, Skärholmen; ☺ 10am-9pm Mon-Fri, 10am-6pm Sat & Sun; bus 173, 707, 710, 748

Ikea doesn't carry the same stigma of yuppiedom here (or, to be fair, in the rest of Europe) as it does in the USA; in fact, it's just the opposite, as the line was developed to be an affordable, populist collection (see Design, p32). Trips to Ikea are a frequent weekend outing for the average Swedish family. On Sundays this recently expanded complex is jammed with kids scoffing mass-produced Ikea hotdogs and parents manoeuvering strollers around various 'solutions for better living'.

# Sleeping

# Sleeping

Whether you choose to sleep in a modern-design showcase hotel, where the rooms are decorated with sound and light, or a creaky old antique sailboat that's been moored after decades of service, you'll find that most of Stockholm's hotels are comfortable and of a high quality, from the ultra-plush to the humblest hostel. Service tends to be top notch, and nearly all of the hotel staff speaks English. Fleapits are fairly hard to find in this city.

Rates at most Stockholm hotels and some hostels include a breakfast buffet, usually vast and varied enough to fuel half a day's sightseeing. Unless otherwise noted, the hotels listed in this chapter all have in-room Internet access (via dataports), and hostels usually have computer terminals available in the lobby. Saunas are common in Swedish hotels; most large places will have one, even if they don't have a pool. Every hotel in Stockholm has non-smoking rooms available; in this chapter, the non-smoking icon indicates that the entire facility is smoke-free. Parking availability is indicated in reviews by the symbol Ⓟ ; be aware that in city-centre hotels there is frequently a charge of Skr75 to Skr95 for parking.

## Accommodation Styles

A large portion of the rooms available in Stockholm are in comfortable but none-too-exciting business hotels, but there are plenty of other options, the best of which we've included here. Travellers can choose to stay on one of several floating hostels, in a former island prison, in a cosy boutique hotel or in one of the city's crisply modern 'design hotels'. There are also plenty of B&Bs and long-term apartment rentals.

## Price Ranges

Prices at Stockholm's major hotels are typically Skr1500 to Skr2000 per night for a double room. The listed price, however, is rarely the lowest available. Nearly all hotel room prices drop by up to 50% on weekends and during July, when practically everyone in Stockholm goes on holiday. The published rates, or 'rack' rates, seldom reflect what you actually have to pay. Always ask about special deals and discounts when booking a room.

### Svenska Turistföreningen

If you stay in a Swedish youth hostel, you'll quickly become familiar with Svenska Turistföreningen (STF; the Swedish Touring Club). The club, affiliated with Hostelling International (HI), has some 340,000 members and is among the largest nonprofit organisations in Sweden, with an annual turnover of around Skr220 million. It was founded in 1885 with the aim of encouraging outdoor activities and travel. The founding members were scientists who worked in the mountains; the first incarnation of STF hostels was a chain of mountain huts built in northern Sweden to house these workers and other mountain travellers.

Once the hut network was established, the STF expanded into youth hostels, with the first at Gränna, on Lake Vättern, opening in 1933. The hostel network grew rapidly after WWII and soon passed the 300 mark. In the 1950s, Dag Hammarskjöld was an active vice president of the STF – even while he was in New York working as Secretary General to the United Nations. Eventually STF joined the IYHF, which later became HI.

Nowadays, all hostels except *af Chapman* & Skeppsholmen, Torrekulla and Tjarö are franchise operations; the STF gets a cut from overnight fees at franchises in exchange for advertising and other promotions. The STF umbrella currently covers 315 hostels, nine mountain lodges and around 40 mountain huts. Nine new hostels across Sweden were added to the network in 2004. There are 84 local associations around the country that organise activities for members, and there's a travel section and publishing department at the STF head office in Stockholm. For more details, or to book a stay at a Swedish hostel, visit www.svenskaturistforeningen.se.

Prices are generally quoted per room, not per person. Rates quoted here are for the high season. In this guide, budget accommodation, listed under 'Cheap Sleeps' for each neighbourhood, includes anything up to Skr350 per person per night.

A night in a Stockholm youth hostel costs Skr150 to Skr350 per person, depending on whether you choose a dorm bed or a private room. A Hostelling International (HI) card will give you discounts on Svenska Turistföreningen (STF) hostel rates; you can buy a card at any of the youth hostels for Skr175. You can also join the STF at hostels and many tourist offices while in Sweden (adults over 26 costs Skr285, 16 to 25 year olds Skr110, children under 16 free and families Skr410). Smoking is prohibited in Swedish youth hostels (though not necessarily in attached bars).

## Longer-Term Rentals

If you're staying in Stockholm for any length of time, it's wise to look into house swaps or long-term rentals. Try these websites for a start.

### HOLIDAY RENTALS
www.holiday-rentals.co.uk
This is a free, searchable database of holiday home rentals with listings organised by country, including several cottages on the Stockholm archipelago.

### HOMELINK INTERNATIONAL
www.homelink.org
Membership in this organisation costs US$75 per year, and only members can view or post listings.

### INTERNATIONAL HOME EXCHANGE NETWORK
www.ihen.com
Membership in this database costs US$39.95 per year (necessary to post a listing), but non-members can view and respond to listings.

### VACATION HOME RENTALS
www.accommodationguide.com/sweden.htm
Listings are paid for by property owners, and anyone can view them. Most of the homes available are in the Swedish countryside.

## Other Resources
### DESTINATION STOCKHOLM
☎ 663 00 80; www.destination-stockholm.com
This discount hotel-and-sightseeing package site offers deals on some of the city's top hotels in the off season. The website is crammed with useful information.

### HOTELLCENTRALEN
☎ 789 24 90; www.stockholmtown.com; Central Station; ⏱ 9am-6pm Mon-Sat, noon-4pm Sun

The accommodation branch of the tourist office books hotels, hostels and B&Bs. There's no charge for bookings made in advance, but a fee of Skr50 (Skr20 for hostels) applies to immediate bookings made in person.

# GAMLA STAN & RIDDARHOLMEN

There are only five hotels on Gamla Stan, and only one – a floating hotel – on Riddarholmen; all are loaded with Old Town character, but are fairly small, very popular and quite expensive, so be sure to book ahead if you want to stay here.

### FIRST HOTEL REISEN
Map pp239–41                                      Hotel
☎ 22 32 60; www.firsthotels.com; Skeppsbron 12; s/d from Skr2293/2543; T-Gamla Stan; P ⓢ
Located in an eight-storey waterfront building with a distinct 'sea-faring' atmosphere, this luxurious hotel features dark wood panelling, wooden floors and sumptuous furnishings in its rooms. The Chapman suite is one of the finest in the city. There's also a popular piano bar, and an extraordinary swimming pool and sauna in the brick-vaulted cellar.

### LADY HAMILTON HOTEL
Map pp239–41                                      Hotel
☎ 50 64 01 00; www.lady-hamilton.se; Storkyrkobrinken 5; s/d/tr from Skr1990/2390/2890; T-Gamla Stan; P
Dating from the 1470s, this quiet and unique hotel lies in the heart of Gamla Stan, next to the cathedral Storkyrkan (p55) and Kungliga Slottet (the Royal Palace, p52). It's packed out with antiques, pictures of Lady Hamilton, rocking horses and art. In the basement there's a sauna and a dipping pool that has been created from an old community well from the 1300s.

## LORD NELSON HOTEL Map pp239–41 *Hotel*

☎ 50 64 01 20; www.lord-nelson.se; Västerlånggatan 22; s/d Skr1690/2050; T-Gamla Stan; Ⓟ

This odd pink-painted building, only six metres wide, features maritime antiques and small rooms with attractive woodwork and brass, each with a model ship. You'll find a 'deck' on the roof. The restaurant only serves a limited buffet breakfast.

## MÄLARDROTTNINGEN

Map pp239–41 *Boat Hotel*

☎ 54 51 87 80; www.malardrottningen.se; s/d from Skr1100/1220, child under 8 free; T-Gamla Stan; Ⓟ

This classy vessel, launched in 1924 and now anchored off Riddarholmen, was once the world's largest motor yacht. The deep blue carpets, the floors, ceilings and chairs of dark wood, and the wonderful restaurant (with a bar in the bridge) create a great maritime atmosphere. All cabins have private bathrooms.

## RICA CITY HOTEL GAMLA STAN

Map pp239–41 *Hotel*

☎ 723 72 50; www.rica.se; Lilla Nygatan 25; s/d/ste Skr1695/1945/2090; T-Gamla Stan; Ⓟ

This 17th-century waterfront building has been a hostel and a Salvation Army headquarters. Its 51 rooms are pretty small and despite the location none have a view of the water, but it's a classy place with unfussy décor and good service. It's in a prime spot for visiting Gamla Stan and the city centre. Half the rooms are non-smoking.

## VICTORY HOTEL Map pp239–41 *Hotel*

☎ 50 64 00 00; www.victory-hotel.se; Lilla Nygatan 5; s/d Skr2190/2590; T-Gamla Stan; Ⓟ ☒

This early 17th-century building is literally full of nautical antiques, grandfather clocks, model ships and art. Most rooms are fairly small, but the museum-like suites are larger. The hotel's restaurant is Leijontornet (see p105).

# NORRMALM & VASASTADEN

The bulk of Stockholm's hotels are here, in the city centre. You'll find everything from standard business hotels to ultra-swank designer showcases to charming little boutique hotels. Some of the best youth hostels are also here, within easy walking distance of the Central Station.

## ADLON HOTELL Map pp236–8 *Hotel*

☎ 402 65 00; www.adlon.se; Vasagatan 42; s/d from Skr1295/1950; T-Centralen; Ⓟ

Located in a fine building dating from 1884 (complete with circular tower and cupola), Adlon Hotel offers 77 modern rooms, with Internet facilities, in a central location.

## BERNS HOTEL Map pp236–8 *Boutique Hotel*

☎ 56 63 22 00; www.berns.se; Näckströmsgatan 8; s/d from Skr2100/2750; T-Kungsträdgården; Ⓟ

Rooms in this boutique hotel, all equipped with CD players, range from 19th-century classical to the latest styles featuring marble and lots of dark wood. The attached restaurant (p107) and club (p134), dating from 1863, is one of the grandest in the city.

## CENTRAL HOTEL Map pp236–8 *Hotel*

☎ 56 62 08 00; www.centralhotel.se; Vasagatan 38; s/d from Skr1625/1750; T-Centralen; Ⓟ

This comfortable and appropriately named hotel features subdued contemporary design, particularly friendly staff and a fine buffet breakfast (but no café or restaurant).

## COMFORT HOTEL STOCKHOLM

Map pp236–8 *Hotel*

☎ 56 62 22 00; www.choicehotels.se; Kungsbron 1; s/d Skr1445/1605; T-Centralen; Ⓟ

This modern business-class hotel in the World Trade Center includes 'Japanese-style' rooms (without windows) and larger multi-bed rooms. There's also a New York-style bar/restaurant.

## FREYS HOTEL Map pp236–8 *Hotel*

☎ 50 62 13 00; www.freyshotels.com; Bryggargatan 12; s/d from Skr1595/1790; T-Centralen

Freys Hotel opened in 1989 and features 115 rooms with '80s furniture and artwork. The reception, updated in 2002, resembles an art gallery. Internet access is available in the lobby only.

## GRAND HÔTEL STOCKHOLM

Map pp236–8 *Hotel*

☎ 679 35 00; www.grandhotel.se; Södra Blasieholmshamnen 8; s/d from Skr2200/3400; T-Kungsträdgården; Ⓟ

The Grand Hôtel is one of the city's most sumptuous lodgings. Some rooms are in royal Gustavian style but others are intriguing traditional/modern mixes. All rooms have Internet access. Room No 701 has a unique

Grand Hotel Stockholm (p156)

tower with a 360-degree view, and No 702 is the astounding Nobel Room, where the literature prize winners stay overnight. It's an impressive stone building with a copper roof and great views of Kungliga Slottet (p52); many public rooms are quite astonishing. Even if you don't stay here, it's worth popping in for a late-night drink at the classy piano bar in the lobby.

### HOTEL GUSTAV VASA Map p230　Hotel
☎ 34 38 01; www.hotel.wineasy.se/gustav.vasa; Västmannagatan 61; s/d Skr950/1200; T-Odenplan; ⊠
Located in a 19th-century building, preserved as a cultural monument, with wrought-iron balconies, this family-owned place has no-frills, modern-style rooms refurbished in 2001, but no restaurant.

### HOTEL ODEN Map p230　Hotel
☎ 457 97 00; www.hoteloden.se; Karlsbergsvägen 24; s/d Skr1060/1320; T-Odenplan; Ⓟ
Hotel Oden occupies the upper six floors above a supermarket in a busy part of town. The characterless brick façade doesn't inspire confidence, but the rooms, in traditional and modern styles, are very pleasant. There's a coffee bar, but no restaurant.

### HOTEL TEGNÉRLUNDEN
Map pp236–8　Hotel
☎ 54 54 55 50; www.hoteltegnerlunden.se; Tegnérlunden 8; s/d from Skr1330/1560; T-Rådmansgatan; Ⓟ

Near the enormous, dramatic Strindberg statue in Tegnérlunden Park, this is a modern hotel with comfortable, functional but unexciting furnishings. There is a café, but no restaurant.

### HOTELL AUGUST STRINDBERG
Map pp236–8　Hotel
☎ 32 50 06; www.hotellstrindberg.se; Tegnérgatan 38; s/d Skr1200/1400; T-Rådmansgatan; ⊠
This quiet, family-run hotel, pleasantly situated in a courtyard, has 21 traditional-style rooms and a spiral staircase. There's a breakfast room, but no restaurant, and some rooms share a bathroom.

### HOTELL BEMA Map pp236–8　Hotel
☎ 23 26 75; hotell.bema@stockholm.mail.telia.com; Upplandsgatan 13; s/d Skr840/910; T-Centralen; Ⓟ
Just north of the city centre and opposite the quiet Tegnérlunden Park, this friendly hotel has 12 very nice twin and double rooms, all with shower and TV. It has the cosy, friendly feel of a Mediterranean-style pensione rather than a large, modern hotel.

### HOTELL HAGA Map p230　Hotel
☎ 54 54 73 00; www.hagahotel.se; Hagagatan 29; s/d from Skr750/995; T-Odenplan
Although it's a rather bland, modern place above a car showroom, this hotel is in a quiet area of town and has 38 comfortable rooms with modern facilities and friendly service.

## ELL LILLA RÅDMANNEN
36–8                                    *Hotel*

☎ 50 62 15 00; www.freyshotels.com; Rådmansgatan 67; s/d from Skr1295/1490; T-Rådmansgatan; P
This 36-room hotel has smallish, tastefully decorated rooms. Staff members are particularly welcoming and the breakfast buffet is excellent.

### KOM HOTEL Map pp231–3          *Hotel*
☎ 412 23 00; www.komhotell.se; Döbelnsgatan 17; s/d from Skr1360/1720; T-Rådmansgatan
Kom Hotel, in a quiet location opposite Johannes Kyrka and just north of the city centre, has interesting contemporary architecture and a notably friendly staff. It's owned and operated by Stockholm's YMCA and YWCA. There is no bar/restaurant, café or room service.

### NORDIC LIGHT HOTEL
Map pp236–8                             *Hotel*

☎ 50 56 30 00; www.nordichotels.se; Vasaplan 7; s/d from Skr2500/2900; T-Centralen; P
Excelling in modern design, the Nordic Light (like its sister hotel, the Nordic Sea, below) features black-and-white design where the single most important element is light. Instead of paintings or artwork on the walls, each room is equipped with its own specially designed light exhibit, which guests can adjust to suit their mood. *Trés chic.*

### NORDIC SEA HOTEL Map pp236–8    *Hotel*
☎ 50 56 30 00; www.nordichotels.se; Vasaplan 2-4; s/d from Skr1290/2400; T-Centralen; P
The Nordic Sea, in a former police station, has an impressive 9000L aquarium in the reception area. Many of the rooms face a quiet internal courtyard. Its bar is the famous Icebar (p125).

## Top Five Hotel Bars/Lounges

- **Grand Hôtel Stockholm piano bar** (p156) Nick a box of matches and pretend you stayed in the Nobel Room.
- **Nordic Sea Icebar** (p158) Everyone looks cute in mittens and parkas.
- **Lydmar Hotel** (p164) Black clothing and cheekbones required.
- **Radisson SAS Royal Viking Hotel SkyBar** (p158) Not quite Valhalla, but it must be pretty close.
- **Rival Hotel** (p162) Wear vintage, pout attractively and carry a *trés chic* cigarette holder.

### PENSIONAT ODEN VASASTADEN
Map pp231–3                             *Hotel*

☎ 796 96 00; www.pensionat.nu; 2nd fl, Odengatan 38; s/d from Skr695/820; T-Rådmansgatan
This small eight-room guesthouse is on the 2nd floor of an ordinary city block. The pleasant rooms feature wooden floors and décor of the early 1900s.

### QUEEN'S HOTEL Map pp236–8       *Hotel*
☎ 24 94 60; www.queenshotel.se; Drottninggatan 71A; s/d from Skr750/780; T-Hötorget; ⊠
In an early 20th-century building on the pedestrian mall, this friendly, old-fashioned hotel has marble staircases and an antique lift. The rooms vary in size and décor; most have the feel of a grandmother's parlour, with chandeliers and charmingly worn-in antique furniture.

### RADISSON SAS ROYAL VIKING
HOTEL Map pp236–8                       *Hotel*
☎ 50 65 40 00; www.radissonsas.com; Vasagatan 1; s/d from Skr2650/2900; T-Centralen; P
Located in a modern tower block, with all the usual luxury mod-cons, this impressive hotel has up-to-date rooms, with 24-hour room service, wireless Internet access, coffee and tea facilities, bathrobes, newspapers and so forth, in fine Swedish style. There's a seafood restaurant attached. The SkyBar on the 9th floor offers great views, and the lobby features glowing blue floor panels and a bar shaped like a Viking longship.

### RADISSON SAS STRAND HOTEL
Map pp236–8                             *Hotel*

☎ 50 66 40 00; www.radissonsas.com; Nybrokajen 9; s/d Skr1850/2300; T- Kungsträdgården; ⊡
Not only does this hotel dominate Nybrokajen with its tower, ivy-covered façade and copper roof, it also has a wonderful glass-roofed courtyard and luxurious rooms with wooden floors, individualistic styles and great views.

### RICA CITY HOTEL KUNGSGATAN
Map pp236–8                             *Hotel*

☎ 723 72 20; www.rica.se; Kungsgatan 47; s/d from Skr1595/1895; T-Hötorget; P
Located in the upper five floors of the PUB department store building (where Greta Garbo started her working career), this hotel has very comfortable rooms furnished in modern Scandinavian style.

Sleeping – Normalm & Vasastaden

## SCANDIC HOTEL SERGEL PLAZA

Map pp236–8                                    *Hotel*

☎ 51 72 63 00; www.scandic-hotels.com/sergelplaza; Brunkebergstorg 9; s/d from Skr1875/2605; T-Centralen; P ⓡ

Situated just off Sergels Torg, this fine establishment has more than 400 rooms and 1980s-style décor. The roofed and carpeted internal courtyard features live piano music. Room rates include three different types of buffet breakfast – the Japanese breakfast is very popular.

## SHERATON STOCKHOLM

Map pp236–8                                    *Hotel*

☎ 412 34 00; www.sheraton.com/stockholm; Tegelbacken 6; s/d from Skr2900/3100; T-Centralen; P

The Sheraton's notoriously grim façade – a face only a Swedish architect could love – conceals a wonderful, modern interior complete with strikingly stylish rooms, an inexpensive café and a top-quality à la carte restaurant.

## WASA PARK HOTEL Map p230    *Hotel*

☎ 54 54 53 00; fax 54 54 53 01; St Eriksplan 1; s/d from Skr525/650; T-St Eriksplan

Reception is on the 1st floor of an ordinary six-storey, yellow painted city block, with an entrance located in the tunnel leading from St Eriksplan to Völundsgatan. There are 15 functional rooms, most with shared bathroom.

# CHEAP SLEEPS

## CITY BACKPACKERS Map pp236–8    *Hostel*

☎ 20 69 20; www.citybackpackers.se; Upplandsgatan 2A; 8-/4-/2-bed dm Skr180/220/245, d Skr245 per person, apt (sleeps 6) Skr1500, breakfast Skr40, sheets Skr50/week; T-Centralen; ⊠ P

City Backpackers (SVIF), one of the cleanest and best-equipped hostels in Stockholm, is 400m from Central Station. It's a friendly place in a bright and airy 19th-century building off a quiet street. The hostel has a kitchen, satellite TV, sauna (free in the morning, Skr20 at night), laundry (Skr50) and free Internet access.

## GOOD NIGHT HOTELL DANIELSSON

Map pp236–8                                    *Hotel*

☎ 411 10 65; fax 411 10 36; Västmannagatan 5; s/d Skr600/800; T-Centralen

This friendly Finnish-Polish, family-run hotel is well placed for the city centre. All of the 20 rooms are decorated in different styles, but none has a phone. Family rooms are available.

The common room has a TV, and free coffee, tea and juice is available.

## HOSTEL BED & BREAKFAST

Map pp231–3                                    *Hostel*

☎ 15 28 38; www.hostelbedandbreakfast.com; Rehnsgatan 21; dm Skr190, s/d Skr375/500, incl breakfast, sheets Skr45; T-Rådmansgatan; ⊠

This is a pleasant, informal and well-equipped basement hostel with a kitchen and laundry (Skr45). The large summer dorm across the street is open June to August.

## HOSTEL MITT I CITY Map pp236–8    *Hostel*

☎ 21 76 30; www.stores.se/hostal.htm; Västmannagatan 13; dm Skr175, private r per person Skr295, incl breakfast; T-Centralen

This SVIF hostel occupies the entire 5th floor of an old-style building on a quiet street and is reached by either stairs or an antique lift. It's a trifle claustrophobic (some rooms have very small windows), but it's clean and friendly. There are no kitchen or laundry facilities.

# DJURGÅRDEN & SKEPPSHOLMEN

Whether you sleep in the lap of luxury on Djurgården or in slightly more austere conditions at the Skeppsholmen hostel, this area puts you in a prime location for exploring most of the best museums and sights in the city.

## SCANDIC HOTEL HASSELBACKEN

Map pp231–3                                    *Hotel*

☎ 51 73 43 00; www.scandic-hotels.se/hasselbacken; Hazeliusbacken 20; r from Skr1890; Bus 44, 47; P

This 1925 building – remodelled in the 1990s – sits on a slope overlooking the amusement park Gröna Lund, just steps away from Djurgården. It's hard to imagine a lovelier setting for a stay in Stockholm, and the hotel's plush amenities (saunas, satellite TV) make it an even more luxurious retreat. The attached restaurant (p113) is top class.

# CHEAP SLEEPS

## VANDRARHEM AF CHAPMAN & SKEPPSHOLMEN Map pp239–41    *Hostel*

☎ 463 22 66; www.stfchapman.com; Flaggmansvägen 8; dm Skr140-210, d Skr420, incl breakfast; Bus 46, 55, 62, 65, 76; ⊠ P

## The History of *af Chapman*

This wonderful, fully rigged sailing ship, launched in 1888 at Whitehaven, England, with the name *Dunboyne*, was the last of this type of three-masted vessel to be built. Initially it worked as a cargo ship for British, then Norwegian, owners. It ended up in Gothenburg in 1915 and was renamed *GD Kennedy*. There it spent a few years as a training vessel, until the Swedish Navy purchased the boat in 1923 and changed the name again to *af Chapman*, in honour of the renowned 18th-century Swedish naval architect Fredrik Henrik af Chapman. The navy used *af Chapman* for training ship's boys until 1934; then it was retired to the Karlskrona naval base. In 1947 Stockholm city council bought *af Chapman* and asked Svenska Turistföreningen to run it as a hostel. It opened two years later, with 136 beds for guests.

Unsurprisingly, given its age and history, the *af Chapman* occasionally needs some tender loving care. It will be closed from September 2004 for extensive airs and renovations. No word on how quickly it's expected to reopen, so call ahead (☎ 463 22 66) to check. The jointly operated Skeppsholmen, on dry land, will remain open throughout.

The large and popular STF boat hostel *af Chapman* will be undergoing repairs from September 2004, so call to find out if it has reopened; meanwhile the adjacent Skeppsholmen hostel is taking up the slack. The *af Chapman* has done plenty of travelling of its own, but it's now well anchored in a superb, quiet location, swaying gently in sight of the city centre (see The History of *af Chapman*, p160). Bunks in dorms below decks have nautical ambience and staff members are friendly and helpful. Apart from showers and toilets, all facilities are on dry land in the Skeppsholmen hostel, where you'll find a good kitchen with a laid-back common room and a separate TV lounge. Laundry facilities and 24-hour Internet access are available. Stays on the boat are normally limited to five nights from May to September.

# KUNGSHOLMEN

Kungsholmen is a mostly residential, non-touristy island, with the exception of the Stadshus (City Hall; p75). Accommodation is fairly minimal, but there's one good option, the classy First Hotel Amaranten, and the area is full of friendly neighbourhood shops and cafés that welcome exploration. It's also not a bad place to look for long-term rentals or apartment swaps (see p155).

### FIRST HOTEL AMARANTEN
Map p230                                    *Hotel*

☎ 692 52 00; www.firsthotels.com; Kungsholmsgatan 31; s/d incl breakfast from Skr1599/2249; T-Rådhuset; P ♿

In this large hotel complex on Kungsholmen, each room is decorated with typically Swedish modern design. There's a sauna, pool and gym with a masseuse and chiropractor. Ideal for business travellers, the hotel has Internet access and even allows you to borrow a laptop from the front desk if you've left yours at the office.

# SÖDERMALM & LÅNGHOLMEN

This area has some of the funkiest hotels in Stockholm, from the incredibly chic, cutting-edge Clarion to the recently revived Rival to the former prison hostel on the island of Långholmen.

*Vandrarhem af Chapman & Skeppsholmen (p159)*

## ALEXANDRA HOTEL Map pp234–5 *Hotel*

☎ 455 13 00; www.alexandrahotel.se; Magnus Ladulåsgatan 42; s/d from Skr935/1195; T-Medborgarplatsen; Ⓟ

The Alexandra is a modern hotel with spacious rooms furnished in fairly standard contemporary style. Its sauna is large and attractive, and an excellent continental breakfast is served in a pleasant dining room.

## CLARION HOTEL Map pp234–5 *Hotel*

☎ 462 10 10; www.clarionstockholm.com; Ringvägen 98; s/d from Skr1695/1895; Ⓟ

Entering this hip new hotel in Söder is like walking into a modern-art museum – in fact the wide ramp leading into the lobby, dotted with stylishly uncomfortable-looking furniture, was modelled on the Tate Modern. The lobby features a huge wall mural and sculptures by Kirsten Ortwed, and the funky lounge bar next to the front desk is full of attractive, well-dressed people. It's almost too much, but it's inarguably impressive. The hotel's 532 rooms maintain the high-design theme, with sleek chaise longues, enormous beds, gaping windows and minimalist décor. Deluxe rooms have a 42-inch wall-TV.

## COLUMBUS HOTELL & VANDRARHEM
Map pp234–5 *Hotel & Hostel*

☎ 644 17 17; www.columbus.se; Tjärhovsgatan 11; s with shared bath Skr1250, d with private bath Skr1550, ste Skr2295, annexe s/d/tr Skr695/895/1095; T-Medborgarplatsen; Ⓟ ☒

Columbus Hotell, in a quiet area just inches from the hub of Söder nightlife, was built in 1780 as a brewery. It has also served as barracks for the city guards (when it was nicknamed 'the sausage pot') and a makeshift hospital during the 1834 cholera epidemic. Each room has clean-lined Swedish décor and a view onto the pleasant cobbled courtyard. The annexe rooms serve as the hostel rooms.

## ERSTA KONFERENS & HOTELL
Map pp239–41 *Hotel*

☎ 714 63 41; www.ersta.se/konferens; Erstagatan 1K; s/d from Skr550/750; ⏰ reception 8am-6pm Mon-Fri, 8am-3pm Sat & Sun; T-Medborgarplatsen; Ⓟ ☒

This hotel has pleasant, old-fashioned rooms, each with phone, desk and TV. Although breakfast is included, there's also a kitchen for self-caterers. The hotel, near the Viking Line terminal, is run by the parish welfare society. There's also a café and restaurant nearby.

## HILTON STOCKHOLM SLUSSEN
Map pp239–41 *Hotel*

☎ 51 73 53 00; www.hilton.com; Guldgränd 8; s/d Skr2700/2900; T-Slussen; ☒ Ⓟ

Perched between the chaotic Slussen interchange and Södermalm's underground highway, Sweden's first Hilton features grand marble staircases and vast, stylish public areas. There's an auditorium where performances, from dance to orchestral to jazz, are frequently held, and several levels of restaurants with excellent views. Rooms are strongly influenced by contemporary design, and lobby furniture is from the Fritz Hansen-Oxford design series.

## HOTEL ANNO 1647 Map pp234–5 *Hotel*

☎ 442 16 80; www.anno1647.se; Mariagränd 3; s/d Skr1595/1995; T-Slussen; Ⓟ ☒

This historical building has labyrinthine hallways and a range of rooms, most with private modern bathrooms and wooden floors. Some rooms have tiled Swedish stoves, toilets with chains, chandeliers or rococo wallpaper. Only a few rooms have good views. There's no elevator or restaurant, but there's a café and bakery on the premises. The swimming pool is in a separate health club 50m away.

## HOTEL TRE SMÅ RUM
Map pp234–5 *Boutique Hotel*

☎ 641 2371; www.tresmarum.se; Högbergsgatan 81; r with shared bath Skr695; bike rental Skr85 per day; T-Mariatorget; ☒

Rooms have gradually been added over the years so that the hotel belies its name (Three Small Rooms) and now has seven rooms, but the charm of this quaint 18th-century hotel in a quiet district of Södermalm hasn't been diluted. With its rough-hewn vanilla-coloured walls, Italian-style décor, high ceilings and wooden floors, it's one of the nicest hotels in Stockholm. And it's hard to beat for value and location.

## MÄLAREN – DEN RÖDA BÅTEN
Map pp239–41 *Boat Hotel*

☎ 644 43 85; www.theredboat.com; Söder Malärstrand, Kajplats 6; hostel dm Skr195, hostel s/d Skr430/490, hostel breakfast Skr55, hotel s/d incl breakfast from Skr675/915; T-Slussen; ☒

'The Red Boat' is a hotel and hostel on two vessels, *Mälaren* and *Ran*. Docked west of the Slussen railway lines, the red boat carried timber around Lake Mälaren from 1914 but became a Göta Canal steamer in the 1920s. It's the cosiest of Stockholm's floating hostels, thanks to lots of dark wood, nautical memorabilia and friendly staff. There are also excellent hotel-standard rooms. The finest is the captain's cabin (s/d Skr785/1200), with nautical paintings, TV, phone and great views across the lake to the Stadshus.

### PENSIONAT ODEN SÖDERMALM

Map pp239–41 *Hotel*

☎ 796 96 00; www.pensionat.nu; Hornsgatan 66B; s/d from Skr695/820; T-Mariatorget

This is a pleasant, early 20th-century-style guesthouse, with wooden floors and 17 rooms, all with cable TV.

### RIVAL HOTEL Map pp239–41 *Hotel*

☎ 54 57 89 00; www.rival.se/undersidor/english1.htm; Mariatorget 3; r standard/deluxe from Skr1990/2550; T-Mariatorget

ABBA's Benny Andersson is one of the three backers behind the newly revitalized Rival Hotel, which includes a vintage 1940s movie theatre, a good café and bakery, a nice lounge, swank cocktail bar and well-preserved retro architecture throughout. Each room is decorated with posters from great Swedish films and comes with a teddy bear to make guests feel more at home; several rooms have views out onto the square, and the deluxe suites on the top floor all have balconies.

### SCANDIC HOTEL MALMEN

Map pp234–5 *Hotel*

☎ 51 73 47 00; www.scandic-hotels.com/malmen; Götgatan 49-51; r from Skr1260; T-Medborgarplatsen; P

This functionalist building dating from 1951 has the only piano bar in Södermalm, complete with blackjack room (although it can get obnoxiously crowded with drunken louts around 1am when the nearby bars close). The pleasant hotel rooms feature the clean lines and up-to-date design typical of the Scandic chain. You couldn't pick a better location for enjoying the Söder nightlife.

### SCANDIC HOTEL SJÖFARTSHOTELLET

Map pp239–41 *Hotel*

☎ 51 73 49 00; www.scandic-hotels.com/sjofartshotellet; Katarinavägen 26; r from Skr1525; T-Slussen; P

Just a few minutes' walk from Gamla Stan, Sjöfartshotellet has a distinctive nautical atmosphere with brass, cherry and oak details and extensive use of blue shades. Views, however, are restricted.

# CHEAP SLEEPS

There are plenty of hostels in and around Södermalm, many within walking distance of both the Viking Line terminal and Centralstationen. Views from the boat hostels are wonderful from on deck and from cabins facing the water.

### GUSTAF AF KLINT

Map pp239–41 *Boat Hostel & Hotel*

☎ 640 40 77; fax 640 64 16; Stadsgårdskajen 153; dm Skr120, d Skr170, hotel s/d Skr395/595, sheets Skr50, breakfast Skr55; ✆ reception 7am-11pm; T-Slussen; ✗ P

This clean and friendly boat hostel, a former naval cartography vessel from 1942, is a little dilapidated but it has atmosphere and it's in a great location.

### LÅNGHOLMEN HOTELL & VANDRARHEM Map pp234–5 *Hostel*

☎ 720 85 00; www.langholmen.com; Långholmsmuren 20; dm from Skr185, cell with private bath from Skr560, breakfast Skr75, sheets Skr40, hotel s/d incl breakfast Skr1155/1455; T-Hornstull then 750m walk, bus 4, 40, 66; P

In a former prison on the small island of Långholmen, off the northwestern corner of Södermalm, this hotel and STF hostel is a very unusual place to stay. It's highly recommended, and most staff members are friendly and efficient. There are good kitchen and laundry facilities, and the pleasant restaurant Långholmens Wärdshus serves breakfast and other meals; there's also a warm little pub and a summer terrace.

### Top Five Hotel Views

- **Tower Suite at the Radisson SAS Strand Hotel** (p158) Gaze over Nybrokajen from the rooftop terrace.
- **Grand Hôtel Stockholm** (p156) You can see Kungliga Slottet (Royal Palace) from rooms fit for a king or queen.
- **Gustaf af Klint** (p162) Gorgeous views of Gamla Stan across the water from the deck of this floating hostel.
- **Ersta Konferens & Hotell** (p161) Check into one of Stockholm's most breathtaking vistas from the Söder Heights.
- **Lydmar Hotel** (p164) This view looks inward, at the hip and gorgeous Swedish yuppies who populate the hotel lounge.

## RYGERFJORD HOTEL & HOSTEL

Map pp239–41                      *Boat Hostel*

☎ 84 08 30; www.rygerfjord.se; Söder Malärstrand, Kajplats 12; hostel dm from Skr180, breakfast Skr62, sheets Skr60, hotel cabins from Skr750; T-Slussen or T-Gamla Stan; P

The *M/S Rygerfjord*, launched in Bergen in 1950 as a *hurtigruten* (coastal steamer) vessel for the Norwegian coast, is now a floating hotel and hostel. The hostel section is rather ordinary, but the public areas, including the restaurant, are very pleasant. Reasonably priced lunches and dinners are also served in the restaurant.

## ZINKENSDAMM HOTELL & VANDRARHEM Map pp234–5      *Hostel*

☎ 616 81 00; www.zinkensdamm.com; Zinkens Väg 20; reception 24hr; hostel dm/s/d from Skr175/440/470, breakfast Skr55, sheets Skr45, hotel s/d incl breakfast Skr1195/1495; T-Hornstull; X P

In the western part of Södermalm, this STF hostel is a large complex in a quiet location by Tantolunden Park. It's well equipped with kitchen facilities and lots of family rooms, but it can be crowded and noisy. The hostel breakfast buffet isn't spectacular, but hostellers can buy the much better hotel breakfast. The comfy Zinkadus bar serves snacks and drinks all day.

# ÖSTERMALM

Östermalm is another convenient, central part of town to stay in – especially if you're interested in Stockholm's exclusive boutique shops and trendiest nightlife – and it has one of the city's hippest hotels in the always-buzzing Lydmar.

## A&BE HOTELL Map pp236–8      *Hotel*

☎ 660 21 00; fax 660 59 87; Grev Turegatan 50; s/d from Skr540/690; T-Östermalmstorg

Situated on the eastern side of the city centre, this small, old-fashioned 12-room hotel on the 1st floor of a city block is good value. Tapestries adorning the hallway create an intriguing atmosphere.

## BIRGER JARL Map pp231–3      *Hotel*

☎ 674 18 00; www.birgerjarl.se; Tulegatan 8; s/d from Skr1645/1860, ste from Skr2850; T-Östermalmstorg; P

One of Stockholm's flagship design hotels, the Birger Jarl is a constant work-in-progress. Its style reflects its origin in the '70s, but each year the hotel brings in new Swedish

---

### Top Five Design Hotels

- **Nordic Light Hotel** (p158) Who needs landscape paintings when you've got a laser light show on the walls of your room?
- **Birger Jarl** (p163) Each of the 'designed suites' showcases a different Swedish designer.
- **Radisson SAS Royal Viking Hotel** (p158) Glowing blue floors, a bar shaped like a Viking longship and a lounge with a view.
- **Rival Hotel** (p162) A film lover's dream, this vibrantly retro-style hotel is partly owned by Benny Andersson of ABBA fame.
- **Clarion Hotel** (p161) So sleek and stylised it's like walking into a copy of *Wallpaper** magazine.

---

designers to add or adjust an element of its interior décor. Many of the rooms are 'design suites' renovated by some of Stockholm's top designers; there's a Svenskt Tenn room with Josef Frank-inspired wallpaper, for example. A stay here doubles as a crash course in current Swedish design trends.

## CRYSTAL PLAZA HOTEL

Map pp236–8                           *Hotel*

☎ 406 88 00; www.crystalplaza.aos.se; Birger Jarlsgatan 35; s/d from Skr1445/1695; T-Östermalmstorg

With an impressive eight-storey tower, neoclassical columns and classical-style artwork, this wonderful hotel offers both old-fashioned and modern rooms with excellent facilities. The circular-plan tower rooms are especially nice.

## HOTEL ESPLANADE Map pp236–8      *Hotel*

☎ 663 07 40; www.hotelesplanade.se; Strandvägen 7A; s/d from Skr1695/2295; T-Östermalmstorg

Built in 1910 and facing a quiet courtyard, this welcoming hotel has individually decorated rooms and a superb Art Nouveau-style breakfast room.

## HOTELL DIPLOMAT Map pp236–8      *Hotel*

☎ 459 68 00; www.diplomathotel.com; Strandvägen 7C; s/d from Skr1895/2495; T-Östermalmstorg; P

This Art Nouveau hotel, dating from 1911, has many different styles of rooms, all luxurious and some with excellent harbour views. In the finest rooms you'll find a Jacuzzi and a sauna. Staff members are attentive and efficient, and the hotel's T/bar is a high-class hang-out, especially in summer, when you can sit on the terrace.

*Reception at Birger Jarl (p163)*

### HOTELL ÖRNSKÖLD Map pp236–8 *Hotel*
☎ 667 02 85; fax 667 69 91; Nybrogatan 6; s/d from Skr775/1275; T-Östermalmstorg
This pleasant, laid-back, 19th-century-style hotel has old but well-looked-after facilities still in good order. Some rooms facing Nybrogatan have wrought-iron balconies.

### LYDMAR HOTEL Map pp236–8 *Hotel*
☎ 55 61 13 00; www.lydmar.se; Sturegatan 10; s/d from Skr1900/2300; T-Östermalmstorg; P
The über-hip and stylish Lydmar, in a functionalist glass and concrete 1930's building, has rooms that vary in style from antique to modern minimalist with heavy emphasis on black. You can choose from 10 choices of music in the lift. The Lydmar is known as much for its ground-level bar and restaurant as for its accommodation; the 'lobby' bar hosts live music several nights a week (see p136), free to hotel guests.

### MORNINGTON HOTEL Map pp236–8 *Hotel*
☎ 50 73 30 00; www.mornington.se; Nybrogatan 53; s/d from Skr1867/2205; T-Stadion
This seven-floor hotel, part of the Best Western chain, has typical upscale modern rooms and a unique library of around 5000 books in the reception area.

### PÄRLAN HOTELL Map pp236–8 *Hotel*
☎ 663 50 70; www.parlanhotell.com; Skeppargatan 27; s/d Skr1075/1275; T-Östermalmstorg
This very popular and homey nine-room hotel has quaint public areas and tastefully decorated rooms with private bath. There's also a balcony with views of the internal courtyard.

### SCANDIC HOTEL PARK Map pp231–3 *Hotel*
☎ 51 73 48 00; www.scandic-hotels.com/park; Karlavägen 43; s/d from Skr1990/2420; T-Stadion; P
Opposite Humlegården Park, this fine 200-room hotel has a wonderful bistro and typically high-quality rooms featuring wooden floors and the renowned Hästens beds.

## CHEAP SLEEPS
### BACKPACKERS INN Map pp231–3 *Hostel*
☎ 660 75 15; www.backpackersinn.se; Banérgatan 56; dm Skr115; breakfast Skr50; sheets Skr40; ☾ late Jun–early Aug, 24hr reception; T-Karlaplan; P
The STF Backpackers Inn, located in a fairly modern school building (during the summer holidays only), has 260 beds in seven-bunk classrooms and 40 beds in four-bed family rooms. There is no kitchen but the cafeteria serves alfresco breakfasts. Showers are in the adjacent sports hall. Street parking is free at night.

### STUREPARKENS GÄSTVÅNING
Map pp231–3 *Hotel*
☎ 662 72 30; www.stureparkens.nu; Sturegatan 58; s/d from Skr520/895, apt Skr1500; T-Stadion; ✗
This older-style guesthouse is on the 4th floor of a featureless six-storey building opposite the small Stureparken. The superior double room has a private bathroom. There's a common room with TV where breakfast is served. There's also a very nice two-room apartment with kitchen, phone, TV and a den area.

### ÖSTRA REALS VANDRARHEM
Map pp231–3 *Hostel*
☎ 664 11 14; fax 664 30 06; Karlavägen 79; dm Skr130 (10% discount with ISIC card); ☾ mid-Jun–mid-Aug, year-round booking by phone/fax; T-Karlaplan; P
You'll feel like a naughty orphan sleeping in the austere dorms at this tremendous old-fashioned school building. Common areas are large and comfortable and have lots of atmosphere. There are no kitchen facilities but there is a cafeteria.

Sleeping – Östermalm

# OUTLYING AREAS

If you're having trouble finding a bed and things get desperate, there are several large, chain hotels just outside of town that provide pleasant accommodation. Most are conveniently located on the *tunnelbana* or *pendeltåg* (J-train) lines, making it a snap to reach the city centre.

## IBIS STOCKHOLM HÄGERSTEN

Map pp228–9                                    *Hotel*

☎ 55 63 23 30; www.ibishotel.com; Västertorpsvägen 131, Hägersten; r Skr690; T-Västertorp, then 500m walk; Ⓟ

This modern hotel is in the southern suburbs, 8km southwest of the city centre and just off the E4/E20 motorway (junction Bredängsmotet). Rooms are small but spotless; all have cable TV, phone and private bathroom. Breakfast is not included but meals are served in the bar/restaurant. There's also a sauna and a fully equipped gym.

## IBIS STOCKHOLM VÄST

Map pp228–9                                    *Hotel*

☎ 36 25 40; www.ibishotel.com; Finspångsgatan 54, Spånga; r Skr520-680; pendeltag J-Spånga, then 1km walk; Ⓟ

This hotel is located near highway E18 in the northwestern suburbs about 15km from the city. Each room has cable TV and private bathroom, and the hotel has a bar/restaurant and a sauna.

## SCANDIC HOTEL TÄBY

*Hotel*

☎ 51 73 54 00; www.scandic-hotels.com/taby; Näsbyvägen 4, Täby; s/d from Skr1195/1395; T-Mörby Centrum, then bus 614 or 691; Ⓟ

If city hotels are full, try the modern Scandic Hotel Täby, located just off the E18 motorway in the northern suburbs. It adheres to the high standards typical of the Scandic chain, with modern Ikea-style décor, spacious rooms, great service and a healthy pro-environment philosophy.

# CHEAP SLEEPS

There are more than 20 hostels in Stockholm's *län* (county) that can easily be reached from the city by SL buses or trains, or by archipelago boats within an hour or so. There are some other cheap accommodation options listed in the Excursions chapter, p167.

## BREDÄNG VANDRARHEM

Map pp228–9                                    *Hostel*

☎ 97 62 00; bredangcamping@telia.com; Stora Sällskapets väg 51; ☽ 8 Jan-21 Dec; dm/r Skr150/450; T-Bredäng, then 600m walk; Ⓟ

A short walk from the Bredäng *tunnelbana* stop, in a pleasant suburb near Lake Mälaren, this is a clean and pleasant hostel with a well-equipped kitchen. When the camping ground is open (early April to late October), laundry facilities, a cafeteria and shop are available there.

---

## Worth the Trip

Two of the most luxurious hotels in the area are a bit outside of town, making for a decadent mini-vacation if you want to pamper yourself and get away from urban life for a while.

**Hasseludden Konferens & Yasuragi** ( ☎ 747 61 00; www.hasseludden.com; Hamndalsvägen 6, Saltsjö-Boo; s/d/ste from Skr1350/2300/3300, Yasuragi packages s/d from Skr1550/2900; boat from Strömkajen or bus 444 to Orminge Centrum then bus 417 to Hamndalsvägen plus 10-min walk; Ⓟ ☒ ) is just 30 minutes from Stockholm by boat. This hotel and spa complex has the only Japanese spa (*yasuragi*) in Sweden. You can visit the spa without staying overnight, but for a real treat, book one of the full-service *ryokan* suites, which include a massage and traditional Japanese bath. All the hotel rooms have meditative views of the sea and include swimsuits, plush robes and slippers, as well as a healthy breakfast buffet. There are meditation classes, all kinds of massages and spa treatments, a sauna and a 'sushi school'.

**Hotel J** ( ☎ 601 30 00; www.hotelj.com; Ellensviksvägen 1, Nacka Strand; s/d/ste from Skr1195/1595/2995; boat from Nybrokajen or Slussen or T-Slussen then bus 404, 443; Ⓟ ) is a popular weekend getaway for Stockholmers, and has serious *The Great Gatsby* overtones. The breezy blue-and-white summer house, built in 1912, is named for the boats used in the America's Cup; the scent of good-natured, nonchalant wealth wafts unmistakably through the air here. Rooms in the two modern annexes are larger than in the original building, with full baths and balconies. Room rates include an extensive buffet breakfast served in the lobby bar. The attached Restaurant J, near the harbour at Nacka Strand, is a beloved destination in its own right, especially in summer when the giant patio is unbeatable for lounging. To complete the picture, you can also rent little boats and catamarans here.

## HOTEL FORMULE 1 Map pp228–9 *Hotel*

☎ 744 20 44; fax 744 20 47; Mikrofonvägen 30; r with shared bath Skr310; T-Telefonplan; P

This budget chain motel, by the Västberga exit on the E4 motorway about 4km southwest of the city centre, is a modern place with basic rooms. Breakfast costs Skr30 extra. Book well in advance.

## KLUBBENSBORG HOSTEL

Map pp228–9 *Hostel*

☎ 646 12 55; www.klubbensborg.nu; Klubbensborgs-vägen 27; dm/s/d Skr170/300/600; T-Mälarhöjden, then 900m walk; P

This wonderful lakeside SVIF hostel has a rural atmosphere and several buildings dating back to the 17th century. The hostel has a kitchen, laundry and camping ground. Breakfast is available in the attached café and there's also an excellent bakery.

## SOLNA VANDRARHEM & MOTELCAMP

Map pp228–9 *Hostel*

☎ 51 48 15 50; www.solna-vandrarhem.se; Enköpings-vägen 16; dm/s/d Skr150/225/380; pendeltåg J-Ulriksdals Station, then 500m walk (follow signs); P

At this 374-bed former barracks in the north-western suburbs, guests stay in prefabricated huts, which are kept well heated in winter. The hostel has a small guest kitchen and an attached restaurant/bar open daily except Sunday.

# Excursions

# Excursions

Gorgeous as the capital city is, some of Sweden's loveliest areas are just outside of it and can easily be reached on a day trip or overnighter. As many Stockholmers themselves will tell you, there's nothing like venturing out into the archipelago on a summer's day. Composed of somewhere between 12,000 and 24,000 small islands ranging from green and forested to jagged and rocky – not to mention frequent sunshine and all that lovely water – the archipelago counts among Stockholm's prime attractions. If you have even a day to spare, you shouldn't miss it. Other worthy attractions near the capital city are some easily reachable palaces, including the impressive Drottningholm, where the royal family live, and three of Northern Europe's oldest and best-preserved historic towns, Sigtuna, Gamla Uppsala and Birka.

## PALACES
The Stockholm area has some of the loveliest and most impressive royal palaces in Sweden. Several of them are clustered fairly close together; on a quick day trip, you can easily view **Rosersbergs Slott** (p180), **Steninge Slott** (p180) and the prettiest of the three, the delicate alabaster **Skokloster Slott** (p180). **Tyresö Slott** (p170) also makes an easy getaway from Stockholm, and don't forget the queen of them all, **Drottningholms Slott** (p177), with its fantastic **Kina Slott** (p178).

## ISLANDS
The Stockholm Archipelago is the favourite time-off destination for locals. On a clear day, absolutely nothing beats hopping on a ferry and getting out onto the water. All the islands are worth visiting and you could almost choose your destination via the dartboard method, but highlights include **Utö** (p176) and **Finnhamn** (p174). **Vaxholm** (below) is a more developed, bustling island, while **Gällnö** (p175) offers peace and quiet.

## HISTORIC TOWNS
You can get a fascinating look at ancient history in the area around Stockholm with a visit to any of its historic towns. Adorable **Sigtuna** (p180) – there's no other word for it – is perhaps the easiest to reach, and has the most accessible ruins. **Gamla Uppsala** (p181) has a great interpretive museum and wonderful parks. And at **Birka** (p178) you'll find one of Sweden's oldest settlements.

# VAXHOLM
Vaxholm is the gateway to the central and northern reaches of Stockholm's archipelago, and it swarms with tourists in summer. Despite that, it's a pleasant place with several attractions and is well worth a visit.

The town was founded in 1647 and has many quaint summerhouses, which were fashionable in the 19th century. The oldest buildings are in the Norrhamn area, a few minutes' walk north of the town hall, but there's also interesting architecture along Hamngatan (the main street).

The traditional island **market day** is held on the third Saturday in August, although some market stalls are open most days throughout June to August in the town hall square. For information about shopping and events in Vaxholm, go to www.visitvaxholm.com/eng/index.asp.

The construction of **Vaxholms Fästning**, located on an unnamed islet just east of Vaxholm, was originally ordered by Gustav Vasa in 1544. The castle was attacked by the Danes in 1612 and the Russian navy in 1719; most of the current structure dates from 1863. Nowadays it's home to the National Museum of Coastal Defence and was renovated in 2002. The ferry across to the island departs from next to the tourist office every 30 minutes while the castle is open.

At the **Hembygdsgård** (an open-air museum), you'll find the finest old houses in Vaxholm, including the *fiskarebostad*, an excellent example of a late 19th-century fisherman's house, with a typical Swedish fireplace.

Around the corner from the tourist office, the **Customs House** is one of the few stone buildings in town and dates from 1736. The other notable stone building is the **church** (Kungsgatan), which is late 18th century. Just off Hamngatan, you'll see the **town hall**, rebuilt in 1925 with an onion dome on its roof; if it's open, take a look inside.

## Transport

**Distance from Stockholm** 34km
**Direction** Northeast
**Travel time** 45min–1¼hr
**Bus** Take No 670 from T-Tekniska Högskolan.
**Boat** In summer Waxholmsbolaget boats depart frequently from Strömkajen (outside the Grand Hôtel Stockholm) between 8.30am and 6.30pm on weekdays, 8am and 6.30pm on Saturday, and 8am and 9.30pm on Sunday and holidays. Cinderella Båtarna sails from Strandvägen (near Nybroplan) to Vaxholm three or four times daily from the third week in April to the last week of September and once daily Friday to Sunday from late September to early November.

## Sights & Information

**Cinderella Båtarna** ( ☎ 58 71 40 00; bokning@stromma.se)

**Hembygdsgård** ( ☎ 54 13 17 20; Trädgårdsgatan 19; admission free; 🕑 11am-4pm Sat & Sun mid-May–mid-Aug)

**Tourist office** ( ☎ 54 13 14 80; Söderhamnsplan; 🕑 10am-4pm Mon-Fri, also Sat & Sun in summer) Ask for the handy leaflet *A stroll through Vaxholm*.

**Vaxholms Fästning** ( ☎ 54 17 21 57; adult/child Skr40/10 incl ferry; 🕑 11.45am-3.45pm early Jun & mid-Aug–Sep, 11.45am-5.45pm late Jun–mid-Aug)

**Waxholmsbolaget** ( ☎ 679 58 30)

## Eating

**Melanders Fisk** ( ☎ 54 13 34 66; Hamngatan 2; lunch Skr65-85; 🕑 lunch 11.30am-3pm)

**Moby Dick Restaurang & Pizzeria** ( ☎ 54 13 38 83; Söderhamnsplan 1; pizza from Skr65) Enchiladas and other takeaway dishes also available.

**Waxholms Hotell** ( ☎ 54 13 01 50; Hamngatan 2; mains Skr115-285) Try the summer herring buffet.

## Sleeping

**Berggrens Hus** ( ☎ 54 13 02 79; Soldatgatan 14; s/d from Skr350/450) About 1km from the harbour.

**Rådhusgatan 18** ( ☎ 54 13 15 55; Rådhusgatan 18; s/d from Skr250/400; 🕑 summer only)

**Vaxholms Camping** ( ☎ 54 13 01 01; 3km west of the harbour; hiker/car with tent Skr85/115)

**Waxholms Hotell** ( ☎ 54 13 01 50; www.waxholmshotell .se; Hamngatan 2; s/d from Skr1200/1400)

# GAMLA TYRESÖ

Gamla Tyresö (Old Tyresö) has a pleasant English-style park with some significant attractions. The **church** on the hill has an impressive square tower and dates from 1641. The **altarpiece** was looted from Poland and shows a remarkable scene of the murder of Bishop Stanislaus of Kraków in 1079. There's also an interesting **votive ship** from 1620, one of the oldest in Sweden.

Work started on **Tyresö Slott** in the 1620s and was completed by 1635. The castle was rebuilt in rococo style in the second half of the 18th century and restored in 17th-century style after purchase by Claes Lagergren in 1892. On Lagergren's death in 1932, the castle and estate were bequeathed to Nordiska Museet and the interiors have been kept in excellent condition since.

Prince Eugene, the royal artist, stayed for 18 summers at the small group of buildings across the stream from the church; the complex has been restored as an excellent youth hostel. Advance booking is obligatory from October to May.

Just south of Gamla Tyresö is the sprawling wilderness of **Tyresta National Park**.

## Sights & Information

**Tyresta Nationalparkernashus** ( ☎ 745 33 94; Tyresta Village; ☉ 9am-4pm Tue-Fri, 11am-5pm Sat & Sun Mar-Oct, 10am-4pm Sat & Sun Nov-Feb; Skr20) The 4900-hectare Tyresta National Park, just south of Gamla Tyresö, is noted for its virgin forest, which includes huge 300-year-old pine trees.

**Tyresö Slott** ( ☎ 770 01 78; adult/child Skr55/25; ☉ guided tours on the hour noon-4pm mid-Jun—mid-Aug, noon-2pm Sun May-Oct, by appointment at other times) The castle has a café and restaurant.

## Sleeping

**STF Vandrarhem Lilla Tyresö** ( ☎ 770 03 04; fax 770 03 55; Kyrkvägen 3; dm Skr150-185)

# SÖDERTÄLJE

Södertälje, a large satellite town 38km southwest of Stockholm, offers a couple of attractions of interest to children and families.

The adventure swimming pool, **Sydpoolen**, has waves, currents, slides, diving, a lagoon for babies and a climbing wall. There's also a fitness centre and a gym.

Discover science and technology for yourself at **Tom Tits Experiment**, with lots of hands-on exhibits.

## Sights & Information

**Sydpoolen** ( ☎ 55 44 28 00; www.sydpoolen.se; Grödingevägen 2; adult/child under 7 1hr Skr60/45, 3hr Skr75/55; ☉ 9am-9pm Mon-Sat, 9am-6pm Sun)

**Tom Tits Experiment** ( ☎ 52 25 25 00; Storgatan 33; adult/child Skr85/65; ☉ 10am-4pm Mon-Fri, 11am-5pm Sat & Sun late Aug—late Jun, 10am-5pm late Jun—late Aug)

# STOCKHOLM ARCHIPELAGO

Depending on which source you read, the archipelago around Stockholm has anything between 14,000 and 100,000 islands, and regular boats offer great possibilities for outings. Having a summer cottage on a rocky islet is popular among wealthy Stockholmers.

While many islands can be visited on a day trip, you'll get a better experience if you stay overnight. Most of the main islands have Svenska Turistföreningen (STF) hostels, but they tend to only open in summer and they're often booked out months in advance. For information on cabin and chalet rental, contact **Destination Stockholms Skärgård** ( ☎ 54 24 81 00; www.dess.se; Lillström, SE-18497 Ljusterö).

Boat frequencies described in this section are for the summer period, mid-June to mid-August. Services are reduced at other times of year and are generally very poor in January and February. Quoted ferry fares are all one way; return tickets are normally just double the one-way fare. We've included transport information for each island; other details for the archipelago are listed following. Most places on the islands don't have formal addresses, but the islands are very small and well signposted.

## Sights & Information

**Cinderella Båtarna** ( ☎ 58 71 40 50; www.cinderella-batarna.com in Swedish; Skeppsbron 22, Stockholm)

**Norrtälje tourist office** ( ☎ 017 67 19 90)

**Strömma Kanalbolaget** ( ☎ 58 71 40 00; www.strommakanalbolaget.com) Operates the popular Thousand Islands Tour, in which the M/S *Waxholm III* calls at Strindberg's island (Kymmendö), Bullerö, Sandhamn and Vaxholm. You get around an hour ashore at each place (except Vaxholm).

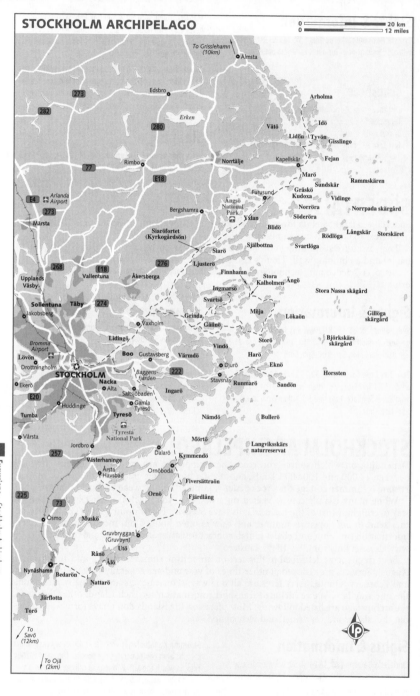

# STOCKHOLM ARCHIPELAGO

0 ═══════════ 20 km
0 ═══════════ 12 miles

**Waxholmsbolaget** ( ☎ 679 58 30; www.waxholmsbolaget
.se) The biggest archipelago ferry operator, with offices
outside the Grand Hôtel Stockholm and at the quay in
Vaxholm. Ask for the free *Stockholm Archipelago Guide*.

# Eating

**Dannekrogen** ( ☎ 50 15 70 79; Utö) Near the Gruvbryggan harbour, next to the bakery and opposite the ICA
supermarket, this places has standard pub food.

**Dykarbaren** ( ☎ 57 15 35 54; Sandön; mains from
Skr135) Standard pub food.

**Pizza Stugan** ( ☎ 50 15 73 50; Utö; pizza Skr65-95)
Located in Edesnäs.

**Sandhamns Värdshus** See Sleeping below.

# Sleeping

**Lotsutkiken** ( ☎ 52 03 41 11; fax 52 03 41 21; Öja;
s/d Skr345/650)

**STF Vandrarhem Arholma** ( ☎ 017 65 60 18; Arholma;
dm Skr120)

**STF Vandrarhem Finnhamn** ( ☎ 54 24 62 12; fax 54 24
61 33; www.finnhamn.nu; Finnhamn; dm Skr165)

**STF Vandrarhem Fjärdlång** ( ☎ 50 15 60 92; fax 50 15
66 34; Fjärdlång; dm Skr125; ☺ early Jun–late Sep) This
collection of chalets on the rocks of remote Fjardlång has
no restaurant, so you'll need to bring your own food.

**STF Vandrarhem Gällnö** ( ☎ 57 16 61 17; fax 57 16 62
88; Gällnö; dm Skr150; ☺ May-Sep)

**STF Vandrarhem Sävö** ( ☎ /fax 015 64 03 46; Sävö;
dm Skr130)

## Transport
**Travel time** 3–5hr
**Bus** Take No 640 from Stockholm Tekniska Högskolan to Norrtälje, then No 636 (or No 637 to Älmsta,
then change to No 636) to Simpnäs (three to five
daily) followed by a 20-minute ferry crossing to
the island.
**Ferry** Once daily from mid-June to mid-August,
**Blidösundsbolaget** ( ☎ 411 71 13) sails directly
from Strömkajen in Stockholm to Arholma (Skr100,
3½ to five hours). Båtluffarkortet (a boat pass, available from Waxholmsbolgaet) is valid.

**STF Vandrarhem Siaröfortet** ( ☎ /fax 54 24 21 49;
Siaröfortet; dm Skr150; ☺ May-Sep, advance bookings
only May–mid-Jun & mid-Aug–end Sep)

**STF Vandrarhem Stora Kalholmen** ( ☎ 54 24 60 23;
fax 57 16 01 25; Stora Kalholmen; dm Skr135; ☺ early
Jun–mid-Aug)

**STF Vandrarhem Utö** ( ☎ 50 42 03 15; fax 50 42 03 01;
Gruvbryggan, Utö; dm Skr200) The Utö hostel, associated
with the nearby Utö Värdshus, is located in a former
summer house. Reception and meals can be found at the
Utö Värdshus.

**Sandhamns Värdshus** ( ☎ 57 15 30 51; lars.mac.gregor
.e@sand hamns-vardshus.se; s/d from Skr550/850)

**Utö Värdshus** ( ☎ 50 42 03 00; receptionen@uto-vardshus
.se; Utö; B&B from Skr800) This is the only hotel on the
island and it overcharges accordingly, but the restaurant
serves fine meals.

## The Right of Public Access

The right of public access to the countryside, *allemansrätten*, which includes national parks and nature reserves, dates
back to common practices in medieval times, but isn't enshrined in law. Full details can be found on the Internet at
www.environ.se.

You're allowed to walk, ski, boat or swim anywhere outside private property but must stay at least 70m from houses
and keep out of gardens, fenced areas and cultivated land. You can camp for more than one night in the same place and
you may pick berries and mushrooms, provided they're not protected.

Don't leave any rubbish or take living wood, bark, leaves, bushes or nuts. Fires made with fallen wood are allowed
where safe, but not on bare rocks. Use a bucket of water to douse a campfire even if you think that it's out. Cars and
motorcycles may not be driven across open land or on private roads; look out for the sign *Ej Motorfordon* (No Motor
Vehicles). Dogs must be kept on leads between 1 March and 20 August. Close all gates and don't disturb farm animals
or nesting birds.

If you have a car, bicycle or you're hitching, look for free camping sites around unsealed forest tracks leading from
secondary country roads. Make sure your spot is at least 50m from the track and not visible from any house, building or
sealed road.

# ARHOLMA

Arholma is one of the most interesting islands in the far north of the archipelago. Everything was burnt down during a Russian invasion in 1719. The lighthouse was rebuilt in the 19th century and is a well-known landmark. The island became a popular resort in the early 20th century, and is noted for its traditional village and chapel.

STF Vandrarhem Arholma offers dorm beds in a renovated cow barn. Advance booking is essential.

Arholma has a summer café and a grocery shop by the harbour.

# ÄNGSÖ

This small island lies 15km south of Norr-tälje and it was declared a national park as early as 1909, despite being only 1.5km long and 600m wide. Ängsö is character-ised by soft meadows, virgin woodland and magnificent displays of wild flowers (especially in spring). You may also see birds such as ospreys, sea eagles and great crested grebes.

## Transport

Travel time 3hr
Bus No 621 runs every hour or two (fewer on week-ends) from J-Åkersberga station (Stockholm) to Norr-tälje and No 632/634 runs six to 12 times daily from Norrtälje to Furusund.

You can't stay overnight in the park, but there are boat trips (from Furusund) and guided walks – contact Norrtälje tourist office for current details.

# SIARÖFORTET

The tiny island, Kyrkogårdsön (Cemetery Island), in the important sea lane just north of Ljusterö (40km due northeast of Stockholm), may be only 400m long but it's one of the most fascinating islands in the archipelago.

After the outbreak of WWI, the military authorities decided that Vaxholm castle wasn't a good enough defensive position. In 1916 construction of a new fort, Siaröfortet, began on Kyrkogårdsön. This powerful defence facility was never used in anger; after renovation in 1996, it's now open as a museum and a visit is highly recommended. You'll see two impressive 15.2cm cannons (incidentally, they're trained on the passing Viking Line ferries!), the officers' mess, kitchen, sleep-ing quarters and tunnels. There are no fixed opening times; contact the managers at the STF hostel to arrange a free tour.

## Transport

Travel time 1½hr
Bus/Ferry Waxholmsbolaget ferries to Siaröfortet depart from Strömkajen in Stockholm and sail to Siaröfortet via Vaxholm once or twice daily.

STF Vandrarhem Siaröfortet is an excel-lent hostel with two saunas. Canoe hire and breakfast are available.

# FINNHAMN

The 900m-long island of Finnhamn has rocky cliffs and a small beach which has good swimming opportunities for families. It's a fairly trendy place and attracts wealthy visi-tors from Stockholm and beyond. You can camp in the woods for free, but note that you'll need to carry all your own water in with you.

The STF Vandrarhem Finnhamn is lo-cated in a large converted warehouse and advance bookings are absolutely essential. There are rowing boats and boats with out-boards for hire. The attached café serves good meals.

## Transport

Travel time 2hr
Ferry You can sail with Waxholmsbolaget from Stockholm (Strömkajen) to Finnhamn. Cinderella Båtarna sails from Strandvägen to Finnhamn two or three times daily.

## STORA KALHOLMEN

Measuring only 700m long by 300m wide, this rocky little islet just south of Finnhamn offers some excellent swimming opportunities.

The STF Vandrarhem Stora Kalholmen is a very nicely located hostel, but it doesn't have electricity or a flush toilet. There is however a gas stove, as well as a sauna – perfect after a long day. Canoe hire is also available. Meals are only available for large groups, so you'll need to bring your own food.

### Transport

**Travel time** 2¼hr
**Ferry** Sailings with Cinderella Båtarna from Strandvägen (via Vaxholm and Finnhamn) run three times daily from Monday to Friday and once on Saturday and Sunday.

## GÄLLNÖ

Gällnö is a strangely shaped island with a long coastline and a small population. It's a great place for swimming and fishing. Camping is allowed in the woods, but bring your own water.

### Transport

**Travel time** 1–2hr
**Ferry** Waxholmsbolaget sails from Strömkajen to Gällnö two to five times daily.

The STF Vandrarhem Gällnö is housed in a former schoolhouse built in the early 20th century, but some rooms are available in adjacent cabins. There's also a sauna. Near the Gällnö hostel is a small shop that serves coffee and cakes.

## SANDÖN

Sandön, with a population of around 100 people, is 2.5km long and has superb sandy beaches that are reminiscent of the Mediterranean on a sunny day. Sandhamn is the northern settlement, but the best beaches are at **Trovill**, near the southern tip of the island.

*Glaciated rock slabs, Utö (p176)*

Excursions – Stockholm Archipelago

The wooden houses and narrow alleys of **Sandhamn** are worth exploring, too. However, the island is a popular destination for party goers and wealthy sailors and many regattas start or finish here. Overall, the place is rather expensive and is best visited as a day trip. Camping is prohibited on the island.

Sandhamns Värdshus first opened its doors in 1672, and it still serves good food. A three-course meal costs Skr263 and main courses cost from Skr139 to Skr191. The Värdshus also offers accommodation.

Situated just 50m from the quay is the popular and rather trendy restaurant/bar Dykarbaren.

## Transport

**Travel time** 2–3½hr
**Bus/Ferry** Waxholmsbolaget sails from Strömkajen to Sandhamn via Vaxholm with the vintage steamer SS *Norrskär* once on Saturday and Sunday. It's also possible to take bus No 433 or 434 from Slussen to Stavsnäs (50 minutes) then sail from there (35 minutes to one hour, six to nine times daily).

Cinderella Båtarna runs boats from Strandvägen to Sandhamn twice daily between mid-June and mid-August (2¼ hours), departing at 9.30am and returning at 2.30pm (6pm on weekends), allowing nearly three hours in Sandhamn (nearly 6½ hours on weekends).

# FJÄRDLÅNG

Fjärdlång is a 4km-long island without roads, and few residents. It's very scenic and is an ideal place to relax and enjoy the archipelago life. Swimming and fishing are both possible, and boat hire is also available. Fjärdlång is also a great place for picking wild berries from July to early August, and for picking mushrooms in late August.

Perched on the rocks, the wonderful STF Vandrarhem Fjärdlång consists of a house and several chalets. There's no shop or meals service, so you need to bring your own food.

## Transport

**Travel time** 1hr
**Bus/Ferry** The Waxholmsbolaget ferry sails from Dalarö to Fjärdlång three or four times daily. Direct boats from Stockholm to Utö stop at Fjärdlång once or twice daily (three hours).

# UTÖ

Utö is a large, delightful island in the southern section of the archipelago – it's 13km long and up to 4km wide. There's a fairly good road and track network, so it's popular with cyclists.

You can purchase a reasonable sketch map of the island from the **tourist office** ( ☎ 50 15 74 10; ۞ 10am-4pm Mon-Fri Apr-Sep), which is in a small cabin by the **guest harbour** ( ☎ 50 15 74 10) at **Gruvbryggan**, also known as Gruvbyn, (the northernmost village). It's open between 10am and 4pm on weekdays, from April to September. At other times, ask at the inn Utö Värdshus, which is just up the hill. There's also a post office in the village centre.

Most of the sights are located at the northern end of the island, near Gruvbryggan. The most unusual thing to see is **Sweden's oldest iron mine**, which opened in 1150 and closed over 700 years later, in 1879. The three pits are now flooded – the deepest, at 215m, is Nyköpingsgruvan. The **mining museum**, which is opposite the Värdshus, keeps variable hours, so make sure you check when you arrive on the island. The well-preserved 18th-century **miners' houses** on Lurgatan are worth a look. The **windmill** is open 11am to 3pm daily. The best **sandy beach** is on the north coast, about 10 min-

## Transport

**Travel time** 2–4hr
**Bicycle** Ask at the guest harbour about bike hire.
**Bus/Ferry** Take the *pendeltåg* from Stockholm Centralstationen to Västerhaninge, then bus No 846 to Årsta Havsbad. From there, Waxholmsbolaget and Utö Rederi ferries connect eight to 10 times daily with Utö, but make sure you know whether your boat stops at Spränga or Gruvbryggan first. You can also sail directly from Strömkajen to Utö (via Saltsjöbaden), once or twice daily; Gruvbryggan is always the first stop.

If you take a ferry from Nynäshamn to Ålö, you'll have to hike most of the length of the island to reach Gruvbryggan (one hour, two to four daily).

utes' walk from the Värdshus, in the direction of Kroka. To see the **glaciated rock slabs** on the eastern coast, walk for about 20 minutes through the pine forest towards Rävstavik.

# ÖJA

In the far south of the archipelago, Öja is 4km long but only 500m wide. Until the 1990s, the island was within a military zone and was strictly off limits for tourists. The village at the southern tip, **Landsort**, has been a pilot station since 1535. The **labyrinth** near the village, whose pattern is believed to be at least 3000 years old, has superstitious origins; it was believed to bring good luck to fishermen, and some locals still say it can't hurt to walk through (but beware, it's also supposed to increase fertility!).

**Transport**

**Travel time** 2hr
**Ferry** The ferry to Öja departs from Torö, Ankarudden, and sails to Landsort two to five times daily.

**Landsorts fyr**, built in 1672, is the oldest preserved lighthouse in Sweden. The light is still operational and can be seen 18 nautical miles away.

The former pilot's house Lotsutkiken now offers B&B and there's a café/restaurant nearby.

# SÄVÖ

About a one-hour drive and a short ferry trip south of Stockholm, tiny Sävö is only 1.3km long and is a great place to escape from the summer crowds. There's a nature reserve on the island. Access is by private car only – there's no public transport.

**STF Vandrarhem Sävö**, in a former pilot's station, is an old wooden building that has great sea views. Breakfast and boat hire are both available. Advance bookings are compulsory from September to May.

**Transport**

**Travel time** 1½hr
**Car** Drive south on the E4 motorway and turn off at Vagnhärad. Follow road No 219 south, then turn off for Tofsö, Källvik and Sävö. By prior arrangement, the STF hostel manager will come to the mainland by boat and pick up overnight guests.

# DROTTNINGHOLM

The royal residence and parks of Drottningholm on Lovön should be among the best tourist attractions in Stockholm, but the real highlights of a visit here are the amazing, Unesco-listed Drottningholms Slottsteater and Kina Slott.

The Renaissance-inspired **Drottningholms Slott** and the geometrical baroque gardens were both designed by the great architect Nicodemus Tessin the Elder. Construction began in 1662, about the same time as Versailles, and the palace is now home for the Swedish royal family. You're advised to walk around yourself, since the hour-long guided tour (at 11am, noon, 1pm and 3pm daily in summer) tends to drag and assumes an in-depth knowledge of Swedish royalty and 18th-century Swedish history.

The **Lower North Corps de Garde** was originally a guardroom but it's now replete with gilt leather wall hangings, which used to feature in many palace rooms during the 17th century. The **Karl X Gustav Gallery**, in baroque style, depicts the militaristic endeavours of this monarch, but the ceiling shows battle scenes from classical times. The highly ornamented **State Bedchamber of Hedvig Eleonora** is the most expensive baroque interior in Sweden and it's decorated with paintings featuring the childhood of Karl XI. The painted ceiling shows Karl X and his queen, Hedvig Eleonora.

Although Queen Lovisa Ulrika's collection of over 2000 books has been moved to the Royal Library in Stockholm, the **library** is still a bright and impressive room, complete with most of its original 18th-century fittings. The over elaborate **staircase**, with statues at every turn, was the work of both Nicodemus Tessin the Elder and Nicodemus Tessin the Younger. The circular **Drottningholm Palace Chapel** wasn't completed until the late 1720s.

The palace has a gift shop and there's an adjacent restaurant.

**Drottningholms Slottsteater** was completed in 1766 on the instructions of Queen Lovisa Ulrika. This is an extraordinary place, since it remained untouched from the time of Gustav III's death (1792) until 1922. It's the oldest theatre in the world still in its original state; performances are held here in summer using the 18th-century machinery, such as ropes, pulleys and wagons. Scenes can be changed in less than seven seconds.

Illusion was the order of the day in here and there's fake marble, fake curtains and papier-mâché viewing boxes. Even the stage was designed to create illusions regarding size.

The interesting guided tour will also take you into some other rooms in the same building. You'll see hand-painted 18th-century wallpaper and an Italian-style room, the **salon de déjèuner**, with fake three-dimensional wall effects and a ceiling that looks like the sky. There are regular performances in the theatre every summer.

At the far end of the gardens is **Kina Slott**, a lavishly decorated Chinese pavilion that was built by King Adolf Fredrik as a birthday gift to Queen Lovisa Ulrika (1753). It was restored between 1989 and 1996 and is now mostly in its original condition. There are 15 rooms, including the excellent **Mirrored Drawing Room** and the **Blue Drawing Room**. The **Octagonal Hall** has a magnificent mid-18th-century Swedish tiled stove. There's a coffee shop on the premises.

On the slope below Kina Slott, the **Guards' Tent** was erected in 1781 as quarters for the dragoons of Gustav III, but it's not really a tent at all. The building now has displays about the gardens and Drottningholm's Royal Guard.

The artist **Evert Lundquist** had his studio in a converted power station between Kina Slott and the lake, but it was converted into a museum when he gave up painting. The museum shows Lundquist's studio exactly as he left it.

## Transport

**Distance from Stockholm** 10km
**Direction** West
**Travel time** 1hr by boat
**Boat** Strömma Kanalbolaget departs from Stadshusbron once or twice an hour from 9.30am to 6pm daily in summer (reduced service from late April to early June & mid-August to early September).
**Bus/Train** T-Brommaplan to bus Nos 301 to 323 (eight minutes).

## Sights & Information

**Drottningholms Slott** ( ☎ 402 62 80; admission Skr60, combination ticket Skr90, chapel free; ☉ 10am-4.30pm May-Aug, noon-3.30pm Sep, noon-3.30pm Sat & Sun Oct-Apr)

**Evert Lundquist studio** (adult/child Skr50/25, pay at Kina Slott; ☉ 5.30-7pm Wed & 11am-2pm Sun mid-May–mid-Aug) Guided tours are held at 4pm on Wednesday.

**Kina Slott** ( ☎ 402 62 70; adult/child Skr50/25, Guards' Tent free; ☉ 11am-4.30pm May-Aug, noon-3.30pm Sep, Guard's Tent noon-4pm early Jun–mid-Aug)

**Slottsteater** (Court Theatre; ☎ 759 04 06; adult/child Skr50/free) There are frequent daily guided tours in English.

**Strömma Kanalbolaget** ( ☎ 58 71 40 00; strommakanal bolaget@stromma.se; Skeppsbron 22, Stockholm; adult/child return Skr110/55, incl admission to Drottningholm Slott & Kina Slott Skr180)

# BIRKA

The Viking trading centre of Birka, on Björkö in Lake Mälaren, is now a Unesco World Heritage Site. It was founded around AD 760 with the intention of expanding and controlling trade in the region. The village attracted merchants and craft workers, and the population grew to about 700 people. A large defensive fort with thick drystone ramparts was constructed next to the village. In 830 the Benedictine monk Ansgar was sent to Birka by the Holy Roman Emperor to convert the heathen Vikings to Christianity, and he lived in Birka for 18 months. Birka was abandoned in the late 10th century when Sigtuna took over the role of commercial centre.

The village site is surrounded by a vast graveyard. It's the largest Viking Age cemetery in Scandinavia, with around 3000 graves. Most people were cremated, then mounds of earth were piled over the remains, but some Christian coffins and chambered tombs have been found. The fort and harbour have also been excavated. A cross to the memory of St Ansgar can be seen on top of a nearby hill.

Excursions – Drottningholm

The excellent **Birka Museum** includes finds from the excavations, which are still proceeding. There are also copies of the most magnificent objects and an interesting model showing the village as it was in Viking times. The museum has a restaurant.

## Sights & Information

**Birka Museum** ( ☎ 56 05 14 45; adult/child Skr65/30, normally incl in ferry tickets; ☹ 10am-6.30pm 30 Jun-19 Aug, slightly shorter hours late Apr–late Sep)

# GRIPSHOLMS SLOTT

Originally built in the 1370s, the castle Gripsholms Slott passed into crown hands by the early 15th century. In 1526 Gustav Vasa took over and ordered the demolition of the adjacent monastery. A new castle with walls up to 5m thick was built at Gripsholm using materials from the monastery, but extensions, conversions and repairs continued for years. The oldest 'untouched' room is Karl IX's bedchamber, dating from the 1570s. The castle was abandoned in 1715, but it was renovated and extended during the reign of Gustav III (especially between 1773 and 1785). The moat was filled in and, in 1730 and 1827, two 11th-century **rune stones** were found. These stones stand by the access road and are well worth a look; one has a Christian cross, while the other describes an expedition against the Saracens. The castle was restored again in the 1890s, the moat was cleared and the drawbridge rebuilt.

Gripsholm is the epitome of castles, with its round towers, spires and drawbridge. It contains some of the state portrait collection, which dates from the 16th century, and you can enjoy exploring the finely decorated rooms.

You can also visit the nearby **Grafikens Hus**, a centre for contemporary graphic art and classical prints.

## Transport

**Distance from Stockholm** 25km
**Direction** West
**Travel time** 30min
**Boat** There are sailings three times daily with **Mälarö skärgårdstrafik** ( ☎ 711 14 57) between Rastaholm (Ekerö) and Birka. Tickets include guided tour and admission to the Birka Museum. Summer cruises to Birka depart from many places around Lake Mälaren, including Västerås, Strängnäs, Mariefred, Södertälje and Stockholm.
**Bus** Nos 311 and 312 from T-Brommaplan stop on the main road about 1.5km from Rastaholm.

## Sights & Information

**Grafikens Hus** ( ☎ 231 60; adult/child Skr40/free; ☹ 11am-5pm daily May-Aug, Sat & Sun Sep-Apr)

**Gripsholm** ( ☎ 101 94; adult/child Skr50/25; ☹ 10am-4pm daily May-Aug, 10am-3pm Tues-Sun Sept, noon-3pm Sat & Sun Oct-Apr)

## Eating & Sleeping

**Gripsholms Grill i Mariefred** ( ☎ 211 51; Gripsholms-vägen 1; pizza from Skr55, fast food from Skr25)

**Gripsholms Värdshus & Hotel** ( ☎ 347 50; Kyrkogatan 1; s/d from Skr1400/1600) Sweden's oldest inn, this place has great views of the castle.

### The Vintage Steamer SS *Saltsjön*

The wonderful old steamship SS *Saltsjön*, launched in 1925, was specifically designed to navigate the narrow sounds between Saltsjön and Baggensfjärden, which lie between Stockholm and Utö in the southern archipelago. The ship was built with a 55HP compound steam engine and could hold 454 passengers. After WWII, SS *Saltsjön* was moved to the northern archipelago and was eventually taken out of regular service in 1968.

Just two years later, it was renamed SS *Björkfjärden* and started taking passengers to Birka on Lake Mälaren, but a boiler fault in 1975 put it out of business.

After being renovated by a group of enthusiasts, the boat started sailing again under its original name. The SS *Saltsjön* can take up to 300 passengers and has a top speed of 11 knots. There's a restaurant on board.

SS *Saltsjön* now sails from Stockholm's Strömkajen to Gruvbryggan (Utö) via the original route on weekends from mid-June to mid-August. Departure from the city is at 9.30am and the return trip is at 8.15pm, allowing three hours on the island. The round trip costs Skr190 and Båtluffarkortet is valid.

STF Vandrarhem Mariefred ( ☎ 361 00; fax 123 50; dm Skr180; ☀ early Jun–early Aug) This hostel, run by the Swedish Red Cross, is only 500m west of the castle.

# SIGTUNA

Sigtuna, founded around AD 980, is the most pleasant and important historical town around Stockholm. It's also the oldest surviving town in Sweden and Stora gatan is probably Sweden's oldest main street. Around 1000, Olof Skötkonung ordered the minting of Sweden's first coins in the town. There are about 150 runic inscriptions in the area, most dating from the early 11th century and located beside ancient roads. Sigtuna has many quaint streets and wooden buildings still following the medieval town

## Transport

**Distance from Stockholm** 70km
**Direction** Southwest
**Train** The nearest station is at Läggesta, 3km west, with hourly trains from Stockholm (40 minutes). A **museum railway** ( ☎ 210 00) from Läggesta to Mariefred runs on weekends from May to September (daily from 25 June to 12 August).
**Bus** Nos 304 and 307 run hourly from Läggesta to Mariefred (five minutes).
**Boat** The steamship SS *Mariefred* ( ☎ 669 88 50) departs from Stadshusbron (Stockholm) for Gripsholm daily except Monday from 13 June to 27 August, and weekends only from 20 May to 12 June and 2 to 12 September (tickets Skr130, 3½ hours).

plan but, apart from the church, the original buildings didn't survive the devastating late-medieval era town fires.

During medieval times, there were seven stone-built churches in Sigtuna, but most have now disappeared. Off Prästgatan is the ruin of the church of **St Per**, originally built in the 12th century, but with a virtually intact tower. The ruin of **St Lars** is nearby. The **St Olof church** was built in the early 12th century, but became ruinous by the 17th century.

The adjacent **Mariakyrkan** (Olofsgatan) is the oldest brick building in the area – it was a Dominican monastery church from around 1250, but became the parish church in 1529 after the monastery was demolished by Gustav Vasa. Inside, look for the excellent 14th- and 15th-century **murals and ceiling paintings** and the magnificent 5m-wide 15th-century German **reredos** (wall hangings). Free summer concerts are held here once a week.

**Sigtuna Museum** looks after several attractions in the town, all of them on Stora gatan and near the tourist office. **Lundströmska gården** is an early-20th-century middle-class home and adjacent general store, complete with period furnishings and goods. **Sigtuna rådhus**, the smallest town hall in Scandinavia, dates from 1744 and was designed by the mayor himself. It's on the town square (opposite the tourist office). There's also an **exhibition hall** next to Systembolaget. The main museum building, at Stora gatan 55, has displays of artefacts (mostly from the 1988–90 excavations), including gold jewellery, runes, coins and loot brought home from abroad. The oddest find is the half-skeleton that turned out to be a mid-11th-century bishop of Sigtuna with a walrus ivory crozier.

Just 2km north of Sigtuna, the **Viby peasants township**, by the manor house Venngarns Slott, is a well-preserved group of 19th-century houses showing how agricultural workers lived before the era of land reforms. They're still in use as private homes and the area is not a museum.

The magnificent private palace **Steninge Slott**, 7km east of Sigtuna, dates from 1705 and was designed by Nicodemus Tessin the Younger. You'll see luxuriously ornate interiors, but there's also a glassworks, ceramic works, candle factory, restaurant and an **art gallery** that usually features impressive temporary exhibitions, including regular displays of local and international glassworks artists.

About 9km southeast of Sigtuna, **Rosersbergs Slott** is a large palace on the shores of Lake Mälaren. It was constructed in the 1630s and used as a royal residence from 1762 to 1860. The interior has excellent furnishings from the Empire period (1790–1820). One of the highlights is **Queen Hedvig Elisabeth Charlotta's conversation room**, an intimate horseshoe-shaped cubbyhole upholstered in plush satiny fabric; one can only imagine the secrets she must have told there.

Around 11km due northwest of Sigtuna (26km by road), there's the exceptionally fine, whitewashed baroque palace **Skokloster Slott**, which was built between 1654 and 1671. The palace has impressive stucco ceilings and collections of furniture, textiles, art and arms. There's a small café onsite. The adjacent **motor museum** has a good collection of vintage cars and motorcycles. There's also a fire engine for kids to play in. The **Skokloster pageant** ( ☎ 38 67 25) lasts five days in mid-July and includes around 350 performances (medieval tournaments, exhibitions, concerts, 18th-century activities etc).

# Sights & Information

**Rosersbergs Slott** ( ☎ 59 03 50 39; adult/child Skr50/25; tours hourly 11am-3pm May-Aug, Sat & Sun Sep)

**Sigtuna Museum** ( ☎ 59 78 38 70; Stora gatan 55; admission Skr20; ☽ noon-4pm Tue-Sun Sep-May)

**Skokloster Motor Museum** ( ☎ 38 61 06; adult/child Skr40/10; ☽ 11am-5pm May-Sep)

**Skokloster Slott** ( ☎ 018 38 60 77; www.skokloster.se; adult/child Skr65/20; tours 11am-4pm May-Aug, 1pm Mon-Fri & hourly noon-3pm Sat & Sun Apr, Sep & Oct) Tours available in English on request.

**Steninge Slott** ( ☎ 59 25 95 00; adult/child Skr30/10; ☽ 11am-4pm Sun-Fri & 11am-2pm Sat early Jun–mid-Aug, 11am-2pm Sat & 11am-3pm Sun Jan–early Jun & mid-Aug–mid-Nov) Located 7km east of Sigtuna.

**Tourist office** ( ☎ 59 25 00 20; turism@sigtuna.se; Stora gatan 33; ☽ 10am-6pm Mon-Sat, 11am-5pm Sun Jun-Aug, shorter hours Sep-May) In an 18th-century wooden house, Drakegården.

## Transport

**Distance from Stockholm** 40km
**Travel time** 1hr
**Bus/Train** SJ or SL train to Märsta, change to bus No 570, 575 or 584 (frequent) just outside the Märsta train station. Bus No 883 runs every hour or two from Uppsala to Sigtuna. The Märsta to Sigtuna bus passes 3km north of Steninge Slott. To Rosersbergs Slott, take SL *pendeltåg* to Rosersberg, then walk 2km to the palace (signposted). For Skokloster, take hourly SJ train to Bålsta, then infrequent bus 894.

# Eating

**Båthuset Krog & Bar** ( ☎ 59 25 67 80; Strandprom-enaden; mains Skr140-250) This floating wooden house out on the lake serves fish, lamb and beef dishes.

**Farbror Blå Café & Kök** ( ☎ 59 25 60 50; Storatorget 14; weekday lunch from Skr65)

**Tant Bruns Kaffestuga** ( ☎ 59 25 09 34; Laurentii Gränd 3; snacks from Skr15, sandwiches Skr50-60) Straight out of a storybook – literally – this saggy-roofed cottage is an unmissable stop just off Sigtuna's main street.

# Sleeping

**Sigtuna Stadshotell** ( ☎ 59 25 01 00; Stora Nygatan 3; s/d Skr1550/2150) This classy, historic boutique hotel has 27 rooms with modern accoutrements.

**Sigtunastiftelsens Gästhem** ( ☎ 59 25 89 00; bokning en@sigtunastiftelsen.se; Manfred Björkquists allé 2-4; s/d Skr800/950) This imposing structure, run by the Christian-humanist Sigtuna Foundation, looks like a cross between a cloister and a medieval fortress; rooms are less austere than you might think and are individually decorated with antiques.

**STF Vandrarhem Ansgarsliden** ( ☎ 59 25 82 00; ansgarsliden@svenskakyrkan.se; Manfred Björkquists allé 12; dm from Skr125; ☽ mid-Jun–Aug) The STF hostel is run by the Swedish church and lies about 1.6km west of the town centre.

**Stora Brännbo** ( ☎ 59 25 75 00; contact@stora.brannbo .se; Stora Brännbovägen 2-6; s/d from Skr900/1000) This modern-design hotel and conference centre has several single rooms with spartan décor but luxurious linens and top-notch services.

# UPPSALA

Uppsala is the fourth-largest city in Sweden, with a population of about 136,000, and is one of its oldest. **Gamla Uppsala** (Old Uppsala) flourished as early as the 6th century; the cathedral was consecrated in 1435 after 175 years of building and the castle was first built in the 1540s, although today's edifice belongs to the 18th century. The city depends on the sprawling university, founded in 1477 and the oldest in Scandinavia.

Uppsala began at the three great **grave mounds** at Gamla Uppsala, 4km north of the modern city centre. The mounds, said to be the graves of the legendary pre-Viking kings Aun, Egils and Adils, are part of a larger cemetery that includes about 300 small mounds and **boat graves**, dating from around 500 to 1100. A 10th-century boat grave in the vicarage garden was excavated in the 1970s and a small oriental statue was found. Important chieftains were often buried in their boats, along with all necessary provisions for their final journey.

The new **Gamla Uppsala Historical Centre** exhibits artefacts excavated from Gamla Uppsala and nearby archaeological sites, including a king's **gilt helmet** and a **necklace** with an image of a Valkyrie.

# UPPSALA

Gamla Uppsala was supposedly the site of a great heathen temple where human and animal sacrifices took place, but there's no evidence to support this. However, Thor, Odin and the other Viking gods were certainly displaced when Christianity arrived in 1090. From 1164, the archbishop of Uppsala had his seat in a cathedral on the site of the present church, which, by the 15th century, was enlarged and painted with frescoes.

Next to the flat-topped mound **Tingshögen** is the **Odinsborg Inn** ( ☎ 32 35 25), a restaurant that is known for its horns of mead, although daintier refreshments are offered in summer.

Construction of **Uppsala Slott** was ordered by Gustav Vasa in the 1550s and it features the state hall where kings were enthroned (and a queen abdicated). Nils Sture and his sons Erik and Svante were murdered in the castle in 1567 – Nils was stabbed by the crazed King Erik XIV, but others finished him off. The clothes Nils was wearing when he was killed are on display in the cathedral – they're the only 16th-century Swedish clothes still in existence. The castle burnt down in 1702, but was rebuilt and took its present form in 1757.

The **Vasa Vignettes** 'waxworks' museum in the death-stained dungeons shows the past intrigues of the castle. Uppsala Slott also houses an **art museum**, which features 16th- to 19th-century and contemporary art, including paintings by Cranach of Martin Luther and his wife.

The remarkable brick manor **Wiks Slott**, with an unusual clock tower and a magnificent park, is one of Sweden's best-preserved

*Uppsala Domkyrkan (below)*

medieval houses and dates from the 15th century. The interior was reconstructed in the 1650s and again in the 1860s. The house is about 20km southwest of the city centre, next to an arm of Lake Mälaren; take bus No 847 (four to eight daily).

The Gothic **Domkyrkan** dominates the city just as some of those buried here dominated their country: Gustav Vasa, Johan III, and Carl von Linné, who established the system of scientific names for species. The **treasury** in the north tower has Gustav Vasa's sword and a great display of medieval clothing, including archbishops' vestments from 1200 onwards. The nearby **Trefaldighets Kyrka** isn't outwardly as impressive, but has beautiful painted ceilings.

The **Gustavianum Museum** has exhibits on the university and the history of science, an excellent antiquities collection and an old 'anatomical theatre'. The **Uppland Museum**, located in a university water mill dating from the 1860s, houses county collections from the Middle Ages.

At the old university library, **Carolina Rediviva**, you'll see a display hall with maps and historical and scientific literature. The pride of the museum is Sweden's most precious book, the surviving half of the **Codex Argentus**, a holy bible written with silver ink on purple vellum in the now-extinct Gothic language in Ravenna in 520.

The excellent **botanical gardens** are below the castle hill. The gardens aren't to be confused with the **Linné Museum** and its **garden**. The museum keeps memorabilia of Linné's work in Uppsala. The garden (Sweden's oldest botanical garden), with more than 1000 herbs, was designed according to an 18th-century plan.

Take sandwiches and sit by the main **Uppsala University** building (which is imposing enough to demand a glance inside) and absorb the ambience of an historic university. On the lawn at the front are nine typical Uppland **rune stones**. On 30 April, the students gather dressed in white to celebrate the Walpurgis Festival in procession and song. There's also a raft race on the river at 10am and a 'run' (starting at the University Library) at 3pm, on the same day.

The old waterworks, **Pumphuset**, has a museum covering all public utilities. The **Museum of Evolution** includes dinosaur fossils and a mineral display. It's also open on weekdays from June to August by arrangement.

There's also the more obscure **Museum of Medical History** and the **Psychiatric Museum**. Both museums are south of the city centre and deal with the historical and developmental aspects of their respective topics.

## Transport

**Distance from Stockholm** 71km
**Direction** North
**Travel time** 1hr
**Bus** The bus station is outside the train station. No 802 departs once or twice each hour from 3.25am to 12.10am for the nearby Arlanda airport. Swebus Express runs to Stockholm (once or twice an hour, fewer on weekends), Sala (one hour, two or three daily) and other cities.
**Train** SJ trains run from Stockholm (40 minutes); X2000 trains require a supplement. Trains to Sala (35 minutes) run roughly once an hour. All SJ services between Stockholm and Gävle, Östersund and Mora stop in Uppsala. SL coupons and travel cards are good as far as Märsta.
**Bus to Gamla Uppsala** Take the direct No 2 departing from Uppsala's Stora torget (four per hour).

# Sights & Information

**Art Museum** ( ☎ 27 24 82; Uppsala Slott; admission Skr30; ☉ noon-4pm Tue-Fri, 11am-5pm Sat & Sun)

**Botanical Gardens** ( ☎ 471 28 38; Villavägen 6-8; admission free; ☉ 7am-8.30pm May-Sep, 7am-7pm Oct-Apr)

**Carolina Rediviva** ( ☎ 471 39 00; Dag Hammarskjölds väg 1; ☉ 9am-4pm late May–mid-Sep, variable hours mid-Sep–late May)

**Domkyrkan** (Cathedral; ☎ 18 72 01; Domkyrkoplan; admission free; ☉ 8am-6pm)

**Gamla Uppsala Historical Centre** ( ☎ 23 93 00; Disavägen; admission Skr50; ☉ 10am-5pm mid-Apr– mid-Aug, 10am-4pm mid-Aug–end Sept)

**Gustavianum Museum** ( ☎ 471 75 71; Akademigatan 3; adult/child under 12 Skr40/free; ☉ 11am-4pm mid-May–mid-Sep, 11am-4pm Wed-Sun late Sep–early May)

**Linneaum Orangery** ( ☎ 10 94 90; Svartbäcksgatan 27; admission Skr20; ☉ 9am-9pm May-Aug, 9am-7pm Sep)

**Linné Museum** ( ☎ 13 65 40; Svartbäcksgatan 27; admission Skr30; ☉ noon-4pm Tues-Sun Jun–early Sep)

**Museum of Medical History** ( ☎ 611 26 10; Eva Lagerwalls väg 8; admission Skr25; ☉ 1-5pm Thu & last Sun of every month, closed Jul-Aug)

**Museum of Evolution** ( ☎ 471 27 39; Norbyvägen 22; admission Skr25; ☉ 1-4pm Tue-Thu & 11am-3pm Sun Sep-May)

**Private Room Agency** ( ☎ 10 95 33; fax 12 82 42; s/d from Skr300/400) This agency organises B&B accommodation around Uppsala.

**Psychiatric Museum** ( ☎ 611 29 48; Eva Lagerwalls väg 10; ☉ 10am-2pm Thu & noon-3pm 1st Sun of every month, closed mid-Jun–Aug)

**Public library** (Svartbäcksgatan 17; ☉ 11am-Sat mid-May–mid-Aug)

**Pumphuset** ( ☎ 27 42 24; Munkgatan 2; adult/under 12 Skr5/free; ☉ noon-4pm by arrangement)

**Royal Cinema** ( ☎ 13 50 07; Dragarbrunnsgatan 44) This multiscreen cinema shows films from Hollywood regularly.

**University hospital** ( ☎ 611 00 00; enter from Sjukhusvägen) The pharmacy at entrance No 70 ( ☎ 611 34 55) is open until 9pm.

**Uppland Museum** ( ☎ 16 91 00; St Eriks gränd 6; admission Skr35; ☉ noon-5pm Tue-Sun)

**Uppsala Slott** ( ☎ 27 24 82; adult/child Skr60/10 incl entrance to Art Museum; guided tours in English 1pm & 3pm Jun-Aug)

**Uppsala Tourism** ( ☎ 27 48 00; tb@uppsalatourism.se; Fyris torg 8; ☉ 10am-6pm Mon-Fri, 10am-3pm Sat, noon-4pm Sun mid-May–mid-Aug)

**Vasa Vignettes** ( ☎ 27 24 82; adult/child Skr40/20; ☉ noon-4pm Mon-Fri & 11am-5pm Sat & Sun May-Aug)

**Wiks Slott** ( ☎ 56 10 00; adult/child Skr35/20; tours 1pm & 3pm Jun–mid-Aug; tours in English on request)

# Eating & Drinking

There's a Hemköp supermarket on Stora torget. Saluhallen, the indoor produce market, is at St Eriks torg between the cathedral and the river, and a small open market is at Vaksala torg, behind the train station (both closed on Sunday). Other options include:

**Café Kvarnfallet** ( ☎ 15 03 33; Fyris torg 4; cakes & sandwiches from Skr35) You'll find abundant charm and old-world romance at this adorable 13th-century cellar near the river, where you can sit and sip in small vaulted rooms or at outdoor tables set up right beside the rapids.

**Domtrappkällaren** ( ☎ 13 09 55; St Eriks gränd 15; weekday lunch from Skr75; ☿ lunch & dinner) Previously a prison, this stylish place has an atmospheric basement and a more ordinary upstairs section.

**Hambergs Fisk** ( ☎ 71 00 50; Fyris torg 8; mains Skr135-250; ☿ lunch & dinner, closed Mon) Hambergs Fisk is an excellent fish restaurant.

**Katalin and all that Jazz** ( ☎ 14 06 80; Godsmagasinet) This excellent place in a former warehouse has regular live jazz and blues, with occasional pop and rock bands.

**Kung Krål** ( ☎ 12 50 90; Gamla torget; mains from Skr75-185; ☿ lunch & dinner daily Apr-Aug, closed Sun Sep-Mar) Good, filling Swedish and international food.

**Ofvandahl's** ( ☎ 13 42 04; Sysslomansgatan 3-5; cakes & desserts Skr15-35; ☿ lunch & dinner, closed Sun) This is the oldest and classiest café in town.

**William's English Pub** ( ☎ 14 09 20; Åsgränd 5) An English-style pub in the university quarter.

# Sleeping

**First Hotel Linné** ( ☎ 10 20 00; Skolgatan 45; s/d Skr1250/1500) This excellent hotel is next to the gardens at the Linné Museum.

**Hotel Svava** ( ☎ 13 00 30; Bangårdsgatan 24; s/d Skr1250/1500) This is a modern, centrally located hotel run by the Ramada chain.

**Hotel Uppsala** ( ☎ 480 50 00; Kungsgatan 27; s/d from Skr700/800) This central option has a range of rooms (all with private bathroom, some with self-catering facilities) and charges extra for breakfast.

**Scandic Hotel Uppsala** ( ☎ 495 23 00; uppsala@scandic-hotels.com; Gamla Uppsalagatan 50; s/d Skr1100/1400) Located 2.5km from the city centre on the road to Gamla Uppsala, with pleasant rooms, a bistro and restaurant.

**STF Vandrarhem Sunnersta Herrgård** ( ☎ 32 42 20; Sunnerstavägen 24; dm Skr180, hotel s/d Skr550/650) The hostel, with two- or three-bed rooms, is in an early 19th-century manor house some 6km south of the centre. Take bus 20 or 50.

*Grave mounds, Gamla Uppsala (p181)*

# VÄSTERÅS

Both an old and a modern city, Västerås is now a centre of Asea Brown Boweri (ABB) industrial technology. The heavy industry, modern shopping malls and sprawling suburbs contrast strongly with the old town centre and the wooden buildings along the Svartån River. You can relax on the shores of Lake Mälaren or visit any of the several historical sites nearby.

Västerås is the sixth-largest city in Sweden and has an international feel – more than 7% of its inhabitants are immigrants.

**Västmanlands Länsmuseum**, in Västerås Slottet manor house, has a strong general historical collection which includes Iron Age gold jewellery, as well as dolls houses and Swedish porcelain. The neighbouring **Turbinhuset** (Turbine House), part of the same complex, was the inducement for ABB to move their business here from Arboga, southwest of Västerås.

The nearby **Konstmuseum**, in the old city hall, has temporary exhibitions of Swedish painters and the permanent collections get an occasional airing. There's a café in the vaulted cellar.

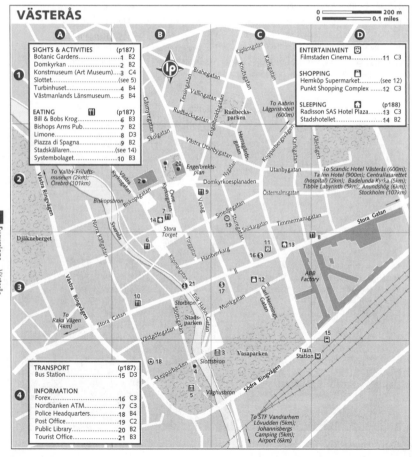

**VÄSTERÅS**

0 ————— 200 m
0 ————— 0.1 miles

| SIGHTS & ACTIVITIES | (p187) | |
|---|---|---|
| Botanic Gardens | 1 | B2 |
| Domkyrkan | 2 | B2 |
| Konstmuseum (Art Museum) | 3 | C4 |
| Slottet | (see 5) | |
| Turbinhuset | 4 | B4 |
| Västmanlands Länsmuseum | 5 | B4 |

| EATING | (p187) | |
|---|---|---|
| Bill & Bobs Krog | 6 | B3 |
| Bishops Arms Pub | 7 | B2 |
| Limone | 8 | D3 |
| Piazza di Spagna | 9 | B2 |
| Stadskällaren | (see 14) | |
| Systembolaget | 10 | B3 |

| ENTERTAINMENT | | |
|---|---|---|
| Filmstaden Cinema | 11 | C3 |

| SHOPPING | | |
|---|---|---|
| Hemköp Supermarket | (see 12) | |
| Punkt Shopping Complex | 12 | C3 |

| SLEEPING | (p188) | |
|---|---|---|
| Radisson SAS Hotel Plaza | 13 | C3 |
| Stadshotellet | 14 | B2 |

| TRANSPORT | (p187) | |
|---|---|---|
| Bus Station | 15 | D3 |

| INFORMATION | | |
|---|---|---|
| Forex | 16 | C3 |
| Nordbanken ATM | 17 | C3 |
| Police Headquarters | 18 | B4 |
| Post Office | 19 | C2 |
| Public Library | 20 | B2 |
| Tourist Office | 21 | B3 |

To Aabrin Lågprishotell (600m)

To Vallby-Frilufts-museum (2km); Örebro (101km)

To Scandic Hotel Västerås (600m); Ta Inn Hotel (900m); Centrallasarettet (hospital) (2km); Badelunda Kyrka (5km); Tibble Labyrint (5km); Anundshög (6km); Stockholm (107km)

To Raka Vägen (4km)

To STF Vandrarhem Lövudden (5km); Johannisbergs Camping (5km); Airport (6km)

Excursions – Västerås

The fine late-14th-century brick **Dom-kyrkan** has carved floor slabs, six altarpieces, the black marble sarcophagus of King Erik XIV and a **museum**.

**Vallby Friluftsmuseum**, off Vallbyleden near the E18 interchange 2km northwest of the city, is an extensive open-air collection assembled by the county museum. Among the 40-odd buildings, there's an interesting **farmyard**, but the highlight is **Anunds Hus**, a reconstructed 11th-century farm, which is 40m long. Take bus No 12 or 92 from Vasagatan.

The city is surrounded by ancient religious sites and the most interesting and extensive is the excellent **Anundshög**, the largest tumulus in Sweden, located 6km northeast of the city. It has a full complement of prehistoric curiosities, such as mounds, stone ship settings and a large 11th-century rune stone. The two main stone ship settings date from around the 1st century and it is thought that the row of stones beside the modern road mark the ancient royal ceremonial road Eriksgata. The area is part of the Badelunda Ridge, which includes the 13th-century **Badelunda kyrka** (1km north) and the odd 16m-wide **Tibble labyrinth**, an intricate series of low-walled paths in the pattern of a cross, made of stone and grass (1km south). Ask the tourist office for the handy map *Badelunda Forntids Bygd*. Take bus No 12 or 92 to the Bjurhovda terminus, then walk 2km east.

## Sights & Information

**Anunds Hus** (in Vallby Friluftsmuseum; admission Skr22; ☺ 1-4pm mid-June–mid-Aug)

**Centrallasarettet** (Hospital; ☎ 17 30 00) Just off the E18 motorway, towards Stockholm.

**Domkyrkan** (Cathedral; ☎ 16 10 06; Biskopsgatan; admission free; ☺ 8am-5pm Mon-Sat, 8am-7pm in mid-May–mid-Aug, 9.30am-5pm Sun)

**Filmstaden** (☎ 12 85 00; Gallerian 34; ☺ 5-10pm) This cinema screens films regularly.

**Forex** (Stora Gatan 18; ☺ 9am-5pm Mon-Fri)

**Konstmuseum** (Art Museum; ☎ 16 13 00; Fiskartorget 2; admission free; ☺ 10am-5pm Tues-Fri, 11am-4pm Sat, noon-4pm Sun)

**Nordbanken ATM** (Stora Gatan 23)

**Post office** (Sturegatan 18)

## Transport

**Distance from Stockholm** 110km
**Direction** Northwest
**Travel time** 1–2hr
**Air** The **airport** ( ☎ 80 56 00) is 6km southeast of the city centre; a taxi will cost around Skr150; connecting buses also run from the airport to the city centre. Skyways/SAS flies regularly on weekdays to Oslo, Malmö and Gothenburg. Ryanair now flies to Västerås from London Stansted.
**Bus/Train** The bus and train stations are adjacent, on the southern edge of the city centre. Swebus Express runs daily to Stockholm (1¾ hours, four to six daily). Upplands Lokaltrafik bus No 804 runs to Uppsala via Enköping. Västerås is readily accessible by train from Stockholm (one hour, hourly).

**Public library** ( ☎ 16 46 00; Biskopsgatan 2) Offers free Internet access.

**Taxi Västerås** ( ☎ 18 50 00)

**Tourist office** ( ☎ 10 38 30; Stora Gatan 40; ☺ 9am-7pm Mon-Fri, 9am-3pm Sat, 10am-2pm Sun mid-Jun–mid-Aug, shorter hours and closed Sun for the rest of the year)

**Vallby Friluftsmuseum** ( ☎ 16 16 70; ☺ 7am-10pm Jun-Aug, 8am-sunset Sep-May)

**Västmanlands Länsmuseum** ( ☎ 15 61 00; Slottsgatan; admission free; ☺ noon-4pm Tue-Sun)

## Eating & Drinking

**Bill & Bobs Krog** ( ☎ 41 99 21; Stora Torget 5; mains Skr85-200) The 'classics' menu includes burgers, pork fillet and Thai-style chicken.

**Bishops Arms** ( ☎ 10 28 00; Östra Kyrkogatan) This is the place to go for a drink, but it also serves English-style pub food.

**Hemköp supermarket** (Punkt Shopping Centre, off Stora Gatan; ☺ 9am-5pm Mon-Sat)

**Limone** ( ☎ 41 75 60; Stora Gatan 4; ☺ closed Sun; weekday lunch Skr65, mains Skr70-195) Fine Italian food.

**Piazza di Spagna** ( ☎ 12 42 10; Vasagatan 26; pizza/pasta from Skr75, mains Skr165-225) Try the fried camembert with cloudberry jam.

**Stadskällaren** (City Cellar; ☎ 10 28 00; Stora Torget; mains from Skr165-200) A pleasant brick-walled restaurant, but it's not really a cellar, as its name would imply.

**Systembolaget** (Stora Gatan 48; ☺ 10am-6pm Mon-Wed, 10am-7pm Thu & Fri, 10am-2pm Sat)

Excursions – Västerås

# Sleeping

**Aabrin Lågprishotell** ( ☎ 14 39 80; Kopparbergsvägen 47; s/d from Skr500/600)

**Johannisbergs Camping** ( ☎ 14 02 79; Johannisbergsvägen; tents/cabins from Skr85/285)

**Radisson SAS Hotel Plaza** ( ☎ 10 10 10; mailbox@vasterasplaza.se; Karlsgatan 9A; s/d from Skr1250/1450) Easily the most impressive hotel in town, the 'glass skyscraper' has superb modern accommodation.

**Raka Vägen** ( ☎ 30 04 00; Hallsta Gårdsgata 1; s/d Skr800/875)

**Scandic Hotel Västerås** ( ☎ 495 58 00; Pilgatan 17; s/d Skr1100/1450)

**Stadshotellet** ( ☎ 10 28 00; stadshotellet.vaesteraas@ elite.se; Stora Torget; s/d from Skr1000/1300) A flash, modern place with marble floors, mirrors and an indoor fountain.

**STF Vandrarhem Lövudden** ( ☎ 18 52 30; Johannisbergsvägen; dm Skr150) About 4km south of the city centre in former factory workers' lodgings; take bus 25.

**Ta Inn Hotel** ( ☎ 13 96 00; Ängsgärdsgatan 19; s/d from Skr700/900)

# Directory

# Directory

## TRANSPORT
### AIR
Direct flights to Stockholm's Arlanda Airport leave daily from Chicago and New York in the US, and from London, Manchester and Birmingham airports in the UK.

### Airlines
Airline offices in Stockholm can be found under *flygbolag* or *flygföretag* in the Yellow Pages. Several airlines share the same address, while others don't have street addresses and can be contacted only by phone at the appropriate airport desk.

**Aer Lingus** (Map pp236-8; ☎ 411 52 62; www.aerlingus.com; Kungsgatan 19)

**Aeroflot** (Map pp236-8; ☎ 21 70 07; www.aeroflot.com; 2nd fl, Sveavägen 31)

**Air Baltic** (Map pp236-8; ☎ 0770 72 77 27; www.airbaltic.com; Terminal 5, Arlanda airport)

**Air France** ( ☎ 51 99 99 90; www.airfrance.com; Terminal 5, Arlanda airport)

**Alitalia** (Map pp236-8; ☎ 796 94 00; www.alitalia.com; Kungsgatan 19)

**American Airlines** ( ☎ 791 59 99; www.americanairlines.com; Kanalvägen 10A, Upplands Väsby)

**Austrian Airlines** (Map pp236-8; ☎ 0200 72 73 73; www.aua.com; c/o SAS, Stureplan 8)

**Britannia Airways** ( ☎ 50 91 00 00; www.britanniaairways.com; Kanalvägen 10C, Upplands Väsby)

**British Airways** (Map pp236-8; ☎ 0200 77 00 98; www.ba.com; Hamngatan 11)

**Delta Air Lines** (Map pp231-3; ☎ 58 76 91 01; www.delta.com; Karlavägen 108)

**Estonian Air** ( ☎ 797 96 30; www.estonian-air.ee; Air France counter, Arlanda airport)

**Finnair** (Map pp236-8; ☎ 020 78 11 00; www.finnair.com; Silja Line & Destination Finland Office, Kungsgatan 2)

**Icelandair** (Map pp231-3; ☎ 690 98 00; www.icelandair.com; Kungstensgatan 38)

**KLM – Royal Dutch Airlines** ( ☎ 58 79 97 57; www.klm.com/uk_en; Vretenvägen 8, Solna)

**Lithuanian Airlines** ( ☎ 59 36 09 05; www.lal.lt; Arlanda airport)

**LOT Polish Airlines** (Map pp236-8; ☎ 24 34 90; www.lot.com; Kungsgatan 66)

**Lufthansa Airlines** (Map pp236-8; ☎ 020 72 75 55; www.lufthansa.com; c/o SAS, Stureplan 8)

**Ryanair** ( ☎ 09 00 20 20 240; www.ryanair.com; Nyköping Skavsta airport & Västerås airport)

**SAS** (Map pp236-8; ☎ 020 72 75 55; www.scandinavian.net; Stureplan 8)

**Skyways** (Map pp236-8; ☎ 50 90 50 50; www.skyways.se; c/o SAS, Stureplan 8)

**Swiss International Airlines** ( ☎ 58 77 04 45; www.swiss.com; Terminal 2, Arlanda Airport)

**Thai Airways International** (Map pp236-8; ☎ 59 88 36 00; www.thaiair.com; Kungsgatan 66)

### Airports
#### ARLANDA AIRPORT
☎ 797 60 00, 797 61 00 (flight information); www.lfv.se/site/airports/arlanda/eng/index.asp; 45km north of Stockholm

Arlanda is Stockholm's main airport, serving some 18 million passengers annually. Terminals 2 and 5 are for international flights; 3 and 4 are domestic; there is no terminal 1 – it was never built. There are services (food, shops) in each of the terminals and a vast selection of each in the Sky City shopping area connecting terminals 3 and 4 with terminal 5.

Some transport options between Arlanda and the city include:

**Arlanda Express train** ( ☎ 020 22 22 24; www.arlanda express.com; adult/child Skr180/90; 4-6 trains/hr; 20min) The quickest way to travel between the airport and Centralstationen.

**Flygbussarna airport bus** ( ☎ 600 10 00; www.flygbuss arna.se; Skr89, taxi Skr115; 40min; every 20min) Runs to Central Station, or – even handier – in combination with a Flygtaxi, which you order in advance at the Flygbus ticket counter in the airport or from the bus driver. The Flygtaxi meets you at one of several drop points and, for a set fee, takes you straight to your front door.

#### BROMMA AIRPORT
☎ 797 68 74; www.lfv.se/site/airports/bromma/eng/index.asp; 8km west of city centre

Bromma is conveniently located, but only a handful of airlines use it. Flygbussarna buses travel between the airport and Cityterminalen (Skr69, 20min); taxis cost about Skr170.

### SKAVSTA AIRPORT
☎ 0155 28 04 00; www.skavsta-air.se; 100km south of city centre

The trip between Cityterminalen and Skavsta takes about one hour with Flygbussarna (about Skr100, every 20min).

### VÄSTERÅS
☎ 020 80 56 10; www.vasterasflygplats.se; 110km from city centre

The airport bus leaves Västerås about 20 minutes after a scheduled flight comes in; it takes around 75 minutes (Skr100) to reach Cityterminalen. In the other direction, the bus arrives at the airport two hours before a scheduled departure.

## BICYCLE
Sweden is a flat country and it's ideal for cycling from May to September. Cycling is an excellent way to look for points of interest in and around Stockholm, such as prehistoric sites, rune stones, parish churches and quiet spots for free camping. You'll find many towns and villages within a day's ride of Stockholm. Bear in mind, however, that Stockholm is a long way from other countries and it's 516km from Oslo, the nearest foreign capital by road.

Airlines may consider your bike as luggage, but check this before booking. International ferries to Stockholm usually charge a small fee for bicycles. Helmet use is compulsory in Sweden.

## Hire
### CYKEL OCH MOPEDUTHYRNINGEN
Map pp231–3

☎ 660 79 59; Strandvägen, kajplats 24; ☺ 9am-9pm May-Sep, call for opening hours Oct-Apr; bicycle hire about Skr150 per day

Rents mopeds and bicycles.

## Bicycles on Public Transport
Generally bicycles are not allowed on public transport. The surface commuter trains, or pendeltåg (with stations marked by a J instead of the underground's T), allow bicycles during off-peak hours, but you can't disembark at Central Station with a bike.

## BOAT
Ferry connections between Sweden and Denmark, Estonia, Finland, Germany, Lithuania, Norway, Poland and the UK provide straightforward links, especially for anyone bringing their own vehicle. In most cases the quoted fares for cars (usually up to 6m long) also include up to five passengers. Most lines offer substantial discounts for seniors, students and children, and other special deals may be available – always ask when booking.

DFDS Seaways (☎ 0990-333000) in the UK can make reservations for Silja Line's Baltic ferry services.

Passengers leaving Sweden by ship don't have to pay a departure tax.

## To/From Estonia
Tallink (Map pp231-3; ☎ 732 40 00; www.tallink.se in Swedish) departs once every two days from Tallinn to its Stockholm terminal, taking around 15 hours (overnight). Deck tickets start at Skr205/265 in September–May/June–August. The company has an office at the Frihamnen terminal building.

## To/From Finland
Silja Line (☎ 09-180 45 10; www.silja.com /english; Bulevardi 1A, POB 659, Helsinki) sails overnight every day of the year from its Stockholm terminal to Helsinki, taking around 15 hours. Cabin berths are no longer compulsory; deck passage starts at €25/12 for adult/child. Cars up to 6m long cost €28 (excluding passengers); bicycles/motorcycles cost €8/16. In summer, breakfast costs €8 and the famous Silja smörgåsbord costs €24. The ships call briefly at Mariehamn in Åland; the islands are exempt from the abolition of duty-free within the EU. Note that there's a lower age limit of 18, unless travelling with parents. There's also a sales outlet in Stockholm (Map pp236-8; ☎ 22 21 40; fax 611 91 62; Kungsgatan 2).

Viking Line operates ferries overnight from Helsinki to its Stockholm terminal (Map pp234-5) via Mariehamn. Tickets cost €29 to €40, depending on whether you get deck passage or a cabin etc; cars (passengers not included) cost from €81. It takes 16 to 17 hours and sails once daily all year. Viking Line also sails from Stockholm to Turku via Mariehamn (11 hours) twice daily all year, including an overnight crossing, for €12 to €18 deck passage.

Buffet meals are served on all Viking Line services. The company has a strict minimum age limit of 20 on Saturday, all public holidays, the 8am Stockholm–Turku departures and the 2.35pm Mariehamn–Stockholm departures. Travelling with parents or evidence in writing giving a valid reason for travelling (studies, visiting relatives, business etc) is acceptable. There are Viking Line offices in **Helsinki** (☎ 09-12351; www.vikingline.fi; Mannerheimintie 14), **Turku** (☎ 02-33311; Hansa-Thalia Aurakatu 10) and at Stockholm's **Cityterminalen** (Map pp236-8; ☎ 08-452 40 00).

Two other companies run daily 'booze cruises' between Stockholm and Mariehamn on Åland. Birka Cruises only offers return fares from Stockholm. However, **Ånedin-Linjen** (Map pp236-8; ☎ 08-456 22 00; fax 10 07 41; Vasagatan 6) runs daily passenger ferries from Stockholm to Mariehamn (six hours). One-way fares start around Skr135 (couchette) and rise to Skr570 for a suite.

**SeaWind Line** (toll free ☎ 98 00 68 00, www .seawind.fi; Linnankatu 84, Turku) sails once daily except Saturday from Turku to Stockholm Värtahamnen (Map pp231-3), via Langnäs (Åland). The trip takes 11 hours, and tickets (from Skr440/860 day/night one way) include a car (maximum length 5m), up to four passengers, a cabin and breakfast (overnight sailings only). The ship isn't suitable for disabled travellers. In Sweden, call ☎ 020 79 53 31.

## To/From Latvia

The ferry service from Riga to Stockholm has been reinstated; it runs three times a week in each direction. Tickets are Skr310/620 through **Latvia Tours** (☎ 07-085005; inese@latviatours.lt; Kalku 8, Riga) or directly from **ScanSov Offshore** (☎ 08-402 56 90, 402 56 00; fax 24 96 89) in Stockholm.

## To/From Lithuania

**Lisco Line** (☎ 06-395050; www.shipping.lt; Perkelos st 10, Klaipeda) sails twice weekly from Klaipeda to Stockholm Frihamnen (Map pp231-3; 17½ hours). Passenger fares, including meals, start at Skr550. You can also contact Lisco Line in **Vilnius** (☎ 02-31 33 14; vilnius@krantas.lt; Pylimo st 4, Vilnius) and in **Stockholm** (☎ 08-667 52 35; stockholm@krantas.lt).

## To/From Poland

**Polferries** (☎ 058-343 1887; www.polferries.pl; ul Przemyslowa 1, Gdansk) sails from Gdansk to Nynäshamn three days per week (19 hours).

Passenger fares start at Skr495 (more for a cabin berth) and car tickets, including the driver's fare, start at Skr920. In Sweden, contact **Polferries** (☎ 08-52 01 81 01; fax 52 0181 20; Färjeterminalen, Nynäshamn).

## To/From the UK

**DFDS Seaways** (UK ☎ 08705 333000; travel.sales@ dfds.co.uk; Gothenburg ☎ 031-65 06 50, info@dfdsseaways.se) has two crossings per week from Newcastle to Gothenburg via Kristiansand (Norway) on its vessel M/S *Princess of Scandinavia*. From Gothenburg, you'll need onward transport by air, rail, bus or car to reach Stockholm (478km). Return fares from Newcastle to Gothenburg begin at £69 in peak season; a car is £72.

## BUS

City buses are run by **Statens Lokaltrafik** (SL; ☎ 600 10 00; www.sl.se). Tickets are good for buses as well as the *tunnelbana* (see p194). Most bus routes operate between 5am and midnight daily. Single tickets can be bought from the driver as you board; prepaid tickets should be stamped by the driver, and SL cards should be shown. Most bus routes include comprehensive maps of routes in the area, including listings of night buses, which operate from midnight to 5am. The main stations for night buses are Odenplan, Slussen, Gullmarsplan, Fridhemsplan and T-Centralen.

**Swebus Express** (☎ 0200 21 82 18; www.swebus express.se) has the largest 'national network' of express buses, but it serves only the southern half of the country. Fares for long journeys are 30% cheaper if you travel between Monday and Thursday (autumn to spring). **Svenska Buss** (☎ 020 67 67 67; www.svenskabuss.se in Swedish) and the cheaper **Säfflebussen** (☎ 020 160 06 00; www.safflebussen.se in Swedish) also connect many southern towns and cities with Stockholm. North of Gävle, connections with Stockholm are provided by several smaller operators, including **Ybuss** (☎ 060-17 19 60; www.ybuss.se in Swedish) from Sundsvall, Östersund and Umeå. Only Swebus doesn't require seat reservations – it always guarantees a seat.

## CAR & MOTORCYCLE

Basic road rules conform to EU standards, using international road signs. In Sweden you drive on the right. Headlights should be dipped but must be on at all times when driving. Seat belt use is obligatory, and children under seven years old should be in appropriate harnesses or in child seats, if fitted.

You only need a recognised full driving licence, even for car rental. If bringing your own car, you'll need your vehicle registration documents. In case your vehicle breaks down, telephone the **Larmtjänst 24-hour towing service** (☎ 020 91 00 40). Insurance Green Cards are recommended. At the time of writing, petrol cost around Skr9.50/L.

The blood-alcohol limit is a stringent 0.02%. The maximum permitted speed on motorways and remote highways is 110km/h. Other speed limits are 50km/h in built-up areas, 70km/h on narrow rural roads and 90km/h on highways. The speed limit for cars towing caravans is 80km/h. Automatic speed cameras are very rare in Sweden, but police can use handheld radar equipment and impose on-the-spot fines of around Skr1200.

The national motoring association affiliated to Alliance Internationale de Tourisme (AIT) is **Motormännens Riksförbund** (☎ 020 21 11 11, 690 38 00; fax 690 38 20; Sveavägen 159, Stockholm).

Driving in central Stockholm is not recommended; traffic is chaotic and fuel and parking are expensive. Illegally parked cars will get a fine; those deemed dangerous will be towed more than 17km out of town and the owners charged around Skr1500. Parking on streets and in carparks usually costs between Skr20 and Skr50 per hour; look for a white 'P' on a blue sign.

## Rental

The following car-rental agencies also have offices at Arlanda and Bromma airports:

**Avis** (Map pp236-8; ☎ 20 20 60, 020 78 82 00; www.avis.se in Swedish; Vasagatan 10B; Map pp234-5; Ringvägen 90; ☺ 6am-6pm Mon-Fri, 9am-2pm Sat & Sun; T-Centralen)

**Europcar** (Map pp236-8; ☎ 21 06 50, 020 78 11 80; www.europcar.se; Tegelbacken 6; ☺ 7am-6pm Mon-Fri, 10am-2pm Sat, noon-4pm Sun; T-Centralen)

**Hertz** (Map pp236-8; ☎ 24 07 20, 020 21 12 11; www.hertz.nu; Vasagatan 26; ☺ 7.30am-6pm Mon-Fri, 9am-3pm Sat & Sun; T-Centralen)

## TAXI

Taxis can be hailed on the street and are easy to find on busy streets or in front of bars at closing time. Cabs that are on duty have a lit 'taxi' sign on their roof. To be sure you're choosing a reputable cab, though, it's best to call one of the companies listed (bookings available 24 hours a day) and arrange a pickup. Most drivers speak at least some English, but if your Swedish is shaky it helps to have an address written down.

Some taxi companies in Stockholm:

**Flygtaxi** (☎ 020-97 97 97; www.flygtaxi.se in Swedish) The airport taxi can be reserved in connection with Flygbussarna (either at the ticket counter or with the bus driver).

**Taxi Stockholm** (☎ 15 00 00)

**Top Cab** (☎ 33 33 33)

## TRAIN

Stockholm's main train station, **Centralstationen** (Map pp236-8; ☺ 5am-12.15am), has good long-distance connections with other parts of Sweden and continental Europe. Lines to Norway and Finland are rather slow in comparison, but the route to Oslo now features modern high-speed trains.

Statens Lokaltrafik (SL; see above) also runs commuter trains from the city centre to outlying areas; most lines leave from Centralstationen, and SL bus and Tunnel-bana tickets are good for the commuter trains as well.

The **Sveriges Järnväg** (SJ; ☎ 020 75 75 75, www.sj.se) domestic ticket-office windows are open 7.30am to 8pm weekdays, 8.30am to 6pm Saturday and 9.30am to 7pm Sunday. International train tickets can be purchased between 10am and 6pm on weekdays only. If your train departs outside these times, you can buy a ticket from the ticket collector on the train, but you are strongly recommended to get your ticket in advance.

The **Tågkompaniet** (☎ 0920-23 33 33 or ☎ 020 44 41 11, www.tagplus.se) ticket office, in the entrance hall, is open 7.45am to 8.15pm daily (closing noon to 3pm weekends).

## Within Sweden

Sweden has an extensive railway network, and trains are certainly the fastest way to get around. There are four long-distance train operators in Sweden, but the national network of Sveriges Järnväg covers most of the main lines. Exceptions are the overnight trains from Stockholm to Boden and Narvik, and the summer-only line from Boden to Haparanda, run by Tågkompaniet. Several counties run regional *länstrafik* train networks.

SJ's flag carriers are the X2000 fast trains running at speeds of up to 200km/h, with services from Stockholm to Gothenburg, Malmö, Karlstad, Mora, Växjö, Jönköping, Sundsvall and other destinations.

Tickets for journeys on X2000 and overnight trains include a compulsory seat reservation; on other trains you're advised to reserve a seat (Skr30). Night train supplements are required for sleepers (from Skr165 per bed) or couchettes (from Skr90), but not for seats. First- and 2nd-class seats and sleepers are available on almost all trains (night trains don't have 1st-class seats).

Bicycles can be carried on many *länstrafik* trains without reservation. On SJ trains, bikes (when allowed) must go as registered baggage (Skr150).

## To/From Sweden

Three trains a day go between Stockholm and Oslo (from about Skr100). Around seven daily X2000 trains run from Copenhagen in Denmark to Stockholm (from about Skr1100, from 5¼ hours) via the new Öresund bridge.

Travelling by train from the UK to Sweden is more expensive than flying, but you can stop en route in either direction. From London a return 2nd-class train ticket to Stockholm, valid for two months, will cost around UK£400. For tickets, contact **Deutsche Bahn UK** (London ☎ 0870 243 5363) or **European Rail** (London ☎ 020-7387 0444).

## TUNNELBANA

The underground network, called *tunnelbana* or *T-bana*, is run by **Statens Lokaltrafik** (SL; ☎ 600 10 00; www.sl.se). It has an **information centre** (🕐 7am-6pm Mon-Fri, 10am-5pm Sat & Sun) in T-Centralen. It's easy to use, quick and very efficient. Single tickets are not recommended; they cost between Skr20 and Skr60 depending on how far you travel (ie the number of zones crossed). A better bet is to buy a multitrip coupon from a Pressbyrån kiosk (Skr60/110 for sets of 10/20). SL sells 24hr passes for Skr80, or 72hr ones for Skr150. Another good option is the weekend pass (Skr220), which allows unlimited travel during four consecutive weekends. If you're going to be in Stockholm for a couple of weeks, it's worth getting a monthly travel pass (*månadskort*), good for all *tunnelbana* trains, most commuter trains (*pendeltåg*, or J-trains) and city buses. At present these cost Skr500 but the price is about to increase to

Skr700, to much public protest. The Stockholm Card also entitles you to travel discounts; see p196). The *tunnelbana* operates from 5am to 1am Sunday to Thursday, and 5am to 3am Friday and Saturday.

## TRAM

There are old trams from 1920–50 that sways their way from Norrmalmstorg to Waldemarsudde on Djurgården (Skr29). The timetable varies, but trams are usually scheduled to go every 12 minutes. The trams are managed by. enthusiastic members of the Swedish Tram Society.

# PRACTICALITIES
## ACCOMMODATION

Accommodation in this guide is listed by neighbourhood, with 'Cheap Sleep' options at the end of each section; these include anything up to Skr350 per person per night (see Sleeping, p153). Prices at Stockholm's major hotels are typically around Skr1500 per night for a double room. The listed price, however, is rarely the lowest available. Most rates drop by up to 50% at weekends and in July, when Stockholmers usually take their .holidays. Always ask about special deals and discounts when booking a room. Prices are generally quoted per room, not per person. Rates quoted in this guide are for the high season, which peaks between June and August.

## Booking Services
### HOTELLCENTRALEN Map pp236–8
☎ 789 24 90; www.stockholmtown.com; Central Station; 🕐 9am-6pm Mon-Sat, noon-4pm Sun
The accommodation branch of the tourist centre books hotels, hostels and B&Bs. There's no charge for bookings made in advance, but a fee of Skr50 (Skr20 for hostels) applies to immediate bookings made in person.

### DESTINATION STOCKHOLM
Map pp236–85
☎ 663 00 80; www.destination-stockholm.com; Nybrogatan 58
This discount hotel-and-sightseeing package site offers deals on some of the city's top hotels in the off season. The website is crammed with useful information.

# CHILDREN

Stockholm and Sweden in general are very child-friendly.

Public transport offers reduced rates for children. SL buses, commuter trains and the metro are free to kids under six, and there's a discount of roughly 40% for kids aged from six to 17 inclusive. Some public toilets have nappy-changing facilities, eg the toilet in the basement at Centralstationen. Breastfeeding in public is rare but is unlikely to cause offence.

Parents can leave their kids at the 'Rum för Barn' inside Kulturhuset (p58) to play while they go off sightseeing. Some hotels and companies (if you're in Stockholm on business) can also assist with childcare.

Many attractions and museums in Stockholm have sections set up specifically for the younger set, usually with toys, hands-on displays and activities. Admission is usually free for children up to about seven years of age and half-price (or substantially discounted) for kids up to 16 or so, although a few museums allow free admission to anyone under 21. See the boxed text 'Stockholm for Children', p48, for more about child-friendly sights and activities.

In Stockholm, there are several public parks with play areas for kids; some restaurants and hotels also have play areas. Hotels and other accommodation options often have 'family rooms' which accommodate up to two adults and two to four children for little more than the price of a regular double. Scandic hotels have an eat-all-you-like children's menu (for children under 14) for around Skr45.

Car rental firms hire out children's safety seats at a nominal cost, but it's essential that you book them in advance. Highchairs and cots (cribs) are standard in many restaurants and hotels. Swedish supermarkets offer a relatively wide choice of baby food, infant formulas, soy and cow's milk, disposable nappies (diapers) etc.

Ask your nearest Swedish tourist office for the brochure *Sweden for Children*. Lonely Planet's *Travel with Children* is also a useful source of information.

# CLIMATE

Stockholm has a cool, temperate climate with moderate precipitation in all seasons. Summer weather is mild and usually sunny, while winters are cold, dark and often snowy. The long-term average temperature for January to March is -2°C; for July and August it's 16°C.

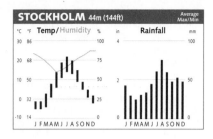

# COURSES

Swedish-language classes for travellers at a wide range of levels and durations are available from the following:

**Medborgarskolan** (Map pp231-3; ☎ 457 57 00; www.medborgarskolan.se/stockholm in Swedish; Hagagatan 23A)

**Stockholms Folkuniversitetet** (Map pp236-8; ☎ 789 41 90; www.folkuniversitetet.se; Bryggargatan 4)

# CUSTOMS

Travellers entering Sweden from outside the EU may bring in limited amounts of certain products duty-free. The allowances are: 1L of spirits (over 22% alcohol content by volume); 2L of fortified wine (15% to 22% alcohol by volume); 2L of wine (3.5% to 15% alcohol by volume); 200 cigarettes, 100 cigarillos, 50 cigars or 250g of smoking tobacco. Tobacco products and alcoholic drinks can be brought into Sweden duty-free only if you're over 18 and 20 years of age, respectively.

Sweden has strict drug laws and you may be searched on arrival, especially if coming from Denmark. All animals, syringes and weapons must be declared to customs on arrival, and if you're coming from outside the EU, you must declare mobile phones, live plants and animal products (meat, dairy etc).

For current customs regulations, ask at your nearest Swedish tourist office or contact **Tullverket** (Customs; ☎ 0771-520520; www.tullverket.se; Box 12854, SE-11298 Stockholm).

# DISABLED TRAVELLERS

Stockholm is reasonably well set up for people with disabilities – there are many special transport services with adapted facilities, ranging from trains to taxis, but always contact the operator in advance. Some SL buses are wheelchair accessible, and **Taxi 020** (☎ 789 24 96; 🕙 9am-5pm Mon-Fri, ☎ 632 90 70 other times) offers taxi tours for disabled people. Public toilets, some hotel rooms and a few museums have facilities for the disabled, street crossings may have ramps for wheelchairs and audio signals for the visually impaired, and even grocery shops may be wheelchair accessible.

You may want to contact your national support organisation and speak with its travel officer, if there is one. These organisations often have complete libraries devoted to travel, and can put you in touch with tour companies that specialise in disabled travel.

## Organisations

For further information on facilities for the disabled in Stockholm, contact Informationsavdelning at **De Handikappades Riksförbund** (☎ 685 80 00; www.dhr.se; Katrinebergsvägen 6, 5 tr, SE-10074 Stockholm).

The UK-based **Royal Association for Disability & Rehabilitation** (RADAR; ☎ 020-72 50 3222; 12 City Forum, 250 City Rd, London EC1V 8AF, UK) can supply general advice for disabled travellers in Sweden.

In the USA, contact the **Society for Accessible Travel and Hospitality** (☎ 212-447 7284; sathtravel@aol.com; 347 5th Ave, Ste 610, New York, NY 10016 USA).

**Special Interest Travel** (www.sitravel.com) has a section for disabled travellers on its website.

## DISCOUNT CARDS
### STOCKHOLM CARD

The Stockholm Card covers all transport and almost all sightseeing needs – it's available at tourist offices, camping grounds, hostels and SL Centres, and costs Skr220/380/540 for 24/48/72 hours for adults, Skr60/120/180 for children. A maximum of two children's cards can be purchased with each adult card. The card covers entry to more than 70 museums and attractions (some are open in summer only – see www.stockholmtown.com for a full list of sights covered by the card), city parking in metered spaces, sightseeing by boat (April to September) and travel on public transport (including the Katarinahissen lift, but excluding local ferries, some city buses and airport buses). To get maximum value, use two 24-hour cards over three days (with a rest day in between) and be sure to plan around opening hours: Skansen remains open until late, whereas royal palaces are open only until 3pm or 4pm (for details of all museums and sights, see the Neighbourhoods chapter, p47).

Students and seniors get discounted admission to most museums and sights without the card, so you'll need to work out if it's cheaper to just get a transport pass and pay admission charges separately.

### STOCKHOLM PACKAGE

This cut-price package basically includes a hotel room and the Stockholm Card. It costs Skr455 to Skr1630 per person per night, depending on the standard of accommodation, the time of your visit and whether a single supplement is required. Up to four children under six years old stay for free when sleeping in extra beds in their parents' room (Skr75 per child aged seven to 17). Travel agencies in other Scandinavian capitals or major Swedish cities can help with arrangements. Otherwise, contact Hotellcentralen in Stockholm (see p194).

### ISIC

The most useful student card is the International Student Identity Card (ISIC; £7 for 15 months), a plastic ID-style card with your photograph, which provides discounts on numerous forms of transport including airlines, international ferries and local public transport, as well as on admission to museums, sights, theatres and cinemas. For information, contact ISIC (www.isiccard.com, downloadable application forms online) or pick up an application from your local Student Travel Office.

## ELECTRICITY

Electricity in Sweden is supplied at 220V AC, 50Hz, and round continental-style two-pin plugs are standard. Equipment set for a different voltage or cycle will not function correctly in Sweden. You're advised to obtain a suitable adapter in advance, as it can be difficult or impossible to find one in Stockholm.

## EMBASSIES, CONSULATES & HIGH COMMISSIONS

Although the following diplomatic missions are located in Stockholm, some of the neighbouring countries also have consulates located in Gothenburg, Malmö and Helsingborg. New Zealand Citizens should contact the nearest **New Zealand embassy** (☎ 31-70 346 9324; Carnegielaan 10-IV, The Hague, The Netherlands).

**Australia** (Map pp236-8; ☎ 08-613 29 00; www
.sweden.embassy.gov.au; info@austemb.se; Block 5,
Sergels Torg 12)

**Canada** (Map pp236-8; ☎ 08-453 30 00; www.dfait
-maeci.gc.ca/canadaeuropa/sweden/menu-en.asp; 7th fl,
Tegelbacken 4)

**Denmark** (Map pp236-8; ☎ 08-406 75 00; www
.danemb.se; Jakobs Torg 1)

**Finland** (Map pp236-8; ☎ 08-676 67 00; www.finland
.se; 6th fl, Jakobsgatan 6)

**France** (Map pp231-3; ☎ 08-459 53 00; www.amba
france.se; Kommendörsgatan 13)

**Germany** (Map pp231-3; ☎ 08-670 15 00; www.stock
holm.diplo.de/de/home/index.html; Skarpögatan 9)

**Ireland** (Map pp231-3; ☎ 08-661 80 05; irish.embass@
swipnet.se; Östermalmsgatan 97)

**Japan** (Map pp231-3; ☎ 08-663 04 40; www.japan
samb.se; Gärdesgatan 10)

**Netherlands** (Map pp239-41; ☎ 08-24 71 80;
www.netherlands-embassy.se; Götgatan 16A)

**Norway** (Map pp231-3; ☎ 08-665 63 40; fax 782 9899;
Skarpögatan 4)

**Poland** (Map pp228-9; ☎ 08-764 48 00; www.polemb
.se; Consulate-General, Prästgårdsgatan 5, Sundbyberg)

**UK** (Map pp231-3; ☎ 08-671 30 00; www.british
embassy.se; britishembassy@telia.com; Skarpögatan 6-8)

**USA** (Map pp231-3; ☎ 08-783 53 00; www.usemb.se;
webmaster@usemb.se; Dag Hammarskjölds Väg 31)

# EMERGENCY

The toll-free emergency number (fire service,
police and ambulance) is ☎ 112.

There are a number of 24-hour police stations located in Södermalm (Map pp234-5;
☎ 401 03 00; Torkel Knutssonsgatan 20) and
in Kungsholmen (Map p230; ☎ 401 00 00;
Kungsholmsgatan 37). There's also a police
office by the (upstairs) Kungsbron entrance
to Centralstationen; it's open 9am to 5pm
weekdays.

The 24-hour pharmacy is **Apoteket CW Scheele**
(Map pp236-8; ☎ 454 81 30; Klarabergsgatan
64). There's also a 24-hour **medical hotline**
( ☎ 463 91 00) and a toll-free **medications hotline**
( ☎ 020 66 77 66).

The nearest thing to a rape crisis centre
is **Kvinnojouren** ( ☎ 760 96 11), the national
organisation that deals with violence against
women.

In case of vehicle breakdowns or towing,
contact **Larmtjänst** ( ☎ 020 91 00 40) for road-
side assistance.

# GAY & LESBIAN TRAVELLERS

Sweden is a fairly liberal country and, along
with several neighbouring countries, allows
gay and lesbian couples to form 'registered
partnerships' that grant marriage rights except access to church weddings, adoption and
artificial insemination. Even so, take note that
homosexual couples are discreet in public.

Up-to-date details of gay restaurants, bars,
cafes, discos, nightclubs and culture (movies
and theatre) are listed in the free monthly
tabloid newspaper **QX** (www.qx.se/english/).
Lesbians can find tourist information (for
nightclubs, bars, coffee shops and restaurants)
on the website www.corky.nu. More general
information for gay and lesbian travellers is
posted on the Internet at thorntree.lonely
planet.com.

**Stockholm Pride** is a four-day event in late July/
early August, mainly based in Pride Park, Tantolunden (Södermalm). The program includes
art, debate, health events, literature, music,
spirituality and sport. There are song contests,
transvestite drag shows, mud wrestling, film
showings and (of course) a parade. For full
details, check the website at www.stockholm
pride.org or contact RFSL (see below).

Gay bars, nightclubs and other venues in
Stockholm are mentioned in the Entertainment chapter (p129), but ask at RFSL for up-
to-date information.

## Organisations

**Riksförbundet för Sexuellt Likaberättigande** (RFSL;
☎ 736 02 13; forbund@rfsl.se; Box 350, SE-
10126 Stockholm) is the national organisation for gay and lesbian rights. It's based at
Stockholm's **Gay-Hus** (Map pp236-8; Sveavägen
57), where there's also a bookshop, restaurant and nightclub. **Riksförbundet för hivpositiva**
(RFHP; ☎ 714 54 10; www.rfhp.a.se; Gotlandsgatan 72) is the national society for people
with HIV. Its website is well worth reading and
presents a new light on 'liberal Sweden'.

# HOLIDAYS
## Public Holidays

There's a concentration of public holidays in
spring and early summer. Midsummer brings
life almost to a halt for three days – attractions
and restaurants may be closed and transport
and other services are reduced (even on Midsummer's Eve). Some hotels and many restaurants and tourist attractions are closed or have

shorter opening hours between Christmas and New Year, and often for a few days leading up to Christmas Eve (24 December).

It's not uncommon for shops, restaurants and hotels to close for several weeks between Midsummer and early August.

Many businesses will close early the day before and all day after public holidays. Public holidays in Sweden:

**Nyårsdag** (New Year's Day) 1 January

**Trettondedag Jul** (Epiphany) 6 January

**Långfredag, Annandag påsk** (Easter) March/April – Good Friday to Easter Monday

**Första Maj** (Labour Day) 1 May

**Kristi Himmelsfärds dag** (Ascension Day) May/June

**Annandag Pingst** (Whit Monday) late May or early June

**Midsommardag** (Midsummer's Day) first Friday after 21 June

**Alla Helgons dag** (All Saints' Day) a Saturday in late October/early November

**Julafton** (Christmas Eve) 24 December

**Juldag** (Christmas Day) 25 December

**Annandag Jul** (Boxing Day) 26 December

**Nyårsafton** (New Year's Eve) 31 December

All public holidays are also school holidays. In addition, students are usually off the first week of January, the last week of December, one week in early spring and from mid-June to mid-August for summer holidays.

# INTERNET ACCESS

Email and Internet services are popular in Sweden, and most tourism-oriented businesses now have access. Internet cafes typically charge Skr1 per minute.

Most public libraries offer free Internet access but you generally need to have a library card, which requires a Stockholm address. At many libraries, Internet access is for research purposes only, and you may be kicked off the computer if you use it for email.

If you're bringing a laptop and hope to access your home Internet or accounts, you'll need a telephone adapter. Since three types of telephone jacks are used in Sweden, universal access will require three types of adapter (or a large combination adapter that incorporates all three). Duplex adapters allow a telephone to be connected in parallel with your modem, so you can dial manually or get an operator connection. A good source of information on adapters is Tele-Adapt (www.teleadapt.com).

You'll also need a reputable 'global' modem, or you can by a local PC-card modem in Stockholm if you're going to stay a long time.

Stockholm is loaded with Internet cafes, including the fun game centre Tilt (see p120). Telltale rows of monitors and red ticket machines mark the ubiquitous self-service Sidewalk Express stands, where you can access the Internet and email for a mere Skr19 per hour (coin-operated only). You purchase a ticket and log in using the code printed on it; if you don't use up all your time, save the ticket and log in again at any Sidewalk Express terminal. The connections are fairly quick when they're working, but the no-frills computers crash often and aren't promptly maintained. The stands can be found at Central Station (near McDonald's) as well as upstairs in Cityterminalen; SkyCity at Arlanda Airport; inside Robert's Coffee at Drottninggatan 33; and inside the shopping centre at Sergelgatan 8-12. Other locations crop up and vanish seemingly at random, so be on the lookout.

Some other places that offer public Internet access:

## INTERNATIONELLA BIBLIOTEK
Map pp231–3

☎ 50 83 12 88; Odengatan 59; 🕑 10am-8.30pm Mon-Thu, 10am-6pm Fri, noon-4pm Sat & Sun; T-Odenplan

This annexe of the city library offers free walk-in 10-, 15- and 30-minute Internet slots and is wheelchair accessible. There's a PC with word processing programs, a scanner and a floppy disk drive (handy for downloading or uploading lengthy text items) downstairs. There are also 60-minute bookable slots available upstairs (Skr15); for reservations call ☎ 50 83 12 89. Print-outs cost Skr2 per page. The 10-minute computers are available from 9am on weekdays year-round. There are other computers (both PC and Mac) in the main library building, nearby on Sveavägen 73; ask which ones allow private email.

## MEDBORGARPLATSEN BIBLIOTEK
Map pp234–5

☎ 50 81 26 90; Medborgarplatsen 4; 🕑 11am-7pm Mon-Thu, 11am-5pm Fri, 11am-3pm Sat; T-Medborgarplatsen

There are three email-accessible PCs here, with booking of free 60-minute slots available up to one week ahead. Two PCs offer short-term Internet access (snabb). Print-outs cost Skr2 per page.

### HORNSTULL BIBLIOTEK Map pp234–5

☎ 50 84 06 52; Hornsbruksgatan 25; ☼ 11am-7pm Mon & Tue, 10am-6pm Wed, 10am-5pm Thu, 11am-3pm Sat; T-Hornstull

This place has four computers with free Internet access. Printing costs Skr2 per page. Bookings can be made 24 hours in advance.

### ACCESS IT Map pp234–5

☎ 50 83 14 89; basement, Kulturhuset, Sergels Torg; ☼ 10am-7pm Tue-Fri, 11am-5pm Sat & Sun; T-Centralen

Currently there are 26 walk-in PCs and a ticket-machine queueing system. Charges are Skr20 per 30 minutes. Print-outs cost Skr2 per page. Ask the staff about downloading onto disk.

### CAFE ZENIT Map p230

☎ 698 57 40; Sveavägen 20; ☼ 10am-6pm Mon-Fri, 11am-5pm Sat, noon-5pm Sun; closed July

This café lets you use one of its four computers free of charge if you make a purchase.

## LEGAL MATTERS

The police in Stockholm are generally friendly and helpful. The chances of being stopped by the police if you haven't been up to something are extremely small. In case of arrest, however, the police can hold someone for up to four days without charge. There may also be a restriction on phone calls if the matter is considered serious enough. The police also have the right to name an *advokat* (attorney), although the criminal justice court may appoint one. The police keep a list of attorneys, and bills for so-called public attorneys may be partly paid for by the state. The proportion of the bill to be paid may depend on the client's country of origin.

Parking is always difficult in Sweden, and a typical fine amounts to Skr700. Although suburban areas have free street parking at night (☼ 5pm to 9am daily), you can be fined for parking during street-cleaning night, which varies from place to place. Fines have been issued in dubious circumstances and readers are advised to bring up these matters with the appropriate authority.

Sweden isn't liberal when it comes to illegal drugs – don't even think of bringing even a tiny amount into the country with you.

The legal drinking age is 18 in bars and taverns, and 20 to purchase alcohol in Systembolaget shops. You must be 18 or older to buy cigarettes or drive a car.

## MAPS

The tourist office sells a range of thematic maps, including *Cykelkarta Storstockholm* (Greater Stockholm Cycling Map; covers eight routes; Skr227), *Nationalstadsparken* (The National City Park; Skr80), *Stockholms skärgård* (an excellent map of the Stockholm archipelago; Skr125) and *Stockholm Trafikkarta* (Stockholm Motorists Map; Skr80). There's also the rather good *Gamla Stan karta* (Gamla Stan map; Skr25) and the 1: 10,000 scale *Stora Stockholmskartan* (Greater Stockholm Map; covering the city, some suburbs and parts of the archipelago; Skr65). The Storstockholms Lokaltrafik (SL) transport maps of the city and Stockholm county are excellent, but at the time of writing were no longer being produced.

The *What's On – Stockholm* tourist booklet, which is available free of charge from tourist offices and hotels, has two basic map pages, but the folded *Stockholms officiella turistkarta* (Skr15, from the tourist office) covers a larger area and is easier to read. Other free maps include the easy-to-use *Besökskartan* (Visitors Map), the *Welcome to Stockholm Map* and *Your Free Guide/Map*. All of these maps can be found at the tourist office.

## MEDICAL SERVICES

The health care system in Sweden is absurdly complicated, not to mention expensive, but it's very modern and almost all doctors speak English. There's no general practitioner system in Sweden so, if it's not an emergency, you're advised to go to the local *sjukhus* (hospital) or visit the local *apotek* (pharmacy). There's a 24-hour pharmacy in the centre of Stockholm, **Apoteket CW Scheele** (Map pp236-8; ☎ 454 81 30; Klarabergsgatan 64). *Hälso och sjukvård* (health and medical care) is listed in the blue pages of the pink-cover business phone book *(Företag)*; this is where you can find your nearest suburban *vårdcentral* (medical centre). You can also contact the **24-hour medical hotline** ( ☎ 463 91 00) or the toll-free **medications hotline** ( ☎ 020 66 77 66). The general emergency number, which includes the ambulance, is ☎ 112.

Dental treatment is also expensive, and costs around Skr700 per hour. Look for *tandläkare* (dentist) in the phone book, or you can visit the drop-in surgery at **St Eriks Ögonsjukhus** (Map p230; ☎ 654 11 17; Polhemsgatan 48, ☼ 7.45am-8.30pm).

## Emergency Rooms

Hospitals with 24-hour accident and emergency (casualty) services:

**Danderyds sjukhus** (Map pp228-9; ☎ 655 50 00; Danderyd; T-Danderyds sjukhus)

**Karolinska sjukhuset** (Map p230; ☎ 51 77 00 00; Haga; bus 52 from Sergels Torg)

**St Eriks Ögonsjukhus** (Map p230; ☎ 672 30 00; Flemingatan 22, Kungsholmen; bus 59 from Sergels Torg) This hospital specialises in the treatment of eyes.

**St Görans sjukhus** (Map p230; ☎ 58 70 10 00; Sankt Göransplan 1, Kungsholmen; bus 52 from Sergels Torg)

**Södersjukhuset** (Map pp234-5; ☎ 616 10 00; Ringvägen 52, Södermalm; bus 43 from Regeringsgatan) The most convenient hospital to the city centre.

## MONEY

The Swedish krona (plural: kronor) is usually represented as Skr (preceding the amount) in northern Europe (and throughout this book) and SEK (preceding the amount) in international money markets, but within Sweden it's just kr (after the amount). One Swedish krona equals 100 öre. Coins come in denominations of 50 öre (you'll see both the small copper-coloured version and the larger silver one) and Skr1, Skr5 and Skr10, while notes are in denominations of Skr20, Skr50, Skr100, Skr500, Skr1000 and Skr10,000.

The Swedish krona has tended to be relatively stable, with an annual inflation rate hovering around 2%. The kronor-per-US dollar exchange value has shifted between about eight and 10 kronor per dollar in the past half-dozen years.

At the time of writing, Sweden wasn't participating in the European single currency, or euro.

## ATMs

With an ATM card from your home bank, Swedish ATMs will allow access to cash in your account. 'Bankomat' and 'Automat' ATMs, found adjacent to many banks and around busy public places such as shopping centres, accept Visa, MasterCard, Plus and Cirrus format bank cards, and Electron and Maestro debit cards. Note that you'll immediately be charged interest using credit cards at ATMs.

## Changing Money

Changing money is easy in Stockholm. There are reliable exchange offices at major transport terminals and banks, and post offices also exchange major foreign currencies. Forex exchange offices usually offer the best exchange rates and low fees – Skr15 per travellers cheque and Skr20 for changing cash. X-Change offices don't charge a fee when you buy currency. Changing money at banks costs up to Skr60 per transaction. Eurocheques aren't accepted anywhere.

Some exchange offices and banks:

**American Express** (Map pp234-5; ☎ 411 05 40; Norrlandsgatan 21)

**Exchange Centre** (Map pp236-8; ☎ 411 29 26; Sveavägen 23; ⏱ 9.30am-7pm Mon-Fri, 10am-3pm Sat) No commissions. This outfit arranges Western Union money transfers.

**Forex** (Map pp236-8; ☎ 411 67 34; Centralstationen, main Vasagatan entrance; ⏱ 7am-9pm)

**Forex** (Map pp236-8; ☎ 21 42 80; Cityterminalen, the city bus terminal; ⏱ 7am-8pm Mon-Fri, 8am-5pm Sat & Sun)

**Forex** (Map pp236-8; ☎ 20 03 89; Sverigehuset, Hamngatan 27; ⏱ 8am-6pm Mon-Fri, 9am-3pm Sat, 10am-3pm Sun)

**Forex** (☎ 59 36 22 71; Arlanda airport, terminal No 2; ⏱ 6am-10.30pm)

**FöreningsSparbanken** (Map pp236-8; Hamngatan 31; ⏱ 10am-4pm Mon-Wed, 10am-6pm Thu, 10am-3pm Fri)

**Handelsbanken** (Map pp236-8; Kungsträdgårdsgatan 2; ⏱ 9.30am-3pm Mon-Fri)

**Handelsbanken** (Map pp234-5; Hornsgatan 140; ⏱ 9.30am-3pm Mon-Fri)

**Nordbanken** (Map pp236-8; Hamngatan 12; ⏱ 10am-4pm Mon-Fri)

**X-Change** (☎ 797 85 57; Arlanda airport, terminal No 5; ⏱ 5.30am-8.30pm)

**X-Change** (Map pp236-8; ☎ 50 61 07 00; Kungsgatan 30; ⏱ 5.30am-8.30pm)

## Credit Cards

Visa, MasterCard, American Express and Diners Club cards are widely accepted. Apart from when you're renting a car, you're better off using a credit card because you'll get a better exchange rate and you can avoid transaction fees. Credit cards can be used to buy train tickets but they're not accepted on domestic ferries, apart from those sailing to Gotland. Electronic debit cards can be used in many shops.

If your card is lost or stolen in Stockholm, as always, you should report it to the appropriate company:

**American Express** ( ☎ 020 79 51 55; ⏲ 8am-5pm Mon-Fri)

**Diners Club** ( ☎ 14 68 78; ⏲ 24hr)

**Eurocard/MasterCard** ( ☎ 14 67 67; ⏲ 24hr)

**Visa** ( ☎ 020 79 31 46 for non-Swedish Visa cards only; ⏲ 24hr)

## Travellers Cheques

Exchange offices, banks and post offices exchange major international brands of travellers cheques. Forex exchange offices are generally the best option. Banks charge Skr40 to Skr50 per transaction for changing travellers cheques. You're advised to shop around and compare exchange rates and fees to ensure you get the best deal.

## NEWSPAPERS & MAGAZINES

International publications are available at all newsstands.

Some Stockholm publications:

**Dagens Nyheter** (DN; ☎ 738 10 00; www.dn.se in Swedish) One of Stockholm's two main daily papers.

**Svenska Dagbladet** ( ☎ 13 50 00; www.svd.se in Swedish) Daily newspaper, slightly more right-leaning than DN.

**Metro** (www.metro.se/metro in Swedish) Free daily tabloid distributed on the *tunnelbana*.

**Aftonbladet** ( ☎ 725 20 00; www.aftonbladet.se in Swedish) Evening tabloid full of gossip.

**Expressen** ( ☎ 738 30 00) Similar to Aftonbladet.

**På Stan** (On the Town) The excellent Friday arts-and-culture supplement to DN.

**Guiden** A pocket guide to clubs and DJ nights, published by Expressen and available free at coffee shops and bars.

**Nöjesguiden** (www.nojesguiden.se in Swedish) A free monthly music-focused entertainment paper with great club listings.

## PHARMACIES

For information on prescription mediation, contact **Läkemedelsupplysningen** (the Medical Information Office; ☎ 020 66 77 66). The central 24-hour pharmacy is **Apoteket CW Scheele** ( ☎ 454 81 30; Klarabergsgatan 64).

## POST

The Swedish postal service has undergone some changes in recent years; you can no longer buy stamps at all the post offices, for example. However, stamps can be bought at Pressbyrån newsagents, tobacconists and bookshops. The longest opening hours are offered by the post office at Centralstationen (Map p236–8), which is open from 7am to 10pm during the week and from 10am to 7pm on the weekend; it also has a fax service (fax 10 25 84). You can pick up poste restante mail at the **central post office** (Map pp236-8; Drottninggatan 53; ⏲ 8am-6.30pm Mon-Fri, 10am-2pm Sat).

The blue postboxes are for local mail (to destinations within Stockholm) and the yellow postboxes for everywhere else.

Sweden has an efficient postal service. Sending postcards and letters weighing up to 20g within Sweden costs Skr5, to elsewhere in Europe costs Skr8 and to the rest of the world costs Skr10.

For airmail prices and other current postal rates, contact the postal service's **customer services** ( ☎ 020 23 22 21 toll-free within Sweden; www.posten.se).

If you want to ship a large package home, some shops may be able to arrange this for you, but a less expensive option is to go to the post office yourself and ask for the 'box and postage' *(kartong med porto)* deal, which allows you to ship up to 10kg for around Skr250 within the EU or Skr385 outside the EU (depending on the size of box and the destination).

If you're sending anything valuable, contact **Federal Express** ( ☎ 0200 25 22 52; Kabelgatan 5-6, Arlanda). It offers a free pick-up service on weekdays only.

## RADIO

BBC World Service broadcasts to Sweden on short wave at 9410kHz from 7am to 10am and 4pm to 11pm daily. Channel P6 (Radio Sweden domestic), which has programming in English, German, Sami, Latvian, Russian and Finnish, is at 89.6FM in Greater Stockholm and at 1179kHz throughout the rest of the country. For current program lists, check the Internet at www.sr.se/rs/schedule (in Swedish only) or contact **Radio Sweden** ( ☎ 784 72 88; info@rs.sr.se).

Some other Stockholm radio stations:

**National Swedish Radio** (96.2FM) Classical music and opera.

**NRJ** (105.1 FM) Latest pop hits.

**Radio Stockholm** (103.3FM) News, traffic reports and discussion programs.

**Rockklassiker** (106.7FM) Rock classics.

# TAX & REFUNDS

Value-added tax or *mervärdeskatt* (VAT, the equivalent of sales tax in the USA), known locally as MOMS, is generally included in the marked prices for goods and services, including books, food and drink, transport, meals and accommodation. The amount varies but it can be as high as 25%.

At shops with the sign 'Tax Free Shopping', non-EU citizens making single purchases of goods exceeding Skr200 (including MOMS) are eligible for a MOMS refund of between 15% and 18% of the purchase price. When making your purchase, show your passport and ask the shop assistant for a Global Refund Cheque. Upon departing the country (and prior to check-in), you should present the cheque along with your unopened purchases (as long as you do this within three months of the date of purchase) to get export validation. You can then cash your cheque at any of the 78 European refund points listed in the booklet *Tax Free Shopping Guide to Sweden*, which is available free of charge from tourist offices.

Some shops are part of the tax-free shopping system but don't display a sign, so it's always wise to ask.

# TELEPHONE

Sweden is an expensive place to use telephones and you can rack up a substantial bill due to so-called toll-free numbers that aren't free at all. It can be very frustrating, but reaching the main phone company (Telia) by phone, ironically, is virtually impossible.

Telia Butik (Telia Shops) exist primarily to sell telephones, but the staff can usually help with other enquiries; the most central **Telia Butik** (Map p230; ☎ 475 17 70) is at Kungsgatan 36.

For directory assistance, charged at Skr11.25 per minute, dial ☎ 11 81 18 (for numbers within Sweden) or ☎ 11 81 19 (for international numbers).

## Mobile Phones

In Stockholm, the Telia Mobiltel GSM system has coverage even in the *tunnelbana*. For details, call ☎ 90350. Comviq and Telia prepaid mobile phonecards can be bought at Pressbyrån newsagents but are valid only in Sweden. Your mobile may be locked onto your local network in your home country, so you need to ask your home network for advice

before taking your mobile phone abroad. If compatible, your phone will program automatically into the local network.

The Telia network charges Skr2.95 per minute for national calls from 8am to 6pm on weekdays (less at other times); calls made to other networks are a little bit more expensive.

Calls from your mobile may be routed internationally (even for local calls within Sweden) so prepare yourself for a substantial bill.

To buy a very basic mobile phone that you can fill up with conversation minutes as often as you need to, you should expect to pay around Skr395. Load up the phone with prepaid minutes at Phone House shops or at Pressbyrån; they're available in denominations of Skr200 to Skr500. If you'll be staying in Stockholm for a long time, you'll get a better deal if you buy a year's service from one of the mobile phone companies and pay by the month.

## Phonecards

Almost all public phones in Sweden are cardphones, but most also take credit cards (although it's not advisable to use a credit card in a cardphone since charges are very high). Coin-operated phones are scarce.

*Telefonkort* (phonecards) cost Skr35, Skr60 and Skr100 (which are worth 30, 60 and 120 units, respectively) and can be bought from Telia phone shops, Pressbyrå kiosks, tobacconists, newsagents, and Expert and OnOff electronic goods shops. International calls with a prepaid Telia phonecard start at around Skr10 per minute (for calls made between 10am and 10pm Monday to Saturday) or Skr8 at other times.

All telephone calls within Sweden (including local calls) cost a minimum of three units, which is quite expensive compared to most other European countries, and is nearly six times the connection charge from a private phone. Telia rates from public phones are around three units per minute between 8am and 6pm on weekdays. National calls are 50% cheaper between 6pm and 8am, and on weekends. Phone calls from hotel rooms, after the owners have added their fee, are little short of extortionate.

## Phone Books

In addition to the Yellow Pages (available on the Internet at www.gulasidorna.se), Telia phone books have purple (information in

English), green (community services), blue (regional services, including health and medical care) and pink (businesses) pages. In Stockholm, the green, blue and pink pages are in a separate phone book, called *Företag* (the business directory). Local *Din Del* phone books are easier to use.

When looking up telephone books, remember that the letters å, ä and ö fall at the end of the Swedish alphabet.

## Phone Codes

Phone calls to Sweden from abroad require the access code, the country code (46), the area code and telephone number, omitting the initial zero in the area code. To make international calls from Sweden, dial ☎ 00 followed by the country code, the area code (usually omitting the initial zero) and the telephone number.

Most Swedish telephone numbers have area codes followed by varying numbers of digits. Numbers beginning ☎ 020 or ☎ 0200 are toll-free (but note that charges apply when these numbers are called from public card phones). You can't call Swedish ☎ 020 or ☎ 0200 numbers from outside the country. Numbers beginning with ☎ 010, ☎ 073 and ☎ 070 are mobile codes.

The telephone area code for Greater Stockholm is ☎ 08.

## TELEVISION

The national TV channels TV1 and TV2 don't have advertising and are almost entirely in Swedish. TV3 and TV5 are commercial satellite or cable channels (not available nationally) which broadcast a lot of English-language shows and films. The commercial channel TV4 has good-quality broadcasting in Swedish and English. Foreign-made programmes and films are always shown in their original language, with Swedish subtitles. Hotels may also have satellite or cable channels such as Euro News, BBC World, Sky News, ABC, NBC, CNN or Euro-Sport, all of which are in English.

## TIME

Sweden is one hour ahead of GMT/UTC, the same as Norway, Denmark and most of Western Europe. When it's noon in Sweden, it's 11am in London, 1pm in Helsinki, 6am in New York and Toronto, 3am in Los Angeles, 9pm in Sydney and 11pm in Auckland. Sweden observes daylight-saving time – the clocks go forward an hour at 2am on the last Sunday in March and back an hour at 2am on the last Sunday in October. Timetables and business hours are quoted using the 24-hour clock, so it's really useful to be familiar with this, but dates are often given by week number (1 to 52).

When telling the time, note that in Swedish the use of 'half' means 'half an hour before' rather than 'half an hour past'.

## TIPPING

Service charges and tips are usually included in restaurant bills and taxi fares, but you will get no arguments if you want to reward good service with a tip. Bargaining isn't customary, but you can get 'walk-in' prices at some hotels and *stugby* (chalet parks).

## TOILET

Stockholm is strictly pay-to-pee. Public toilets in parks, shopping centres, libraries, and bus or train stations cost Skr5; it's a really good idea to keep a few Skr5 coins on you for emergencies. Except at Centralstationen and Åhléns department store (where there are attendants), pay toilets are coin-operated. You'll even have to pay at the main tourist office at Sverigehuset! Toilets in restaurants are for patrons only – although if you're friendly and you ask politely first, some places will show mercy. There are free gents' urinals in the following locations: in the basement at Centralstationen (it's signposted *urinoar*, but it's fairly revolting); near Tegnérlunden Park; in Kungsträdgården, opposite Arsenalsgatan; in Odenplan; and in the basement of Kungliga biblioteket (the Royal library).

## TOURIST INFORMATION

The main tourist office and excursion shop of the **Stockholm Information Service** (☎ 789 24 90; info@stoinfo.se) is normally located on the ground floor of Sverigehuset (Sweden House) at Hamngatan 27, near Kungsträdgården. Sverigehuset has been under repair, however, so the main tourist office is temporarily located on the ground floor of Kulturhuset (Map pp236-8), supposedly until November 2004 – but the expected moving date has changed a few times, so it's best to check. Its services include booking hotel rooms, theatre and concert tickets, as well as packages for such things as boat trips to the archipelago. There's also an Internet terminal where you can search the tourist office website. The office is open from 8am to 7pm on weekdays and 9am to 5pm on weekends from June to August; during the rest of the year it's open between 9am and 6pm (between 9am and 3pm on weekends in May and September, and 10am and 3pm on weekends from October to April). Telephone inquiries are answered only during office hours.

Located in the same building as the tourist office is a Forex currency exchange office and a travel agency specialising in travel to the Finnish province of Åland. Upstairs you'll find the Sweden Bookshop, which has information in English about Swedish life and culture provided by the Swedish Institute. Again, since the building is undergoing repairs, the bookshop can be found in its temporary location at Slottsbacken (see Shopping, p144) until November '04.

Perhaps more convenient for newly arrived travellers is **Hotellcentralen** (Map pp236-8; ☎ 789 24 90; hotels@stoinfo.se), located at Centralstationen. It's open between 7am and 9pm daily from May to September (between 9am and 6pm daily from October to April). In addition to tourist information, you can reserve hotel rooms and hostel beds, buy both the Stockholm Package and Stockholm Card, book sightseeing tours and buy maps, books and souvenirs.

Both tourist offices charge Skr50 plus 10% deposit for hotel reservations and Skr20 for hostel, chalet or camping reservations, but only for walk-in bookings; reservations for future dates made by phone are free. Many of the office's publications and leaflets are free, including the useful booklets What's On – Stockholm (issued monthly in summer, and every two months at other times), Hotels & Youth Hostels in Stockholm (issued annually) and Stockholm Restaurangguide (issued twice yearly).

The head office of the **Swedish Travel & Tourism Council** ( ☎ 08-725 55 00; info@visit-sweden.com; Box 3030, SE-10361 Stockholm) can provide you with general information about Sweden.

The **Stockholm Information Service** (www.stockholmtown.com) manages the main tourist information website, but you may find the site short of detail. Alternatively, information for tourists is available at the Swedish-language website www.alltomstockholm.se, which is definitely the best information source about Stockholm. There's a plan to include instructions in English to assist navigation around the Swedish pages, but no word as to when this might happen.

Details of the main city museums, including temporary exhibitions and events, can be found on the Internet at www.stockholmsmuseer.com. Although this site is only in Swedish, there are links to museum homepages, some of which have information in English.

For information in English about the Stockholm archipelago, go to the Archipelago Foundation Internet pages at www.skargardsstiftelsen.se. You'll find Stockholmskartan, an excellent street map of the city, at www.map.stockholm.se/kartago – use the zoom-in button repeatedly to get the best resolution. The text is in Swedish but it's easy to navigate through this site.

Yellow Pages directories of business phone numbers can be found on the Internet at www.gulasidorna.se and www.bizbook.se (both in Swedish).

## Books

One of the finest guidebooks in English about the city is Close to Stockholm, by Magdalena Korotyska and Karin Winter (1998), an unusual picture book covering most of Stockholm, with hand-painted panoramas. It includes a detailed and well-researched guide to 160 buildings that are worth visiting.

Another unusual book, The Stockholm Time Walk by Michael Tongue (1996), suggests a walking tour that takes you past 50 points of interest, mostly in Gamla Stan but also in some neighbouring parts of Norrmalm and Södermalm. The book contains text and photos of these areas as they were around 100 years ago as well as clear maps of the route today.

Cultural Walking Tours, by Elena Siré and Sten Leijonhufvud (1998), covers 10 walking tours that explore the city's architectural and historical heritage. Although aimed at the disabled, this handy little book is also useful for other visitors.

An essential guide for architecture buffs is The Complete Guide to Architecture in Stockholm, by Olof Hultin et al (1998), which describes 400 buildings from the earliest times up to the present, using colour photos, detailed text and maps.

## VISAS

Citizens of EU countries can enter Sweden with a valid passport or national identification card and stay up to three months, but nationals of Nordic countries (Denmark, Norway, Finland and Iceland) can stay and work in Sweden for an indefinite period. If you're not from a Nordic country and you want to stay for more than three months and up to five years, you'll need to apply for a free *uppehållstillstånd* (residence permit) on arrival in Sweden. For an application form, contact the **Swedish Immigration Office** ( ☎ 470 97 00; fax 470 9930; Solnavägen 96; Box 507, SE-16929 Solna) or the **Swedish Migration Board** (Migrationsverket; ☎ 011-15 60 00; migrationsverket@migratio nsverket.se; Tegelängsgatan 19A, SE-60170 Norrköping).

Citizens of other countries can also enter Sweden with a valid passport or national identification card and stay up to three months. However, 90-day tourist visas, which cost Skr250 and must be obtained from your nearest Swedish embassy before entering Sweden (allow two months for processing), are required by nationals of many Asian and African countries (including South Africa), Croatia, Serbia and Montenegro, Bosnia-Hercegovina, Bulgaria, Colombia and Guyana. Visa extensions aren't easily obtainable. Non-EU citizens can also obtain residence permits, which are valid for six months and longer. You must apply for these permits before entering Sweden and you'll be interviewed by consular officials at your nearest Swedish embassy – allow up to eight months for this process. Normally you'll have to be married or cohabiting with a permanent resident of Sweden and you may have to send in your passport to get it stamped.

Foreign students are granted residence permits if they have comprehensive health insurance, can prove acceptance by a Swedish educational institution and are able to guarantee that they can support themselves financially.

For details about the current visa situation, check the Internet at www.swedish -embassy.org.uk.

## WOMEN TRAVELLERS

Sexual equality is emphasised in Sweden and there should be no question of discrimination. **Kvinnojouren** ( ☎ 760 96 11), based in Stockholm, is the national organisation that deals with violence against women. Local Kvinnojouren centres are listed in the green pages of telephone directories or on the Internet at www.gulasidorna.se.

Pregnant women with health emergencies should contact the nearest *mödravårdcentral* (maternity hospital); you can find contact details in the blue pages of the pink-cover business telephone directory (which is listed by municipality).

Some Stockholm taxi firms offer discounts to women at night, so be sure to ask when booking.

Recommended reading for first-time solo women travellers is the *Handbook for Women Travellers*, by Maggie and Gemma Moss. It's published by Piatkus Books but is now out of print, so may be difficult to track down. *Safety and Security for Women Who Travel*, by Sheila Swan and Peter Laufer (1998), is also useful and widely available in paperback.

There are several good websites for women travellers, including those at www.passionfruit .com and www.journeywoman.com, and the women travellers page on the Lonely Planet website's Thorn Tree (http://thorntree.lonely planet.com).

## WORK

Most foreigners require a work permit in advance in order to undertake paid employment in Sweden. Non-EU citizens need to apply for a work permit (and a residence permit for stays over three months), enclosing confirmation of the job offer from the prospective employer on either form AMS PF 1704 or form AMS PF 1707, as well as a completed form SIV 1040.U (available from Swedish diplomatic posts), a passport photo and passport. Processing of the permit takes between one and three months and this must be done before entry to Sweden. There's no fee, except for the cost of returning your passport by post, if necessary. EU citizens need to apply for a residence permit within three months of arrival only if they find work, they can then remain in Sweden for the duration of their employment (or up to five years). For the latest details, check the website at www.swedish-embassy.org.uk under Consular Affairs and Work Permits.

Unemployment is still fairly high and work permits are granted only if there's a shortage of Swedes with certain skills (eg technical manufacturing areas). Speaking Swedish fluently is essential for most jobs. No one is looking for builders or people with social services or care skills, and service work opportunities are minimal. Go to the local branch of Arbetsförmedlingen (the Employment Office), which may be able to help, and which will have some literature in English. Arbetsförmedlingen's website (www.ams.se) has information in English on: starting a business in Sweden; working, studying and living in Sweden; details of unemployment insurance; and job vacancies listed by region or profession.

Students enrolled in Swedish institutions can take summer jobs, but such work isn't offered to travelling students.

For volunteer opportunities in Stockholm, check the frequently updated listings on the Internet at www.volunteerabroad.com /Sweden.cfm.

# Language

# Language

It's true – anyone can speak another language. Don't worry if you haven't studied languages before or that you studied a language at school for years and can't remember any of it. It doesn't even matter if you failed English grammar. After all, that's never affected your ability to speak English! And this is the key to picking up a language in another country. You just need to start speaking.

Learn a few key phrases before you go. Write them on pieces of paper and stick them on the fridge, by the bed or even on the computer – anywhere that you'll see them often.

You'll find that locals appreciate travellers trying their language, even if you're in a country where many or most speak English. Your efforts will be appreciated no matter how muddled you may think you sound. So don't just stand there, say something! If you want to learn more Swedish than we've included here, pick up a copy of Lonely Planet's comprehensive but user-friendly *Scandinavian Phrasebook*.

Note: The Swedish alphabet has three more letters than the English alphabet: **å, ä** and **ö**. These fall at the end of the alphabet. This book uses Swedish alphabetical order throughout.

## SOCIAL
## Meeting People
Hello.
Hej.
Goodbye.
Adjö/Hej då.
Please.
Tack.
Thank you (very much).
Tack (så mycket).
Yes/No.
Ja/Nej.
Do you speak English?
Talar du engelska?
Do you understand (me)?
Förstår du (mig)?
Yes, I understand.
Ja, jag förstår.
No, I don't understand.
Nej, jag förstår inte.

Could you please ...?
Kan du vara snäll ...?
| | |
|---|---|
| repeat that | och upprepa det |
| speak more | och tala lite |
| slowly | långsammare |
| write it down | och skriva ner den |

## Going Out
What's on ...?
Vad händer ...?
| | |
|---|---|
| locally | i närheten |
| this weekend | denna helgen |
| today | i dag |
| this evening | i kväll |

Where are the ...?
Var finns ...?
| | |
|---|---|
| clubs | klubbarna |
| gay venues | gay-klubbarna |
| places to eat | restaurangerna |
| pubs | pubbarna |

Is there a local entertainment guide?
Finns det en lokal nöjesguide?

## PRACTICAL
## Question Words
| | |
|---|---|
| Who? | Vem? |
| What? | Vad? |
| When? | När? |
| Where? | Var? |
| How? | Hur? |

## Numbers & Amounts
| | |
|---|---|
| 1 | ett |
| 2 | två |
| 3 | tre |
| 4 | fyra |
| 5 | fem |
| 6 | sex |
| 7 | sju |
| 8 | åtta |
| 9 | nio |

| | |
|---|---|
| 10 | tio |
| 11 | elva |
| 12 | tolv |
| 13 | tretton |
| 14 | fjorton |
| 15 | femton |
| 16 | sexton |
| 17 | sjuton |
| 18 | arton |
| 19 | nitton |
| 20 | tjugo |
| 21 | tjugoett |
| 22 | tjugotvå |
| 30 | trettio |
| 40 | fyrtio |
| 50 | femtio |
| 60 | sextio |
| 70 | sjuttio |
| 80 | åttio |
| 90 | nittio |
| 100 | ett hundra |
| 1000 | ett tusen |
| 2000 | två tusen |

## Days

| | |
|---|---|
| Monday | måndag |
| Tuesday | tisdag |
| Wednesday | onsdag |
| Thursday | torsdag |
| Friday | fredag |
| Saturday | lördag |
| Sunday | söndag |

## Banking

I'd like to ...
Jag skulla vilja ...

| | |
|---|---|
| cash a cheque | lösa in en check |
| change money | växla pengar |
| change some travellers cheques | växla resecheckar |

Where's the nearest ...?
Var är närmaste ...?

| | |
|---|---|
| ATM | bankomat |
| foreign exchange office | utländsk valuta |

## Post

Where is the post office?
Var är posten?

I'd like to send a ...
Jag skulle vilja skicka ett ...

| | |
|---|---|
| letter | brev |
| parcel | paket |
| postcard | vykort |

I want to buy a/an ...
Jag skulla vilja ha ett ...

| | |
|---|---|
| aerogram | aerogram |
| envelope | kuvert |
| stamp | frimärke |

## Phones & Mobiles

I want to buy a phone card.
Jag skulla vilja ha ett telefonkort.
I want to make a call (to ...)
Jag skulle vilja ringa (till ...)
I want to make a reverse-charge/collect call.
Jag skulle vilja göra ett ba-samtal.
(*ba* is pronounced like B.R. – 'bee-ah')

Where can I find a/an ...?
Var finns ...
I'd like a/an ...
Jag skulle vilja ha ....

| | |
|---|---|
| adaptor plug | en adapter |
| charger for my phone | en laddare till min telefon |
| mobile/cell phone for hire | mobil telefon till hyra |
| SIM card for your network | ett SIM-kort till detta nätverk |

## Internet

Is there a local Internet café?
Finns det något Internet-kafé i närheten?

I'd like to ...
Jag skulle vilja ...

| | |
|---|---|
| check my email | kolla min e-mail |
| get online | koppla upp mig till Internetet. |

## Transport

What time does the ... leave?
Hur dags går ...?

| | |
|---|---|
| bus | bussen |
| ferry | färjan |
| plane | planet |
| train | tåget |

What time's the ...?
När går ...?

| | |
|---|---|
| first bus | första bussen |
| last bus | sista bussen |
| next bus | nästa buss |

Are you free? (taxi)
Är du ledig?
How much is it to ...?
Vat kostar det till ...?

Can you take me to (this address).
Kan du köra mig till (denna adress)?

# FOOD

| | |
|---|---|
| breakfast | frukost |
| lunch | lunch |
| dinner | middag |
| snack | mellanmål |
| eat | äta |
| drink | dricka |

Can you recommend a ...?
Kan Ni recomendera ...?

| | |
|---|---|
| bar/pub | en pub |
| café | ett kafé |
| restaurant | en restaurang |

Is service/cover charge included in the bill?
Är serveringsavgiften inräknad?

*For more detailed information on food and dining out, see 'Eating' on p99.*

# EMERGENCIES
It's an emergency!
Det är ett nödsituation!

Could you please help me/us?
Kan du hjälpa mig/oss?
Call the police!
Ring polisen!
Call the a doctor/an ambulance!
Ring efter en doktor/en ambulans!
Where's the police station?
Var är polisstationen?

# HEALTH
Where's the nearest ...?
Var är nämaste ...?

| | |
|---|---|
| chemist (night) | (natt)apotek |
| dentist | tandläkare |
| doctor | doktor |
| hospital | sjukhus |

# Symptoms
I have (a) ...
Jag har ...

| | |
|---|---|
| cough | hosta |
| diarrhoea | diarré |
| fever | feber |
| headache | huvudvärk |
| pain | ont |
| sore throat | ont i halsen |

## Glossary
You may encounter some of the following terms and abbreviations during your travels in and around Stockholm. See also the Language chapter and the Food section in the Places to Eat chapter. Note that the letters å, ä and ö fall at the end of the Swedish alphabet.

**allemansrätt** – 'every man's right'; a tradition allowing universal access to private property (with some restrictions), public land and wilderness areas
**apotek** – pharmacy

**bad** – swimming pool, bathing place (usually *äventyrs bad*)
**bakfickan** – literally 'back pocket', an ordinary low profile eating place associated with a gourmet restaurant
**bankautomat** – cash machine, ATM
**barn** – child
**berg** – mountain
**bibliotek** – library
**bil** – car
**biljet** – ticket
**biljetautomat** – automatic ticket machines for street parking
**bio, biograf** – cinema
**bro** – bridge
**bryggeri** – brewery
**buss** – bus
**båt** – boat

**centrum** – town centre
**cykel** – bicycle

**dagens rätt** – daily special, usually only on lunch menus
**domkyrka** – cathedral
**drottning** – queen

**ej** – not
**ekonomibrev** – economy post
**etage** – floor, storey

**flygplats** – airport
**folkdräkt** – folk dress
**folkhemmet** – welfare state
**frukost** – breakfast
**fyr** – lighthouse
**fågel** – bird
**färja** – ferry
**färjeläge** – ferry quay
**fästning** – fort, fortress
**förening** – club, association
**förlag** – company

**galleria** – shopping mall
**gamla** – old
**gamla staden, gamla stan** – the 'old town', the historical part of a city or town
**gatan** – street (often abbreviated to just g)
**glögg** – spicy mulled wine
**grundskolan** – comprehensive school

**gruva** – mine
**gymnasieskolan** – upper secondary school
**gård** – farm
**gästhamn** – 'guest harbour', where visiting yachts can berth; cooking and washing facilities usually available
**gästhem** – guesthouse

**hamn** – harbour
**hembygdsgård** – open-air museum, usually old farmhouse buildings
**hjortron** – cloudberries
**hus** – house, sometimes 'castle'
**husmanskost** – traditional Swedish fare; what you'd expect cooked at home when you were a (Swedish) kid
**hytt** – cabin on a boat
**hälsocentral** – clinic

**i** – in
**inte** – not (or ej)
**is** – ice; ice cream
**ishall** – ice-hockey stadium

**jul** – Christmas
**järnvägsstation** – train station

**kaj** – quay
**karta** – map
**klockan** – o'clock, the time
**kommun** – municipality
**konditori** – baker and confectioner (often with an attached cafe)
**konst** – art
**kort** – card
**krog** – pub or restaurant (or both)
**krona** (s), **kronor** (pl) – Swedish currency unit
**kung** – king
**kyrka** – church
**kyrkogård** – graveyard
**källare** – cellar, vault

**landskap** – region, province, landscape
**lasarett** – hospital
**lilla** – lesser, little
**loppis** – second-hand goods (usually junk)
**län** – county

**mat** – food
**midsommar** – midsummer; first Friday after 21 June
**MOMS** – value-added tax
**museum, museet** – museum

**nedre** – lower
**norr** – north
**ny** – new
**nyheter** – news
**näs** – headland

**och** – and

**palats** – palace
**pendeltåg** – local train
**pensionat** – pension or guesthouse

**P-hus** – multistorey car park
**polis** – police
**post** – post office
**på** – on, in
**påsk** – Easter

**RFSL** – Riksförbundet för Sexuellt Likaberättigande; national gay organisation
**riksdag** – parliament
**rådhus** – town hall
**rökning förbjuden** – no smoking

**SJ** – Statens Järnväg (Swedish Railways)
**sjukhus** – hospital
**sjö** – lake or sea
**skog** – forest
**skål!** – cheers!
**skärgård** – archipelago
**slott** – castle
**smörgåsbord** – Swedish buffet (lunch or dinner)
**stark** – strong, hot (spicy)
**STF** – Svenska Turistföreningen (Swedish Touring Association)
**stor** – big, large
**strand** – beach
**sund** – sound (geography)
**Sverige** – Sweden
**svensk** – Swedish
**Systembolaget** – state-owned liquor store
**söder** – south

**tandläkare** – dentist
**teater** – theatre
**telefonkort** – telephone card
**toalett** – toilet
**torg, torget** – town square
**torn** – tower
**trädgård** – garden open to the public
**tunnelbana** – underground railway, metro
**turistbyrå** – tourist office
**tåg** – train

**vandrarhem** – hostel
**vik** – bay or other inlet
**vuxen** – adult
**vårdcentral** – hospital
**väg** – road
**värdshus** (or **wärdshus**) – inn
**väst** – west (abbreviated to v)
**västra** – western
**växel** – money exchange, switchboard

**wärdshus** – see *värdshus*

**å** – stream, creek, river

**ö** – island
**öl** – beer
**öst** – east (abbreviated to ö)
**östra** – eastern
**övre** – upper

# Behind the Scenes

## THE LONELY PLANET STORY

The story begins with a classic travel adventure: Tony and Maureen Wheeler's 1972 journey across Europe and Asia to Australia. There was no useful information about the overland trail then, so Tony and Maureen published the first Lonely Planet guidebook to meet a growing need.

From a kitchen table, Lonely Planet has grown to become the largest independent travel publisher in the world, with offices in Melbourne (Australia), Oakland (USA), London (UK) and Paris (France).

Today Lonely Planet guidebooks cover the globe. There is an ever-growing list of books and information in a variety of media. Some things haven't changed. The main aim is still to make it possible for adventurous travellers to get out there – to explore and better understand the world.

At Lonely Planet we believe travellers can make a positive contribution to the countries they visit – if they respect their host communities and spend their money wisely.

## THIS BOOK

This 2nd edition of *Stockholm* was written and updated by Becky Ohlsen, based on the 1st edition, which was written by Graeme Cornwallis. This city guide was commissioned in Lonely Planet's London office, and produced by:

**Commissioning Editor** Amanda Canning, Alan Murphy
**Coordinating Editor** Emma Koch
**Coordinating Cartographer** Simon Tillema
**Coordinating Layout Designer** Indra Kilfoyle
**Editors** Kristin Odijk, Miriam Cannell, Carly Hall
**Layout Designers** David Kemp
**Cover Designer** Sophie Rivoire
**Artwork** James Hardy
**Series Designer** Nic Lehman
**Series Design Concept** Nic Lehman, Andrew Weatherill
**Managing Cartographer** Mark Griffiths
**Mapping Development** Paul Piaia
**Project Manager** Glenn van der Knijff
**Language Editor** Quentin Frayne
**Regional Publishing Manager** Katrina Browning, Amanda Canning
**Series Publishing Manager** Gabrielle Green
**Series Development Team** Jenny Blake, Anna Bolger, Fiona Christie, Kate Cody, Erin Corrigan, Janine Eberle, Simone Egger, James Ellis, Nadine Fogale, Roz Hopkins, Dave McClymont, Leonie Mugavin, Rachel Peart, Ed Pickard, Michele Posner, Howard Ralley and Dani Valent
**Thanks to** Glenn Beanland, Ryan Evans, Wayne Murphy

**Cover photographs** View of Stockholm Town Hall across the water at sunrise, Chad Ehlers/alamy (top); Ornate decorative detail on building in Stortorget, Wayne Walton/Lonely Planet Images (bottom); Gate at entrance to Hagaparken, Jonathan Smith/Lonely Planet Images (back).

**Internal photographs** by Jonathan Smith/Lonely Planet Images except for the following: p2 (#2), p66 (#1, 3) Anders Blomqvist/Lonely Planet Images; p97, p173, p185 Graeme Cornwallis/Lonely Planet Images; p66 (#2) Jon Davison/Lonely Planet Images; p65, p66 (#4) Veronica Garbutt/Lonely Planet Images; p8, p59 (#1, 4) Wayne Walton/Lonely Planet Images; p183 Christopher Wood/Lonely Planet Images. All images are the copyright of the photographers unless otherwise indicated. Many of the images in this guide are available for licensing from Lonely Planet Images: www.lonelyplanetimages.com.

## ACKNOWLEDGMENTS

Many thanks to Storstockholms Lokaltrafik for the Stockhom Transport Systems Map.

## THANKS
### BECKY OHLSEN

Thanks to: commissioning editor Amanda Canning; cartographer Mark Griffiths and his crew; Jennifer Sjöberg, Mats Sjöberg and Gunnel Nordling; Peter Kvarnestam and his kittens; Jonas Thorell and the Venue; Charlotte Reinhard; Stuart Gaston; Viatchislav Jefimov; that clerk at the 7-11 on Odenplan; Wicklow Mick Lavin; The Loft; Veysel Akbulut; White Hassle; Tom Downs; Lello Primavera; Bob and Dorothy Ohlsen; Karl Ohlsen; Zachary Hull, Patrick Leyshock and

---

## SEND US YOUR FEEDBACK

We love to hear from travellers – your comments keep us on our toes and help make our books better. Our well-travelled team reads every word on what you loved or loathed about this book. Although we cannot reply individually to postal submissions, we always guarantee that your feedback goes straight to the appropriate authors, in time for the next edition. Each person who sends us information is thanked in the next edition – and the most useful submissions are rewarded with a free book.

To send us your updates – and find out about LP events, newsletters and travel news – visit our award-winning website: www.lonelyplanet.com.

Note: We may edit, reproduce and incorporate your comments in Lonely Planet products such as guidebooks, websites and digital products, so let us know if you don't want your comments reproduced or your name acknowledged. For a copy of our privacy policy visit www.lonelyplanet.com/privacy.

Tom Burnett; John Taboada; and Hill's Svensk-Engelsk Fickordbok. Most of all, tusendubbling to mormor and morfar Elisabeth and Arne Odeen, Aunt Kristina Björholm (the Jultomte), and my parents, Joel and Christina Ohlsen.

# OUR READERS

Many thanks to the travellers who used the last edition and wrote to us with helpful hints, useful advice and interesting anecdotes. Your names follow:

Patrik Aqvist, Leif VS Balthzersen, Biljana Bedzovska, Suzanne Bush, Claire Chambers, Roy Coates, Candida D'Arcy, Tony Fagan, Tony Fuller, Marcelo Gameiro de Moura, Lotta Gollas, A Kearn, Christina MacPherson, Damir Madunic, Duncan Maggs, Ronald Newman, Robin O'Donoghue, Montjovent Pascal, Adam Rattray, Nat Robbins, Jacob Hale Russell, Salvador Sanchez, Sage Savage, Davide Secci, Barry and Birgitta Shay, Mary-Louise Sloan, Michael Stiles, Lisl Swinehart, Naylora Troster, Fredrik Tukk, Marianne Undberg, Murray Verran, Oscar Virot, Henrik Waldenstrom, Ann Wallace, Sarah Wintle.

# Notes

# Notes

**Notes**

**Notes**

Notes

# Index

See also separate indexes for Eating (p225), Drinking (p225), Shopping (p225) and Sleeping (p226).

Index

225

## MAP LEGEND

### ROUTES

| | |
|---|---|
| Freeway | One-Way Street |
| Primary Road | Unsealed Road |
| Secondary Road | Mall/Steps |
| Tertiary Road | Tunnel |
| Lane | Walking Tour |
| Track | Walking Path |

### TRANSPORT

| | |
|---|---|
| Ferry | Rail |
| Metro | Rail (Underground) |
| Cable Car, Funicular | Tram |

### HYDROGRAPHY

| | |
|---|---|
| River, Creek | Water |

### AREA FEATURES

| | |
|---|---|
| Airport | Land |
| Area of Interest | Mall |
| Building, Featured | Park |
| Building, Information | Cemetery, Christian |
| Building, Other | Sports |
| Building, Transport | Urban |

### POPULATION

| | |
|---|---|
| ✪ CAPITAL (NATIONAL) | ◉ CAPITAL (STATE) |
| ● Large City | ● Medium City |
| ● Small City | ● Town, Village |

### SYMBOLS

| Sights/Activities | Drinking | Information |
|---|---|---|
| Beach | Drinking | Bank, ATM |
| Castle, Fortress | **Entertainment** | Embassy/Consulate |
| Christian | Entertainment | Hospital, Medical |
| Islamic | **Shopping** | Information |
| Jewish | Shopping | Internet Facilities |
| Monument | **Sleeping** | Police Station |
| Museum, Gallery | Sleeping | Post Office, GPO |
| Ruin | Camping | **Geographic** |
| Swimming Pool | **Transport** | Lookout |
| Zoo, Bird Sanctuary | Airport, Airfield | Mountain, Volcano |
| **Eating** | Bus Station | National Park |
| Eating | Taxi Rank | River Flow |

# Map Section

A B C D

1 Skälby

Barkarby

To Västerås via E18 (85km)

Hjulsta

Kista 279

To Sigtuna (35km); Uppsala (55km)

To Edsbacka Krog (8km); Scandic Hotel Täby (12km); Vaxholm (25km); Norrtälje (55km)

Norrtäljevägen

Klingsta

Danderyds Sjukhus

Tensta

Hjulstavägen

Nationalstadsparken 12

18

21 30

Skälbyvägen

Lunda

26

Avestagatan

Spånga

Spånga Kyrkväg

Rinkeby

Kymlingelänken

Kälvesta

Solhem

Rissne

E18

Enköpingsvägen

28

Ulriksdal

E18

Bergshamra

Bergshan

Vinsta 275

Flysta

Rissne

Hallonbergen

Råstasjön

Brunns viken

2 Hässelby Gård

Johannelund

Nälsta

Sundbyberg

Näckrosen

Solna

Haga parken

Vällingby

Duvbo 17

Duvbo

Solna

6

8 7

Bergslagsvägen

Bergslagsvägen

Vällingby

Eneby

Ballstavägen

15

11

Lövstavägen

Räcksta

Spångavägen

279

Sundbybergs Centrum

31

Solna Centrum

Hagalund

E4

2

Norra Ängby

Bromma

Vreten

Huvudsta

See p230

Uppsalavägen

Blackeberg

Islandstorget

Kyrksjön

Bromma Airport

Huvudsta

Västra Skogen

Karlberg

5

Judarn

Ulvsundasjön

Karlberg

3 Södra Ängby

Ängbyplan

Åkeshov

275

Lillsjön

Traneberg

Sankt Eriksplan

Stadshagen

Rörbyvägen

Brommaplan

Abrahamsberg

Stora Mossen

Alvik

Kristineberg

Thorildsplan

Fridhemsplan

261

Åkeslund

Alléparken

Alvik Strand

Nockeby Torg

Stora Essingen

Lovö Kyrkallé

Nockeby

Nockeby

Olovslund

Ålstensgatan

Klövervägen

Stora Essingen

Lilla Essingen

Långholmen

4

Höglandstorget

Äppelviken

Essingeleden

Gröndal

Hornstull

Lovön

Kärsön

Ålstens Gård

Smedslätten

Gröndal

Trekanten

Liljeholmen

261

Fågelön

27

Hägersten

Aspudden

Söderleden

Årstadal

Årstaberg

Kungshatt

Axelsberg

Örnsberg

Midsommar kransen

Mälarhöjden

Mälarhöjden

Telefonplan

23

Bredäng

24

See pp234–

Fiskarfjärden

Sätra

Bredäng

25

Västertorp

Hägerstensåsen

E4 E20

Västberga

Liseberg

5 Sätra

Södertäljevägen

Fruängen

Solberga

Älvsjö

Älvsjövägen

Vårberg

Skärholmen

22

Fruängen

Herrängen

Längsjön

Örby

E4 E20

Vårberg

Huddingevägen

Hagsätra

226

Högdalen

6 Vårby Gård

Sergeltorp

Snättringe

Magelungsvägen

Rågsved

Vårby

To Södertälje (16km); Nyköping (130km)

Masmo

Glömsta

Gömmaren

Milsten

Stuvsta

Stuvsta

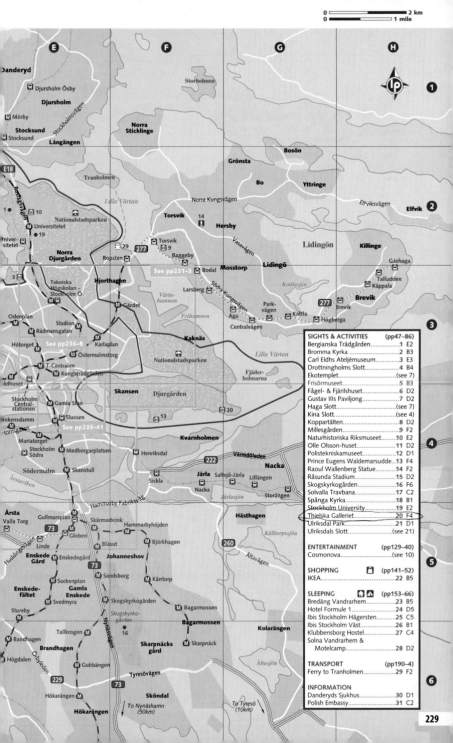

0 ———— 2 km
0 ———— 1 mile

**SIGHTS & ACTIVITIES** (pp47–86)
Bergianska Trädgården.............1 E2
Bromma Kyrka .........................2 B3
Carl Eldhs Ateljémuseum..........3 E3
Drottningholms Slott.................4 B4
Ekotemplet..........................(see 7)
Frisörmuseet.............................5 B3
Fågel- & Fjärilshuset.................6 D2
Gustav IIIs Paviljong.................7 D2
Haga Slott..........................(see 7)
Kina Slott...........................(see 4)
Koppartälten...........................8 D2
Millesgården............................9 F2
Naturhistoriska Riksmuseet......10 D2
Olle Olsson-huset...................11 D2
Polistekniskamuseet................12 D1
Prince Eugens Waldemarsudde..13 F4
Raoul Wallenberg Statue..........14 F2
Råsunda Stadium.....................15 D2
Skogskyrkogården...................16 F6
Solvalla Travbana....................17 C2
Spånga Kyrka.........................18 B1
Stockholm University................19 E2
Thielska Galleriet.....................20 F4
Ulriksdal Park..........................21 D1
Ulriksdals Slott.....................(see 21)

**ENTERTAINMENT** (pp129–40)
Cosmonova.........................(see 10)

**SHOPPING** (pp141–52)
IKEA.....................................22 B5

**SLEEPING** (pp153–66)
Bredäng Vandrarhem................23 B5
Hotel Formule 1......................24 D5
Ibis Stockholm Hägersten.........25 C5
Ibis Stockholm Väst.................26 B1
Klubbensborg Hostel................27 C4
Solna Vandrarhem &
   Motelcamp........................28 D2

**TRANSPORT** (pp190–4)
Ferry to Tranholmen.................29 F2

**INFORMATION**
Danderyds Sjukhus...................30 D1
Polish Embassy........................31 C2

229

# KUNGSHOLMEN & VASASTADEN

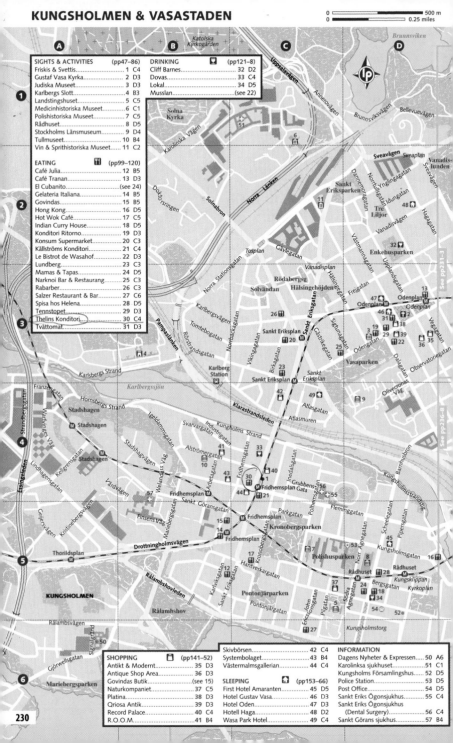

| SIGHTS & ACTIVITIES | (pp47–86) | |
|---|---|---|
| Friskis & Svettis | 1 | C4 |
| Gustaf Vasa Kyrka | 2 | D3 |
| Judiska Museet | 3 | D3 |
| Karlbergs Slott | 4 | B3 |
| Landstingshuset | 5 | C5 |
| Medicinhistoriska Museet | 6 | C1 |
| Polishistoriska Museet | 7 | C5 |
| Rådhuset | 8 | D5 |
| Stockholms Länsmuseum | 9 | D4 |
| Tullmuseet | 10 | B4 |
| Vin & Sprithistoriska Museet | 11 | C2 |

| EATING | (pp99–120) | |
|---|---|---|
| Café Julia | 12 | B5 |
| Café Tranan | 13 | D3 |
| El Cubanito | (see 24) | |
| Gelateria Italiana | 14 | B5 |
| Govindas | 15 | B5 |
| Hong Kong | 16 | D5 |
| Hot Wok Café | 17 | C5 |
| Indian Curry House | 18 | D5 |
| Konditori Ritorno | 19 | D3 |
| Konsum Supermarket | 20 | C4 |
| Källströms Konditori | 21 | C4 |
| Le Bistrot de Wasahof | 22 | D3 |
| Lundberg | 23 | C3 |
| Mamas & Tapas | 24 | D5 |
| Narknoi Bar & Restaurang | 25 | C3 |
| Rabarber | 26 | C3 |
| Salzer Restaurant & Bar | 27 | C6 |
| Spisa hos Helena | 28 | D5 |
| Tennstopet | 29 | D3 |
| Thelins Konditori | 30 | C4 |
| Tvättomat | 31 | D3 |

| DRINKING | (pp121–8) | |
|---|---|---|
| Cliff Barnes | 32 | D2 |
| Dovas | 33 | C4 |
| Lokal | 34 | D5 |
| Musslan | (see 22) | |

| SHOPPING | (pp141–52) | |
|---|---|---|
| Antikt & Modernt | 35 | D3 |
| Antique Shop Area | 36 | D3 |
| Govindas Butik | (see 15) | |
| Naturkompaniet | 37 | C5 |
| Platina | 38 | D3 |
| Qriosa Antik | 39 | D3 |
| Record Palace | 40 | C4 |
| R.O.O.M. | 41 | B4 |

| Skivbörsen | 42 | C4 |
|---|---|---|
| Systembolaget | 43 | B4 |
| Västermalmsgallerian | 44 | C4 |

| SLEEPING | (pp153–66) | |
|---|---|---|
| First Hotel Amaranten | 45 | D5 |
| Hotel Gustav Vasa | 46 | D3 |
| Hotel Oden | 47 | D3 |
| Hotell Haga | 48 | D2 |
| Wasa Park Hotel | 49 | C4 |

| INFORMATION | | |
|---|---|---|
| Dagens Nyheter & Expressen | 50 | A6 |
| Karolinska sjukhuset | 51 | C1 |
| Kungsholms Församlingshus | 52 | D5 |
| Police Station | 53 | D5 |
| Post Office | 54 | D5 |
| Sankt Eriks Ögonsjukhus | 55 | C4 |
| Sankt Eriks Ögonsjukhus (Dental Surgery) | 56 | C4 |
| Sankt Görans sjukhus | 57 | B4 |

0 — 500 m
0 — 0.25 miles

KUNGSHOLMEN

Roslagsvägen
Brunnsviken
Hjorthagsparken
Trollättevägen

Roslagstull
Norra Djurgården
Uggleviksvägen
Planterhagsvägen
Fiskartorpsvägen
Storängsvägen

Brunnsviken
Ruddammsvägen
Brunbärsvägen
Ruddammsvägen
Ruddammsparken

Cedersdalsgatan
78

Vanadislunden
Roslagsgatan
Freigatan
Tuleetgatan
71

Sveavägen
Hagagatan
40

Teknika Högskolan – Stockholm Ö
Valhallavägen
Korsbärsvägen
Drottning Kristinas Väg
Teknikringen

Östra Station
Gustaf Backen
Trackportsvägen
Drottning Sofias Väg

Lidingövägen
Olaus Petriparken
Sandelsgatan
Strindbergsgatan

Surbrunnsgatan
Odengatan
Östermalmsgatan
Karlavägen
Teknika Högskolan – Stockholm Ö
Stadion
61

Artillerigatan
Erik Dahlbergsallén

Spelbomskans Torg
62
18
46
52 68
44 39
Markvardsgatan
93
58

Jarlaplan
Jarlaparken
Danderydsplan
Floragatan

Stadion
76

Odenplan
90
33
42
Luntmakargatan
72
Rehnsgatan
Kungstensgatan

Engelbrektsgatan
Runebergs plan
92
75

Grev Turegatan

Jungfrugatan
Östermalmsgatan
77
91

Observatorielunden
Rådmansgatan
21
66
82
Observatoriegatan
63
43
53
49
Dalagatan
64
65
67
37 35
Eriksbergsparken
Runebergsgatan
Eriksbergsplan

Karlaplan
Karlaplan
Karlaplan

Humlegården
69
88
Stadion

See pp236–8

Rådmansgatan
Tegnerlunden
57
36
59
73
12
Jutas Backe
Kommendörsgatan

Tegnérgatan
Upplandsgatan
Hollandergatan
Saltmätargatan
Engelbrektsplan
David Bagares Gata
Humlegårdsgatan
Sturegatan
Braheegatan

Norra Bantorget
Norra Järnvägsgatan
Barnhusgatan
Wallingatan
Olof Palmes Gata
Apelbergsgatan
Hötorget
Oxtorget
Hötorget
Brunnsgatan
Kungsgatan
Sturegatan
Stureplan
Östermalmstorg
Östermalmstorg

Sibyllegatan
Artillerigatan
Skeppargatan
Riddargatan
Grevgatan
Styrmansgatan
Grev Magnigatan
Storgatan
Narvavägen

Master Samuelsgatan
Jakobsbergsgatan
Smålandsgatan
Norrmalmstorg
Nybrogatan

T-Centralen
T-Centralen
Sergels Torg
Klarabergsgatan
Drottninggatan
Regeringsgatan
Hamngatan
Norrmalmstorg
Berzelii Park
Raoul Wallenbergs Torg
Nybroplan

Styrmansgatan
Strandvägen
79

Kungsbron
Terminalslingan
Klara Norra Kyrkogata
Brunkebergstorg
Kungsträdgården
Kungsträdgården
Nybrokajen
Nybroviken
Ladugårdslandsviken

Blekholmsterrassen
Klarabergsviadukten
Central-plan
T-Centralen
Vattugatan
Herkulesgatan
Karl XII's Torg
Stallgatan
Kungsträdgården
Nybrokajen

Galärparken
13

Stockholm Centralstationen
See pp239–41
Jakobsgatan
Gustav Adolfs Torg
Strömgatan
Norrström
Museiparken
32
19

Kungsholmen
Hantverkargatan
Samuel Owens gata
Ragnar Östbergs Plan
Norr Mälarstrand
Blekholmsfaret
Rödbodtorget
Tegelbacken
Helgeandsholmen
Slottskajen
Kunglig Slottet

Skeppsholmen
Amiralitetsparken
Svensksundsparken
Gröna Gången

Centralbron
Vasabron
Mynttorget
Slottsbacken
Gamla Stan
Stortorget
Skeppsbron

Riddarfjärden
Evert Taubes Terrass
Birger Jarls Torg
Riddarholmen
Stora Nygatan
Lilla Nygatan
Skomakargatan
Prästgatan
Österlånggatan
Skeppsbrokajen
Strömmen
Gamla Stan

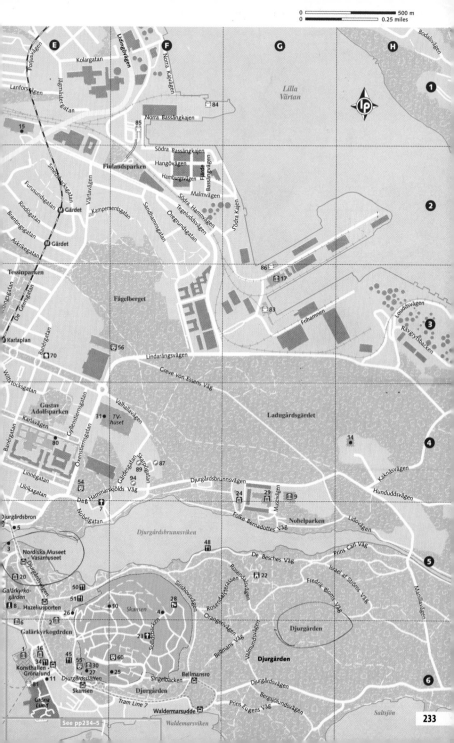

0 ⊏⊐ 500 m
0 ⊏⊐ 0.25 miles

**E** Kolargatan

Pilotgatan
Lanforsvägen
Jägmästargatan
15

Lidingövägen
Norra Kajvägen
84 **F**

**G**

*Lilla Värtan*

Bodalsvägen

**H**

**1**

85 Norra Bassängkajen
Södra Bassängkajen
Hangövägen
Finlandsparken
Hamburgsvägen
Flärde
Södra Bassängkajen
Malmvägen
Södra Hamnvägen
Tegeluddsvägen
Öregrundsgatan
Södra Kajen

Smedsbacksgatan
Furusundsgatan
Vårdavägen
Kampementsgatan
Sandhamnsgatan
Rindögatan
Gärdet
Brantingsgatan
Gärdet
Askrikegatan

**2**

86 17
83 Frihamnen
Louddsvägen
Rävgryfsbacken
**3**

Tessinparken
De Geersgatan
Fågelberget
Banérgatan
Karlaplan
70
56 Lindarängsvägen
Greve von Essens Väg

Wittstocksgatan

Gustav Adolfsparken
Karlavägen
Gyllenstiernsgatan
Valhallavägen
31 TV-huset
Ladugårdsgärdet
14

**4**

Banérgatan
80
Oxenstiernsgatan
Cardellgatan
Skarpögatan
89
94
87
Kaknäsvägen
Hunduddsvägen

Linnégatan
54
Djurgårdsbrunnsvägen
24
29
9
Mastvägen

Ulrikagatan
Dag Hammarskjölds Väg
7
Folke Bernadottes Väg
Nobelparken
Lidovägen

Djurgårdsbron
5
Nobelgatan
*Djurgårdsbrunnsviken*
48
De Besches Väg
Prins Carl Väg

**5**

3
Nordiska Museet
- Vasamuseet
Djurgårdsvägen
22
Rosendalsterrassen
Rosendalsvägen
Israel af Ströms Väg
Fredrik Bloms Väg

Manillavägen

20
Galärkyrko-gården
50
8 Hazeliusporten
51
10
Skansen
4
28
Sirishovsvägen
Orangerivägen
*Djurgården*

6
Galärkyrkogården
26
23
Sollidsbacken
Bellmansvägen
Valmundsvägen
**Djurgården**

1
16
45
34
55
30
60
27
25
Bellmansro
Singelbacken
Djurgårdsvägen
Bergsjölundsvägen
**6**

81
11
Konsthallen - Grönalund
Djurgårdsslätten
Skansen
*Djurgården*
Tram Line 7
Waldemarsudde
Prins Eugens Väg
*Saltsjön*

Gröna Lund

See pp234-5
*Waldemarsviken*

233

# SÖDERMALM

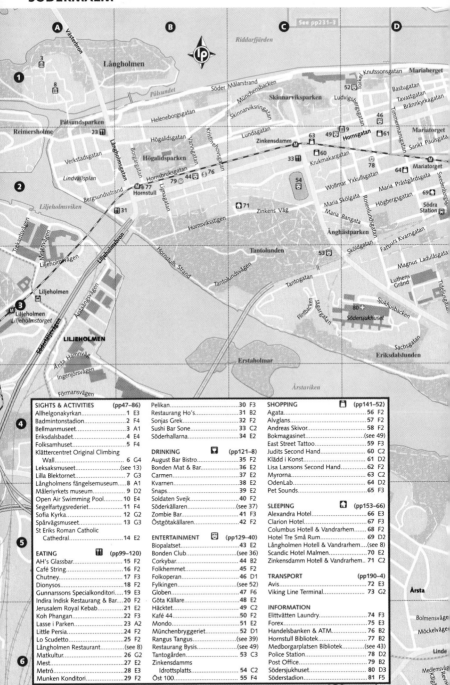

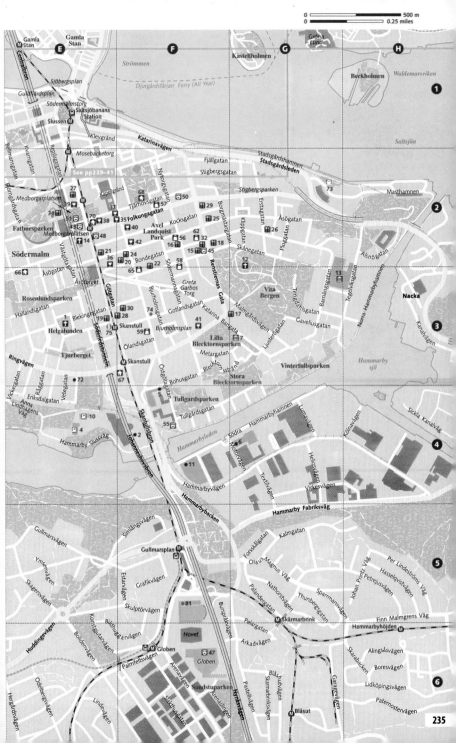

Gamla Stan
Gamla Stan
Centralbron
Sjöbergsplan
Guldfjärdsplan
Södermalmstorg
Saltsjöbanans Station
Slussen
Klevgränd
Mosebacketorg
See pp239–41
Medborgarplatsen
Fatbursparken
Medborgarplatsen
Södermalm
Rosenlundsparken
Hallandsgatan
Helgalunden
Tjurberget
Ringvägen
Eriksdalgatan
Anna Lindhagens Väg
Hammarby Slussväg
Huddingevägen
Johanneshovsbron
Gullmarsvägen
Ymsenvägen
Skagersvägen
Gullmarsplan
Grafikvägen
Skulptörvägen
Estradvägen
Konstgjutarvägen
Bidingsgårdvägen
Palmfeltsvägen
Globen
Globen
Arenavägen
Sandstuparken
Slakthusgatan
Hovet
Odelbergsvägen
Hergärdsvägen
Lindevägen

Strömmen
Djurgårdsfärjan  Ferry (All Year)

Kastellholmen

Gröna Lund

Beckholmen          Waldemarsviken

Saltsjön

Katarinavägen
Fjällgatan
Stigbergsgatan
Nytorgsgatan
Kapellgränd
Tjärhovsgatan
Folkungagatan
Kocksgatan
Axel Landquist Park
Bondegatan
Greta Garbos Torg
Gotlandsgatan
Renstiernas Gata
Katarina Bangata
Blekingegatan
Skanstull
Bjurholmsplan
Ölandsgatan
Skanstull
Östgötagatan
Bohusgatan
Tullgårdsparken
Tullgårdsgatan

Stadsgårdshamnen
Stadsgårdsleden
Stigbergsparken
Borgmästargatan
Erstagatan
Åsögatan
Skånegatan
Klippgatan
Ploggatan
Vita Bergen
Malmgårdsvägen
Lilla Blecktornsparken
Metargatan
Blecktornsstråd
Stora Blecktornsparken
Hammarbyhamnen
Södra      Hammarbyhamnen
Hammarbyvägen
Hammarbyleden
Forssadalgatan
Kalmgatan
Olaus Magnus Väg
Nathorstgatan
Thunbergsvägen
Sparrmansvägen
Textilvägen
Virkesvägen
Heliosgatan
Lumavägen

Masthamnen
Alsnögatan
Barnängsgatan
Tegelviksgatan
Nacka
Norra Hammarbyhamnen
Hammarby sjö
Vintertullsparken
Kölnavägen
Sickla Kanalväg
Hammarby Fabriksväg
Per Lindestoms Väg
Hasselqvistvägen
Johan Printz Väg
Finn Malmgrens Väg
Skärmarbrink
Hammarbyhöjden
Palandergatan
Pelargatan
Arkadvägen
Blåsvughsvägen
Skarmarbrinksvägen
Pastellvägen
Nynäsvägen
Garagevägen
Skaraabacken
Alingsåsvägen
Boresvägen
Lidköpingsvägen
Paternostervägen
Blåsut

Nacka
Pellmangatan
Kvarngatan
Borgmästargatan
Mariagatan
Repslagargatan
Vintvägen
Wollmar Yxkullsgatan
 Åsögatan
Västgötagatan
Götgatan
Södermannagatan
Bjurholmsgatan
Luntgatan
Lusteldgatan
Gaveliusgatan
Tengdahlsgatan
Åstorget
Åsögatan
Skulptörvägen
Buhlingsgatan
Bråvallavägen

0 ———— 500 m
0 ———— 0.25 miles

**235**

A B C D

1 2 3 4 5 6

See p230

Upplandsgatan
Teknologatan
Rådmansgatan
Tegnérlunden
Tegnerlunden
Västmannagatan
Tegnérgatan
Kammargatan
Dalagatan
Torsgatan
Norra Bantorget
Östra Järnvägsgatan
Klarastrandsleden
Kungsbron
Vasagatan
Blekholmsterrassen
Kungsbro Strand
Kaplanstrappan
Kaplansbacken
Bolindersplan
Serafimerstranden
Kungsholmen
Hantverkargatan
Samuel Owens Gata
Ragnar Östbergs Plan

Tegnérgatan
Hollandergatan
Drottninggatan
Sällskapsgatan
Wallingatan
Adolf Fredriks Kyrkogata
Barnhusgatan
Olofsgatan
Apelbergsgatan
Kungsgatan
Mäster Samuelsgatan
Klara Norra Kyrkogatan
Gamla Brogatan
Vasaplan
Terminalslingan
Klarabergsviadukten
Centralplan
Stockholm Centralstationen
Blekholmsfaret
Stadshusbron
Tegelbacken
Norr Mälarstrand

Rosengatan
Kammakargatan
Luntmakargatan
Sveavägen
Olof Palmes Gata
Hötorget
Sergelgatan
Slöjdgatan
Klarabergsgatan
Klara Västra Kyrkogatan
Klara Östra Kyrkogatan
Vattugatan
Herculesgatan
Klarabergsviadukten
Drottninggatan
Beridarebansgatan
Brunkebergstorg
Sergels Torg
T-Centralen
Kulturhuset
Klarabergs Rödbodgatan
Rödbodtorget
Tegelbacken
Klara Mälarstrand
Centralbron
Norra Järnvägsbron

Johannesgatan
Jutas Backe
Regeringsgatan
Malmskillnadsgatan
Brunnsgatan
Oxtorget
Oxtorgsgatan
Hötorget
Hötorgsfaret
Malmskillnadsbron
Malmtorgsgatan
Fredsgatan
Vasabron
Strömborg
Norr Mälarstrand

Torgatan
Norra Bantorget
Hötorget
Sergels Torg
Kulturhuset
Brunkebergstorg
Rödbodtorget
Stadshuset (City Hall)
Ragnar Östbergs Plan
Klara Sjö
Kungsholmen
Riddarfjärden
Norrström

See pp239-41

140 136 35 45 26 1 117 137 138 134 46 93 5 154 33 42 2 128 65 60 147 132 38 176 72 171 57 150 111 78 37 101 172 186 164 51 119 110 113 100 85 90 77 70 124 114 129 174 95 170 127 131 144 123 12 145 83 109 157 15 181 168 151 166 148 10 182 40 163 178 155 173 11 34 152 19 159 20 47 24

Kaplanstrappan

236

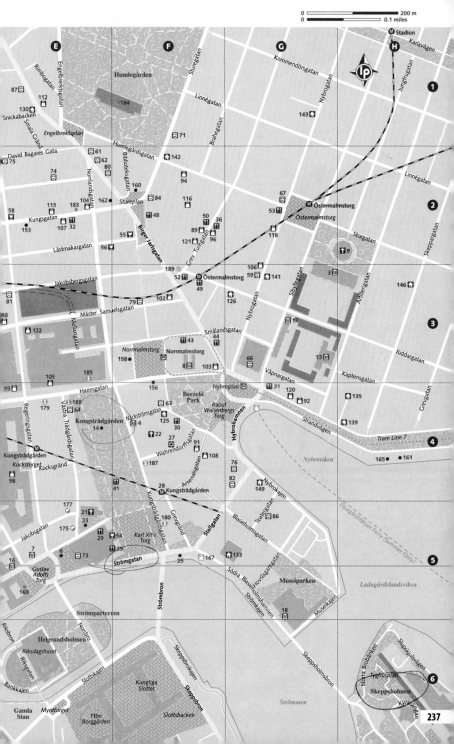

Centralplan

Ⓐ Herkulesgatan

Ⓑ Jakobsgatan

Operan

Ⓒ Strömkajen

Strömgatan

Ⓓ

Vasagatan

Sheraton Hotel

Rödbodtorget

Fredsgatan

Gustav Adolfs Torg

Strömbron

Rosenbad

Strömparterren

• 38

▥ 24

Tegelbacken

Blekholmsfarten

❶

Klara Mälarstrand

Ruskbron

Norrbro

Skeppsholmen

• 39

Rosenbad

Helgeandsholmen

Centralbron

Norra Järnvägsbron

Norrström

Riksgatan

• 30

Bankkajen

Slottskajen

13 ▥

Skeppsbron

Strömsborg

Strömborg

Vasabron

Rådhusgränd

Myntgatan

Mynttorget

25 ▥

Kungliga Slottet

22

▥ 33

Strömbron

❷

Norra Riddarholmshamnen

Schering Rosenheims Gränd

Arkivgatan

Riddarhustorget

6

29

Riddarhustorget

Storkyrkobrinken

48

85

105

Prästgatan

Trångsund

104

Källargränd

Yttre Borggården

31 •

97

Slottsbacken

3 •

37

7

10

20

Slottsbacken

41

60

Telegrafgränd

Skeppar Karls Gränd

19

54

Bredgränd

100

Nygränd

55

Kråkgränd

63

Brunnsgränd

Stortorget

Köpmangatan

93

Skottgränd

Sankt Hoparegränd

Ferkens Gränd

❸

• 5

Riddarholmen

Evert Taubes Terrass

• 44

Birger Jarls Torg

35

28

121 ◷

76

56

Lilla Nygatan

115

59

27

58

Munkbrogatan

106

Södra Riddarholmshamnen

Riddarfjärden

71

83

70

Västerlånggatan

Stora Nygatan

65

Tyska Brinken

Leijonstedts Gränd

109

Gamla Stan

Stortorget

Köpmangatan

79

Svartmangatan

Stora Nygatan

89

43

Kindstugatan

Själagårdsgatan

Tyska Skolgränd

90

98

Österlånggatan

Johannesgränd

Packhusgränd

50

42

Gamla Stan

47

61

46

Kornhamnstorg

67

Järntorget

12

Norra Bankogränd

Södra Bankogränd

68

Tullgränd

Munkbroleden

Södra Järnvägsbron

Centralbron

Sjöbergsplan

Slussplan

117

Slussen

❹

111

107

Söder Mälarstrand

Stadsgårdsleden

Guldfjärdsplan

Torkel Knutssonsgatan

Mariaberget

Bastugatan

Pryssgränd

Pilgatan

102

Guldgränd

72

Södermalmstorg

73

▥ 14

Tavastgatan

Blecktornsgränd

Brännkyrkagatan

Bellmansgatan

78

88

95

87

84

69

Saltsjöbanans Station

118

18

81

36

62

Slussen

51

❺

Timmermansgatan

91

Hornsgatan

23

Mariagränd

103

120

Katarinavägen

112

108

64

▥ 21

66

110

Mariatorget

92

96

94

77

4 ▥

Klevgränd

Urvädersgränd

Slussen Ⓜ

Höskens Gata

Mosebacketorg

75

32

Krukmakargatan

Sankt Paulsgatan

Sweaborgsgatan

Björngårdsgatan

Wollmar Yxkullsgatan

Fredmansgatan

Kvarngatan

Repslagargatan

Söderledstunneln

1

86

82

49

Svartensgatan

Götgatan

80

53

Högbergsgatan

Östgötagatan

Mariatorget Ⓜ

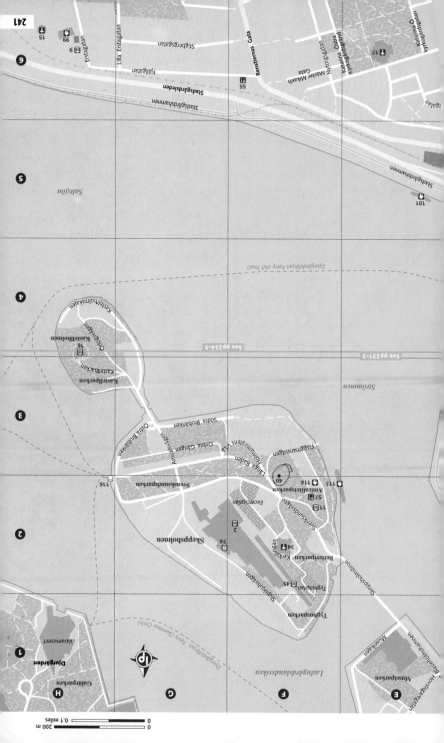

# STOCKHOLM METRO MAP

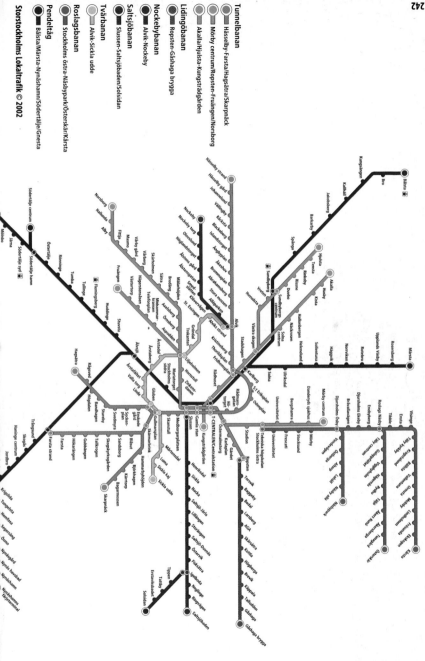

**Tunnelbanan**
- Hässelby-Farsta/Hagsätra/Skarpnäck
- Mörby centrum/Ropsten-Fruängen/Norsborg
- Akalla/Hjulsta-Kungsträdgården

**Lidingöbanan**
- Ropsten-Gåshaga brygga

**Nockebybanan**
- Alvik-Nockeby

**Saltsjöbanan**
- Slussen-Saltsjöbaden/Solsidan

**Tvärbanan**
- Alvik-Sickla udde

**Roslagsbanan**
- Stockholms östra-Näsbypark/Österskär/Kårsta

**Pendeltåg**
- Bålsta/Märsta-Nynäshamn/Södertälje/Gnesta

**Storstockholms Lokaltrafik © 2002**